*My Life
as a
Soviet
Defense
Attorney*

FINAL

Dina Kaminskaya

JUDGMENT

TRANSLATED FROM THE RUSSIAN BY MICHAEL GLENNY

SIMON AND SCHUSTER

NEW YORK

Copyright © 1982 by Dina Kaminskaya
English language translation copyright © 1982 by Michael Glenny

All rights reserved
including the right of reproduction
in whole or in part in any form
Published by Simon and Schuster
A Division of Gulf & Western Corporation
Simon & Schuster Building
Rockefeller Center
1230 Avenue of the Americas
New York, New York 10020

SIMON AND SCHUSTER and colophon are trademarks of Simon & Schuster
Designed by Eve Kirch
Manufactured in the United States of America

1   3   5   7   9   10   8   6   4   2

Library of Congress Cataloging in Publication Data

Kaminskaya, Dina.
Final judgment.

Includes index.
1. Kaminskaya, Dina.   2. Lawyers—Soviet Union—
Biography.   I. Title.
Law   345.47'05044'0924   [B]   82-19120
             344.70550440924   [B]
             ISBN 0-671-24739-5

The author wishes to express her gratitude to Alfred Friendly, Jr., for assistance in working on the English
translation of this book.

To the memory of my parents,
Olga and Isaak

Contents

PART
ONE

PART
ONE

1. Defense Attorneys in the Soviet Union

I STOOD in a vast and ancient building with high, vaulted ceilings—so high they seemed to fade out of sight. The walls were hung with portraits of men wearing black robes and white wigs, their features full of dignity and strength. And all around me were live men and women dressed in the same black robes and wigs.

It did not strike me as strange that in the late twentieth century people should be unself-consciously walking to and fro in curled wigs, that the women too were wearing black robes with two white bands at the neck. I did not find it anachronistic or comic, just as one does not see religious ritual as outdated or absurd. For I was in a temple—the temple of British justice, the Law Courts of London—and those garments symbolized the age-old dignity of their wearers' function.

For the first time in my life I was going into a courtroom not to work but to look and listen. Punctually at two o'clock, the usher declared the court in session. The judge took his seat on the high dais, alone, raised above us all, and the trial began.

I listened to a trial conducted in a foreign language, under laws that were strange to me, and according to rules I did not know. As I listened to the questions put by an excellent barrister named John Macdonald, I was painfully envious of him. I wished that I were standing up in that court in a black gown, and that I were asking those questions.

At the same time I recalled my long hours in the dark, dirty little rooms that are allotted to defense counsel in even the best courthouses of Moscow.

I remembered because the dirt, the interminable waiting, the rudeness of the clerks, and the bright dresses of the women lawyers were our Soviet equivalent of wig and gown; they too were a symbol, a pointer to the Soviet attitude toward the institution of justice. If I envied my London colleagues, it was not simply for the surroundings of the courtroom and for the magnificent building in which everything breathes respect for justice, or because the lawyers' robes were a witness to their prestige: I envied them because I greatly love the profession to which I have devoted thirty-seven years of my life.

I was seventeen years old when I entered law school in 1937. I had only the vaguest idea either of jurisprudence or of the kind of work I would do once I acquired my degree. My choice was undoubtedly influenced by the fact that my older sister was about to graduate from law school. My father, too, had been trained as a lawyer, and often discussed legal problems at home. My sister went on to graduate school and eventually became an academic lawyer, doing postdoctoral research at the Institute of State and Law of the Academy of Sciences until she died. I, however, though I had no notion of what it would entail, thought I would work in the procuracy, the Soviet government's prosecutorial system.

As an undergraduate at the Moscow Institute of Law, I discovered that my favorite subject was the criminal trial. The course was taught by Professor Boris Arseniev, who had previously held a number of senior posts in the Russian Republic's state procuracy. His lectures were clear, entertaining, and instructive. In our third year at the institute, when the time came for our first practical work, we were allowed to choose either the judicial system or the procuracy, which includes the investigatory apparatus. The overwhelming majority of my classmates asked to be sent to the procuracy, and a few wanted trial work, but I can remember no one in those days who planned to specialize in advocacy. A partial explanation for this, of course, was that we were all so influenced by the lectures of our beloved and respected Professor Arseniev. If the defense attorney was ever mentioned in those lectures, it was only in the role of a wretched, defeated opponent. I am sure that it was also because, although we had not yet fully realized how abysmally low in status the profession of defense counsel was, we were very well aware of its unpopularity among the public at large.

For my practical training I was assigned to the procuracy of the Leningradsky District of Moscow, which at that time was in the outskirts of the city. There I was put under the supervision of an experienced investigator, who taught me how to conduct a criminal investigation, including the interrogation of witnesses and accused and all investigatory procedures, from inspection of the scene of the crime and searching the premises on to framing the charge. Seated beside a state prosecutor, I also took part in several trials.

It was during this training period that I first began to feel a genuine interest in legal work, in studying a case, in coming to an independent conclusion. However, the romantic aura of detectives and investigators created by books, movies, and above all by our lectures at the institute, grew noticeably dimmer when compared with everyday reality. I soon discovered that the vast bulk of the cases handled by the procuracy's investigators were not in the least interesting or intellectually demanding. Instead, the investigators were literally overwhelmed with cases of petty larceny from the factories and offices of the Leningradsky District. These cases were completely straightforward, because as a rule the accused were workers or office staff detained by security guards at the factory gates, where everyone entering and leaving was subjected to a compulsory body search. The clumsily hidden booty was removed on the spot, and the work of the investigator was limited to listing the pilfered goods.

For me the glamor of the investigator faded as I found myself increasingly interested in the prospect of trial work. Most of all, I think, I was thrilled by the competitive, duel-like aspect of trial procedure, and my speeches in court as a trainee prosecutor convinced me that I could become a good forensic orator. Thus when I graduated from the institute I had a choice between two aspects of the legal profession which I found equally stimulating: to be a prosecutor acting for the state, or an advocate defending the individual against accusation.

I am grateful that, young as I was, some sixth sense—some combination of upbringing and intuition—prompted me to choose the profession that answers to a fundamental need in my nature—the job that has enabled me to defend so many people against the arbitrary and often cruel power of the Soviet state. Yet even then I had intimations that the role I chose would be a hard one.

Two months of student practice were enough to show me the utterly unenviable status of the advocate in the Soviet legal system. No one bothered to conceal it, either in the courtroom or outside. During a trial the judge would rudely interrupt an advocate or forbid him to put questions whose necessity was obvious even to me. Yet the same judge would never permit himself to treat a prosecutor that way. During a recess the prosecutor would freely and confidently head for the judge's chambers, which no advocate could enter. I was present in judges' offices when the judge, the prosecutor—and often the investigator—discussed the case on trial. Together they would weigh up the evidence and not infrequently they would settle the defendant's fate then and there, not only the question of guilt but even the sentence. The constitutionally established parity of the two sides in court, the equality of rights between prosecutor and defense counsel, were never observed; no attempt was made to camouflage or to make less obvious the preeminence granted the prosecutor as the representative of the state.

What were the reasons for the advocate's total lack of prestige? First of all, in the system of government that prevailed under Stalin, far more violations of the law were the direct result of Communist Party and state policy than were caused by errors and excesses of individual officials. Thus the profession of advocacy itself existed to defend people not so much against state prosecution as against the state's flouting of its own laws. Advocacy was alien to the state. Tolerated as an anachronism, necessary for the Soviet Union's prestige abroad, it was never admitted to have any value for the internal life of the country.

The very structure of the profession—a self-governing association in a totally regulated society—underscored its alien character and its consequent lack of prestige. The original members of the Colleges of Advocates, which replaced the private law practices abolished after the Revolution of 1917, were former private lawyers. Very few of these were Party members and their social and political attitudes were therefore, in the state's view, extremely dubious. From the beginning, then, the authorities had no respect for the profession and did not trust advocates collectively or singly.

As I became aware of this background, I saw certain other things. I noticed that, almost without exception, the advocates who had to submit to humiliation by smug and boorish judges and prosecutors were far better educated and had a far higher standard of professionalism. There was an explanation for this too. In the years before the Second World War, investigators, prosecutors, and judges were drawn from among the so-called "promotees"—industrial workers rapidly promoted to positions of authority as part of the Party's aim to further the dominance of the working class. Many of them not only lacked legal training but had not even completed the minimum ten grades of schooling. They combined their highly responsible legal work with attendance at night school or specially organized law courses. By contrast, many of the advocates had received a first-class university education before the Revolution of 1917.

It also became clear to me that the advocates who were humiliated in the courtroom were actually much freer than the judges and prosecutors who insulted them. The advocate himself decided on his approach to a case, without the need to refer to any higher authority, whereas the state's prosecutor, who behaved with such lordly independence during a trial, was obliged to report in advance on the case and on his handling of it to the District Procurator, and the views of his superiors were binding. If ever a prosecution case was refuted or seriously shaken during a trial, the prosecutor, obliged by law to withdraw his case, could not do so on his own initiative. In such a situation, if the prosecutor asked for a recess before making his closing speech, we all knew he was on his way to ask the District Procurator's permission to change his position.

My spell of practical work as a student also provided some knowledge beyond the scope of purely professional training. It was my first encounter with the harsh realities of life, a part of my education that was not merely of practical value but was essential to my growth as a human being.

From my earliest years my family, my friends, and my schooling placed me in an extremely fortunate position in comparison with the vast majority of Soviet youngsters. These circumstances favored my development into an intelligent, well-educated person, but at the same time they sheltered me from real life, deprived me of any knowledge of it and of the possibility of understanding it.

I was nineteen when I had my first contact with the harsh realities of life. What did I believe in? What circumstances had formed my character and inclinations? What determined my choice of profession and the subsequent course of my life?

Many times, looking back as a mature woman, I have marveled at the happy way in which my early life unfolded. My parents lived to a ripe old age without ever being exiled or imprisoned. This was a rare piece of good fortune in their milieu of intellectuals and professional people. It was even more astonishing in view of my father's youthful membership in the Social-Revolutionary Party and, just before the Revolution, in the party known as the Constitutional Democrats, the "Cadets." He never concealed his political past: whenever he had to fill out an official questionnaire, in the column headed "Political Affiliation" he invariably wrote "Former S. R.; former Cadet." But, amazingly enough, during the Soviet period, right up until the height of Stalin's purges of 1936–38, he—a nonparty professional —held a very senior and politically sensitive job as a director of the Industrial Bank of the USSR, which was responsible for financing industrial investment throughout the entire country.

My father and mother came from poor Jewish families in the provinces; each of them was a person of the highest spiritual sensitivity and irreproachable honesty. In my mother's case this was by virtue of a natural goodness and a certain innate delicacy and nobility, for which one needs neither education nor special knowledge. All my friends loved and admired her. Her face was remarkably beautiful in an understated, pastel-colored way, and her beauty endured long past her youth. Although she changed and aged with the years, even at eighty she amazed everyone who came to our house with her singular good looks and her kindness and serenity, the simplicity of the natural aristocrat. Mother was an astonishingly tactful person. By nature extremely gentle, she endured misfortunes and illnesses with fortitude and strength of character. The only thing she feared was the prospect of lapsing into helpless senility. She was fortunate to die quite suddenly, at eighty-six, having retained to the last a lucid mind and a remarkable degree of physical strength.

My father was exceptionally reserved, stern and ascetic; he had no friends and, far from seeking friendship, actively avoided it. Perhaps his character was formed by his hard life as a young man; in any event, he possessed a fantastic capacity for work and great fixity of purpose. Not only did he never complain of being tired, he never *was* tired. I am convinced that, had it not been for the Revolution, he would have gone very far indeed, because his evident ability combined with his character enabled him to make early and rapid progress in both politics and business.

My father graduated from the law school of Kharkov University, then started work in the southern branch of the Russo-Asiatic Bank and very soon became its vice-president. His intelligence, his political flair, and his gifts as an orator insured his nomination in 1918 as a Cadet Party candidate for election to the All-Russian Constituent Assembly.

He did not accept the Revolution, not because it deprived him of position or wealth (he was never rich) but because of its bloodshed and violence, its lawlessness and its lying. And he maintained that view up to his death.

His outward appearance corresponded remarkably to his inner nature. He was tall and thin, with a straight-backed military bearing which he retained all his life, though he had never been in the army. Yet the features I remember above all were his deep-set, intelligent eyes; his thin, tightly closed lips; and the permanent twitching of his head. This nervous tic, which began soon after the Revolution, was always in the same direction: horizontally, from right to left, a repeated gesture of negation. Once he consulted a distinguished neurologist who examined him carefully and said, "Something exists which, inwardly, you decisively reject. You must do everything possible to remove it, and your tic will immediately disappear." The tic was indeed an involuntary negation of everything that constituted the external framework of his life. It was a "no" to lying and violence. My father's last words were, "I am tired of living in this atmosphere of lies."

After the Revolution, all my father's political intelligence, all his purposefulness became centered on the inner dimensions of his life. Literature, music, painting, philosophy, biology, and especially religion—these were his interests. Books were his fanatical concern, and he collected a magnificent library of Russian idealist philosophy and poetry. He himself sometimes laughed at the intensity of this passion, but he was unable to rid himself of it.

At the beginning of the war our whole family was evacuated from Moscow to the Urals, except for my sister, who moved from Moscow to Uzbekistan with the Institute of State and Law. The following year, 1942, my father was the first of us to return to the capital, where he found that the greater part of his library had been plundered. Most of our furniture and carpets, and our piano, had disappeared too, but his attitude to these losses was one of calm indifference. His library, though, had to be restored at any cost. Every day after work he would set off on his rounds of the second-hand bookstores, where he looked for books bearing his own bookplate and bought them back. He also filled up the gaps by buying new books, until in approximately a year he had almost completely reconstituted his library. But at what a price! He sent almost the whole of his modest salary to my mother, keeping just enough to feed himself, so that to buy books he had to restrict his purchases of even the most essential foodstuffs. Yet there was still not enough money for books, so he began selling the meager bread ration (about a pound a day) that was issued on each person's ration card. Malnutrition ensued, his legs swelled and he had attacks of dizziness, but he could not stop. His health was not restored until I, and then my mother, returned to Moscow.

My father was particularly fond of small, pocket-sized editions, which he could carry around with him and read when traveling or during our invariable Sunday walks in the countryside around Moscow.

Every Sunday in summer we would get up early, take a few plain sandwiches, and set off. Father was a tireless walker and never made any concessions to me. Neither tears nor my assurances that I was about to drop dead with fatigue made the slightest impression. The most commonly used word when addressing me was "must": you *must* eat fish (which I hated), you *must* get up early (till the age of forty I slept late every chance I had), you *must* solve those damned math problems (which I never could understand). His love for me was strong. I never felt rejection, although he never kissed me or even went out of his way to comfort me or make my life easier. He believed that my own strength would grow through self-discipline. Perhaps, however, a kind of subconscious protest against his emotional asceticism led me to take on more of my mother's character. I enjoy the warmth of human contact. I have always needed friendship and am devoted to its cultivation. I love all the unspiritual pleasures and comforts of life. My house was known as one of the most hospitable in all Moscow, and I always delighted in a beautifully set table, delicious food, and the company of close friends.

A love of art and literature, however, was something that my father not only aroused in me but made an essential part of my life. I realize now that everything I have found in art and culture was first shown to me by him. All the museums which I loved so much—and still love in recollection—I first visited in his company; it was from him that I first heard the poetry of Pushkin, Zhukovsky, Goethe, Heine, Byron, and Shakespeare; it was he who first introduced me to Bach and Mozart.

To me, not only the intellectual but the moral authority of my parents was indisputable. My outlook on life was formed by the nature and style of personal relations within my family, where no one ever envied anyone else; where careers and money were not only disregarded as aims in themselves but were rarely discussed at all; where the concept of "useful" or "expedient" acquaintanceships simply did not exist.

Despite the fact that my father did not accept the Bolshevik Revolution, he consciously avoided raising me in an anti-Soviet spirit and indeed went so far (I later realized) as to refrain from ever expressing any political judgments in my presence. I grew up a thoroughly "Soviet" child. At the appropriate age I joined the Young Pioneers, the Communist Party organization for children, and enjoyed all their activities at school.

The height of Stalin's mass terror of the thirties coincided with my late teens and entry into law school. I remember my father coming home and telling of the latest series of arrests among his colleagues; I remember the arrest of parents of my school friends, then of my classmates at the institute; I remember the disappearance of professors who had lectured to us, and even of students whom I knew; I remember the fear whenever the doorbell rang at night. Yet at the time none of this really impressed itself on my mind—I must even admit that it failed to cast a shadow over my life. Nor, to be honest, was I really troubled by the fact that my father lost his job, that for a long time he lived under constant threat of arrest, or that it took him a year to find a very humble job as legal adviser to an industrial organization. Unconscious of the reality of this threat, I simply went on living my carefree student life.

Many years later I recalled those years in talks with a close friend of mine, whom I had first met in 1937, the peak year of Stalin's "Great Purge." Our reminiscences began with my telling her how happy my childhood had been, how the real life of those years passed me by without leaving a mark on my mind or my emotions. She agreed with me, saying that she too now agonized over her inability to understand that extraordinary phenomenon whereby almost our entire generation had consciously or unconsciously deprived itself of the natural human capacity for doubt. We had simply failed to perceive the horror and despair that gripped our parents' generation. Then she in turn told me of an episode from her own life, one that was typical of the circumstances of the time and of our generation's attitude to them.

In 1938, when she was still a student, she came home late from one of the usual student parties to find that she had forgotten her door key. There was nothing for it but to ring the bell and wake up her parents. For a long time there was no response, so she rang a second time. Soon she heard footsteps and the door was opened. There stood her father, dressed as though he had not been to bed at all but had just come in or was on the point of going out again. He was wearing a dark suit, a clean shirt, a neatly tied necktie. On seeing his daughter he stared at her in silence and then, still without a word, slapped her across the face.

I knew her parents; her father was an intelligent, cultivated, totally nonviolent man. At the time she told me this story, we both understood only too well why no one had opened the door for so long, why her father was dressed as he was, and why he had stared at her unable to believe his eyes. We knew now how people interpreted a midnight doorbell; we knew that while she stood outside the door her father had been getting dressed on the assumption that he was leaving home forever. He had no doubt that the authorities had come for him, that this meant his arrest and, ultimately, certain death. At the time it happened, however, her only reaction was to feel shocked and insulted at his assault. Overcome by self-pity, she burst into tears and reproached her father, but after a while she completely forgot about the incident. Years passed before she recalled her father's pale face, his silence, and that blow—no doubt the only time in his life he ever hit anyone. She told me this story with great pain, wracked by guilt at her own incomprehension and that of our whole generation.

Yet we were neither indifferent nor intimidated. We were able and ready to react to any example of injustice. With the uncompromising certainty of youth we condemned any behavior by our contemporaries that we regarded as "uncomradely." We loved and respected our parents, and if the worst had befallen them we would not have renounced them but would have believed in their innocence. Our mental blindness was due to good rather than bad qualities. Our intellect and emotions were simply unable to entertain the possibility of such appalling evil as the conscious, purposeful destruction of innocent people. That is why we could not share the fear and alarm our parents felt—for we knew that *they* were innocent.

"I have no wish to erase those years from my memoirs. It is not that I refuse to suppress sad memories; the fact is that my memories of that time are not sad at all: we enjoyed life . . . we found love and true friendship." I include this quotation from Yevgeny Gnedin's *Catastrophe and Rebirth* because I am astonished at the almost word-for-word correlation between his attitude and mine, especially since he is considerably older than I. Gnedin was forty in 1938, he had worked for years in the press department of the Ministry of Foreign Affairs, of which he had become director of the department. He was infinitely better informed than I was, and he knew personally many of the innocent people who were arrested and liquidated. He was present at the most notorious of the political show trials and noticed "certain inconsistencies" in the indictments; yet even he did not realize at the time that he was witnessing "a judicial farce and the tragedy of innocent people."

After that, is the blindness and incomprehension of my generation really so astonishing? Can it perhaps be explained entirely by our youth, our ignorance of life, the circumstances of our upbringing? But we need to understand something far more difficult: how a combination of two kinds of hypnosis—the hypnosis of revolutionary idealism and the hypnosis of cynical, barefaced lies—was capable of dulling the senses of an entire nation, depriving it of the desire to see and comprehend what was happening.

In 1925, when I was five years old, my parents were allocated an apartment in a newly built housing project in what were then the distant outskirts of Moscow, a district mainly inhabited by horse-cab drivers, jockeys, trainers, and gypsies. Nowadays it is occupied by a huge industrial complex and the printing plant and editorial offices of *Pravda;* then it was a large plot of land, surrounded by a wooden fence, on which stood more than thirty newly built frame houses supplied with modern comforts that were a fantastic luxury for the period, and especially for that area (piped water, sewers, even bathrooms). The place was owned by the People's Commissariat of Finance; the houses were divided into apartments and rented to senior officials of the Commissariat. We occupied half of one of these houses, that is, three large rooms, which was a great privilege. Even more fortunate, however, was the fact that I found myself living among children from educated families. We all got to know each other when we were five or six years old, we grew up together, we helped form each other's interests, and most of them remained my friends until the very end of my life in Moscow. It was the greatest possible stroke of good luck.

We spent all our free time together (and during the scholastic year a lot of school time too, since we were all bad pupils and played hooky). There was everything we could wish for: ski trips, singing and dancing, expeditions to the movies or the theater, and interminable poetry readings. We pooled our lunch money so that two of our friends could go on a walking tour of the Crimea in summer; we celebrated New Year's Eve together; on Sundays we all went swimming together or hiked in the woods.

The interests and pleasures of our young lives became all the more intense after 1934, when Pavel Kogan joined our circle and became its leader. Pavel died in the war, having enlisted as a volunteer, but his name is still known among today's generation of Moscow students. When I first met him he was sixteen years old and already a poet. Our group's love of poetry took on a new quality: now we had our very own poet, whose verse captivated us at first hearing. He wrote about all the things that young lyric poets write about, but he also wrote about us—about our lives, our friendships, our first loves. All of us were under his influence. We sang our own songs, whose words were written by Pavel and the music by another friend of mine. At least one of these songs, called "Brigantine"—a romantic song about the "fierce and untamed" men who "despised the cheap comforts of a life ashore"—is still sung by young people all over the Soviet Union.

Yet even in such well-educated circles as ours, a young man as intelligent, as passionate, and as uncompromising in his moral judgments as Pavel could in those ghastly years of the Terror write a song that contained the lines:

> Believing in our country is so easy,
> Breathing in our country is so free:
> Our glorious, beloved Soviet land . . .

And we, in 1936 and 1937, sang it rapturously.

I remember lines like these, too, which we chanted with delight:

> Our Soviet life is so good and so bright
> That children in ages to come
> Will probably cry in their beds all night
> Because they weren't born in our time . . .

And I remember how we celebrated New Year's Day, 1940. The student poets Sergei Narovchatov and Mikhail Molochko left that New Year's party to go straight for the front line of the Soviet-Finnish War. How thrilled we were at their bravery, what heroes they were in our eyes! It never once crossed our minds that that war was the result of shameless Soviet aggression, that they were going off to kill Finns simply because that small but brave country refused to submit to the threats of its huge, powerful neighbor.

I realize now that from childhood I was surrounded by the most appalling human suffering—beggars on the streets during the Ukrainian famine, horrifying stories about collectivization, the arrest and death in forced-labor camps of people whose innocence I should never have doubted. And with that realization comes awareness of what a dreadful myopia afflicted me and my circle of friends.

The school in which I studied for ten years had far less influence on me than my family and friends. In putting me into this school, which was an hour's walk from our home, my parents were banking on its location to insure better teachers and better pupils than in our neighborhood, with its population of gypsies and cab drivers. The school was in a city neighborhood where there were no factories; the only large plant was the *Izvestiya* printing works. Consequently most of my schoolmates were children of white-collar workers, engineers, skilled technicians, and teachers.

Later the school was granted the special status of "model school." Among its pupils were Vassily and Svetlana Stalin; the daughter of Polit-buro member Lazar Kaganovich; the daughter of Bubnov, Commissar of Education; and many other offspring of highly placed parents. One of my classmates was Galya Kuibysheva, daughter of the deputy chairman of the Council of People's Commissars (the Soviet cabinet).

I was in the seventh grade when the school's status was changed, and in our class at least there was no alteration in the general spirit of egalitari-anism. At first we stared at the very plainly dressed little Svetlana Stalin and the children of other famous Party leaders, but after a few days we lost all interest in these celebrities. Our relationship with Galya Kuibysheva was on a basis of absolute equality. I cannot recall that her father's position set her apart among her classmates or her teachers.

One incident at my school was characteristic of the time. A teacher in one of the lower grades named Leonova was awarded the title "Honored Teacher of the Republic." The event in itself was of no interest to me or my classmates, but the rumors that went around about that award thrilled us. I don't know whether what we were told was entirely true or not, but I can vouch for the accuracy of its retelling. Among the staff were many excellent teachers whose names were well known and respected, but we older students had simply never heard of Leonova and could not fathom why she was chosen for this honor. Then some friends in the senior class told us, quoting a teacher as their source. Leonova, it seems, was the home-room teacher of Stalin's son, Vassily. Dissatisfied with both his behavior and his grades, she had written a note to his father, Joseph Stalin, firmly requesting him to give more attention to his son's upbringing and see to it that he did his homework. Stalin was apparently so delighted by Leonova's boldness and adherence to principle that he immediately gave orders for her to be given the title.

It is hard for me to judge the courage of Leonova's action in those days when the Party leaders still maintained a semblance of the egalitarian tradition that survived from the 1920s. I am certain, however, that only a few years later it would have been simply impossible; no one would have dared write such a note.

My school milieu gave me an opportunity to observe the life of the better-off, better-educated, and more privileged stratum of Soviet society. It was not until I did my stint of practical legal work that I saw the reality of life for the working class, the class in whose name the Revolution had been made, for whose well-being "socialism" was being created. This happened in 1940, twenty-three years after the successful Revolution, in the land where almost total equality was said to have been established.

That was when I first saw those horrifying slumlike wooden huts, without piped water or sewerage, divided into tiny cell-like rooms in which adults and children, young and old, slept side by side. I had gone there with an investigator to search for property that was to be confiscated from those wretched workers who were officially branded "enemies of the people." They were women who had tried to bring home to their starving children a few lumps of sugar or spoonfuls of jam from the "Bolshevik" candy factory where they worked; they were men and women arrested for pocketing a spool of thread, a few packs of cigarettes, a hunk of bread. Under the notorious Soviet law of August 7, 1932, they were dangerous criminals liable to ten years of imprisonment. We were entitled to seize all the furniture except for one table per family, one chair per person, and one bed, but in almost every one of these cases we recorded our statement that there was no property worthy of distraint.

What I saw was not poverty but utter destitution. I had seen it before, in the movies, and had read about it in books, but the films and books always referred to the distant past, to the time covered by the blanket term "before the Revolution" and to the wretched condition of the working class under czarism. Now for the first time I encountered human misery that was not caused by some temporary, external catastrophe such as disease, the death of a close relative, or a natural disaster. This was misery that accompanied people all their lives. It was the first absolutely real, concrete discrepancy between what I saw with my eyes and what I had seen in movies and read in books and newspapers about the life of the Soviet working class.

During that year of practical work I came to realize that work in the legal arm of the government, the procuracy, was incompatible with my character. This was not merely because the investigators and prosecutors I met amazed me by their indifference to human suffering. The main reason was that, having seen the living conditions, the food and the clothes of the people who were prosecuted for petty larceny and other minor offenses, I began to doubt whether the state was acting justly by punishing hungry people with savage prison sentences. I realized that punishment must follow crime; when those same investigators arrested murderers, professional thieves, and violent offenders, who were then convicted and severely punished, I regarded this as inevitable and even just. Yet exactly the same scale of punishment was decreed for minor pilfering, and only because the stolen bread or sugar was called "socialist property" (and therefore anyone who laid hands on it was an "enemy of the people").

When I pictured myself standing up in court and demanding in the name of the state that these people be mercilessly punished, I realized that I simply could not do it.

It was then that I began to doubt whether I had chosen the right career. And again I was faced with the question—what was I to become? The more I thought about that, the more I inclined toward the idea of advocacy. I don't think I was motivated (at least not consciously) by that essential quality of genuine compassion for every person, even the guilty ones, that the Soviet advocate defends. This ability to empathize with other people's misfortune came to me only later, after years in the profession. At the beginning I merely wanted to appear in court and to make speeches (all of which, I was sure, would be good); but I intended to do so only under conditions of maximum independence and intellectual freedom.

The form in which the profession of advocacy is organized offers the greatest possible degree of freedom (although, of course, it is far from total) that exists in the Soviet state. Soviet advocacy is described in official phraseology as a "self-governing social organization." Unlike the overwhelming majority of all other working citizens of the Soviet Union (with the exception of collective-farm peasants), advocates are not state employees and receive no salary or other monetary reward from the state.

The advocates in each *oblast*, or province, and in a few of the largest cities of the USSR, are organized in bodies known as "colleges." Thus there is a College of Advocates for the city of Moscow, which includes about a thousand members, approximately half of whom are women. The professional, financial, and administrative functions of each college are discharged by an elective body, the Presidium of the College of Advocates. The Presidium has real and effective powers over each advocate: it decides on the acceptance of new members; it dismisses members who have committed serious infringements of professional discipline; it nominates the head of each "consultation," or local office, which is the smallest collective unit of the profession.

The chairman of the Presidium and his two deputies represent the College in all dealings with Party and government organizations. These three people are the "free" members of the Presidium, that is, they receive a salary payable out of deductions from the earnings of each advocate in the College.

Like every Soviet organization, the Presidium has to coordinate its work with the appropriate governmental and Party bodies: at government level, the Advocacy Division of the Ministry of Justice, or the justice department of the executive committee of a provincial or municipal Soviet; in the case of the Party, the administrative divisions of the provincial or municipal committees of the Communist Party of the Soviet Union. The Presidium members, however, are entirely responsible for the way a specific problem is referred to outside authority; for the degree of firmness with which they defend the interests of the College; for the acceptance of new members; and for all other matters affecting the everyday professional lives of the advocates.

Elections to the Presidium are important events for College members. In Moscow, the Presidium is chosen at special electoral conferences to which delegates have been elected. Each "consultation" has the right to send a certain number of delegates (proportionate to the number of advocates working in the office, which averages between fifty and seventy). After a preliminary discussion at a meeting of the Party bureau of the office, a full meeting of all advocates in the law office is presented with a prepared list of candidates. The meeting decides by open vote which of the candidates to leave on the list and proposes substitutes for those who are rejected. Great importance is attached to the number of candidates who are Communist Party members, because it is through the delegates who are Party members that the Moscow City Committee of the Party directs the working of the electoral conference. For the past sixteen or seventeen years, another percentage quota has also been applied to the delegates, and I was in this quota for Jews.

None of the voters is indifferent to the results of this election. It is vital to them that the places on the Presidium be occupied by people who have the interests of the college at heart, who know and love the profession of advocacy—and this applies equally to the non-Party majority and those who are Party members.

Until I began to get into trouble for my defense of dissidents, I was a delegate to all the electoral conferences. This was partly because of good relations with my colleagues, but also because I was on good terms with many advocates from other Moscow offices. This was very important in the choice of a delegate. Officially there was no such thing as an election campaign; we did not even know in advance the names of the candidates running for office. An unofficial election campaign, however, began several weeks before the conference. Wherever we met—usually in courthouse corridors

—we discussed the prospects for the election, trying to guess which candidates the Party would propose, which of them could be left on the list, which should be voted off, and who should replace them.

But the real electoral horse trading took place at the conference itself, and especially on its second day. Early that morning the delegates who were Party members held a meeting to discuss the list of candidates for the Presidium approved by the Moscow Party Committee. This meeting was usually chaired by no less a personage than the head of the Administrative Division of the Moscow Committee. At the meeting, proposals for candidacy were decided by open vote, and generally the Party's list was accepted *in toto* or with only minor changes.

The rest of us, nonmembers of the Party, crowded in the corridor awaiting the emergence of our Party—and therefore better informed—colleagues. As soon as they appeared, the real discussion of the candidacies began. The most difficult and important matter was to reach agreement among the delegates on which of the (ethnically) Russian Party-member candidates we should vote for, and which of them should definitely be blackballed. The candidacies of non-Party Russians or of Jews interested us considerably less; none of them could ever become chairman of the Presidium. Only an ethnic Russian who was a member of the Communist Party could be elected to that post.

It was precisely at this stage that it was important for a delegate to be known and trusted by advocates from other offices. All the Communist delegates were bound under Party discipline to adhere, at least publicly, to the list already chosen at the Party meeting; in a few hours, however, they would be able to vote against any of those candidates they disapproved of, since the final voting was secret.

I began my career in the City of Moscow College among advocates who retained the traditional attitudes to the profession, the old approach to trial procedure, the old conceptions of legal defense. Many of them were outstanding lawyers and brilliant orators. I worked in many trials with an old Moscow lawyer whose career antedated the Revolution. Leonid Zakharovich Kats was a master at trial work and a compelling speaker. He was a handsome man, tall, well proportioned, with a small, neatly trimmed beard, and he dressed elegantly and conservatively. As the years went by he looked increasingly aristocratic. Among ourselves we lawyers nicknamed him "the English lord."

Kats stood out among the many lawyers I worked with for his impeccable knowledge of the trial material. No matter how many volumes of records it involved, and whether or not it had any relevance to his client,

Leonid Zakharovich knew all about it. His questions were always brief and to the point, and he formulated them well. He approached the solutions to problems from the broadest possible viewpoint, but the answer to any subsequent question logically followed the answer to the preceding one.

Kats's speeches were a model of court oratory: articulate exposition of the case, superb analysis of the evidence, and flawless logic. He spoke with great emotion and used all the oratorical devices properly: voice modulation, gesture, and appropriate quotations. The only fault I found with Kats was that his speeches were too practiced in their emotionalism.

Especially interesting to me were the trials in which both Kats and Nikolay Nikolayevich Milovidov appeared. Milovidov was the favorite of the Moscow bar and, more important, of the Moscow judges, as much as an advocate could be. He was good-looking too, not as refined as Kats, but no less aristocratic and ingenious. Milovidov was a *barin*, a lazy Russian gentleman—a high liver, a hard drinker and a lover of good restaurants. He did not ask many questions during trial. I always thought he was not too well acquainted with the material, and once he confirmed it by telling me, "I'm sure I'll hear in court everything I need for the defense." But he absorbed like a sponge everything that went on in the courtroom, storing in his memory the minutest details, the smallest nuances in the depositions of witnesses or defendants which would become significant to his defense.

Milovidov's speeches lacked frills or ornaments, but he too was an orator of the highest order. He would rise slowly at the defense table, turn without haste to face the court, and begin to speak in a low, calm voice. Rather than an address, this was like an intimate conversation between the court and himself. Frequently Milovidov would step to the center of the courtroom and stop just in front of the judges. He did not seem to care whether there were other people in the courtroom, or if anybody else listened to him. All he wanted was direct contact with the court.

"Only God knows how he manages," Ivan Klimov, one of the most terrifying judges in Stalin's time, told me once. "One listens to him, and believes everything he says."

Milovidov's calm speeches, filled with such tremendous inner tension, were somehow captivating, bewitching. I felt that every single word uttered by him was the only one capable of expressing his thought, and that to replace it with some other word would be impossible. The thoughts he formulated seemed to flow by themselves, naturally, as a matter of course, and I would wonder why I had not thought of that line of argument myself. I am convinced that if there were trial by jury in the Soviet Union, Milovidov would never have known a defeat.

I dreamed of the time when I would be able to conduct interrogations like Leonid Kats and deliver speeches in the dignified and noble fashion of Nikolay Milovidov.

In the years just before I joined the College of Advocates, most of the newer members were former investigators of the NKVD (now the KGB) or judges who had been dismissed from the bench and by order of the Party were fixed up with jobs in advocacy. Some of these people were undoubtedly talented; they quickly mastered the necessary professional skills. But many of them not only lacked any legal training but were almost illiterate. This new group had, however, one enormous advantage over the older advocates: they were all, no matter where they came from, members of the Party. It was from their ranks alone that heads of law offices were recruited, and through them that Party control was exercised over all members of the profession. Despite having been dismissed from more respected jobs as punishment for misdeeds, they were still counted by the Party as belonging to "us."

For these people the switch to advocacy meant a sharp drop to the very bottom of the hierarchical pyramid, and it denied them any chance of further advancement, either professionally or in the ranks of the Party.

I knew advocates who had been investigators assigned to important cases in the Procuracy of the USSR; others had been members of the Supreme Court of the RSFSR or presided over courts-martial at Military District Headquarters. In all my career, however, I can recall only one instance when an advocate left the profession and went into the judiciary, the procuracy, or a Party appointment. Vassily Samsonov moved from Presidium chairman of the Moscow College of Advocates to the Supreme Court of the RSFSR. But that was in 1967, twenty-seven years after I entered advocacy.

The Soviet advocate's earnings come from the fees that clients pay to the office cashier, which are calculated according to current rates for the various legal services provided. Each fee is credited to the advocate who handles that case. At the end of the month these fees are totaled up and paid, after deducting the taxes paid by all Soviet citizens and other fixed sums, such as the individual's share of the office rent and the salaries of the officers and permanent staff of the College of Advocates. All in all, these deductions average out at between twenty and thirty percent of an advocate's gross earnings.

For conducting a normal, straightforward criminal case, in which the court hearing runs no longer than two days, the advocate may charge no more than twenty-five rubles. After all deductions the advocate gets about nineteen rubles (roughly $27) for such a case, which includes time spent on studying the documentary material, talks with the client in prison, two days of courtroom hearings, another visit to prison after a guilty verdict, study of the trial record, and then, perhaps, preparation of an appeal. The fees in civil cases are equally paltry. For legal advice given to a client in the office, the fee is one ruble (sixty-six kopecks after deductions); the fee for a written opinion on a legal problem or drawing up and certifying other legal documents is no more than three rubles.

Even so, by working very hard indeed (which, in my view, is inevitably detrimental to the quality of his or her work), an advocate who concentrates on minor cases lasting one to three days each can earn considerably more than, say, the average engineer, teacher, or doctor—certainly much more than can be earned as legal adviser to an organization, and more than the salary of a judge at the lowest judicial level, the people's courts, or an investigator in a district procuracy (the pay for judges and investigators was 110 to 130 rubles monthly, at least before the increase awarded to the latter in the 1970s).

Paradoxically enough, the lawyers who are in the worst position are the more qualified advocates who handle longer and more complicated cases requiring intensive preparation. An advocate in a case that lasts several months is paid at the rate of ten rubles per day of the judicial hearing. Days of recess, inevitable in any trial, are five rubles per day. Thus the absolute maximum that defense counsel can earn for a month's work in a long trial is between 170 and 180 rubles, minus the usual deductions. Since the time spent mastering a brief is unrecompensed, advocates' official earnings are certain to be grossly inadequate. (For comparison, the average salary of Soviet workers, blue-collar and white-collar, was 179 rubles in 1980. At the same time university professors received 400 rubles a month.)

Unofficially, however, a system has arisen that provides advocates with substantial payments. The system is permanent and almost universal in the Soviet Union. It is also illegal. Advocates refer to it as *mixt*.

Mixt is the jargon term for the supplementary, unrecorded fees which the client pays directly to the advocate and which is the major portion of his or her income. *Mixt* is not a bribe, and it is not based on the outcome of a case, because that does not depend on the advocate. It is a fee for services rendered. Although this system hardly redounds to the credit of Soviet advocacy, whose interests and prestige remain dear to me, I have no right to pass over this topic in silence.

Most advocates do not see anything immoral in receiving this supplementary reward; in their view, the blatantly unjust official scale of payments gives them the right to redress the balance in their favor. Naturally, a free, open, and legalized system of direct agreement with the client on fees would be preferable to this highly dangerous method of payment. The advocate who accepts *mixt* is put in a position of humiliating dependence on the client, because if a client informs anyone that extra fees have been paid directly to the advocate, the latter will inevitably be expelled from the College of Advocates.

Because the risk is so great, some advocates demand enormously high fees that bear no relation to the work involved. The amount of *mixt* depends on the need and the means of the client, and on the nature of the case, but chiefly, I think, on the character of the lawyer. Some advocates name the figure themselves, and will accept a case only on those terms, while others rely on the client's "conscience"; but in all my years as an advocate I knew very few colleagues who took no *mixt* at all.

Despite the risk involved in *mixt*, advocates discuss the matter quite openly among themselves. Judges and prosecutors are well aware of the practice, and in private they do not condemn it but consider it just and reasonable. For this reason people who find their careers in the state's legal institutions terminated are glad to accept a place in advocacy. They have lost forever the chance to shine in public life, but in exchange they will have a higher standard of living.

I do not believe, however, that *mixt* is the primary reason why the profession of advocacy has become more attractive now than when I joined it. Many university graduates now seek admission to the College of Advocates, and enrollment in the college is a great prize, not attainable by many of those who apply. A law degree is now required for every new advocate, and advocates have begun to be elected deputies to local soviets, to be invited to prestigious conferences and included in delegations of lawyers sent abroad on official visits (though even now, there is not a single advocate to be found in the higher governmental and Party bodies). I think the desire of young lawyers to become advocates is motivated less often by purely material considerations than by a conscious, purposeful urge to organize their professional lives as far as possible outside the framework of the official system, in conditions of relative independence from the state. As before, investigators, judges, and prosecutors still transfer to advocacy, but whereas most of these used to be the rotten apples in the barrel, today's recruits include prosecutors who can no longer tolerate submission to higher authority and prosecution of people whose guilt is unproven; they include former judges convinced that the independence of the judiciary is a sham. These people have faced the choice of whether to accept unquestioningly what is called in the Soviet Union "punitive policy" (not the law, be it noted, but specifically *policy*) or, voluntarily or under compulsion, to resign from the bench or the procuracy.

The average professional level among the Moscow advocates has undoubtedly risen, but it has also leveled out; there are no more vivid personalities like the ones that flourished in the early stages of my career, when we beginners would make a special effort to attend trials in which these striking figures were defending. Indeed, today's young advocates have no time for that: they have to reach an obligatory financial goal, and that means moving from case to case without enough time either to prepare any of them properly or to complete their professional training in a satisfactory manner.

But that is a problem of the present day. My first encounter with Soviet advocacy occurred at a time when it was both underpaid and without status. Linked with this was—and still is—the fact that the legal rights and privileges of a Soviet advocate are far more restricted than those of defense lawyers in Europe and the United States. Under Soviet law, an advocate may accept a brief in any civil or criminal case to be tried in any court in the country. He or she can travel anywhere to defend any sort of case before a People's Court, a city or regional court, or a Supreme Court in any national union republic of the USSR. In reality, however, the rights of advocates and defendants alike are grossly infringed by the state itself under the system known as "access."

The essence of this system is that in all cases in which the investigation is conducted by the KGB (this includes all political cases, as well as cases of illegal currency dealings involving foreigners, and certain other types of case), only advocates granted special permission may plead in court. Foreign experts in Soviet law will search in vain among the legislative statutes for any mention, even a hint, of the "access" system. Both the Code of Criminal Procedure and the Statute on Advocacy, which defines advocates' legal status, are based on the premise of total equality for all members of the profession. Neither seniority nor experience nor ability confer any advantages, either in the right to plead in a particular court, the right to accept any case, or the size of the fee. In fact, however, inequality does exist; it is determined by what the Party perceives as an advocate's degree of political reliability. "Access" is the formal indication of that reliability.

The Presidium of a College of Advocates, in consultation with the KGB, lists the proportion of advocates to whom access is granted (in Moscow it amounted to about 10 percent of the total, that is, between 100 and 120 advocates).

Access is always given to members of a College Presidium, to all office heads, and to all secretaries of Party bureaus or offices. In addition, it is granted to three or four rank-and-file advocates in each office, usually Party members. For several years I was allowed access (no doubt I was not the only non-Party member to have it, but I cannot recall any others who did). I submitted an official request to the chairman of the Presidium of the

Moscow College of Advocates and was then summoned to appear before the personnel secretary of the Presidium, who gave me a special questionnaire to fill out. In addition I had to write a detailed autobiography that included the names of relatives living and dead.

It should be stressed that an advocate's access to cases investigated by the KGB is not the same thing as access to secret documents, which is given to Soviet citizens who work in secret establishments. It is not equivalent because the majority of cases for which advocates need access contain no secret information or documents and are, indeed, often tried in open court. The rationale for the system is that the state, which strictly controls any public pronouncement that may have ideological or political content, is unwilling to allow use of the courtroom forum by an advocate who has not passed an extra test of political obedience.

When I was deprived of access, it was not because I had divulged any secret information—there was none in any of the cases I handled—but because I failed the test of political obedience.

The illegality of the access system first came to international attention during the political trials of the 1970s, when Western newspaper reports about the cases of Anatoly Shcharansky, Yurii Orlov, and others invariably mentioned that these defendants were unable to avail themselves of the services of lawyers of their choice. The Kremlin leadership then realized that the prestige of Soviet justice had suffered a blow. The authorities have not abolished the system; instead they have done everything possible to make its existence less obvious. In 1971 the chairman of the Presidium of the Moscow College of Advocates did not hesitate to reply in writing to Vladimir Bukovsky's mother that Advocate Kaminskaya would not be allowed to defend her son again, in his second trial, because the right to defend was restricted to advocates on the KGB-approved list. No such written comment was made to a similar request in June 1977 by Shcharansky's mother. She too was deprived of the right to choose defense counsel for her son, but in her case it was done verbally. What's more, I was reprimanded by the deputy chairman of the Presidium: "Why did you have to mention 'access' in public and raise all this unnecessary furor? You should have said you were sick or busy, and given that as the reason you couldn't take the case."

Thus there is an extremely important category of cases in which some 90 percent of Soviet advocates may not take part. In all other instances, however, an advocate's right to accept any criminal or civil case is unquestioned. Usually the advocate's participation in a criminal case begins only when the preliminary investigation is completed (in cases where the accused is a minor, and in certain other very rare cases, it begins at the moment the charge is framed). If the defendant is in pretrial detention, this is the first time the advocate meets the client, either in the presence of the investigator or, with the latter's approval, alone. It is also the first time the advocate sees the case documents, the records of investigations and interrogations, as well as the charges themselves. Advocates study these documents with their clients and alone, making notes and transcriptions as best they can.

After the case has gone to court, the principal stage begins, with the preparation and the conduct of the defense. I always reread the dossier in the courthouse, to make sure I had not overlooked anything and to make any further transcriptions from the documentary material that might be necessary in the final preparation of my own brief. These documents, however, must remain in the courthouse, and that is why we worked in these buildings. In the building of the Supreme Court of the USSR, there is a special room where the advocates compile their briefs. This is Room No. 13. Sitting at five small tables, so close they are almost touching, the advocates study their complex, multivolume cases. There is neither natural lighting nor fresh air, nor, of course, air conditioning, but we sat there for hours, days, and weeks.

In the Moscow City courthouse the advocates' room has a window onto the street, but it is always cold, because of a defect in the heating which in thirty years no one has been able to fix. In any case, no one is interested in fixing it; it is only the advocates' room. In the courthouse of the Moscow Provincial Court and in most of the people's courts there is no place at all for the advocates to study their cases. Here we run up and down stairs, lugging our dossiers, looking for an unoccupied courtroom. If we are lucky we can sit down there and work, until the clerk of the court appears and says, "Comrade advocate, we are starting the trial . . ." So we pick up our coats, briefcases, notes, volumes of documentation, and set off again from floor to floor to find an empty room. And if we're unlucky, we work in the corridor, perching on a bench or a window ledge. These are the conditions in which Soviet defense counsel prepare their briefs, copying out page after page of the records by hand.

During the years I have lived in the West, I have visited lawyers' offices as well as courtrooms. Again my first feeling is envy, not for their luxury, but for the comfort, convenience, and calm in which their occupants work. Anyone who has been in lawyers' offices in the United States, England, or France must completely erase the memory of them to imagine the law office of the Leningradsky District of Moscow when I began my career. It was a very small, one-story wooden house. Four or five broken steps led up to the front door, through which the client walked straight into the main room.

There at a desk sat the office secretary (both the only typist and the cashier). The room contained three other desks, where all the advocates' work was supposed to be done, although there were always at least a dozen advocates assigned to that office. As a rule, the three desks were occupied by the duty advocates, those whose turn it was, under the duty roster, to receive clients coming for advice or with requests to take on a defense brief (this is the "off-the-street" part of the practice, as opposed to the "personal" meetings, when the client comes to see an advocate he has already selected).

In the daytime, when many of the advocates were in court and most clients at work, there was some chance of being able to work normally. But in the evening—how can I describe the bedlam into which that room was transformed? It was occupied by the three duty advocates, the secretary, and ten or twelve other advocates and their clients. Interviews with clients were chiefly conducted standing in the small space between the door and the secretary's desk. The only way to avoid this was to receive "personal" clients at the lawyer's home, but this was always—and still is—treated as a serious infringement of professional discipline.

Since those days many Moscow law offices have been given new, more suitable premises. Facilities, though limited, are available for advocates to see their clients in private. The large room, still found in all law offices, is divided by plywood partitions into little booths, each about the size of a shower stall. The walls stop short of the ceiling to allow air to circulate. In each booth there is room for a small table, a chair for the advocate, and a maximum of two chairs for clients. Although this is a great improvement, there are still evenings when an advocate may have to wait hours for a desk or a booth. Nevertheless, perching on window ledges, moving from room to room, interviewing our clients in crowded offices or little booths, we managed to master our briefs quite as well (and sometimes, I thought, even better than) our Western confreres.

And no wonder. A thorough knowledge of the materials in the case— the dossier compiled during the pretrial investigation—is essential for conducting a conscientious and effective defense in the Soviet courts. The Soviet advocate cannot rely on refuting the prosecution by presenting new evidence during the trial or by calling new witnesses, because he or she never knows in advance whether this will be permitted. Consequently the first aim of the defense is to undermine the court's confidence in the evidence gathered by the investigator.

The members of the court have a natural prejudice against the accused. I say "natural" because before trial they see only the investigator's carefully collated evidence supporting the prosecution's version of events. It is this material that shapes the judge's psychological attitude toward the defendant who pleads not guilty. Thus a good advocate must have an exhaustive knowledge of the materials in the case; a capacity for logical thought; the ability to react with lightning speed to any development during a trial; the skill to formulate questions with absolute precision; prudence and caution in putting questions (because no one can predict the answers); and the gift of oratory. In contentious cases, of course, a Soviet judge is liable to be much more impressed by logic and facts than by the emotional coloring of a speech.

In court, prosecution and defense are at least theoretically endowed with equal rights and equal scope for action. Implementation of the defense's rights in ordinary (nonpolitical) criminal cases often depends to an equal degree on the firmness and courage of the advocate and the personal qualities of the trial judge. Naturally, the preeminent status of the prosecutor makes itself felt in court; the prosecutor's requests are refused less often than those of the defense, not because they are any better founded, but because behind the prosecutor stands the full authority of the state—he is, after all, the "state's prosecutor."

The farther away from Moscow, the stronger and more open is that inequality. The Party apparatus controls everyday life in outlying towns with a heavier hand than in Moscow and other major cities. At the same time the provincial judges, procurators, and advocates depend on the local authorities to a much greater extent. And anywhere in the country, the lower the court, the harder it is, as a rule, to achieve an effective defense. Even so, it would be unjust not to observe that in recent decades the standards for conducting trials have risen notably; especially in Moscow, defense confrontations with rude and ignorant judges have become less and less frequent. I think judges who still adopt a scornful attitude to all defense counsel are not doing so in obedience to some secret Party or state directive, but because of both long-standing tradition and prejudice against the accused. That being so, they treat all defense requests as unnecessary and time-wasting, when it would be much easier to wind up the trial by transcribing the indictment verbatim into the verdict, merely adding the length of sentence to prison or labor camp. While showing no respect for advocates, judges also envy them, regarding their job as both easy and lucrative.

For me the work was never easy. Although I loved it, I also found it agonizing. It would never let me out of its clutches: no matter what the hour, whether I was studying a case, or going home on the subway, or sitting over a late supper alone with my husband, somewhere in my subconscious another, parallel process of thought was at work.

When the Criminological Society of the Moscow College of Advocates honored me with a meeting to discuss a murder case I had just finished—the Case of the Two Boys, as we called it—someone asked me to describe my methods of work. I was unable to tell my colleagues anything in the least startling. My method was simply exhaustive study of each case (I have always been spurred on by the irrational feeling that the page I fail to read will turn out to be the most important one); lengthy reflection; and trying to understand the psychology of the person I was defending. I never complained when a trial was delayed or postponed, and never regarded this as time lost, because I could always make good use of it. It might mean, for instance, that I could go to the prison and have another talk with my client; sometimes we might discuss things that were irrelevant to the case but increased my understanding of the person. Actors use the expression "getting under the skin of a part"; I always needed to get under the skin of a case.

As for my speeches, I never wrote them out in full, but they were never delivered impromptu either. My favorite and most effective method of pulling together all my strands of thought in the final preparation of a speech was to play solitaire. For most of my career, while my parents were alive and living with us, and before our son and daughter-in-law emigrated to the United States in 1973, I used to work at night in the kitchen. Later I was able to have a study of my own with a beautiful antique mahogany desk, but I never worked at this desk. My real workplace was a small sofa in the corner, with an oval table in front of it. I would stack my notes in heaps on the sofa and lay out my solitaire on the table along with a few scraps of paper on which to make notes and sketch the plan of my speech. Sometimes I would sit for hours, dealing my games of solitaire and mentally testing out the plausibility and logic of my defense plea, trying to put myself in the judge's place and to hear my speech with his ears.

But in all those years of working in crowded offices, dismal courtrooms, and lonely kitchens, and for all the agonizing over cases, I never regretted the choice I had made as a student. My profession was not only compatible with my abilities and character, it made me, intellectually and morally, a better person.

2. Why I Became a "Political Advocate"

"COMRADE ADVOCATE, why do you defend so many of these people? And not because you're told to, but from choice."

The question was put to me by Judge Pisarenko, a member of the Tashkent City Court, where in 1970 I defended Ilya Gabay against charges of slandering the Soviet system.

"Why do you bother to defend these 'politicals'?" asked a colleague in our law office, an experienced old advocate. "You'd do better to defend store clerks—it pays better and, even more important, it means a quieter life."

What could I say in reply?

My answer was that I defended anyone who needed my help; that it was my profession, and I saw no reason to withhold my help from Gabay or Vladimir Bukovsky, Pavel Litvinov or Yurii Galanskov. Even though my own political views influenced me, I acted basically from ethical convictions, from a simple sense of professional duty.

When I agreed to defend Bukovsky in 1967—his first trial and my first political case—I knew nothing about his political beliefs or his human qualities. To me he was a person who had taken part in a peaceful demonstration and for this had been accused of committing a crime. I would have agreed to defend him whether I shared his political views or not, and I was guided by the same principle when I accepted the defense brief in other, similar cases.

My decision was influenced to some extent, of course, by the fact that my clients' views largely coincided with my own, and that some of them were not simply clients but people for whom, by defending them, I strove to show my admiration and respect. But even when I did not share the views they proclaimed and upheld, this did not influence my decision. What advocate, after all, is obliged to sympathize with the motives of a client's actions or share all a client's views? I would accept without a moment's hesitation the defense of certain dissidents whose chauvinistic and nationalistic beliefs were profoundly alien to me. I saw it as my job to defend the right of free speech—a right guaranteed by the Soviet Constitution and violated every time the authorities prosecute someone for expressing dissident views.

Why would a professional advocate decline the brief in such a case and thereby neglect his or her duty? I am certain the chief reason is fear—an entirely justified and understandable fear of disbarment, which excuses the refusal in the eyes of one's friends and especially one's colleagues.

The period of these political trials was, after all, the second half of the 1960s. The Stalin era of mass arrests and mass terror was over. In taking on the defense in these cases I was never once afraid of being arrested. I believed that if I conducted the defense within the framework provided by the law, I was not endangering my freedom. I am certain that my colleagues —both those who did and those who did not take political cases—were not afraid of arrest or condemnation either; they feared, and with absolute justification, that if they conducted such a defense ethically (that is, a defense based on the materials in the investigator's dossier and an analysis of the relevant Soviet legislation), they would be expelled from the College of Advocates. Although they might be able to find other work, they would lose forever the right to practice their profession.

I do know of instances when, by direct order of higher authority, the Moscow College of Advocates has reinstated advocates expelled for serious offenses against discipline or even for gross professional incompetence. Advocates have also been readmitted to the college after being unjustly convicted during Stalin's terror and subsequently rehabilitated. But advocates expelled for politically incorrect speeches in court are never reinstated.

How great is the potential sacrifice for an advocate who agrees to defend in a political trial and conducts that defense in accord with his professional duty? By what yardstick should it be measured?

When Alexander Solzhenitsyn refused to allow the social stratum to which I belong the right to call itself "intelligentsia," he described us as "an educated rabble." I cannot quarrel with him, because the overwhelming majority of the Soviet intelligentsia has deserved almost everything he has written about it in such anger. And he has the right to call upon all men and women of conscience to make a "conscious, voluntary sacrifice."

"What one must be prepared to lose," he writes, "is not caviar—which nowadays is hardly to be found outside museums—but oranges and butter." That is, of course, a sacrifice, and not such a little one if it lasts a long time, but not so great that many of those I knew in my circle of the "educated rabble" refused to make it. There is, however, another kind of sacrifice, a spiritual one, which has not been taken into account either by Solzhenitsyn (one of the most spiritually sensitive people of present-day Russia) or by his adherents and followers; and that sacrifice is greater than the one Solzhenitsyn calls upon us to make.

Once a very close friend of mine, who had made the "sacrifice," said to me in a confidential talk, "You know, I have been dead for a long time."

This was said by a man who never regretted that he had acted according to his conscience, who, if the same circumstances were to arise again, would do exactly the same, knowing what the consequences would be, knowing that because of it he would be "dead." Yet after his expulsion he had a job, which gave him not just bread and butter but a car as well; he had his splendid family and many close, dear friends. His sacrifice, therefore, really was greater and of a different order than the one Solzhenitsyn himself made voluntarily and consciously, for Solzhenitsyn, despite all his sufferings, did not have to pay for his spiritual freedom at the price of his creative work. He was also fortunate in being able to fulfill the most natural and vital wish of every writer: to have readers. He had readers both when his books were published in large editions and when not only his writings but his very name was under the strictest ban.

Of course neither I nor my friends and colleagues who were faced with the choice of whether to take part in political trials possess the degree of talent with which God has endowed Solzhenitsyn, nor his significance for the spiritual rebirth of his country. Yet none of that makes the sacrifice, to which Solzhenitsyn summons all the "educated rabble," any less hard than the sacrifice he would have had to make if he had been forced to give up forever the joys and agonies of his work. But the magnitude of the sacrifice is not determined by the size of the talent; rather it is by the value to each individual of the thing he sacrifices.

That is why I not only understood but never dared condemn those who refused to take political cases. For the same reason, having agreed to defend such clients, I always gave the most careful thought to the wording of everything I proposed to express in my speeches and appeals. I believed for a long time that I could avoid the terrible danger that threatened me— the danger of losing my profession, the only work that was truly mine, which I knew I could do and which brought me in every case (whether I won it or lost it) the feeling of being needed. Although I estimated the magnitude of the possible sacrifice quite correctly, I never deliberately made that sacrifice. When I appeared for the defense in political trials it was not only because my clients wanted me to, but equally because I myself needed to do it, for both principle and profession.

It is necessary here to say a few words about fear. The innocent, defenseless individual's fear of arbitrary arrest first became an inescapable element in my life during the final years of Stalin's rule.

The years of the "Great Terror," 1936 to 1939, were those of my childhood and adolescence, a time that for me was chiefly one of carefree happiness. Then came the war. The fear I felt then was natural and nothing to be ashamed of. It was fear for my country, which I greatly loved; it was fear of fascism, which I hated; it was fear for the lives of those near and dear to me.

The kind of fear I want to describe, and my personal revulsion for much of Soviet life, began with the campaign against "rootless cosmopolitans" that was unleashed by the authorities in 1948. It was an open and unbridled campaign of persecution of Jews, yet at the same time the leaders of the Communist Party and the Soviet government swore their undying fidelity to the Marxist-Leninist principles of "proletarian internationalism" and the equality of all the nationalities comprising the Soviet state. The obviously anti-Semitic character of the campaign was only faintly camouflaged by not calling the victims of this persecution "Jews" but "rootless cosmopolitans" —a smear implying that these people had no real homeland and were linked by certain mysterious ties into a single international conspiracy.

The campaign was organized and directed from above. Nearly every day newspapers and magazines published articles in which the most ridiculous yet terrible accusations were made against Jewish writers, scholars, movie directors, actors, and artists, illustrated by caricatures of miserable, shifty, dwarfish creatures with large hooked noses engaged in squalid little dealings. In the spring of 1949 a spate of meetings occurred in all universities and in scientific and learned institutions, at which selected and well-rehearsed speakers denounced Jewish scholars for their "cosmopolitan" machinations. Every such meeting ended in the adoption of a unanimous resolution that censured the "rootless cosmopolitans" and demanded their expulsion—and the expulsions invariably followed without delay. Jews were dismissed from their jobs, and no one, of course, was prepared to employ them anywhere else. The next phase was the publication of a series of newspaper articles about the sinister, mysterious agents of "The Joint"

—meaning the Jewish Joint Distribution Committee, the international organization of "Jewish espionage."

The anti-Semitic campaign reached its apogee with the so-called "doctors' plot." In 1952 a group of distinguished doctors was arrested in Moscow: luminaries of medical science, they were (with one exception, I believe) all Jews. They were accused of purposely and with murderous intent giving incorrect treatment to several of their most highly placed patients, members of the government and the Politburo of the Communist Party. The role of *agent provocateur* in this affair was entrusted to the woman assistant of one of the doctors, a certain Lydia Timoshuk, who on orders from the NKVD "unmasked" their villainy.

The front pages of every newspaper were adorned with pictures of this "noble Russian patriot," and her services were rewarded by decoration with the country's highest honor, the Order of Lenin. On January 13, 1953, the newspapers published an official communiqué about the affair, announcing that the criminals had confessed to all their loathsome felonies and would soon be put on trial. I will remember that day forever; January 13 is my birthday, and that evening, in keeping with long-standing tradition, relatives and friends always came to our house to celebrate with me. Since our marriage in 1942, my husband, Konstantin Simis, and I had prepared for the occasion together. In our largest room the long table was set with food and drink for some twenty-five people. The evening drew on, but not a single person—literally not one—came to the party or telephoned us.

We guessed that a catastrophe had occurred, but we learned the whole truth only much later. At the time we did not know, for instance, that the doctors' confessions were extracted from them by the most horrible tortures; that a plan was ready whereby, after the open trial of the "murderers in white coats," as they were led out of the courtroom, they were to be torn to pieces by a crowd of NKVD agents simulating the "just wrath" of the Russian people; that after this the Supreme Soviet of the USSR would issue a decree ordering the deportation of all Soviet Jews to concentration camps in Siberia and Kazakhstan to "protect" them against "righteous Russian anger"; and that the huts for these concentration camps were already built. Only Stalin's death in March prevented these plans and others from being carried out, but his death did not end the terror.

All this we were to discover later, but on that January day, my husband and I sat alone and silent in our brightly lighted room at the festive table, and in silence we drank to my birthday. We realized that our normal life was over, that something terrible was in store for us, as it was for all Soviet Jews. Our friends, Russians and Jews alike, understood this too; that was why not one of them had felt able to come to an evening of celebration.

Those were terrible years—terrible and hard to bear. For our family, as for thousands of other Jewish families, they were hard times in the material sense too. My husband, who since 1945 had been a professor at the Higher Diplomatic School and the Institute of International Relations, was fired without explanation and remained unemployed until the summer of 1953, despite his willingness to do even the most menial work. My sister was dismissed from the Institute of State and Law of the Academy of Sciences and could not find legal work anywhere in the country. Neither her higher degree, her published work, nor her reputation as a gifted scholar were of any help to her. For almost seven years she and her teenage daughter survived only because of the money my parents gave her every month, in addition to occasional scholarly work for friends, which they published under their names and for which they handed her the fees. Fortunately, my parents did not lose their positions as dentist and legal adviser.

Yet when I recall those years as being the grimmest period of my life, I do not think of the material privations. I continued to work, and my earnings provided us—my husband and our son, who was born in 1947—with a very modest existence. Instead I remember it as a time when the most disgusting falsehoods reigned supreme, lies that were devoid of even a hypocritical attempt at plausibility. Arrests, once more on a mass scale, were made on accusations that were breathtaking in their absurdity. For example, one of our friends, a Jew, was arrested and sentenced to many years in a labor camp for "servile admiration of bourgeois Western art": at some gathering he had referred enthusiastically to the films of Charlie Chaplin. Everywhere the persecution of Jews became ever more open and unrestrained.

I am a Jew. I learned this in the Soviet Union during the campaign to fan the flames of anti-Semitism and direct the people's discontents against Jews. Now, having left the Soviet Union, I am once again unsure who I am. My native language, the only one I know, is Russian, my culture is Russian, the history I remember is Russian history; but I suffered during the anti-Semitic campaign against "cosmopolitanism" more painfully and intensely than many Russians. I was more vulnerable than they were. Anti-Semitism tended to pick out the Jews from the rest of society and push us into the line of fire. Ethnic origins per se became a threat, and hence a greater source of fear for self, for family, and for Jewish friends.

My revulsion was not stronger because I was a Jew. Many times since then I have asked myself, "If it had not been the Jews who were humiliated, insulted, and persecuted, would I have felt contempt quite so strongly, would I have found it equally repellent?" My answer is not merely that I hate racism; I am simply incapable of being a racist. I believe that true national pride and self-respect is incompatible with hatred or scorn for people of another race or ethnic group.

The bitterest emotion of all those I have experienced is especially painful because it is not directed against the Soviet regime, which I long ago recognized as wholly amoral. My quarrel is with a fairly appreciable section of the Russian intelligentsia for depriving me of my native land. It is not with those intellectuals living in the Soviet Union who see anti-Semitism as a means of furthering their careers and for whom anti-Semitism is a convenient means of removing talented competitors. My quarrel is with those, whether living in exile or in the USSR, who claim to be concerned about the future of their country, who call for the individual to seek moral perfection, who seek a way for the spiritual regeneration of Russia—and who combine this with anti-Semitism; those who strive to brand every Jew—be it Osip Mandelstam or Boris Pasternak—on grounds of blood as a "rootless cosmopolitan."

Other members of the Russian intelligentsia are different. I remember an occasion, at the height of the 1948–49 wave of anti-Semitic hysteria, when *Izvestiya* that morning had published the usual scurrilous anti-Semitic feature article, accompanied by an anti-Semitic cartoon. An old Russian advocate, a truly cultivated man in the great Russian tradition, approached me in a courtroom during a recess. As he came up to me he said loudly and distinctly, "I want you to know that I feel a deep sense of shame. Today I am ashamed of being a Russian." I also remember another distinguished Russian advocate saying to me in the same period, "It's disgusting. It's worse than it was under czarism. And it's more disgusting, because in those days it was done by people who were openly anti-Semitic but now it is by so-called intellectuals who claim to be internationalists."

These advocates never published anything in *samizdat* or abroad. They never made public statements as spokesmen for national honor and dignity. They were simply decent people, and not even especially brave.

To return to my theme of fear: The moment when our family found itself in immediate danger was in 1952, when a close friend of ours, a gifted young legal scholar named Valentin Lifschitz, was arrested. His story, which had a significant influence on my own development, also reflects the life of my country during those terrible last years of Stalin's rule.

Valentin Lifschitz was arrested and condemned to execution by firing-squad for an attempt on Stalin's life.

Valentin was younger than we were. He had been a graduate student at the Institute of State and Law of the Academy of Sciences; we met at the institute when my husband was teaching there in early 1945, and later they made friends with a well-known historian of Russian law, Professor Serafim Pokrovsky, a man of outstanding talent and erudition. Pokrovsky bore an amazing resemblance to Dostoyevsky, which he did everything possible to stress: he grew a small spade beard, in winter he dressed in a careful copy of a nineteenth-century fur overcoat with a beaver collar, and he wore a tall beaver hat.

Both Valentin and my husband were absolutely captivated by this man. Very soon he became their regular companion, a friend whom they trusted completely. I disliked Pokrovsky on sight. It was an instinctive revulsion. I could not find a single rational cause to justify it. The only thing I could say to Konstantin and Valentin, and which I said frequently, was: "What does he want from you? You're both still boys, and he's a middle-aged man. Why does he insist on trying to be so close to you?" I cannot say that I suspected him of being a provocateur. I simply didn't trust him. It was the only time I ever said, "I don't want that man in our house," and I kept to it. My husband and Valentin, however, continued to meet Pokrovsky, and the three of them spent a large part of their spare time together.

Then came the "anticosmopolitan" campaign. My husband found himself out of work in 1950 and had to go to Rostov-on-Don, where he had the chance of teaching a single course at the university. A year later he was fired again and came back to Moscow. Meantime, Valentin defended his master's dissertation brilliantly but was not kept on at the Institute of Law. As a Jew, he was lucky to get a very modest job at a branch of the All-Union Correspondence School of Law in the city of Gorky.

My husband's friendship with Serafim Pokrovsky broke off naturally, but Pokrovsky and Valentin became absolutely inseparable. Whenever Valentin was in Moscow, he spent the whole time with Pokrovsky. In summer Pokrovsky lived out at Valentin's weekend *dacha*, explaining that he had quarreled with his wife, and he often spent the night at Valentin's apartment in town. Then, early in 1952, Valentin was arrested in Gorky, where he lived alone. No one ever saw the warrant; no one knew why he was arrested.

Valentin's mother, an elderly woman who was a retired professor, tried without success to find out about his fate. We learned only months later that certain friends of Valentin and of ours had been summoned to the NKVD and ordered to give evidence on Valentin's anti-Soviet views. Among them was Serafim Pokrovsky.

Valentin was tried in late December 1952. The trial was a court-martial —itself a sign of the gravity of the charge—behind closed doors (not even Valentin's mother was allowed to attend), and without defense counsel, since under the laws of that time advocates were not permitted in espionage, sabotage, and terrorism cases. All we knew was that only two witnesses had been called: a young woman to whom Valentin had been engaged, and Pokrovsky. Sentence was pronounced on December 31, 1952: Valentin was convicted of an attempted act of terrorism against Stalin and sentenced to execution by firing squad.

I cannot describe what a terrible shock and grief that was to us and to everyone who knew and loved Valentin. I can only say that no one ever doubted for a minute the utter absurdity of such a charge. Not only was Valentin prevented by circumstances from ever even seeing Stalin; he was a person totally incapable of any kind of violence. He was, above all, a serious scholar wholly dedicated to learning.

Soon after Valentin's conviction, I talked with one of his oldest and closest friends, a man of irreproachable integrity. Quoting Valentin's fiancée, Nastya, who had been at the trial as a witness, this friend told us that Valentin was convicted on the testimony of Serafim Pokrovsky. Nastya said that when she saw Valentin in court she did not recognize him at first. He had gone completely gray (he was not yet thirty), and his swollen face looked like a heavily powdered mask. For the whole time she was giving her evidence—after which she was immediately removed from the courtroom—Valentin sat hunched up, his hands covering his face. Only when he answered a question from the president of the court did he raise his head.

The news that it was Serafim Pokrovsky who had destroyed Valentin appalled us. Even I could not imagine that this man was capable of such treachery. We decided that since there had been only two witnesses at the trial, one of them must be the culprit and each would naturally accuse the other, so we had no right to believe one rather than the other.

At the end of April 1953, Valentin's mother succeeded in getting an interview with a deputy of Lavrenty Beriya, the powerful head of State Security. He assured her that Valentin was still alive, that his case would be reviewed and his life was no longer threatened. This was entirely plausible; after Stalin's death an amnesty for criminal prisoners had been proclaimed, and everyone was expecting some lightening of the lot of political prisoners too. What we could not know was that when Beriya's deputy was assuring Valentin's mother that her son's life was no longer in danger, Valentin was dead, shot in the cellars of the Lubyanka on April 16. A month later his mother was told that her son had committed suicide (something that was utterly impossible inside the "internal prison" of the security forces).

We learned the real circumstances of Valentin's case three years later, after the Twentieth Party Congress in 1956 exposed some of the crimes of the Stalin regime. A Moscow advocate who reviewed the case to effect

Valentin's posthumous rehabilitation told us the horrifying truth about the part Serafim Pokrovsky played. Valentin's fiancée, Nastya, had said nothing in her evidence to incriminate Valentin, and the only witness for the prosecution had been Serafim Pokrovsky, whose testimony was the sole foundation for the fatal charge of attempted assassination of Stalin. Pokrovsky had stated that in conversations with him Valentin had said he wished Stalin would die an early death. (In those days that was quite enough to indict someone for attempted terrorism.)

Even that was not the worst. Pokrovsky, it turned out, was not merely an informer who had betrayed his trusting friend but an *agent provocateur* who had fabricated evidence under orders from the NKVD. In addition to tape recordings, the evidence supporting the charge against Valentin included a threatening letter addressed to the Central Committee of the Communist Party that had been typed on Valentin's typewriter. But when our friend studied the material, he established beyond doubt that the letter had been typed by Pokrovsky. Left alone in Valentin's apartment one day, he had composed the letter, typed it out, and mailed it off to the Central Committee.

After Valentin had been posthumously declared innocent by the Military College of the Supreme Court of the USSR, "due to the absence of a *corpus delicti*," Valentin's grief-stricken and by now totally blind mother decided to try to have Pokrovsky punished in some way. By now everyone at the institute knew he was an *agent provocateur* and had caused Valentin's death, yet they continued to shake hands with him. Some did so out of fear —the familiar, deep-rooted fear that had become second nature. Others were morally indifferent. Valentin's mother appealed unavailingly to the director of the institute and to its Party bureau for Pokrovsky's discharge and for his expulsion from the Party.

She then wrote to the Board of Control of the Moscow Committee of the Communist Party demanding his expulsion, and the Board of Control held a special session in which Pokrovsky confessed that he had purposely incited Valentin to make politically compromising remarks, and had fabricated the letter to the Central Committee. His excuse was that he had done this on direct instructions of the NKVD and had regarded it as his duty as a citizen and a Party member, and the Board of Control agreed he had acted in conformity with the duty of a Party member.

In the winter of 1957–58, Valentin's mother finally succeeded in having her appeal examined by the Board of Control of the Central Committee of the CPSU. The national board did not limit itself to questioning Pokrovsky but listened to all the tape recordings of his conversations with Valentin in bars and restaurants, as well as recordings of Pokrovsky's conversations in a cell of the NKVD's prison, where he had been planted as a stool pigeon during the days just after Stalin's death. The provocative nature of all these talks was obvious; this time, Pokrovsky was expelled from the Communist Party.

I don't know how many ruined lives Pokrovsky had on his conscience, but I do know that his choice of Valentin as a victim was not fortuitous. I am even certain that he did not find the choice an easy one, for, monstrous as it may seem, he was genuinely attached to Valentin and regarded him as highly gifted. However, during the notorious campaign against "cosmopolitanism," the NKVD devised a number of big anti-Jewish affairs which were intended to complement the "doctors' plot" in other fields. One of these was to have been the "exposure" of several leading Jewish lawyers as terrorists and saboteurs, and Pokrovsky, of course, was to be the chief provocateur.

Valentin Lifschitz was the first and only victim of this plan. The chain was to start with him partly because he was so close to Pokrovsky, which simplified the task of manufacturing evidence against him, but chiefly because he had been the favorite student of two of the Soviet Union's most distinguished legal scholars, both Corresponding Members of the Academy of Sciences, Aaron Trainin and Mikhail Strogovich. They had been selected to be the principals in the fabricated plot of Jewish lawyers, and Valentin was to be forced to provide testimony against them.

What courage, what honor and nobility Valentin must have possessed, to withstand torture without naming a single name, implicating a single person. We understood now why in the courtroom his face had been a powdered mask and his hair gray.

Nearly thirty years have passed since these events. My profession has taught me to understand people better and to be readier to forgive them. Time and death should have effaced the contempt and hatred I felt for Serafim Pokrovsky, but they have not; I have been unable to forget or forgive him, and I am not ashamed of it.

I hope this story of how our friend was destroyed will help explain the fear that overcame us all during those years. We were so paralyzed by fear that the first, instinctive emotion I felt at hearing the radio announcement of Stalin's last illness was also one of fear. When my husband said to me, "What are you afraid of? The tyrant, the murderer is dying, isn't he?" I agreed with him, realizing that he was right, but I was still afraid. An epoch was dying, and I did not know what the future would hold.

The liberalization that followed Stalin's death gradually freed people from fear. They began to sleep easily at night, they stopped being afraid of late phone calls and footsteps on the staircase in the small hours. Still, there were many people in whom that fear, with its corollary of unquestioning obedience, remained implanted for the rest of their lives. I myself cannot say I succeeded in completely banishing that lurking fear. Perhaps that is why I never became a dissident in the heroic sense of the word that I mean when I describe Larisa Bogoraz-Daniel, Vladimir Bukovsky, Pavel Litvinov, and others as dissidents. I did, however, try very hard not to let my actions be guided by fear. I was old enough to know I must heed the prompting of my own conscience, and the moral blindness of my youth was no longer possible.

Oddly enough, the feeling of personal responsibility and guilt at participation in any form of injustice or lawlessness, even when sanctioned or imposed by the state, was first impressed upon me as a clearly defined moral imperative by an American movie I saw in the early 1960s. *Judgment at Nuremberg*, the famous film about the postwar trials of the Nazi leaders, shook me with its moral force and with the similarity of the situations created by the Soviet and the Nazi legal systems. It had a powerful influence on me and I thought about it often, because it posed and answered the same problems that occupied me at the time and continued to cause me agonies of indecision. Was there a place for me as an advocate in the Soviet legal system? Was I an accomplice in its injustices? Whether or not I was in some degree responsible for what had happened and was still happening in Soviet justice depended on the resolution of those questions.

On January 12, 1968, after the verdict was handed down in the second trial of Alexander Ginzburg, who was convicted with Yurii Galanskov and other dissidents, my colleagues and I were standing in the hallway of the Moscow City Court. The trial was over, all the other participants had dispersed, and only we four advocates remained in the building. We stood there, crushed by the harsh and unjust sentences, even though their severity and injustice were not unexpected. When I thought that we must now go out on the street and face the people waiting there in the ferocious January cold, not counting on justice yet still hoping for it, I was deeply, deeply ashamed.

Yet perhaps one of my colleagues was right when he said, "You have no cause to feel ashamed. We were not part of what the court did. We are not responsible for its injustice."

We went out to the street, where we were met by the crowd of exhausted, frozen people, fenced off from the court building by a cordon of police. They had already heard the verdict but they had not dispersed. They wanted to see us.

And they shouted, "Thank you, thank you" as they handed each of us a bunch of fresh flowers. (Later I thought to wonder how they had managed to keep them fresh for so long in a temperature of minus 40° Celsius.)

Seated in a taxi, my friend, the remarkable advocate Boris Zolotukhin, and I drove away in silence. Then he said to me, "You see, they too understand that we are not the court's accomplices."

"But why are you so quiet?" I asked him.

"You know, it's stupid, but I feel ashamed too."

What did he have to be ashamed of, when only the day before he had given a brilliant speech in defense of Alexander Ginzburg? A speech that was quoted in foreign newspapers as an example of a courageous and principled defense; a speech for which, a few months later, he was to be expelled from the Communist Party and from the College of Advocates.

I am certain that this shame was in some measure a result of the mere fact of his professional involvement with the Soviet legal system. Some of my colleagues, when refusing to defend in political cases, used to say that they did not decline this work out of fear. They believed that participation by an advocate whom the accused had chosen created the illusion of a fair and just judicial system, and they did not want to be parties to such a deception.

I shared that viewpoint, but nevertheless I always accepted political cases. I knew I would be reduced to despair by awareness of my own impotence, by disgust at the cynical farce and an irrational shame at being connected with it. I also knew, though, that if I were to refuse I should feel even more ashamed, and that this shame would be fully justified.

Advocacy was my place in life, my means of participating in it. However shameful the trials in which I appeared, I did not feel able to stand aside from them and thereby absolve myself of responsibility.

The time of my youthful illusions had long since passed. Nor could I believe that the lawlessness, cruelty, and contempt for the human personality in my country were merely a consequence of the "violation of socialist legality" during the years of Stalin's "cult of personality." After the terrible revelations at the Twentieth Party Congress and the sworn assurances of the new rulers that none of it would ever be repeated, I saw the development of a new "cult of Khrushchev." Once more it was bound up with lies and arbitrary disregard of the law, and it unleashed persecution of the great poet Boris Pasternak as well as the suppression of freedom to create, to think, and to speak.

The Soviet dissidents whom I defended were neither terrorists nor extremists. They were people struggling, within the law, to induce the state to observe legitimate human rights. I believed they were fighting, openly and from a sense of duty, for something that we lawyers must fight for in the very nature of our profession. In defending them I felt that I too was in some degree taking part in that struggle.

Although I knew the outcome of these cases would not be affected by what I said in court, that the verdicts had been decided in advance, I did not regard my participation in political trials as pointless. I am convinced that I helped my clients both morally and professionally, and that my help was of value to them. I am convinced also that it is thanks to the advocates that the illegality of the dissident trials in the Soviet Union has become glaringly obvious to the whole world. The scope of the defense in Soviet political trials is extremely limited, not only because of the cramping self-censorship which weighs upon all of us, but because of the law itself. Since no Soviet court is empowered to recognize the unconstitutionality of any law, an advocate cannot point out that articles of the Criminal Code about anti-Soviet agitation and propaganda or slandering the Soviet state and social system conflict with the Constitution, and are *ipso facto* unlawful. When, however, an advocate in open court gave a legal analysis of these articles and affirmed that even under these laws the accused had not committed a crime, or that criticism of or disagreement with any action of the Soviet government and its leaders is the right of every Soviet citizen, and that an individual's convictions cannot in law be regarded as slander, then the advocate accomplished not only a legal but a political defense.

I have never called myself a dissident, not when I was living in the Soviet Union and still less since I have left the country. I have always been conscious of the difference in the kind of courage needed for someone to walk into Red Square and demonstrate in protest at the occupation of Czechoslovakia and the courage required by someone like me, whose function was to defend that person. In defending dissidents, however, I believed I was playing a part in developing a respect for the law among Soviet people and helping to support the whole "defense of legality" movement.

3. Soviet Justice

I N SOVIET JURISPRUDENCE the trial is only the culminating stage of the legal process. It is preceded by a lengthy preliminary investigation (often lasting several months) conducted by bodies that are organizationally independent of the courts. These are the procuracy, the police, the Ministry of Internal Affairs, and—in cases that fall within the competence of the security services—the KGB. Police work of course includes both preventing crime and making inquiries to identify suspects once a crime has been committed.

Soviet police, like all police forces, run a network of undercover agents and maintain covert observation of known malefactors and the criminal underworld in general. The main work in unraveling crime, however, is done by officials of the investigatory departments of the procuracy, the Ministry of Internal Affairs, and the KGB. They can initiate or discontinue investigations, and they have complete independence to conduct all necessary investigations.

Under Soviet law, all relevant material must be recorded in writing in the dossier of each case. This includes the testimony of all witnesses questioned, regardless of its relative importance, and the records of all such procedures as searches, confiscations, examinations of material evidence, and inspections of the scene of the crime. The sum total of the preliminary investigation is the indictment, which is compiled by the investigator and confirmed by the procurator. This is the most important evidentiary document, and its transmittal to the court marks the beginning of the judicial process.

In the indictment the investigator must indicate the charge against each accused, the article or articles of the law that have been infringed, and describe precisely all the evidence indicating guilt. If the accused denies guilt, the investigator must provide a transcript of that testimony as well as all the arguments that refute it. Insufficient evidence, resulting from incomplete investigation, gives a court the right to remand the case for supplementary investigation. Any criminal case of the slightest complexity thus takes many months to investigate.

Soviet law allows suspects to remain at liberty before trial, in which case the suspect is required to sign an undertaking not to leave the locality without the investigator's permission. This is the usual procedure for minor offenses, and in particular where the accused is underage, sick, or the mother of small children. Theoretically, a suspect under investigation can also remain at liberty on payment of bail, but in all my legal career I never encountered a case where bail was granted. I am certain that bail has not been granted in the Soviet Union for the past forty years.

In the overwhelming majority of cases, the accused are held in prison in the strictest isolation, without privilege of correspondence, without meetings with their families, and without the right to consult a lawyer until the investigation is completed. The prison diet is extremely meager; food parcels may be received only from close relatives and only up to a maximum weight of five kilograms per month. These prisoners, who have not yet been found guilty by a court, may be kept in these conditions for several months. The regular period of pretrial detention is two months, but if the investigation of the case is not completed in that time, the detention period may be extended for up to four months longer. After that time has elapsed, the General Procurator of the USSR is empowered to extend the pretrial detention another three months.

Pretrial detention is thus limited by law to a maximum of nine months, and in case of a guilty verdict with a prison sentence, the detention time is counted as time served. In the late 1950s, however, extensions began to be granted by special decrees of the Presidium of the Supreme Soviet. This practice continues, and in 1978, when the Soviet government needed to prolong the trials of Shcharansky and Ginzburg for political reasons, the Presidium simply extended their period of detention.

When the investigation is completed, the investigator must present to the accused (and to his defense counsel, if the accused so wishes) all the materials in the case for him to study, including the exact written records of the testimony given by all witnesses.

At this stage the advocate's task consists chiefly in studying the case materials. This is an unconditional right, which I have always been able to exercise to the full. The advocate also has the right to present evidence, that is, documents relevant to the case; to submit requests (for supplementary investigation, for the calling and questioning of witnesses, for arranging confrontations or the provision of further expert evidence); and to submit pleas for altering the deductions drawn from the investigation, altering the framing of the indictment, the total withdrawal of criminal charges, the exclusion of specific incidents from the indictment, and so on.

An advocate, however, has only the right to ask; the investigator is in no way bound to fulfill such requests. The only requests that raise no objections are those that will not shake the basic conclusions of the investigation (such as requests to include certificates about a person's state of health, the existence of children, positive comment on the accused's performance at work, or evidence of government awards). Other defense requests are rarely granted. This is partly because no investigator wants to add material that might weaken or undermine the existing version of the indictment, which represents months of work, and also because the investigator simply does not have the time to fulfill serious requests—the legally permitted detention period of nine months is an effective deadline.

Thus the pretrial functions of defense counsel are limited by law to a study of the documentary material and the joint planning of defense tactics by advocate and client. There were, of course, instances in my own practice and those of my colleagues when some of our really important requests were granted by the investigator, but that occurred only when the officials appreciated the absolute incontestability of our arguments, and realized that to refuse would inevitably lead to the case being remanded for further investigation.

During my last year as an advocate a friend asked me to defend a woman journalist he knew. She was accused of complicity in pilfering state property and was liable to a prison sentence of up to seven years. The sequence of events in the case was very simple and there was no doubt that a crime had been committed. The journalist had wanted to repair the parquet floor in her apartment. The chances of acquiring parquet flooring in a store were zero (in everyday Russian speech, the verb "to acquire" is used much more frequently than the word "to buy," because it is far more difficult to find what one wants in the stores than it is to pay for it). She then decided to do what millions of other Soviet people do in a similar situation: she went to the nearest construction site and made a deal with the workmen to buy from them the necessary quantity of wooden flooring blocks. She knew, of course, that the workmen did not own the parquet, but would be stealing it from the construction site.

At the moment they were loading the wooden blocks into the trunk of her car, they were all arrested by the police. The outcome of the case depended on the value of the stolen parquet. If its value did not exceed 100 rubles, the case would fall outside the scope of the criminal courts. The prosecutor, however, had arranged for the flooring to be commercially evaluated, and as a result its worth was stated as 284 rubles.

When I began to study the case, two things caught my attention. First, the evaluator had not actually been shown the goods in question, but had simply calculated their value from the current price list. This was an error on the investigator's part. Second, the stolen parquet had not been wrapped in the manufacturer's packaging. This struck me as odd. Obviously it would have been far simpler to load up the trunk of a car with neatly wrapped packages of wooden blocks rather than to unpack them, carry them out in big bags, and then load them, loose, into the car. The only reasonable explanation was that the workmen had simply collected a quantity of loose blocks at random—blocks that for one reason or another had been rejected when the floors of the new building were laid. I realized that we were probably dealing with substandard, scrap flooring.

This was only a guess. The simplest way to verify it was to question the workmen. I asked the investigator to question them, but he refused. I asked to be shown the parquet. The investigator was legally obliged to fulfill this request, but that too he refused. I then submitted a request for the goods to be reevaluated, this time with a physical examination of all the stolen flooring. Again my request was refused. The investigator said he understood the grounds for my request, but his investigation was taking too long and there was simply no time for another evaluation.

Next morning, however, the investigator phoned and asked me to come out at once to the procuracy. He explained that the procurator had instructed him to comply with my request and conduct the second evaluation, because otherwise there was a risk that the case would be remanded for supplementary investigation. The evaluator and I met in the investigator's office, and sat down on the floor with a huge pile of loose parquet between us. As we examined it block by block, I pointed out to him every knot and crack in the wood, and we divided the pieces into two piles, the good blocks stacked up on the left, the scrap ones on the right. The job took about two hours, during which I noticed with delight that the right-hand pile was getting bigger all the time. Finally the whole lot was sorted out. The decisive moment had arrived.

The investigator and I were equally nervous, he because judgment was being passed on his handling of the investigation, I because my client's fate was being decided. Finally the evaluator completed his calculations and announced the result. The total value of the stolen goods was ninety-three rubles seventy-five kopecks. I now had the right to request that the status of the crime be reduced to the theft of a "trivial" amount. A day later I received the official reply: a criminal charge would not be preferred.

This relatively small case demonstrates the kind of work that an advocate has to do at the preparatory stage. Although an advocate's contribution is limited in scope, it is by no means useless.

While preparing for the trial, alone or with his advocate, the accused is able to construct a defense in full knowledge of everything that is being used to substantiate the charges. Furthermore, the indictment, which must be given to the accused at least seventy-two hours before the trial, provides defendant and advocate with the argumentation on which the prosecution will be based.

Similarly, the court, by studying the dossier before the hearing, is informed in advance of the testimony of all the witnesses who will be called, as well as the expert evidence and the arguments of the prosecution, which in due course, sometimes with changes but more often absolutely unaltered, it will hear at the end of the trial in the prosecutor's summation. Thus the judicial process is, in the main, a verification of everything that has already been collated by the investigator and confirmed by the prosecutor.

Both the 1936 "Stalin" Constitution and the new "Brezhnev" Constitution of 1977 (Article 151) enumerate the levels of the Soviet judiciary: Supreme Court of the USSR; Supreme Courts of each of the republics; provincial courts; city courts; people's courts. Provision is also made for courts-martial, which judge all cases of crimes committed by members of the armed forces. The people's courts try the bulk of all civil and criminal cases. The city and regional courts and the Supreme Courts try the more complicated and important cases, and also function as courts of appeal.

All criminal cases in the Soviet Union, irrespective of their importance or the gravity of the charge, are tried by a court consisting of three people —a judge and two "people's assessors." Appeals courts also have three judges, but they are all professionals. The people's assessors are endowed by law with the same powers as the judge. Elected at factories and other work places, they are not only entitled to take an active part in eliciting evidence during a trial; they also decide, with the judge, all the points of law: whether the charge is correctly framed; whether it is proven or not proven; and what punishment should be imposed if the charge is proven. All questions during the trial and the finding of a verdict are decided by majority vote, and the verdict is final even if the professional judge disagrees with the two people's assessors.

In theory, the people's assessors are both judges and a "jury of peers." Thus the law itself guarantees both a fair hearing and a democratic method of reaching a verdict. It would, however, give a distorted picture of the Soviet courts to say that criminal cases (or even civil cases) were actually tried on a basis of complete equality among the members of the court. In practice, the role of the people's assessors is marginal at best. The fact that the people's assessors discuss all aspects of the case with the judge inevitably places them in a position of dependence. The judge influences them by his professional authority, and especially by the fact that the assessors have no legal training, and are incapable, without the judge's help, of understanding legal terminology or correctly evaluating the accused's actions in terms of the law.

Many years in the profession have convinced me that only in exceptional, sensational cases do the assessors act as genuine participants in the trial. Only two such cases occurred in my own career. In the first, one of the assessors was a professional lawyer with an advanced degree, and in the second, one of them was a journalist who had published several articles on legal matters.

The usual state of affairs, in which the people's assessor is a silent and sometimes dozing figure, derives not only from the tendency of Soviet citizens to subordinate their own opinions to those of people in authority, but from the fact that assessors have been purposely endowed with powers they are incapable of exercising. In other countries, the members of a jury faced with the questions "Is this person guilty, and if so does he or she deserve clemency?" need a certain maturity, combined with intelligence, conscientiousness, and a genuine desire to unravel a case and give a correct decision. Their numbers (usually twelve) and the fact that they make their decision in a separate place, away from the professional judge, provide for an independent, many-sided exchange of opinions and the arrival at a fair verdict. But if a jury consists of only two people, if instead of deliberating in private they must make all decisions with the judge, and if they are also obliged to specify the particular law under which the accused should be convicted, how can they avoid relying on the professional judge? And is not the legally established "collectivity" of judgment thereby reduced to a fiction?

The fundamental principle of all justice is the absolute independence of the judiciary from the state. Officially, the Soviet Union adheres to the principles of complete judicial independence and the court's subordination to the law alone. Sadly, I must say that in all my years as a practicing lawyer I never encountered a truly independent judge. The judiciary's complete subjection to Party and governmental directives on penal policy has always existed in the Soviet Union and remains unchanged to this day. As for a judge's impartiality in trying specific cases, here the degree of dependence on higher authority has fortunately lessened with the years.

Many factors combine to prevent a Soviet judge from being independent. First of all, a position on the bench is elective. People's court judges are elected directly by the voters, but the members of provincial courts and the Supreme Courts of the union republics and of the USSR are elected correspondingly by the provincial Soviets and by Supreme Soviets of the union republics and of the USSR. The term of a judgeship, at whatever level of the judicial hierarchy, is limited to five years. Furthermore, all candidacies for judicial office must be put forward and approved by the Party authorities. In practice, therefore, every judge knows that the approval of his candidacy for reelection, and consequently his continuance in the profession, depends on the Party's assessment of his record. Every judge also realizes that he can count on reelection only if he has strictly followed both the general Party directives and the specific instructions of the Party committee to which he is immediately subordinate. Any show of independence and genuine impartiality is bound to evoke the dissatisfaction of the Party authorities and, in consequence, the loss of judicial office.

Each Party body appoints a special official who watches and directs the performance of the local court and procuracy in the name of the Party. In addition, all Soviet judges without exception are members of the Communist Party, and for this reason alone they are obliged to obey all decisions of the relevant Party bodies.

Periodically the bureaus of district and provincial Party committees hold obligatory hearings at which the chairmen of the bench of the appropriate courts (people's courts or provincial courts) report on the work of each judge, noting defects in their performance and pointing out how such failings can be corrected. These Party pronouncements contain comments to the effect that such-and-such a judge has been "showing liberalism" (this is an accepted Party cliché, which means that the judge in question has been awarding too many mild sentences); and if that judge wants to keep his job, he will start handing down stiffer sentences. It may also be pointed out that a court is paying insufficient attention to the need to combat a particular form of crime, such as vandalism or bribery; thereafter, all judges in that district or province are obliged to give harsher sentences for such offenses.

Judges are dependent on the superior courts as well as the Party bodies. No attempt is made to conceal this, and about once a week the superior court summons all judges in the city or province to an instructional conference. In Moscow, for example, the judges of the city's people's courts assembled in the Moscow City Courthouse every Wednesday to hear the president of the City Court or one of his deputies inform them of Party or governmental directives by which they must be guided in trying criminal and civil cases. These directives are binding on the judges. The conference discusses the work of the various district courts and of individual judges, which is assessed in terms of how regularly and obediently they are putting the directives into effect.

This system of control means that all Soviet judges administer justice in accordance with superior directives, whether or not these go against their own convictions or even against the interests of society.

When Nikita Khrushchev was in power, he urged Soviet judges to take a more humane approach, on the principle that a person should be deprived of freedom only when all other disciplinary measures had been exhausted. During that brief "thaw" judges were summoned to instructional seminars given by local Party committees, and the results of these instructions were felt at once, if only temporarily.

Not all judges accept these political swings without inner resistance, without understanding the baseness of their position and the fact that it is a perversion of justice.

I would like at this point to tell the story of a judge who wept.

This happened in a People's Court in Leningradsky district during that short period of Khrushchev's liberalism. I had gone to the courthouse to get a permit for a prison interview with my client. The judge who was to give me the permit was alone in her chambers. She had just finished a criminal trial, and she looked so exhausted that I felt compelled to ask if she was all right or needed help. Suddenly she burst into tears. It was astonishing—a judge who had never been known for sentimentality or softheartedness was sobbing in despair over a sentence she herself had passed.

"This is terrible," she said, "and they make us do it! I had to give a suspended sentence to two bandits. Real bandits who will assault somebody else tomorrow. It's monstrous, but I couldn't act otherwise."

I did not ask her who was forcing her, nor why she could not act otherwise—I knew.

This judge's tribulations did not last long. As circumstances changed, so did the directives from above. And she, no longer sobbing, was again sentencing women with small children or a teenager who had stolen a guitar to years in prison. Unjustified harshness was dearer to her woman's heart than unjustified liberalism. It must be said that the harshness of sentences is a distinctive feature of Soviet justice. And the people's court women judges (more than 35 percent) are not distinguished from their male colleagues by greater compassion.

The need to execute "justice" under constant pressure from above and in accord with ever-changing political directives has resulted in the cynicism and indifference to the fate of human beings that is characteristic of many Soviet judges. I am convinced that this is a major cause of the corruption of the judiciary, which became a noticeable feature of Soviet life during

World War II and increased until it was a glaring and all-embracing phenomenon by the 1950s. Constantly obliged to flout the law, judges lost all respect for it; having to infringe the law on orders from above, they inevitably became ready to break it for money as well. Judges, investigators, and prosecutors then received extremely low salaries. The monthly net earnings of a judge in the provinces, for instance, was 90 to 100 rubles ($125 to $140), while a judge in Moscow earned 100–110 rubles ($140 to $155). This wretched pay scale could barely keep a family above the starvation line.

In the late 1950s a wave of so-called economic crimes hit the Soviet courts, mainly connected with small factories that belonged to the network of producer cooperatives. The accused in such cases were managers and workshop foremen, sometimes the directors and accountants of such small-scale enterprises. As a rule their crime was that, having delivered their planned quota of production to the state, they went on to manufacture a considerable volume of extra goods which were not recorded in the books and were sold through accomplices working in state-owned stores. The profits were shared among the participants. The defendants were often extremely rich by now, and the judges were probably encountering real wealth for the first time in their lives; the money, of course, remained in ready cash, stashed away in various hiding places, since it could not be banked and there was practically no way of spending it. Given these circumstances, only a belief in justice and the sanctity of the law, an inner conviction that the law is paramount, could save a judge from temptation. When that belief had been destroyed by the state itself, all barriers to bribery were gone.

In the immediate post-Stalin years, in Moscow alone practically the entire body of investigators and prosecutors of Moscow Province, many judges of the Moscow Provincial Court, officials of the Kalininsky district procuracy headed by the district procurator himself, and several people's court judges of the same district were arrested and tried for bribery and corruption. Almost the entire People's Court bench of the Kievsky district of Moscow was arrested and tried for bribe taking; nor did this epidemic spare the Moscow City Court and the Moscow City procuracy. The situation was at least as bad in some provincial courts and procuracies; judges who did not take bribes were a phenomenon so unusual as to be incredible. Clients who came to my law office for help were often not looking for defense counsel so much as intermediaries who might channel bribes to the judge. Thus several advocates, too, were drawn into the general corruption of justice.

The link between the judge's total dependence on his political masters and the mass corruption of the judiciary was the basis for a defense plea I once made before the Supreme Court of the RSFSR.

The long, cold, badly lighted courtroom was very familiar to me. The accused were about to be led in, an equally familiar sight. How different they all must have been when they were free; now, though, they all had that same special prison pallor, hands behind their backs, heads bowed. And the women! Stockings hanging down in loops (we had no panty hose in those days, garter belts were forbidden in prison, and women prisoners simply rolled their stockings down below the knee, as peasant women used to do), no makeup (banned in prison), hair twisted into short plaits and tied with scraps of material (combs and hairpins were also forbidden). How old were these women being escorted through the halls under guard? Later, as I listened to their testimony, I caught myself thinking, "She's younger than I am, and so is that one, too . . ." and, looking at them, I couldn't believe it.

On that day, all the normally familiar sights were unfamiliar. The prisoners to be escorted into the courtroom were people I knew, people whom I had faced across many other courtrooms, to whom I had explained my arguments and delivered speeches for the defense while they—today's prisoners—sat on high-backed oak chairs adorned with the coat of arms of the Soviet Union. Among them was a man who had often been my opponent in criminal trials, who in the name of the state had demanded punishment of the guilty and sometimes of the innocent; this was Raphael Asse, one of the most experienced prosecutors in Moscow, and he was now my client, accused of having systematically taken money in exchange for insuring the favorable outcome of a case. Part of the money went to the judges and part he kept for himself. Sometimes it had involved very large sums—tens of thousands of rubles—and sometimes, in minor cases, no more than three or four thousand.

Asse had distinguished himself not only by his high professionalism but simply by his attitude and behavior—he was a civilized, well-mannered person. When I heard that he had been arrested, I was shocked. I could not believe he was guilty.

On the way to my first meeting with Asse in prison, I wondered what he would be like after the many months of imprisonment. I was sure that no matter what his physical condition was, I could count on his full assistance in preparing the defense strategy; after all, he was a practicing lawyer, well acquainted with investigative and judicial work. But the man whom the guard showed into the office was a completely demolished person. The meager jail ration had reduced him to skin and bones, and his fear and despair were so strong that he was completely disoriented. His deposition was surprisingly pathetic. Believing the threats and promises of the investigators, who convinced him that they had irrefutable (though unspecified) proof of his guilt, Asse had pleaded guilty a few days after his arrest.

The first and most natural thought was that he had repented, that once in jail he had found relief in telling the truth, although he knew he would be punished with many years in prison. But I soon discovered that there was no repentance, no moral self-condemnation. This man had long ago forgotten how to respect law and justice, and his crimes did not seem immoral to him. As we discussed his deposition he revived enough to try to persuade me that justice as such suffered no harm when judges took bribes, because they were accepted only for the purpose of giving fair sentences.

It became extremely painful to familiarize myself with the case and then hear it again in court. I felt disgust and despair when I read and then heard the depositions of witnesses who specified where, when, and by whom the bribes were passed, when I came to realize that "justice" had been decided in a little wooden beer hall long before a trial. I thought of the time, energy, and nervous strain of each case—and then an indifferent judge, with a blank look on his face, would utter the customary, "The verdict remains in force."

I had heard this from the very judges who, that first day of the trial, were brought into the courtroom under guard.

How can you defend a person when you yourself can find no grounds for acquittal?

I pitied Asse when I saw how he had changed, how miserable and confused he looked, sitting there fenced off from the world by the wooden barrier. I could make an absolutely sincere speech by appealing for mercy, but I needed a line of approach that would enable me to understand how this could have happened to Asse, to discover why he, of all people, had become a bribe taker. He had not been driven to it by need or material privation; he had no children, and his wife earned a good salary. They had adequate means and a good home. I was convinced after reading the testimony of many witnesses that my picture of his life and habits was correct: he never took part in the drinking bouts and orgies that some prosecutors and judges indulged in, he had no mistresses, and he never gambled.

In an attempt to get to the bottom of this puzzling affair, I had asked my client to describe his view of some of the criminal cases we had both participated in over the years. He recalled many cases which had been resolved unlawfully, not in the courtroom but before the trial, in the office of the secretary of the Leningradsky District Committee of the CPSU. Asse discussed this calmly, as though it were something natural and normal. I realized that, surrounded by people who had started taking bribes long before he had, Asse had gradually lost his repugnance, had finally come to accept bribery as he accepted ideological intervention. After that, the only remaining obstacle to his own corruption was fear, an emotion which, in my view, has never been a reliable guardian of law and order.

My speech in defense of Asse, which was what I have written here put into legal language, was a success. Everything I said was bold and unexpected in a Soviet court. It aroused the interest of my hearers and, most important, of the court. I think it had its effect on the sentence: Asse got four years, the shortest sentence of any of the defendants. And although this was a criminal case, I believe it was then, and not during my defense of Vladimir Bukovsky many years later, that I set out on my career as a "political" defense counsel.

The era of wholesale bribery in which Asse and his colleagues were involved came to an end, but bribery among judges, investigators, and prosecutors persists to this day. The number of those who take bribes has decreased, especially in Moscow and certain other large cities, and it is no longer so open. But it still exists. One example came to light in 1975–76, when the Supreme Court of the RSFSR convicted a group of investigators of the Ministry of Internal Affairs, who had taken bribes in exchange for dropping cases under investigation or for not bringing charges against people under preliminary observation.

In spite of all I have said, the judicial system in the Soviet Union does work, and not only convictions but verdicts of acquittal have been given— less often than true justice required, but given they were. I can think of many cases in which a guilty person received a far more severe sentence than I considered just or expedient, but such punishments were always within the legal limits. I also remember many times when the court agreed with the prosecutor's interpretation of the accused's actions and arbitrarily rejected well-founded defense counterarguments. At the same time, I re-call cases in which the defense succeeded in winning the legal argument, and such occasions were by no means infrequent.

Nevertheless, an acquittal is always a notable event in the career of a Soviet advocate. Sometimes we achieved it right away, in the court of first instance, but more often victory came only after a lengthy progress through the higher courts. Each of my acquittals was a noteworthy event in my life, a moral reward for the hard work which I feel entitled to call the justifica-tion for my whole life.

PART
TWO

1. The Case of the Two Boys

AT THE BEGINNING of February 1967 a defense attorney named Lev Yudovich telephoned me. We had known each other for many years, and although we were not close friends we respected each other.

"I have a dangerous proposal," said Lev. "I want you to join me in an exceedingly interesting case. Two boys, Sasha and Alik, are charged with the rape and murder of a fourteen-year-old girl, a classmate of theirs. I've studied the papers at the state procurator's office and both boys are completely innocent. They've been committed for trial. Will you defend Sasha?"

"It sounds fine. I'm prepared to believe the case is interesting, but why is it dangerous?" I asked in astonishment. "It's a criminal case without the slightest hint of a political element. Just the usual contest between prosecution and defense. How can it possibly be dangerous for an advocate?"

"The fact is that both at one point confessed their guilt. Then they both withdrew their confessions. My client, Alik, has kept on denying everything, but Sasha later told the prosecution investigator that it was his lawyer who had persuaded him to renounce his confession and that in fact both he and Alik are guilty. Irina Kozopolyanskaya was taken off the case and is under threat of expulsion from the College of Advocates. Then a few days after that Sasha wrote a statement asserting that on the urging of the investigator he had lied about his lawyer, that he was quite innocent, and that all his previous confessions were false. Irina asked one of her colleagues to take over Sasha's defense"—here Lev named one of the best advocates in Moscow—"but he refused. He said he would never put his career in the hands of a stupid, confused boy who had already shown no compunction in slandering his own attorney. That's why the case could be dangerous for you. Think it over, but bear in mind that it is a remarkably interesting case, perhaps the most interesting of my whole career."

"I've thought it over," I said. "Tell the parents to come to my office at six o'clock."

That was how I came to defend Sasha Kabanov.

Not far from Moscow is the little village of Izmalkovo. It stands on a high bank overlooking a chain of small lakes known as the Izmalkovo-Samarinsky Ponds. A long, narrow, wooden plank bridge links the village with the far bank and the famous "writers' village" of Peredelkino, where Pasternak lived and is buried. Beyond it runs the "Generals' Road," with its "generals' houses," so called because their owners are mostly senior army officers. These are beneficiaries of Stalin's decree, shortly after the Second World War, that his generals and marshals should all be given country houses, *dachas*, with large plots of land. The house nearest the lake belongs to Ruslanova, a popular folk singer. There too is the *dacha* of Marshal Semyon Budyonny, the legendary leader of the Red Cavalry in the days of the civil war.

In 1965 Budyonny's dacha had some repairs made to it. Each morning an army truck from a nearby military unit brought a load of construction materials and a squad of soldiers who were being used as workers. Then in the evening the truck came back and returned the men to their unit.

On June 17, 1965, three soldiers were working on the site: Bazarov, Zuyev, and Sogrin. They finished their work earlier than usual and decided to go to the playground in the village, where local young people usually gathered in the evening. Sasha and Alik, who were both fifteen, also went to the playground, along with some girls about their age. The young people and the soldiers all played volleyball together.

Around eleven that night the soldiers decided to leave (the truck was already waiting for them), and the teenagers agreed to walk with them across the plank bridge toward the Generals' Road. Some of the girls—Nina and Nadya Akatova, Lena Kabanova (Sasha's sister), and Ira, who lived in one of the *dachas*—went on ahead with the three soldiers, while Sasha, Alik, and Marina Kostopravkina came a few minutes later. Alik wanted to take his accordion home; Marina went to fetch a sweater; and Sasha stopped to tell his mother where they were going. After five minutes, or perhaps seven, the three were all walking together down the main street of Izmalkovo, past the only two-story apartment house in the village, known as the "Big House." It is a large wooden building, each room occupied by one family. Every window in the house was open—it was a very hot evening—and the lights were still on in every room.

Alik, Marina, and Sasha had known each other since infancy and were classmates at school. They walked along, happy and laughing, toward the home of the Akatova sisters, not suspecting that those few minutes were to be fateful for all of them, that just ahead lay a hideous death for Marina, years in prison for Sasha and Alik.

The Akatova girls, it turned out, were not at home, so the three friends concluded that Nina and Nadya had gone on to the bridge and were waiting for them there. The way from the Akatovs' house to the bridge was also down the main street. The last house on the left-hand side of the street belongs to the Bogachev family; behind it is an orchard stretching along the shore of the lake, then a small gully, and beyond that an old wooden fence that separates Ruslanova's property from the village. To walk down the road from the Akatovs' house to the bridge takes no more than five minutes.

A short while later Sasha and Alik came back to the Akatovs', but without Marina. All the other girls were now there: they told the two boys that they had gone by a different way, because they had wanted to get away from the soldiers and prevent them from finding out where the girls lived. After another few minutes (how anxiously those minutes were later to be counted!) the girls—Nadya and Nina Akatova and Lena Kabanova—and Sasha and Alik were walking across the plank bridge toward the Generals' Road. They were seen by fishermen sitting on the bank (these ponds are famous for their carp, and there were a lot of fishermen); they were also heard by the inhabitants of the nearby house, because the children were singing and laughing loudly.

Singing as they went, they crossed the bridge. One of the girls asked, "Where's Marina?" and one of the boys replied: "She decided to go on ahead and catch up with you on the Generals' Road; she didn't want to come back with us." To which one of the girls (later none of them could remember who) said, "Oh, Marina always does things *her* way," and nobody mentioned her again.

It was quite late that night when the children finally got home, and only at dawn next morning did Marina's mother start to go from house to house asking whether anyone had seen Marina.

Marina had not come home.

The news of Marina's disappearance traveled around the village with incredible speed. One after another the villagers came to the Kostopravkins' house. Among them were some who had seen the children playing volleyball the previous evening, some who had heard the children's voices as they crossed the bridge; and there were the fishermen who had seen them, either from the bank or from a boat, and had even recognized their voices; the Akatov sisters, after all, were the two best singers in the village and there was no mistaking them.

From early morning a policeman was installed in the Kostopravkins' house to take statements. He carefully questioned everyone who came to the house and meticulously noted down all testimony, fixing the precise times when the children had left the volleyball court, and when the fishermen and the people in the neighboring houses had heard them. He questioned Alik, Sasha, Nadya, Nina, Ira, Lena, and many others, recording all their statements.

The policeman was particularly searching in his questioning of Alik and Sasha—they, after all, were the last people who had seen Marina. Only they could tell why they had suddenly left her, why she had gone on ahead alone, and why she hadn't wanted to come back with them. But neither Alik nor Sasha could give any reasons. "She didn't come with us, that's all," and, "She just didn't want to," these were the only explanations they offered that first day and the many subsequent days.

Meanwhile, policemen and local volunteers were combing the banks of the lake and the orchard, examining every bush, every path. They searched until darkness, but no trace of Marina was found.

On June 19 the search was renewed early in the morning, and that evening the searchers came across a small clearing in the gulley near Ruslanova's *dacha*. There, under some low bushes amid heavily trampled grass, they found Marina's sweater; nearby was a button torn from the swimming shorts she had been wearing underneath her clothes. A little farther away was a man's old peaked cap and a white button, of the kind sewn onto the cheapest sort of men's underwear, including the kind issued to troops of the Soviet Army.

Frogmen came to Izmalkovo and searched underwater for Marina's body—in vain.

Again there followed days of interrogating everyone who had been in the village that evening, and all the inhabitants of nearby villages about whom the police might possibly harbor suspicions.

The first suspects were the soldiers. Their stories about how they had returned to their unit after the game of volleyball were contradictory. The investigator was made particularly skeptical by the evidence of the truck driver who had taken the soldiers back to their base. He insisted that he had arrived at the agreed time of eleven, but that the soldiers had not been there; they did not show up, he claimed, until 1:00 A.M., and when they did, they begged him not to tell anyone about their late arrival. Soldiers, however, are subject only to military law; they are dealt with by their own military procuracy and tried by court-martial. The military procurator refused to arrest them, on grounds of insufficient evidence of guilt. The longer the case continued, the more the soldiers' testimonies came to resemble each other and the shorter became the period of their unauthorized absence.

A week passed. On the morning of June 23 Sasha and some of his friends went rowing on the lake, and they talked about Marina. Sasha was telling the others how they had walked together toward the Akatovs' house and what they had talked about on the way. Suddenly he stopped and, in the words of his friends, turned so pale that they were all frightened (this pallor was later interpreted by the investigator as proof of his guilt). Beside the boat, almost touching it, a ghastly, bloated corpse was floating. It was Marina. According to the medical experts, Marina died of "asphyxia caused by drowning." They also indicated that death had been preceded by forced sexual intercourse.

Marina's funeral was attended by the whole village, including the school and all the teachers. Class after class filed past the grave to say their last farewells. It was a funeral at which the grief was unfeigned, as was the urge for vengeance on the as yet undetected murderer.

More time passed. During the month after Marina's death on June 17, uniformed and plainclothes police of the district arrested twenty-eight people who for various reasons were potential suspects. Among them was a certain Sadykov, a man with a previous record of convictions for theft and disorderly behavior, who lived in a small village not far from Izmalkovo. On the night of June 17–18 he had not spent the night at home; his wife had found him next morning in a shed, dead drunk, with torn and bloodstained clothes. He was detained in the police cells for the legally permitted period of three days, the maximum period the police may detain a suspect before he is turned over to the courts. Friends of his, however, confirmed to the investigator that they had been drinking with him that night, that a drunken brawl had broken out and that was the reason for the bloodstains. So Sadykov was released.

Later, studying the prosecution's dossier on the case, I was amazed at the incompetence of the investigator, who dithered from one version to another, from one set of suspicions to another, without subjecting any of them to thorough checking. On every occasion he conducted no more than the most superficial interrogation. He made no attempt to find out the reasons for contradictory evidence (as in the case of the soldiers). He did not send Sadykov's bloodstained shirt for tests, preferring to accept the testimony of the man's drinking companions. Even after the pathologist's report came in, he failed to carry out biological tests on the clothing of any of the suspects, despite the importance of determining whether or not the garments showed traces of semen. The passing of time was inexorably working against the investigator and against the likelihood of justice being done. The testimony of suspects grew ever more confident, fewer and fewer contradictions appeared in their statements, and they were able to call upon an ever greater number of corroborative witnesses who confirmed their innocence. By early August 1965, the number of people being summoned for interrogation had dwindled almost to zero. The investigation was clearly up a blind alley.

Suddenly, during the third week of August, the news flashed around the district: the murderer had been found and arrested. He was a hardened criminal, a recidivist previously convicted of both rape and murder. His name was Nazarov. Then came more news: the suspect had confessed. He had told the investigator how he had battered and raped Marina, then had killed her and thrown her body in the water.

The natural urge for revenge, the thirst for retribution that is always aroused by a violent crime, came to obsess the thoughts and emotions not only of Marina's mother, Alexandra Kostopravkina, but of most inhabitants of Izmalkovo. They began to count the days to the completion of the investigation and the opening of the trial. The words "death penalty" and "firing squad" were on everybody's lips.

But time passed, and there was no sign of the investigation being closed. At the end of December 1965 came a staggering new announcement: "The investigation into the death of Marina Kostopravkina has ceased because of the absence of a suspect."

A delegation from the village went to the procurator to demand an explanation. What did this mean? A criminal suspect had been detained, and he had confessed. No one was satisfied by the procurator's explanation that the confession was false, that Nazarov had retracted his original statement, saying it had been made when he was confused, and that there was no other evidence of his guilt. All this was even harder to believe because it was now common knowledge that he was shortly to be tried for raping another girl and for a series of robberies.

Soon letter after letter, petition after petition was going to the Central Committee of the Communist Party with a single demand: "Find and punish the criminal." It was now 1966. Nearly a year had passed since Marina's death and still nothing was heard from the investigators. They would not reopen the case, they said, "for lack of a suspect." The letters to the Central Committee had done no good.

Then the villagers decided to enlist the writers in the struggle. The writers' settlement, Peredelkino, was, after all, just across the lake. So the writers too petitioned the Central Committee, demanding that the criminal be found and punished.

June 17 was the anniversary of Marina's death. Again the Kostoprav-kins' relatives and neighbors gathered at the village cemetery, together with the teachers and children who had been Marina's friends. This time there were fewer tears than a year ago. The children stood in silence while the adults drank vodka "in memory of Marina." Tears were not lacking, however: for this purpose the family had invited an old inhabitant of the village, Yekaterina Marchenkova, who was a *plakalshchitsa*, a professional mourner. Standing at a little distance from the crowd around the grave, a thin, gray little woman in thick-lensed spectacles, a large black kerchief on her head, she drained her final glass of vodka and began. At first she spoke in a low, singsong voice, then gradually her lamentation grew louder and faster.

She spoke of how clever and beautiful Marina had been, and how an evil man had destroyed her. Soon there were tears in her voice, and her words were interrupted by loud sobs. Alexandra Kostopravkina began to join in and repeat after her: "My darling daughter, my pretty little girl, who was the villain who murdered you, my sweet one . . ."

Marchenkova's keening grew louder and more agonized:

Marina, Marinochka, my darling!
Forgive me, a stupid old woman!
Release me from my guilt.
Why do I dream of you every night?

By now everyone was weeping and Marchenkova's words could hardly be heard.

It was only later, on the way home, that Marina's godfather, Zakharov, asked Alexandra Kostopravkina whether she had heard how, in her lamen-tation, Marchenkova had said that she felt guilty about Marina because she could have saved her and did not.

That evening Kostopravkina invited Marchenkova to her home for the wake. Again the vodka circulated, and Kostopravkina asked the old woman what she knew about Marina's death and why she had said that she could have saved her and did not. At first Marchenkova simply denied having said any such thing at the cemetery. They drank some more, and before leaving to go home she said that exactly a year ago, late in the evening, she had been sitting in her room on the second floor of the "Big House." The window was open, and while she was eating supper she heard a loud conversation in the street.

She recognized Marina by the sound of her voice: "Alik! Leave me alone! Stop pestering me! You ought to be ashamed. Sasha! Let go, what do you want with me? Leave me alone, both of you!" In reply, one of the boys had laughed loudly.

"I didn't think anything of it," Marchenkova went on. "I just thought they were fooling around and I went to bed."

Indeed, to a sensible, uninvolved person who chanced to hear this story, there was nothing sensational about it. Even if one believed that Marchenkova really had overheard this conversation, precisely on June 17, and that she had indeed recognized Marina's voice, the fact was that neither of the boys had denied walking past the house on that evening. They had themselves, the very next day, described their route to Marina's mother and to the policemen. Furthermore, the wording of the conversation, as recalled by Marchenkova, in no way incriminated either Sasha or Alik. Marina had not been crying, nor had she called for help, although they had been walking down the main street of the village, with people in every house who would have come to her assistance. The words she spoke to Alik or Sasha, "Leave me alone!," might have been a normal reaction to any boyish joke.

So too reasoned the district procurator, to whom Alexandra Kostopravkina next day presented a statement declaring that she and others had found the murderers—Sasha Kabanov and Alik Burov. Indignant at her reception by the district procurator, Kostopravkina then addressed her complaint to the procuracy of Moscow Province, and was told that the investigation into Marina's death had been entrusted to an experienced investigator by the name of Yusov.

A tall, thin man with a long, pale, oval face, Yusov wore a large pair of spectacles in front of his small, almost slitlike, nearsighted eyes. Yusov called Kostopravkina to see him without delay. He listened to her carefully, questioning her in particular detail about Marchenkova's story. His final words were to assure her that now "everything will be handled differently." The case was under the special aegis of the Central Committee of the CPSU (a reaction to the writers' petition), to which he had been ordered to report the results of his inquiries. He would find the criminals at all costs.

On June 22, 1966, Sasha Kabanov was sixteen years old, the age at which he had the right to receive his internal passport, an identity card that every Soviet citizen is required to have. All the necessary certificates had already been handed in to the police station. Sasha was told he would receive his passport on August 31.

Dressed in a new shirt bought for the occasion and a pair of pants carefully ironed by his mother, he went to the police station. Meanwhile at home a special festive meal was prepared for his return—the family was celebrating the coming of age of yet another son. Their eldest son was already married and lived away from home, the second son was serving in the army, their daughter Lenochka was also working by now, and soon it would not be long before it was Sasha's turn to join the army for his compulsory three years of military service. The Kabanov family was not only a large one; it was a loving, united family, and above all—what is extremely rare in rural Russia—all its members were teetotalers.

By the time Sasha returned from the police station, the whole family had gathered. Suddenly, two unexpected visitors arrived. One of them was well known—he was the inspector in charge of the local police station; the other man was a complete stranger: tall and thin, wearing large spectacles, with thin, tightly closed lips in a pale face. He introduced himself as the new inspector from the Ministry of Education.

The inspector's manner was polite, concerned and friendly. He asked Sasha about his schoolwork, about the books that he was reading, and asked to be shown the new textbooks and exercise books that Sasha had already prepared for the opening of school the next day. He thanked the family for their invitation to join them at dinner but regretted that he had no time. He had to go and visit all the other houses in which the new senior-class students lived.

"Perhaps Sasha could help me by showing me the way to the house of his nearest classmate. Then he can come straight home, he won't be late for dinner . . ."

And so they went out—the new inspector, the local police officer, and Sasha.

An hour passed before Sasha's mother heard from neighbors that both Sasha and Alik had been driven off in a police car. It was only after four days of long and anxious searching—because no one knew where the two boys had been taken—that the parents finally discovered that one of the boys was in the remand cells in the town of Zvenigorod and the other in the cells of the village of Golytsino, and that they had been arrested and held on the orders of Yusov, senior investigator of the procuracy of Moscow Province.

The next day, the mothers of Alik Burov and Sasha Kabanov took the train to Moscow to see the procurator. In an office on the second floor of the handsome old procuracy mansion sat the man they had met as an inspector from the Ministry of Education. This time, however, he was not smiling in friendly fashion, nor did he ask about anyone's grades. He was now Senior Investigator Yusov, and he replied tersely to the amazed women. He declared himself convinced that Alik and Sasha had killed Marina, although the two boys had not been formally charged. He listened with an ironic expression as the mothers assured him that their sons were completely innocent. He could not predict when the case would be ready for trial, nor could he say when the parents could engage a lawyer, though he would certainly inform them when the time came. Soviet justice would never allow children to be deprived of legal aid; everything would be done according to the law. Naturally, the boys could not receive any correspondence—that was strictly forbidden.

More days passed, during which Alik and Sasha were still detained. The parents did not complain, because they did not know that the maximum permitted period of detention under such conditions was three days. Nor did they know that on September 3 Yusov had received a written order from the procurator to transfer the boys to a prison in Moscow that had facilities for minors.

On September 6 Lena Kabanova received a phone call at her job in the city. The caller was Yusov, who told her to meet him at her subway entrance so he could give her a letter from Sasha. When she arrived at the station Yusov handed her a sealed envelope and instructed her to open it only in the presence of her parents.

Lena hurried into the station to catch her train; if she missed it, there would be an hour's wait before the next one. From the Bakovka stop she hurried along the road through the woods, ran across the plank bridge, up the main street and past the volleyball court, arriving at home breathless.

"A letter from Sasha! Yusov gave me this letter from Sasha!"

What happiness—news from their son, the first word from their boy, who had been taken away by a trick which had prevented even a goodbye to him. The letter was written on one large sheet of paper:

> Sept. 6, 1966
>
> Dear Mama and Papa, Lenochka, brothers, and Aunt Marusya,
>
> Don't worry about me, I'm being well treated. I have told them what Alik and I did to Marina. We raped her and then drowned her. Please send me a clean pair of pants and some dried crusts. Investigator Yusov has promised they will be delivered to me. Forgive me. I expect we'll be seeing each other soon.
>
> Your son,
> Sasha

Sasha's mother, Klavdia Kabanova, told me that after they read this letter none of them even cried. They just sat in silence. Unable to think, they felt only the emptiness of total despair. But when they were able to think and talk again, not one of them believed for a moment that what Sasha had written was the truth.

Knowing the family well, I believed what she said. These completely uneducated, simple people were awesome in the dignified restraint with which they endured the grief that had overwhelmed them. Klavdia Kabanova never ceased to amaze me; this woman had raised six children in the dauntingly hard conditions of rural Russia—living in a wooden shack heated only by a wood-burning stove, with no piped water (all their water was fetched from the well in buckets), no sanitation, no gas stove; working seven days a week from morning till night on the state farm as well as at home—yet she never became embittered, always behaved with dignity. Somehow she managed to command the respect not only of her children, who invariably obeyed her without a murmur, but also of her fellow villagers; and she even managed to retain the fresh looks and youthful walk of a real Russian beauty, with her ash-blond hair that showed scarcely a trace of gray and her small but piercing and brilliantly blue eyes.

She was the undoubted head of the family, yet she never gave orders— indeed, she hardly ever so much as asked for anything to be done: somehow her family automatically knew what was needed and how they should act. Sasha's father worked as a truck driver in Moscow; he came home late at night and saw his family only on Sundays.

Late that same evening of September 6, Alik's mother arrived, breathless from running, at the Kabanovs' house. Yusov had sent a letter from Alik too. Both families now sat down to read and reread the two letters. Alik's letter was as follows:

September 6

Dear Mama and Papa and Galya,
    Don't worry about me. No one has done me any harm. I have told the investigator that Sasha and I raped Marina, then threw her into the lake. Send me my new cap and lots of dried crusts, please. Investigator Yusov says you will be allowed to deliver them. Forgive me.

Your son and brother,
Alik

The promise of food packages was as spurious as the confessions. Klavdia Kabanova tried to deliver the parcels to Yusov, but he was not in, to her at least, the next day.

The day after that came a new development: Alik was brought to the village under escort. He walked the whole length of the village from the volleyball court to the lake. Beside him, never more than a pace away, was Yusov, while policemen with guard dogs flanked them on either side. Behind followed a group of strangers (sworn in as "official witnesses" to testify that the operation was procedurally correct) and a man with a movie camera.

Everyone in the village, children and grownups alike, ran to watch. They heard Alik, unhurriedly and with amazing calm, point out the route he and Marina had followed from the playground, down the main street, past the "Big House" and past the Akatovs' house.

Alik went on talking. It was near the Bogachevs' house, the last in the street, that he and Sasha had attacked Marina, twisting her arms behind her back. She had tried to shout, but they had gagged her with Alik's new cap (the one he asked his mother to send him). Then they had dragged her a little way along a path into the orchard, where they pushed her to the ground under a tree.

At the investigator's suggestion, Alik, without an instant's hesitation, pointed out the tree beneath which first he and then Sasha had raped Marina. They had then strangled her, picked her up by her arms and legs, and dragged her to the side of the lake. He walked to the lakeside (all this, of course, was being recorded by the camera) and pointed out the spot where, after first swinging Marina's body back and forth a few times, they had flung it into the lake.

Alik was not merely calm; he seemed completely unembarrassed by the crowd of neighbors, who stood in absolute silence, shattered by the terrible story complete with revolting details of the violent rape, and by Alik's dispassionate, unemotional description of the murder, told without a trace of remorse. As he was being escorted back to the car, Alexandra Kostopravkina ran up, shouting: "Murderer! Vicious brute—you should be torn to pieces!" Even then Alik remained calm.

Then early on September 9 a policeman came to Izmalkovo and invited the mothers of the two boys to go with him at once to the police station at Zvenigorod, where Investigator Yusov was waiting to see them.

They collected the food they had bought and drove off in the police car. They were not allowed into Yusov's office but were asked to wait in the corridor. Their food parcels were taken from them, and they waited for several hours. Finally Yusov appeared, accompanied by a tall, stout man whom he introduced: "This is your defense counsel, Advocate Borisov. I have just questioned your sons in his presence and I have charged them, under Article 102 of the Criminal Code, with first-degree murder. You may now talk to your lawyer."

This was completely unexpected. Burova and Kabanova had decided they would retain two lawyers, one for each boy, and, most important of all, that they would seek their defense counsel in Moscow. Since the investigator had told them only a few days ago that it was still too early to engage lawyers and that he would warn them when it was time, why had he himself suddenly appointed a lawyer for Alik and Sasha? As though anticipating this question, Yusov added, "Don't worry. Comrade Borisov is a very experienced advocate, and he is not just an ordinary lawyer, he is in charge of a law office. You may have complete confidence in him. I must go now, I'm late. We'll talk another time."

The consultation with Advocate Borisov did not take much time either: "The boys have confessed to everything," he said. "They did it in a moment of foolishness. No, there can be no doubt about it. They really are guilty— if they weren't, they wouldn't have confessed. No, they have not been beaten up. Investigator Yusov is a good man and he has treated the boys well. Why are you so upset? They are both minors, they won't be executed. The law permits only a ten-year maximum prison sentence. Now let's go to my office; you must pay the first part of my fee to the cashier." As the women entered his modest office they noticed a plate on the door:

A. S. Borisov
Head of Legal Consultancy

Yusov, it seemed, had not deceived them: he really had chosen a senior lawyer to defend the boys.

Next morning Sasha was brought to Izmalkovo. Again everyone came running to watch him; again the boy was escorted by Yusov, policemen with dogs, official witnesses, a movie cameraman. Once more the same story was told with the same dispassionate calmness, with the same appalling details. The only difference in his version was that he had not strangled Marina; he thought she had choked to death when Alik rammed his cap into her mouth. This time not only Kostopravkina but the entire crowd shouted, "Murderer! Brute!" Without looking at them, Sasha went on slowly telling his story; only Yusov turned to the angry crowd and told them not to disturb the official party while it was trying to do its work.

Sasha was taken straight from Izmalkovo to the remand cells at Zvenigorod, where he was questioned in the presence of Mrs. Volkonskaya, a teacher whom he greatly liked and respected. There too he calmly told the same story, no more and no less, all details identical.

Every day thereafter the authorities requestioned everyone who had seen the children at the volleyball court on June 17, 1965, as well as the children themselves. Each witness was questioned about the precise timing: when had they started playing? When had they stopped playing? How long had it taken them to walk home? How soon did Alik and Sasha join them?

By now the witnesses were being summoned to Moscow for questioning; on September 17, Alik and Sasha had been transferred to the prison with a special section for minors.

Nina and Nadya Akatova, Ira Klepikova, and Lena Kabanova were being interrogated by the investigator almost daily. Just as they had done when questioned during the days just after Marina's death, they affirmed that no more than fifteen to seventeen minutes had elapsed between the moment they left the volleyball court and the boys' arrival at the Akatovs' garden. Yusov, however, tried to convince them that they were mistaken, that the interval could not have been so short. To commit such a crime in a mere quarter of an hour was impossible, and the boys had, after all, confessed that they had done it.

"You won't help them, and you might be getting yourselves into trouble. You could be charged with perjury," was Yusov's argument, although under Soviet law, persons under sixteen cannot be held criminally responsible for perjury. At the time of the questioning, only Lena Kabanova was sixteen, so the other girls were not liable to prosecution for perjury.

The girls stuck obstinately to their story until they were brought face to face with Sasha. In their presence he described, as calmly and unemotionally as before, what Alik and he had done to Marina and how they had killed her. He stated that he and Alik had been absent for thirty-five minutes. Immediately the investigator asked the girls, "Do you corroborate the testimony of the accused?" Nina, Nadya, and Ira replied: "Yes, we do."

Only Lena, Sasha's sister, answered the question with a firm "No." And despite Yusov's order not to speak directly to the accused, she asked Sasha, "Why are you lying, Sasha? I was there myself, and I *know* it was only fifteen minutes."

For this the investigator shouted at her, ordering her to sign the indictment and leave his office.

Then suddenly the questioning of witnesses in front of the boys ceased. In vain their mothers asked to be interrogated in the boys' presence, so that they might at least be able to see their sons and hear for themselves what they had to say. The investigator refused to permit either this or a prison visit by the mothers.

After a few more days Yusov announced that the investigation was completed. This time the two mothers firmly refused to accept Borisov as defense counsel and said they wanted their boys to be defended by lawyers from Moscow, especially since the trial was to be held there.

This was how Lev Yudovich and Irina Kozopolyanskaya came to take on the case. It was from these lawyers that the mothers learned that Alik and Sasha were going to plead not guilty; that Yusov had forced them to make their confessions; and that they were wholly innocent.

Marina's mother heard of this too; she heard it, in fact, from Yusov, who told her that the two lawyers had been bribed by the boys' relatives to persuade them to retract their confessions. All this would be brought out into the open at the trial, and the court would sort out the facts.

By now, no one in Izmalkovo was neutral. The whole village threw itself into the battle for retribution against the boys and their parents, who continued to believe in their innocence, and, of course, against those corrupt and dishonest lawyers who had tried to shield the two confessed—and therefore unquestionably guilty—criminals. By now, too, everyone had forgotten that before the boys' arrest they had been regarded as a couple of decent kids (of the two, Sasha was better liked, because Alik was apt to be cheeky to grownups), and that it had never entered anyone's head to suspect their complicity in Marina's terrible death.

That was how the case stood when I said, "I've thought it over," and undertook Sasha's defense.

2. Pretrial

I T WAS ONLY ABOUT TWO WEEKS before the start of the hearing, and I realized that the whole of that time would have to be devoted to a study of this complex case.

On day one I began my work in the courthouse of the Moscow Provincial Court. Alone in an empty courtroom, I sat down at a table and opened the indictment—thirty-four pages of dense, single-spaced typescript, about half of it made up of lengthy passages from the testimony of Alik and Sasha when they had confessed themselves guilty.

> Walking down the road, before we reached the village water pump, Sasha suggested to me that I should rape Marina. I said I wouldn't. We met Marina at the pump, and walked on together toward the bridge. We walked past the two-story "Big House" and the Akatovs' house. There was no one there, so we went on as far as the last house, where Nadya Bogacheva lives. At the corner of the fence we made a grab at Marina and started twisting her arms. Marina said she would scream. I stuffed my cap into her mouth and we dragged her to an apple tree in the orchard. Sasha pulled her by her left arm, I used my left hand to pull her right arm. I was holding my cap in my right hand, and I used the cap to gag her mouth.

There followed several more pages of Alik's evidence, describing in minute detail how they had dragged Marina to the second row of apple trees and pushed her to the ground, how Sasha had held her legs while Alik raped her, how Sasha had then strangled her, and how they had carried her body to the lake. After that came several pages quoting Sasha's testimony, in which he too had confessed his guilt:

Alik and I walked from his house to the pump. Marina was standing there. On the way to join Marina, Alik suggested raping her, and I agreed. Together with Marina we went as far as the "Big House," and there Alik made a grab at Marina. She said: "Leave me alone," and we walked on downhill.

There was no one at the Akatovs' house, so we went on. We stopped near the Bogachevs', the last house in the street, and Alik jumped on Marina and stopped her mouth with his cap. We grabbed her by the arms and went into the orchard.

The rest consisted of the same details given in Alik's statement, except for Sasha's assertion that when they had finished raping the girl,

Alik said to Marina: "Get up." She didn't reply. We tried to make her get up, but she didn't get up. Alik took his cap out of Marina's mouth. We decided that she was dead, but we didn't know why. Perhaps she had suffocated. Alik said we had better bury her, so that nobody would find her, but then we decided to carry her down to the lake.

And so on for page after page, with only the most trivial points of difference; the kind of testimony, packed with detail, that looks so convincing.

At the very end of Volume III appeared a deposition written in a childish hand—Sasha's holograph statement:

I have decided to tell the truth because I want to go out into the world with a clear conscience. I have committed a crime, but I will take the consequences of it and I don't want to be tortured by my conscience for not having repented of what I did. I do repent of it and will never do such a thing again, because it was just done for a stupid dare suggested by Alik Burov. On my own, I would never have thought of doing such a thing. (Vol. III, p. 224.)

More and more often I found myself thinking, "Perhaps they really did do it."

I knew both Lev Yudovich and Irina Kozopolyanskaya, and I did not believe they had improperly persuaded Alik and Sasha to change their testimony and retract their confessions. Lev and Irina were both principled people, incapable of such a breach of professional ethics. They were also experienced, level-headed lawyers, well aware of the consequences for themselves if the court ever found out that the radical alteration in the defendants' testimony was the result of improper influence by their defense counsel.

I also realized, however, that in these pretrial months both boys had acquired a new sort of experience in prison; and that if their "confession" was the outcome of unlawful pressure by the investigator, it was equally possible that their retraction of it might have resulted from the influence of more experienced cellmates.

Just as these thoughts were passing through my mind, the door of the courtroom opened and a man came toward me.

"Good morning, comrade advocate. I heard you were studying the case of the two boys, and I decided to come in and introduce myself. I don't think you have pleaded in my court before." He was Judge Kirilov.

Kirilov was a relatively young member of the Moscow Province bench. Lawyers who had appeared before him invariably commented on his intelligence and the soundness of his legal training, but they also remarked on the harsh, almost despotic way he conducted his trials and said he was often curt and even rude to defense counsel. I was pleasantly surprised that he had taken the trouble to say hello. No such tradition existed in the Moscow courts; indeed, a judge in whose court you had appeared many times would often walk past without even nodding.

Kirilov went on, "I'm glad you're involved in this case. It's a very interesting case, but also very distasteful. Don't you think, Comrade Kaminskaya, that the case is very distasteful?"

"I think all murder cases are distasteful. And in this one the accused are mere boys. It certainly is extremely distasteful."

"That's true, of course. But there are several peculiar features here. It is, so to speak, a contest between the honor of the procuracy and the honor of the bar. Because, as you know, either someone induced these boys to make a false confession or someone else persuaded them to retract truthful testimony and slander the investigator."

"The honor of Investigator Yusov is not the same as the honor of the procuracy, just as the behavior of Advocate Kozopolyanskaya cannot be equated with the behavior of the bar as a whole."

"You misunderstand me, comrade advocate. This is a very difficult and unpleasant case. Have you read Volume I of the prosecution dossier? You haven't? You must at least glance through it before you visit your client. By the way, when were you planning to go?"

"Tomorrow morning. As it happens, I was just about to go and look for you to get your permission for the visit. My request is made out. Here it is."

Suddenly Kirilov's face turned to stone, and in a harsh voice that brooked no objection he said, "I cannot give you permission today. You will not go to the prison tomorrow. Come and see me tomorrow at the end of the working day and I'll give you permission. You can go see him the day after tomorrow."

Nothing like this had ever happened in all my professional career. An advocate's right to visit the client before the trial at any time convenient to the advocate has always been respected, and the only limitation is that the visit must take place during the prison's working hours. No other judge in my experience had ever concerned himself with the day or the time at which an advocate went to see his client.

I instantly made up my mind that I would obtain that permission today and no later. If the refusal was simply motivated by this man's arbitrary whim, then he must be made to realize that I was able to insist on my rights. Otherwise a judge of this stamp, once he sensed weakness or pliancy in an advocate, would disallow important questions and overrule pleas that were essential to the defense. If, on the other hand, more weighty reasons lay behind this blunt refusal, then it was up to me alone to decide the correct course of action.

In what I thought was an equally tough and uncompromising tone of voice, I replied, "You are mistaken, Comrade Kirilov. I shall go to the prison tomorrow. It happens to suit my convenience, and no one has the right to prevent me. I must therefore ask you to sign my request for a prison visit immediately. You know it's my right and your refusal would be illegal."

"I don't propose to discuss with you what is legal or illegal. You will get your permission tomorrow."

As soon as I could get there I was in the office of the deputy chairman of the bench of the Moscow Provincial Court, Judge Chernomorets. He knew me from the many cases in which I had appeared before him. He greeted me and listened attentively.

"There has obviously been some misunderstanding, Comrade Kaminskaya. Don't worry. I'll speak to Kirilov right away and clear it up. No one in this court has any intention of restricting your rights."

I went out into the anteroom. Five, ten, fifteen minutes went by. At last I was called back into the judge's office.

"Comrade Kaminskaya, do you *have* to go tomorrow of all days? Why don't you postpone your visit to any other day that suits you? Comrade Kirilov and I have agreed that he will sign your permission today, but the date of its validity will be the day after tomorrow. So you won't have to make another journey to the courthouse just to get your permission."

Chernomorets was clearly embarrassed. I said firmly, "Until I know why my right to see my client is being restricted, I will not change my decision, and I demand to be given permission today for a visit tomorrow."

"Please don't be offended, comrade advocate. We have nothing against you personally. But you know, of course, that the bar as a whole has been somewhat compromised where this case is concerned. A judge must exercise caution and prudence . . ."

I listened to him uncomprehendingly. If they didn't trust me, why did this distrust extend only to tomorrow and no further?

"Please tell me without beating about the bush—why should a judge wish specifically that I shouldn't see my client *tomorrow?*"

Still embarrassed, Chernomorets said, "Kirilov has already signed a permission for Advocate Yudovich to visit *his* client tomorrow. He considers it unsuitable that you should both be in the prison on the same day."

I must admit that this explanation was totally unexpected. It had not occurred to me, chiefly because it was so absurd. Judge Kirilov knew as well as I did that prisoners detained on the same case are carefully kept in complete isolation from each other. It was immaterial whether Yudovich and I were in the prison simultaneously or at different times, because the prison authorities would routinely arrange our meetings in such a way that Alik and Sasha would not even glimpse each other. Therefore the judge's real reason for objecting to our simultaneous visit was that he was afraid of contact between the two lawyers. He was trying, in this blatantly improper way, to prevent—or at least to hinder—counsel from devising joint tactics for the defense.

"So what are you really afraid of? The chance that I may meet and confer with Yudovich? His possible influence on me?"

Chernomorets made no reply.

"I am going to that prison tomorrow. I want you to understand quite clearly that if I consider it necessary to exert any influence on my client, I am perfectly capable of doing it on my own. And if I wish to discuss my position with Yudovich, I shall do it today—and I shall do it at home and not in the prison."

Chernomorets stretched out his hand. "Give me your permit. I'll sign it myself. This whole business really is ridiculous."

As I walked down the corridor of the courthouse, I suddenly remembered that the secretary had kindly offered me Volume I, a volume I had thought I didn't need at that stage; I also remembered that Judge Kirilov had insisted that I look at it before I went to see Sasha. I went back into the empty courtroom, sat down at the table again, and reached for Volume I. I would at least glance at the contents list on the first page.

The whole of the first page consisted of one large photograph, a full-face portrait in close-up. The smiling face was looking straight at me: a girl with clear, sparkling eyes, a look of pure, ingenuous happiness. It was Marina.

I slowly turned the page and there was another photograph, this time of a hideous, bloated corpse with black, unrecognizable features. A few scraps of clothing were sticking to the upper part of what had once been a body. That, too, was Marina.

Again came the thought: "Perhaps they really did do it. And I will be helping them to evade responsibility, to evade any kind of punishment for having done this. That would be terrible."

Late that evening Lev Yudovich called me at home.

"Well, have you had a look at the case?"

He could sense my mood from my tone of voice.

"That feeling will pass, Dina," he said. "It will pass as soon as you have talked to Sasha, as soon as you begin to study the material really thoroughly. Believe me. At first I was in even greater despair than you are."

Lev then described how, at Yusov's suggestion, he had begun his study of the case by listening to the tape recording of the boys' confessions and the confrontation between them that followed.

"It was awful," he said.

I believed him. Although I had only read their testimony, I could nevertheless imagine those voices:

". . . Sasha suggested it. I didn't want to, and it was only later that I agreed. Sasha strangled her, while I stood aside . . ."

". . . Alik suggested it. Why did you talk me into it? It was your idea in the first place, and I only agreed out of stupidity. You're lying—I didn't strangle her. Nobody strangled her. Why did she die? I don't know why she died. How should I know? Maybe because she suffocated, maybe because of something else. . . ."

This not only made sense, the wording was all too plausible. I had the impression of two cornered animals, each attacking the other in the hope of slightly mitigating his own guilt. All the passion, all the emotional force was directed at an attempt to claim the role of secondary accomplice. I was shocked. How dare Borisov defend both boys! By law an advocate can defend two or more persons in the same case only if there are no contradictions between them.

Next day I left home early. In the prison I was assigned to Visitors' Room No. 30. At the end of a corridor, large and light, with windows onto the street, it is a convenient place to work; it has big desks with drawers in which I was able to hide the sandwiches and chocolate Sasha's family had given me. It is sometimes possible to pass food to a prisoner during an interview; the guards may turn a blind eye, provided the prisoner takes nothing back to the cells with him.

Sasha was brought in.

It is difficult for me now to separate that first impression from all the subsequent impressions, from the time when I knew him well, when his face seemed familiar and dear, when he eventually learned to smile when talking to me.

Sasha was tall, with black hair and dark brown eyes. I was surprised by what struck me as his very long arms, and realized only later that this was because the sleeves of his prison uniform were too short for him. His hands, reddened with cold, protruded awkwardly. He had on clumsy workman's boots without bootlaces (forbidden by prison regulations), so that his feet clumped as he walked. His pants were short, too. The whole effect was gawky and angular. He glared sullenly at me from beneath lowered brows. I gave him news of his parents, of his brothers and his sister, family details that I had learned for his benefit. I knew how much he needed this news; more than two months had passed since his last meeting with Irina Kozopolyanskaya, his previous lawyer, and in all that time he had been allowed no meetings and no letters.

This conversation, however, was not only for his benefit. I needed to have a good look at him, to get used to his way of speaking and his ability to express himself, to establish some kind of personal contact before getting down to the real matter at hand.

Sasha spoke very slowly, scarcely raising his head. I offered him a sandwich, a chocolate bar, but he refused. When I lit a cigarette, he asked for one, "Only don't tell my mother, she'd be upset."

Suddenly he asked, "Do you know Kozopolyanskaya?"

"Yes, I do. She asked me to send you her regards."

"I understand she won't be defending me now. I feel so ashamed at what I did to her."

I was glad to hear him say that word—ashamed. It is not one that you hear spoken very often in prison. I remained silent, however, and Sasha went on telling about his life at home, about school, about how much he had to do around the house, because when he was not actually in school he was in sole charge of his younger brother. He told me how much he loved animals —dogs, cats, rabbits, birds—and how he worried about his favorite kitten and his dog. "No," he said, "he's no special breed, just an ordinary mutt, but very intelligent. I guess he must be missing me."

He was silent for a moment, then without the slightest change of tone he suddenly said, "Surely you don't believe I strangled Marina with these hands?"

His red, chapped hands lay palms up on the desk and he stared intently at them. How sincerely he said those words, and how much I wanted to believe him, but inwardly I could hear his voice saying, "Alik suggested raping her and I agreed . . . Alik said we had better bury her, so that nobody would find her, but then we decided to carry her down to the lake."

Instead of replying I asked him to tell me everything that had happened the evening Marina was killed. I told him that I had absolutely no interest in what he might have said to Yusov or to other investigators; I didn't want to know why he had confessed and why he had subsequently changed his mind. I simply wanted to hear from him about the game of volleyball and the walk to the lake, and what had happened when they parted from Marina.

"Only please," I begged him, "tell the story in as much detail as possible. Try and remember every little thing—what you talked about as you walked down the street, whether you met anybody on the way. Try and remember it *all* and tell me just as it was."

So once again, very slowly, pausing after each word, he began to describe that day from the very beginning. He would finish a sentence and stop. Then the next sentence would invariably begin, "Well, you see . . ."

It was almost noon, and he was still telling me how he went to the store and what he bought, how he went to fetch the milk from his Aunt Marusya.

What was it going to be like in court if he spoke as slowly as this? I could already imagine the irritated comments of the prosecutor and even of the judge. Inwardly I could hear the prosecutor's voice saying, "Why are you dragging out your evidence this way? When you agreed to commit the crime you could talk fast enough—now, it seems, you've almost forgotten how to talk!"

Or the judge: "At this rate your case will take three months. Talk faster!"

I simply had to teach him to talk a little more rapidly, and without the perpetual "Well, you see . . ." and "It's like this . . ."

That day, however, I did not hurry him or question him, except that when he finished his story I said, "You told me that after Marina had left you, you didn't go back to the Akatovs' house at once but stood waiting behind the 'Big House' for ten minutes. So why, when you and Alik gave one of your statements, did you say you went to the clubhouse in those ten minutes?"

"We didn't go."

"Then what made you say you *did* go?"

Sasha was silent.

"You must tell me. If you don't, how can I help you?"

"Well, you see, it was like this. We agreed to tell the girls we'd gone to the clubhouse if they asked why we were late. Once we had told that story to the girls, we had to tell it to the police."

"But why didn't you want to tell the girls you'd been waiting behind the 'Big House'?"

Another pause, another "Well, you see . . . We went into a shed behind the 'Big House' and smoked a cigarette. I didn't want the girls to find out about that, because my sister Lena was with them and she would have told my mother."

"Didn't your family know you smoked?"

"Well, you see, I wasn't really smoking then, just trying it. I smoke now, but not much. My mother doesn't know, she doesn't send me cigarettes in her parcels. My cellmates give me some, anyway. It's enough."

Our meeting came to an end. Sasha obviously expected me to say that I believed him and now realized he was innocent. Instead I told him I was going to help him but he must tell the truth. It would be his only defense.

"I really am telling you the truth," he said. "We didn't do it."

I rode home in the rush hour, first in a jam-packed bus and then in the overfilled subway, then in another bus, and I noticed nothing during the journey. All I could see was Sasha's face and his hands as he spread them out on the desk. By now my inner voice of doubt, prompted by the terrible details of the boys' confession, was almost silent.

It is very important for me to believe sincerely in the cause I defend in court. No doubt that is why we lawyers so readily incline to believe our clients. And the advocate's speeches are primarily based on analysis of the evidence and on a watertight argument. At the same time, important elements of any courtroom speech are the manner of delivery, the timbre of the voice, the use of gesture, and even sometimes, when you are facing the judge, the way you look at him. When I speak in court, I use very simple language. I am convinced that even the most complex thinking, the subtlest nuances of emotion can be expressed in simple words. But this style—devoid of all ornamentation—forbids the slightest falsity. I believe that I have the ability to detect even the slightest note of falsity, and that it functions not only when assessing the speeches of my colleagues but, much more important, when gauging my own speeches. A strange feeling used to come over me, when I would suddenly begin to hear my voice as though I were speaking in an empty room: I knew it was my own voice, yet it was detached from me, living a life of its own that was alien to me. This happened only when I was not sincerely convinced of the moral rightness of my position. It is the reason why, when I took on Sasha's brief, I needed not just to believe him but to be absolutely convinced of his innocence.

The days of preparation went on. I evaluated every document, every piece of evidence from the standpoint of the prosecution. I tried to see each of them in the worst possible light for Sasha, then to refute the prosecution argument, totally ignoring the confessions. And every day I became more and more convinced that the only evidence of guilt lay in these confessions.

It was up to the defense to show that they were not corroborated by incontestable proofs of guilt, and to convince the court that the confessions in no way corresponded to the objective facts of the crime. But the only facts outside the boys' testimony which could be accepted as incontestable were the following: (1) There had been a volleyball game, in which Marina had played, but whose exact duration had never been established; (2) after the game, the young people had divided into two groups; (3) the Akatov sisters, Ira Klepova, Lena Kabanova, and the three soldiers had walked on ahead; (4) Alik, Sasha, and Marina had, for various reasons, been delayed in the village; (5) after a certain lapse of time Alik and Sasha had gone to the Akatovs' house without Marina; (6) the other girls had gone for a walk with Alik and Sasha along the Generals' Road; (7) Marina had not returned home; (8) on June 19 her sweater had been found in the gully; (9) her corpse had been found on June 23; (10) according to the technical reports she had entered the water alive and had drowned.

Everything else listed in the indictment as "objective fact" was wholly derived from the boys' confessions. Even the pathologist's report about Marina's rape and the hydrologist's report about her drowning were conjectural and based on the confessions. If the two confessions were true, then the boys' testimony reflected the actual, objective circumstances of Marina's death.

But what if they had not told the truth? How were we to prove that the testimony of Alik and Sasha contradicted the real circumstances of Marina's death, when no one knew what those real circumstances were?

Yudovich and I decided to visit the scene of the crime, even though it was now late in January; the lake was frozen over and the orchard lay deep in snow.

We drove along the Generals' Road, then turned off at the store, where the road leads to the writers' settlement. We walked down to the lakeside. There was the long, narrow plank bridge, and leading straight uphill from it was the main street of Izmalkovo, the road to the playground. To the right of the Bogachev house and immediately behind it was the "orchard," a few widely spaced rows of apple trees. To walk through the orchard and down to the lake was impossible—we would have sunk into loose, powdery snow well above our knees. So we drove back to Moscow.

But the trip was not a waste of time. We had seen how close together everything was: the apple tree, under which Marina had allegedly been raped, the Bogachevs' house, the Akatovs' house, the main street, the lake.

We calculated the time needed to walk from the Big House to the orchard. I had taken four minutes to cover the distance, Lev only three. The investigator had been calculating on the same amount of time when he stated that the boys had sufficient time to commit the murder: three to four minutes from the Big House, two from the orchard to the lakeside, five from the lake to the Akatovs' house. That left thirty minutes, a period in which, according to the investigator, there was ample time to rape Marina, strangle her, haul her body to the lake, swing it back and forth by the arms and legs, and throw it from the high bank into the water.

How on earth was it possible to determine whether those minutes were enough for two fourteen-year-old boys to do all that, return to their friends, and then, thirty minutes later, to go walking along the Generals' Road singing cheerfully? Since the investigator gave prime significance to the time factor as indirect proof of the boys' guilt, we also had to analyze it very carefully and collate, scrap by scrap, every possible fragment of information about the time that elapsed between the end of the volleyball game and Sasha's and Alik's return to the Akatovs'.

The witnesses' statements had all been approximate: "We finished the game at 10:40," "We finished the game at 10:35," "We finished the game at 10:45." Which of these times would the court take as the starting point? If it were 10:45, then the boys could not have done it; if it were 10:35, then they would perhaps have had enough time.

We found another time indicator. The girls had told the investigator that when they arrived at the Akatovs' house they put on a long-playing record to learn the words of a new song. The boys had arrived when the girls had listened to approximately half of one side of that record.

Lev and I listened to that same record: one side ran eighteen and a half minutes. Alik and Sasha had therefore reached the Akatovs' house nine to ten minutes after the girls got there. To go from the volleyball court to the Akatovs' by the route the girls took was a matter of five to seven minutes. Therefore from the moment when the boys parted from the girls to the moment when they met again, no more than seventeen minutes had elapsed —and in that length of time they could not have committed the crime and rejoined the girls. However, a certain amount of time had been taken up in carrying the record player from one room to another and in putting on the record. And before putting it on the girls had probably said something like, "Say, there's a new song just out, let's listen to it." How long might that conversation have lasted? Five minutes? If so, then the boys were innocent. But suppose it had lasted ten minutes; the time would then have been just sufficient for the crime.

According to the strict letter of the law, the court should choose the variant that was most favorable to Sasha and Alik, on the principle that the accused should always have the benefit of the doubt. Yudovich and I were well aware, however, that we had to find something much firmer than these minute-by-minute discrepancies, something that would force the court to reject the confessions as inadmissible.

It was no less important to establish the reasons why both of the accused had simultaneously denied their earlier testimony and confessed; furthermore, the explanation had to be so convincing that the court would be left in no doubt that such reasons had been strong enough to induce the boys to accuse themselves out of their own mouths.

From then on, all our talks with our clients were devoted to searching for those reasons.

"Sasha! On September 6, the day you first confessed, why did you state that you raped Marina on the *opposite* bank of the lake from the orchard?"

"Well, you see, I didn't know where she had been raped. So I just pointed to a place near the spot where I saw her corpse floating in the water."

"But why did you say you had raped Marina under the second apple tree in the orchard?"

"Yusov told me Alik had said that. He even showed me a piece of paper, a little scrap of gray paper, on which Alik had written it down. So I just confirmed it."

I produced a copy I had made of the plan of the orchard, which showed the position of the apple trees and the footpath down to the lake. I found the second apple tree from the Bogachevs' house and asked Sasha to show me the route from that tree to the spot where, according to the testimony, they had thrown Marina's body into the water.

He looked at me in perplexity. "Why from that tree? I pointed out a different tree."

He then confidently placed his finger on the second apple tree—but the second tree counted from the other end of the orchard, from the end where it was bounded by a small ditch and a fence surrounding Ruslanova's property.

"Are you sure you pointed to *that* tree? Remember, the official witnesses came to the orchard with you, and the court may call them to give evidence."

"I remember pointing to exactly that tree."

Two days before that conversation, while plowing through Volume I of the dossier, I had noticed an error that Investigator Yusov had allowed to escape his attention when compiling the record of his visit to the scene of the crime with Sasha.

In the record of his "site visit" with Alik, Yusov had written: "Walked to the Bogachevs' house. Turned left. After a further 13.5 meters, pointed to the second apple tree from the Bogachevs' house, the tree standing at a distance of 6 meters in a straight line from the footpath."

In the record of Sasha's site visit, however, Yusov's statement read:

"Walked to the Bogachevs' house. Turned left. Walked along the footpath as far as the second apple tree from the far end, and pointed to it as the spot where he and Burov raped Marina."

Thereafter, in all the documents, Yusov had stated that Alik and Sasha had pointed to the *same spot*—the second apple tree from the far end of the orchard—as being the place where the crime was committed.

Yet although I noted that error, at this stage I did not regard it as having any serious significance. I thought it was probably due to sheer carelessness; Yusov had, after all, compiled that record after Sasha had confessed and was going to plead guilty. Under such open-and-shut circumstances, documents are often drawn up somewhat negligently. But when I mentioned the discrepancy to Lev Yudovich, he said, "You don't know Yusov. I've been observing him carefully ever since I started work on this case. He's a scoundrel, but he's a stickler for the formalities and an experienced investigator. I'm sure he did this on purpose for some reason we need to find out."

Lev's suspicions received their first confirmation the next day, when I sat down again in the empty courtroom to study Volume I, which contained all the photographs taken during the site visits. There was the volleyball court, the village street with the Big House, the Bogachevs' house. Finally came a photograph of Alik. He was standing beside the tree and pointing to it with outstretched arm. It was a big apple tree, with widely spreading branches and dense foliage. Only the thick lower branches could be seen through the leaves. In the background, visible against the sky, was a tall wooden pole carrying electric power cables.

Sasha, in his photograph, was standing in the same pose, arm outstretched. The apple tree, however, looked smaller, and to the right of it, just visible in the grass, was the stump of a felled tree. There was no light pole to be seen, but the photograph was poor and its entire upper part was blurred.

Next morning, studying Volume II, I noticed that the testimony of the official witnesses who had been present during Sasha's site visit was not on file. This could not be regarded as a chance omission. Apart from indirectly confirming Sasha's statement that he had pointed to a different tree, it also indicated something more.

Very often an investigator selects his official witnesses from among people familiar to the police, minor officials whose functions bring them into direct contact with the police force. It is easy for an investigator to influence such people; they will not give the game away if there is ever any question of an investigator having infringed the procedural regulations. The fact that Yusov had not taken statements from the official witnesses at Sasha's visit might indicate that they were ordinary people, outsiders, whom he could not or dared not try to pressure. The defense would therefore have to ask the court to call these people to the witness stand for questioning, a request that no court had ever refused.

As I continued to study the case, I found myself noticing a succession of details that at first seemed quite trivial but gradually forced me to examine them. For instance, one of the first witnesses stated that after their game of volleyball the boys and girls went to the well to clean the ball and wash their hands. The investigator had calculated that the time for this would be two minutes. But why on earth did they wash their hands, and not only their hands but the ball as well? I knew that on June 17 the weather had been fine and sunny, warm enough for the children to have gone swimming that day. If during the game the ball had landed in the mud, it might have been necessary to wash it, but then only the person who picked up the ball would have needed to wash afterward, and the boys, at least, would probably have wiped their hands on their clothes.

I could therefore assume that there had been a heavy rain the day before —heavy, because despite the warm weather the mud had not dried out. And if the mud had not dried in the village itself and on the playground, where people were constantly walking, it must have been even muddier in the orchard and on the path to the lake. If one allowed that the boys had followed the route ascribed to them in the indictment, then they could not possibly have arrived at the Akatovs' house clean or dry.

In my next talk with Sasha he confirmed that it had indeed rained hard the day before, and he added that the place from which Marina's body had supposedly been flung into the water was always very muddy and swampy. Sasha also said that Mrs. Akatova was extremely houseproud, and if he and Alik had had muddy shoes she would never have allowed them to come indoors.

We thus had a further request to the court—another one that would not normally be refused—to admit in evidence data on the weather for the days preceding June 17, 1965.

The main question in our conversations, however, was why they had decided to plead guilty.

Sasha never complained of being badly treated or beaten up, nor about the harsh conditions in which he had been kept before his transfer to Moscow. They had distressed him much less than if he had been a city-bred boy, used to the comforts of urban living. Tough though it was to sleep uncovered on bare wooden bunks, to eat nothing but dry food (no kitchens are provided for remand cells), to freeze at night and gasp for air in the unventilated cells by day, none of this made him plead guilty.

Yusov did not threaten Sasha. He simply gave him, against the law dealing with underage prisoners, an adult cellmate, a sort of "Uncle Vanya," who told Sasha horrifying tales of the prison attached to the Moscow Criminal Investigation Department, the notorious No. 38 Petrovka. He described how they beat you up there, how not only the investigators and guards but even the other prisoners taunted and humiliated you. Every day Yusov told Sasha that a confession from him would determine which prison he was sent to while awaiting trial: if he confessed, they would put him in a decent one; if not, it would be No. 38 Petrovka. Furthermore, Yusov told Sasha that if he pleaded guilty he would not even be held in detention before the trial. Uncle Vanya was news to me; he was not mentioned once in the dossier, and, needless to say, had vanished the day Sasha confessed.

Hour by hour, day and night, Uncle Vanya pressured Sasha to confess. He persuaded the boy to confess not because he was guilty, but because, so the old man convinced him, no one would believe in his innocence: "You have no other course. If you don't plead guilty, they'll transfer you to 38 Petrovka, and there they'll make you confess whether you like it or not. And they'll take it out on you in other ways: you'll get a longer sentence, and when you get to be eighteen they'll send you to the worst prison camp in Siberia. You'll be among murderers who play cards for other prisoners' lives and who think nothing of killing and disfiguring someone if they lose the game."

Uncle Vanya lifted up his shirt and showed Sasha an enormous scar which ran from his chest right across his stomach. "See what they did to me? It was a miracle I survived."

Every day Yusov summoned Sasha for interrogation and asked, "Well, have you changed your mind? Are you going to confess? If not, go back and think it over again. I'm not in a hurry. I can wait." When Sasha tried to protest that he was genuinely innocent, Yusov replied that he was not interested in listening to fairy tales; he didn't believe it, and no court would believe it either.

Back Sasha would go to his cell, where Uncle Vanya was waiting to tell him how lenient the courts were to minors who pleaded guilty, and how they would let him off lightly. "If you confess, you won't get more than five years. In fact, because of your age they might even let you go altogether. The school will give you a character reference, and you come from a good, hard-working family. They might even let you go scot free."

And so it went every day, while Sasha still insisted, "I'm not guilty."

The turning point was Alik's statement, in which he wrote that he had committed the crime at Sasha's suggestion. "You see, Sasha," said Yusov, "now you have no alternative. If you persist in claiming innocence, Alik will throw all the blame on you. The court will grant him all possible mitigation, because he was the one who confessed and repented, and the full weight of punishment will fall on you."

Sasha now had no doubt that Yusov and Uncle Vanya were right. After Alik's confession, who would believe they hadn't raped the girl, hadn't killed her? And he had to confess today, so his admission would not be dated later than Alik's. Then he might hope for mitigation too. He would say that Alik had suggested the rape first and that he, Sasha, had not strangled Marina, for he well knew from Uncle Vanya that the principal accused or instigator of the crime—known in the underworld as the "locomotive"—always got a much stiffer sentence.

On that day Alik became Sasha's deadly enemy in the struggle to be in second place. But Sasha did not know that a few days after the terrible confrontation between him and Alik, the struggle was over; that Alik had retracted his confession and declared that he had falsely incriminated both Sasha and himself under the pressure of Yusov and cellmate "Uncle Victor."

Also on September 6, Sasha heard with relief Yusov's assurance that no one would ever know Alik had submitted his confession first, and that as soon as Sasha confessed he would be allowed to write a letter home. Then, no doubt very soon, Yusov might be able to let Sasha go home until the trial.

Such was Sasha's explanation to me of the reasons for his false confession.

Was it convincing?

Was it convincing that his sense of total helplessness, of the impossibility of breaking out of that vicious circle of Yusov-Uncle Vanya, and his loss of all hope that anyone would believe his innocence, were enough to make him assume the guilt for a dreadful crime? Perhaps for the adults arrested on suspicion of having murdered Marina (the soldiers Sogrin, Zuyev, and Bazarov, even the drunken lout Sadykov) these reasons might not have been sufficient. Grown men might possibly have had enough strength of will, common sense, and hard-won experience to withstand the interrogations and the illegal psychological pressure that Yusov used. They might have scoffed at Uncle Vanya and they might not have believed Yusov's promises.

Alik and Sasha were unable to withstand that pressure. They had neither the strength of character nor the education nor the worldly experience. They were just a couple of ordinary country boys, never before separated from their parents, brought up to obey adults and trust in the authority of an educated man.

I am convinced that no one can define the limit of an individual's power of psychological resistance. It is a hard thing to assess, even in oneself. The only yardstick is the subjective, emotional opinion of the observer, and I believed Sasha.

At once I was able to understand the logic behind all Yusov's gross infringements of the law. He had only one reason: confession. Taking over the case more than a year after the victim's death, Yusov saw this as the one way of pursuing the investigation. He knew that the boys had already been questioned many times before the case was entrusted to him, and he also knew that other people had been detained on suspicion. Yet, realizing that after such a long time lag he could get a confession only by breaking the will of someone who had not yet been formally accused and exonerated for lack of evidence, and that breaking the will of one of the adults would be more difficult, he chose to concentrate on Sasha and Alik. Thereafter, all Yusov's infringements of the rules were part and parcel of his method of pressuring the teenagers until they broke.

Yusov was a very ambitious man. After a successful career as an investigator, he had been transferred from Moscow to the provinces for some violation of official rules. The case of Alik and Sasha was one of his first cases (if not the first) after his return to the central office of the procuracy of Moscow Province. It was meant as a test of his ability, a touchstone of his career prospects. A satisfactory solution would mean rapid promotion for him, especially since the case was under the immediate scrutiny of the Central Committee.

Yusov was prepared to risk breaking the law because he was banking on the fact that a solution of the crime based on voluntary confessions would save him from having to answer for his illegal acts ("generals who win battles don't get court-martialed"). Two factors were inextricably linked, Yusov's need to further his career and his fear that the procedural misdeeds would become known. If Yusov's position had been different, he need not have worried. Investigators have been forgiven for even worse sins. In his case, however, the outcome might be another transfer to somewhere in the wilds, and this time without the slightest hope of an eventual return to Moscow. That is why falsification of evidence became the basic method of his conduct of the case.

3. The First Trial

B Y THE TIME THE TRIAL BEGAN, Sasha and I had complete rapport. During our talks I tried to prepare him in such a way that, as far as possible, no question from prosecution or defense would come as a surprise. At every meeting he practiced giving evidence to me as if he were in court. I had to teach him how and when to stand up in front of the court, when and to whom he could put questions. I asked innumerable questions which the prosecutor or the judge would be sure to ask him.

All this was necessary because contact between advocate and client during the trial is made very difficult. An advocate can talk to his or her client before and after a hearing and during recesses, but only in the presence of a guard. Even under these conditions, it is possible to give practical advice and to clear up confusion about what is actually going on in the courtroom, but it is far from satisfactory. And this is the only form of communication allowed between the defendant and people he trusts, because contact with family or friends is forbidden. The advocate is effectively the only person a prisoner may even look at.

I warned Sasha that we would be allowed to talk every day, but bearing in mind the clash I had already had with the judge, we agreed that Sasha himself would ask permission for each meeting.

And so came the first day of the trial.

In the Soviet press there is no reporting of criminal cases until the trial is scheduled. All investigation by police and procuracy is conducted in secret, and this secrecy is preserved by a special law. Any person divulging information about pretrial investigation can be held criminally responsible. But in the case of the two boys, Investigator Yusov himself constantly and purposely divulged to every witness he summoned the material of his investigation. He described the case in his own terms and showed the experts' reports. If any of the villagers expressed doubt whether Marina could have drowned at the spot Alik and Sasha had indicated, they were invariably impressed by the learned hydrologists' report and agreed that it was perfectly possible for someone to have drowned at that place. Yusov also showed photographs of the clothes that were on Marina's corpse—the shredded pants of a warmup suit—and he would say, "See how they tore these pants when they undressed Marina."

Later, during the hearing, the defense was able to counterbalance this with other expert evidence, which reported that the damage to the clothing might equally have been caused in the water, especially in view of the heavy growth of bushes along the banks and the fact that the bottom of the lake was littered with junk. The witnesses, however, tended to accept Yusov's explanation as incontestable.

Yusov revealed to the witnesses only those parts of the boys' testimony in which they admitted their guilt, and he mentioned only those points in the other evidence which, in his opinion, confirmed that guilt. He also created a special category of witness: people who were called to testify that Yusov had interrogated Alik and Sasha politely and calmly, that the boys had not been mistreated and had confessed voluntarily.

Aside from this special group, all the other witnesses thus became biased witnesses, on whose objectivity we could not rely. The facts they actually knew became overgrown with so much detail and supposition, suggested to them by Yusov, that they became unable (and in some cases unwilling) to separate fact from assumption. Hence their testimony became protracted and increasingly categorical.

The defense needed to insure that the witnesses told the truth and testified only to what they actually knew. The time the volleyball game ended; the time they heard the children singing from the direction of the plank bridge; how Sasha had turned pale when he saw the floating corpse of Marina ("Only a murderer could have turned so pale"); how Alik's parents were bad people and of course couldn't be expected to raise a good son.

But the court would question them all—a total of a hundred people— and day after day, hour after hour the emotional charge of hatred and desire for revenge, with which almost every one of them was filled, would inevitably have its effect. It would fortify the court's prejudice against the accused and add to that underlying distrust which is always generated by the very fact of being indicted on a criminal charge.

The case was heard in the largest courtroom of the Moscow Provincial Court. Among all those witnesses not a single face was familiar to Yudovich and me. We had never seen any of them before, never heard the sound of their voices. Yudovich and I stared at the crowd of people and tried to guess which one was Marchenkova, which Marina's mother, which the mother of the Akatovs. Suddenly we noticed one woman standing in the middle of a group of other witnesses and explaining something to them—a short, thickset, almost square woman, her gray hair curled into countless small ringlets, with a large comb thrust into it. I think Lev and I spoke simultaneously: "Berta Karpovna Brodskaya."

What made us remember that name so clearly, the name of a witness who was no witness at all? In the period immediately after Marina's death, Brodskaya was away on vacation. When she did return to Izmalkovo, the first passions had died down and people were returning to their everyday affairs. Brodskaya, who lived alone, had an unquenchable urge for involvement in public affairs which had for a long time lacked an outlet. She was one of that distinctive class of people called—not officially, but among the public at large—Old Bolsheviks.

This was not merely because of her membership in the Party. She was a recognizable type, whose appearance is often similar to Berta's: the hair cut short, pulled straight back and held in place by a comb, and a way of dressing reminiscent of the early years of the Revolution. But Old Bolsheviks are chiefly recognized by a mental attitude, the inflexible attitude of a person who is never prey to a single doubt. Such people do not hesitate or qualify; their judgments are always categorical. At work, they often cause trouble and unpleasantness for their colleagues. When they retire, they get involved in community or public affairs. This gives them the right to meddle, to act as self-appointed guardians of the "moral tone" of their neighbors, to be the judges of other people's lives in the court of public opinion. Berta Brodskaya was just such a person.

In including her in his list of essential witnesses, Yusov knew that Brodskaya could give no evidentiary testimony. She had been away from the village at the time of Marina's death; she had not been at the cemetery during Marchenkova's lamentations, nor in the village when Yusov took Alik and Sasha there. Yusov was calling her so that "the people's anger" would be heard from her mouth, and so the court should hear her demanding the most merciless sentence.

This old Communist battleax had become the foremost instigator of hatred and ill will. She wrote the petitions demanding capital punishment for the boys (which was forbidden by law because they were under eighteen); the first signature on these petitions was always hers. Her deposition to Yusov stated: "I have no doubt whatsoever that they are the murderers. I am convinced of it, and I demand that capital punishment be inflicted upon them."

When pronouncing sentence, the judge would take into account the fact that the case was being carefully watched by the Central Committee and that his sentence would be reported to the appropriate Party official. He also knew that if the sentence failed to satisfy people like Berta Brodskaya, it would produce a flood of indignant protests.

As we stood in the corridor Lev Yudovich and I could sense the hostility of all these people, which had expanded to include counsel for the defense.

The case of Alik and Sasha was heard three times in courts of the first instance. Altogether, the court hearings alone took up five months of concentrated drama and intensive work. Not even the stenographic record fully reflects the emotional intensity of a courtroom: the way the judge listens or does not listen to the witness; the tone in which the judge or the prosecutor puts questions, kindly or threatening or perhaps blatantly sarcastic; how the judge looks at the accused and what the accused sees in that look. The pause, too—a live, significant, minute-long silence in the courtroom, when a glance or a gesture can speak volumes—is meaningless in the stenographic record.

In this case, most difficult and most tense of all was that first trial in the Moscow Provincial Court.

We were prepared; we realized that it would involve a great deal of tough cross-examination, that Judge Kirilov's bullying would create an extra element of nervous tension, all the harder to bear because it was not judicial but personal.

The session of the court was declared open and the indictment was read.

Then followed the first question invariably put to the accused in the form prescribed by law: "Citizen Burov, do you understand the indictment that has been read to you? Do you plead guilty?"

Sitting behind Yudovich, Alik was about to stand up and reply. Everyone knew he would plead not guilty; there would be nothing unexpected in his reply. As Lev Yudovich turned his head slightly to see Alik, an order was suddenly barked out: "I forbid you to look at Burov! How dare you turn around!"

This was not a guard shouting; it was Judge Kirilov's style of addressing counsel for the defense.

When Lev gets excited, he turns pale. When he is angry, his nostrils dilate. He leaped to his feet, pale, with tightly clenched jaws and nostrils flaring. Again came a bark: "Comrade advocate, sit down! I will not allow you to enter into an altercation with the court."

"I demand that the court permit me to make a statement. I wish to object to the conduct of the chairman and that objection to be entered in the court record."

"Comrade advocate, sit down! I will give you such permission at an appropriate time."

And Lev was forced to submit. The chairman of the bench is the boss, and both defense and prosecution are obliged to obey instructions which may be not only illegal but senseless. I had no doubt that Lev would find a suitable moment to return to this matter, and that the incident would be entered in the court record. Now, however, he acted quite correctly in not allowing the conflict to develop into an open wrangle.

After Alik pled as expected, everyone awaited Sasha's reply. He had not revoked his confession until the very end of the investigation, right after his talk with his first lawyer, Kozopolyanskaya. He had then admitted his guilt again, and later repudiated that deposition.

Fortunately I did not have to turn around to see him. He was sitting near the three judges' desk, at an oblique angle from me, and I could see his face perfectly well.

"Citizen Kabanov, do you understand the indictment that has been read to you? Do you plead guilty?"

I could sense the general tension.

Sasha slowly stood up. His face looked paler than usual, and I noticed that the judge looked him straight in the eye.

Suddenly Sasha turned his back on me, so that he was not turned half-way from the judge but directly facing him. From behind I could see that he was holding his head up, which meant that he was returning the judge's intent look (as I had taught him to), and he said firmly, "I plead not guilty."

"Not guilty on all counts?"

"On all counts."

A sigh was heard. In that courtroom, in which the only audience was the families of the accused, Marina's mother, and a few other people who had been given permission to attend, every sound was very audible. The sigh of relief came from Sasha's parents, followed by a hiss of "Murderer!" from Alexandra Kostopravkina, Marina's mother.

I waited for the usual "Sit down, Kabanov."

Instead, Kirilov asked the guard to bring the defendant close to the judge's desk. There stood Sasha, alone in that empty space. In pants that ended well above his ankles, a gray cotton prison uniform jacket, he looked gawky and pathetic.

Rising from his seat, Kirilov leaned across the desk and said very distinctly, "Answer my question again—do you plead guilty? Take your time, think about it. We can wait."

Again came Sasha's "Not guilty."

"Don't listen to anyone who may have told you to lie. The court can distinguish lies from truth."

Sasha said nothing.

"Why are you silent? Who told you to tell lies? If you tell the truth, you have nothing to fear."

I did not move. I sensed that my intervention at this moment would only increase the court's lack of confidence in Sasha's testimony.

Lev's reaction was the same. "Keep quiet. Let Kirilov question him if he wants to; he may be more inclined to believe him."

"Has anyone been prompting you to tell lies?"

"Yes, they have."

"Who?" shouted Kirilov.

"Who?" came like an echo from the prosecutor.

"Uncle Vanya."

"Who in the world is Uncle Vanya? Someone you invented?"

"No, I didn't invent him. He was put into my cell as soon as I was arrested. He told me, 'The investigator will never believe you didn't do it, nor will the judge. It'll only be worse for you if you plead not guilty. Your only hope at the trial is to confess. All judges like it when a defendant confesses . . .' "

"We don't need you to tell us what judges like and what they don't," Kirilov interrupted. "Sit down."

The prosecutor was Voloshina, a woman who combined stupidity and lack of legal education to a remarkable degree. She was rude and ill mannered; her only way of maintaining the prosecution's authority was to ask questions as loudly as possible and in a carefully rehearsed tone of crushing sarcasm. Outside the courtroom she was a completely different person. She talked to us amiably and complained incessantly about her menopausal mood swings and hot flashes. These swings tended to occur very suddenly, sometimes when she was in the middle of examining a witness. Whenever this happened, the proceedings ceased to have any resemblance to a judicial hearing. She was unable to listen to the replies to her questions, she would interrupt the witness in mid-sentence, and she intervened with questions when a defense attorney was examining a witness. Her lack of legal training did, however, give her one advantage: she was never hampered by the rules of procedure because she simply didn't know what the rules were.

The omens for the trial were not good. We had an irascible, autocratic judge, a hysterical prosecutor, the resentful mother of the victim—and the "people's prosecutor," a woman teacher at the school where Marina, Sasha, and Alik had studied, who was convinced of one thing: "They are guilty. If they confessed, they must be guilty." * Nothing could shake that passionate belief, and the help she gave the prosecutor was invaluable. Every day, during every recess, she kept watch on the defense advocates. She tried to eavesdrop on everything we said to each other, and she saw to it that the witnesses did not speak to us, did not even look in our direction. This was the atmosphere of suspicion, covert observation and unconcealed malevolence in which we were obliged to work for the six long weeks of the first trial.

On the first day, the accused were asked no further questions. The court discussed various requests for extra witnesses and similar purely procedural matters. Next morning they would begin questioning Sasha, and I wanted to boost his morale a bit as well as discuss tactical points. As I have already mentioned, permission to talk to our clients in the presence of guards is given as a matter of course. It is one law the authorities do not break.

When I asked Kirilov's routine permission, he said, "Comrade advocate, you may talk to your client only in prison, and only after the prosecution's examination is finished. I will not allow you a meeting before then. That applies equally to Advocate Yudovich. Understood? That is all. This session of the court . . ."

He was about to declare the session closed and so deprive Lev and me of the opportunity of lodging an official objection. I interrupted him, to put forward a firm argument in support of a meeting with my client, quoting the articles of the law which gave me that right. I had to insure that the clerk entered my objection in the court record. This was a move aimed at the court of higher instance. If Kirilov were to convict the two boys and we appealed the conviction, then Kirilov's refusal of my request would be regarded as a serious infringement of the Procedural Code. This, in conjunction with other infringements, in particular the dubious nature of the entire prosecution case, might lead to a quashing of the conviction.

Kirilov heard me out calmly, with a faintly condescending smile. "Is that all, comrade advocate? Have you finished?" Looking at Yudovich, who was also on his feet, he went on, "You, of course, associate yourself with your colleague's objection? Will it suit you if we put you on record as making a similar request?"

Again Kirilov was interrupted. This time it was Sasha. He also stood up

---

* People's prosecutors and people's defenders may participate in criminal trials as representatives of public opinion. They are elected by colleagues of the defendant or the victim (if the defendant or victim is a worker or a student), or by the community where the defendant or victim lives. These prosecutors and defenders have the same rights and functions as the government prosecutors and advocates.

This institution was established in 1958.

and asked permission to address the court. "Well, what have you got to say? Your counsel has already spoken on your behalf."

"I want to say," said Sasha, "that I decline to have any meeting with my lawyer until you yourself suggest it. I don't want you to think I am being prompted."

There followed a pause—a long pause, in which the chairman of the bench looked Sasha straight in the eye. I had the impression that this time there was no threat in that look, but a genuine and lively interest. Well done, Sasha! I thought. He had spoken with courage and dignity.

All the same, it was essential for us to meet, and I must find a way. At the same time I was watching the clerk of the court to make sure she was entering Sasha's statement in the record; this was very important, because in the appeals court an advocate can quote only the actual text of the trial record.

How long did that pause last—seconds or minutes? It seemed very long to me. Kirilov looked in silence at Sasha, who continued to look Kirilov straight in the eye.

"Very well, Kabanov. I accept that condition. I will say when you can talk to your lawyer. We have finished our work for today. Tomorrow we will begin with your examination. Think that over. And let me remind you once again—tell us the truth."

Lev and I stayed on in the empty courtroom, profoundly depressed by the way things had gone—the rudeness of the judge, the insults hurled at us by Marina's mother, and above all by the court's open flouting of the law. How were we to do our job when our clients were totally isolated from us? All defendants, even mature, educated adults, look forward impatiently to the meetings with their advocates after a day's session, if only to ask: "Well, how's it going? What's your opinion? Was I right when I said . . . ?"

Lev and I drafted the wording of the written protests we would submit to the court. We were in absolute agreement on the need to record in black and white every infringement of the Code of Procedure committed by the court, every instance of blatant rudeness by the judge toward both defendants and their counsel. We agreed, however, to tolerate everything that might be said by Kostopravkina, Marina's mother, a woman blinded by terrible grief. Out of respect for her suffering we were prepared to forgive her, but when we made that decision, we had no conception of what, in fact, we would later be obliged to hear from her lips without protest.

In that first trial the main force of Kostopravkina's hatred was directed at Lev Yudovich, so it was more difficult for him to keep our private agreement to tolerate this woman's attacks. It was made even harder by the fact that the judge not only failed to restrain her outbursts but obviously took genuine pleasure in watching Kostopravkina standing in front of the bench with arms akimbo, no doubt the pose in which she was accustomed to stand when quarreling with her neighbors. She was a strong, solidly built woman, still young, her eyes glittering with anger from underneath the black head-scarf of mourning.

In a loud voice, almost shouting, she would say to the court, "I refuse to answer that hired lawyer's questions. My daughter's been killed, but he earns money for what he's doing, and eats pork . . ."

"Why pork?" I asked Lev.

He shrugged his shoulders in amazement. But we discovered later that Kostopravkina and Brodskaya had concocted a statement to various Party and government officials in which they complained that Alik's parents had killed their pig and were keeping Yudovich supplied with pork.

Marina's mother at least answered my questions. Standing with her head turned away from me and her lips firmly shut, she would invariably ask the judge, "Do I have to answer her?"

"Yes, you do," Kirilov would reply, though with a hint of sympathetic regret in his voice.

So it continued for days on end, until Lev and I finally realized that our decision to tolerate her had been wrong, that we had not only overestimated our own capacity for tolerance, but that Kostopravkina took our silence as a sign of weakness, permission for her to continue this behavior.

Meanwhile, both Sasha and Alik were examined. The court heard about the conditions under which they had been detained, about Yusov's methods of deception and persuasion. Sasha described how, having already confessed, he had shown the investigator a scene of the crime that was completely different from that shown by Alik. The court decided to call the official witnesses of the site visit, to obtain a statement from the police in charge of the remand cells about who else had been placed in the boys' cells, and to get data on the weather for the days preceding Marina's death. Despite objections from the prosecutor, all these requests of ours were granted.

By now, Kirilov was beginning to listen to Sasha's testimony more calmly and even, so we thought, with interest. Of the questions he put, many were genuinely reasonable and necessary. It became clear that he too had done his homework.

Examination of the witnesses was just about to begin when suddenly Kirilov announced a twenty-four-hour recess and, turning to Sasha, added, "Kabanov, I shall keep my word. I now propose that you have a meeting with your advocate. Comrade advocates, I will today give you permission to meet your clients. All of tomorrow is at your disposal."

What a good omen this seemed to us! But much more often during the six weeks of the trial we were seized with despair, when it seemed that our cause was hopeless and the court was listening only to the other side.

I spent the morning of the recess day in the courthouse, having decided to go to the prison in the afternoon. As I came out of the courthouse I met Yudovich, who was just on his way to the prison. I got into Lev's car right at the courthouse and off we went. As we drove away, we saw Voloshina, the prosecutor, who was staring at us very hard.

Next morning I was smoking a cigarette on the courthouse landing when I heard the loud voice of our prosecutor: "Well, we'll really give it to them today! This will be a nice little present for them."

A few seconds later I saw Voloshina and Kostopravkina coming up the stairs. "Good morning, comrade advocate. How did you get on with your client yesterday?" said the lawyer, while Kostopravkina walked past me without turning her head.

What could this "little present" be? I did not have time to talk to Lev about it, as he arrived just on time.

The members of the court entered and the session was declared open. We all sat down, except Voloshina, who remained standing: "I wish to lay before the court a very important document and request that it be added to the material in the case," she said, and gave the court a small scrap of greenish paper.

Having read it, Kirilov handed it in silence to one of the people's assessors, who nodded meaningfully; he then passed it to the other assessor, who had the same reaction. It was now the turn of the people's prosecutor. She took it and without even looking at it said, "Please put this on file."

What could it be? Surely it wasn't an affidavit from the police certifying that no other person had been kept in the remand cells with the boys? That really would be a blow. This thought flashed through my mind while the judge was saying the customary, "Comrade advocates, you may acquaint yourselves with this document."

The piece of paper was in our hands. It was a statement, stamped with the official seal of Penal Institution No. 1, where the boys were detained during trial:

At the request of the Moscow Provincial Procuracy it is hereby confirmed that according to data in the Register on February 24 of this year Advocate Yudovich was admitted for a meeting with his client Burov (time of arrival: 3:35 P.M.; time of departure: 6:20 P.M.) and Advocate Kaminskaya was admitted for a meeting with her client Kabanov (time of arrival: 3:35 P.M.; time of departure: 7:50 P.M.). Permission for visits granted by Moscow Provincial Court.

We had no time for reflection, nor was it necessary. The illegality and irrelevance of this application were obvious. In going to the prison together we had broken no law, no regulation, no rule of professional ethics. I looked at Lev. As I expected, his face was pale and his nostrils flaring. He was about to plunge into the fray. I decided I would give the reply.

I sometimes wonder what my face looks like when I am not just excited but angry. My own impression is that my looks do not change; I know I never turn pale and never blush. There is only a slightly stony feeling in the muscles of my face and I speak a little more slowly than usual, rapping out each word with extra precision. At this moment it was very important not to lose self-control, because the prosecutor's application was not as harmless as it might seem at first sight. It contained no personal threat either to Lev or to me, but it was a "long shot" aimed at a possible future occasion when the verdict might be quashed and the case referred for supplementary investigation. Then, if the certificate was on file, the investigator could call Yudovich and me for questioning, simply to confirm whether the information in it was factually correct. And that would constitute grounds for removing us from the case, because a witness cannot appear as defense counsel in the same case.

That is why I now stood to face the court and requested—very calmly, as I thought, and speaking very distinctly—that the state's prosecutor should specify to exactly which count of the indictment against Burov and Kabanov she wished this certificate to be attached. Kirilov was sitting with his head against the high back of his chair; he looked expectant as I began to speak, and there was a short pause after my query. He had been waiting for me to explode in a tirade. Then he turned to Voloshina and said, "The advocate's question is justified. You have not offered the court any grounds for your application. Which facts in the case of Burov and Kabanov would, in your opinion, be confirmed by the inclusion of this document?"

I stayed on my feet and asked permission to continue. I asked that the state's prosecutor also specify the statutory basis on which she had started making independent inquiries while the matter was *sub judice*. I had every reason, I said, to believe that such inquiries could not have been sanctioned by the court, which had on its own initiative offered us meetings with our clients on the same day. If I were mistaken in this belief, I wished to be shown the text of the prosecutor's application and the court's ruling upon it. Again leaning back in his chair, Kirilov looked at me and I looked at him. There was another brief moment of deathly silence in the courtroom, then the judge spoke.

"You are not mistaken, comrade advocate. The court knew nothing of this application."

Turning to Voloshina, he asked with a certain exasperation, "Do you still insist on it, comrade prosecutor? Will you offer grounds for your application?"

"Yes, I request that the court discuss my application. I consider it justified. I have nothing further to add."

There followed the usual exchange of nods with the two assessors, and, "Please enter this in the court record," Kirilov said to the clerk. "After consultation *in situ*, the bench rules as follows: the procurator's application is refused. The document is to be returned as irrelevant to the case."

Lev now stood up and protested with all his considerable force. He asked the court to point out to the prosecutor that her action was inadmissible and illegal. He also said that throughout the trial we had exercised great tolerance and restraint in not reacting to the insults directed at us by Kostopravkina, and that we had done so out of sympathy for her grief and distress. We had a right to expect that the chairman of the bench would himself make clear to Kostopravkina that her behavior was impermissible, but our expectations had been in vain. We must now insist that the court uphold a normal standard of behavior that would allow us to do our work properly and to shield us from any further insults.

Nods to left and right, then Kirilov said, "Kostopravkina, the court warns you: you must behave decently during a trial. Comrade prosecutor, the court hereby reprimands you." From then on the disgraceful scenes of the first days of the trial did not recur.

A few days later the entire court, including the defendants, their relatives, and Kostopravkina, adjourned to a small room with heavily shuttered windows to hear the tape recordings of the boys' testimony and see the films of the site visits. All the equipment was in place—a movie projector and a tape recorder, and a screen was hung on one wall.

The first shots appeared, flickering, with speeded-up movements like an old silent movie. Among the people and the German shepherd guard dogs I had some difficulty in making out the figure of Alik, with Yusov standing slightly in front of him. One could make out individuals as they passed in front of the camera, but it was blurred and indistinct.

We saw Yusov stop, then Alik stopped immediately behind him, stretched out his arm, and . . . the film stopped. Only the white light on the screen and the clicking of the projector indicated more to come.

Again we saw the village street, with people walking down it. Sasha was in the middle, surrounded by guard dogs. He was walking along with bowed head, Yusov beside him, his hand on Sasha's shoulder. Now they had reached the Bogachevs' house, turned left, and . . . again nothing but a clattering noise and a white screen.

The prosecutor explained that there was a fault in the film. It had been shot by an amateur. Now we would see the next sequences.

A crowd of people. Yusov standing beside Sasha. Sasha's outstretched arm. Where was he pointing? What route had they followed from the Bogachevs' house? It was infuriating that just this disputed section of the route was not shown, presumably spoiled by an incompetent photographer.

As evidence, this film provided absolutely nothing for or against the prosecution case, but it did have an emotional impact. For me it marked the first time I saw Alik and Sasha as they were paraded in their shame in front of their neighbors, friends, and schoolmates. I saw their attitudes of submissiveness and obedience; I was made even more keenly aware of their helplessness and I pitied them all the more.

Immediately after the film we listened to the tape recording. The room was silent. The first words, spoken by Yusov, were heard clearly. It was the confrontation between the two boys. Yusov announced that the proceedings would be tape recorded and that Advocate Borisov would be present. I recognized Alik's voice at once. He sounded calm as he gave a detailed account of the game of volleyball. I heard him say, "Sasha was the first to suggest raping Marina, I didn't want to. The three of us walked down the main street . . ." Then Alik's voice grew more muffled, the words less distinct. Some kind of noise, distant at first and then growing louder, was making it difficult to hear. Soon it was clearly not just a noise—it was music. The beautiful melody of Oginsky's "Polonaise" resounded in our temporary courtroom, and through it, barely audible, came the terrible words that had so pained me when I first read them, "You were the first! Why are you telling such lies about me? You suggested it . . ."

Again the music made it impossible to make out any more that was said.

"What's happening?" Kirilov was asking the prosecutor. "What's happening, comrade prosecutor?"

"It's quite simple. The investigator forgot to switch off the radio. The music was playing very quietly and did not disturb the proceedings. Unfortunately the microphone was standing just beneath the loudspeaker. But it doesn't matter. There is a record of the meeting, written by Yusov himself. It corresponds exactly to the tapes."

There was indeed a written record. In it the boys' testimony was written down very exactly, with a mass of details about the rape. It stated how they undressed her and how they carried Marina's body, dropping it on the way. All this was reproduced in the indictment as incontrovertible proof of the boys' guilt. But not one of those details reached me through the stirring strains of the "Polonaise."

During a recess, Lev and I decided to ask permission to hear the tape again at any time that suited the court, during a trial session or after it, or early the next morning. We had to transcribe that tape and make sense of its contents.

The law that allows tape recordings to be made during questioning stipulates certain conditions which the investigator must observe. It categorically forbids the making of a partial or fragmentary record; the testimony must be covered in full, from the opening words of the investigator announcing the date and place to the final words of the person being questioned, stating that he has nothing further to add.

The law also states categorically that the investigator must make a normal written record simultaneously with the taping. Theoretically this written record is supposed to correspond exactly with the tape, but everyone realizes that this is a practical impossibility. As a participant, the investigator is simply unable to write down a verbatim transcript. The tape recording is therefore always fuller and longer than the written record.

We wanted to establish the full text of the tape recording, to get every minor detail in the stories the boys had told at that confrontation, but there was also another reason. Both Lev and I had the impression that if Yusov's written record were to be read aloud at the same tempo as the tape recording, it would prove to be longer; ergo, it contained material that was not on the tape—words that the boys had never spoken.

We had no way of discussing these suspicions with Alik and Sasha because we could not predict when, if ever, Kirilov would grant us another meeting with our clients. The best solution we could devise was to record that tape on another recorder and then, in our own time and without delaying the trial, decipher it for ourselves.

We presented an application to this effect as soon as the hearing resumed, but, as we had feared, it was refused.

The usual nods were exchanged between the assessors and Kirilov, who instructed the clerk of the court to enter in the record: "The application by the defense is refused on the grounds of the obvious defectiveness of the tape recording." And turning to us he added, "I think, comrade advocates, that the grounds for this ruling will satisfy you."

Kirilov was informing us that he was binding the court to a decision that the tape recording was inadmissible; that he rejected it as evidence of the defendants' guilt; and that in consequence the court could make no reference to the tape recording when reaching its verdict. This did not satisfy us, however, because we knew that if the court were to find the boys guilty, it would be on the basis of the written record of that confrontation, and the defense was now deprived of any opportunity to contest that document.

The girls with whom Alik and Sasha had played volleyball were examined next. They all affirmed that the boys were absent for no more than fifteen minutes between the end of the game and their next meeting at the

Akatovs' house, and that they had agreed to a longer time of absence only because Yusov insisted on it during the investigation. They were questioned and intimidated in court in a grossly biased fashion, not only by the judge and prosecutor but by the people's prosecutor, their own teacher. She made such threats as "Don't slander a Soviet investigator! You'll answer for it if you do."

The defense lodged objection after objection, complaining against improper methods of influencing underage witnesses and against the court's failure to put a stop to the illegal procedure. With increasing frequency Kirilov would interrupt us: "Your objection will be entered in the record. Comrade people's prosecutor, you may proceed."

It was now obvious that the boys' confessions dominated this trial, and the formula "Once he's confessed, he's guilty" was the cement holding together the whole faulty structure of the prosecution case.

Only the testimony of Sasha's and Alik's teacher, Mrs. Volkonskaya, could damage this structure. She had been invited by Yusov to assist as a school representative at Sasha's interrogation. In the court Mrs. Volkonskaya was asked by the state prosecutor to confirm that during this interrogation Sasha had confessed voluntarily, that Yusov had not put pressure on him. After she confirmed all that, Voloshina asked her, "Well, do you want to tell us anything else?"

To this question Volkonskaya answered: "When the interrogation was over, Sasha asked Yusov: 'Are you going to let me go now?' It seemed to me odd to the point of absurdity. But I was even more surprised by Yusov's answer: 'Oh come, Sasha, you don't think I can let you go now, do you? Marina's relatives are here, you know.' "

So Sasha's explanation that he had confessed partly because Yusov had promised him he would not have to be held in detention before the trial unexpectedly got very important confirmation.

And then came a witness of a very different kind. When Berta Brodskaya was called, she entered the courtroom confidently and replied to the court's questions with equal composure. "Yes, I know they"—she never once mentioned the boys' first or last names, although she had known both of them since birth—"they killed Marina. Marina was a remarkable girl. She was of the stuff of which heroes are made. And they tormented her like Fascists. They have not only deprived a mother of a beloved daughter, they have deprived the whole Soviet people of a wonderful person of whom it would have been proud. Her death is a loss for all of us, and in the name of us all I demand that this court—a court chosen by the people—show no mercy to these murderers. They have no right to be walking this earth."

This speech drew applause from the people's prosecutor and Kostopravkina. Applause is not permitted in the courtroom during judicial proceedings, but no one was admonished.

It was now our turn to crossexamine her.

"I came here to make a statement to the court. I have no wish to talk to anyone else here," said Berta Brodskaya calmly and confidently, with a triumphant expression on her face.

"Comrade chairman, you have cautioned the witness regarding her obligation to speak the truth, but you have apparently not reminded her of her other obligation, to answer questions. I request that you make this clear to witness Brodskaya; that you warn her that refusal may render her liable to a charge of contempt of court, and that if she still refuses to answer she must make a signed statement in the court record to that effect."

Kirilov immediately warned her to listen to the questions and answer them.

Nevertheless, after each question Brodskaya asked the judge whether she was obliged to answer it, and each time Kirilov snapped, "Answer!" The court could not disallow a single one of our questions. With pedantic exactitude we asked only those directly related to specific points in the indictment:

"Witness Brodskaya, did you yourself see what Burov and Kabanov were doing between 10:00 P.M. and 11:00 P.M. on June 17?"

"Were you in the Akatovs' home on the evening of June 17?"

"Did you yourself see Burov and Kabanov arrive in the Akatovs' yard?"

"Can you describe what Burov and Kabanov were wearing that evening?"

Over and over she was forced to answer, "No . . . I didn't see them . . . No, I wasn't there . . . No, I didn't hear them . . ." And so it continued, through every count of the indictment, until an infuriated Berta Brodskaya almost shouted at the judge, "No, I didn't see anything! I came here to give the court my opinion, the opinion of an old Communist."

Brodskaya did not know, of course, that the law specifically forbids a court to admit *opinion* as evidence. From that moment on, whatever the verdict might be and on whatever grounds it might be based, the name of Brodskaya could not figure in it. Kirilov was intelligent enough not to admit such obviously irrelevant testimony.

Marchenkova's examination proceeded quite differently. The old mourner's whole appearance seemed to say, "What do you want with me? Can't you see what a sick, frightened old woman I am?" Her clothing, her walk, and her barely audible voice stressed how aged and feeble she was; her hands, shaking with nervousness, and the stick she leaned on combined to arouse pity.

When the court put its first question to her, Marchenkova gave no reply at all. When the question was repeated she slowly pushed back her wool headscarf, cupped her hand to her left ear, and said, "Please speak very loudly. I can hardly hear."

I barely caught a rapid exchange of glances between the judge and Voloshina, the prosecutor, after which the latter looked questioningly at Kostopravkina, who shrugged her shoulders.

This little scene was equally unexpected for Lev and me. How could it be that neither Alik, Sasha, nor their parents had ever mentioned to us that Marchenkova was almost stone deaf? She was, after all, the prosecution's star witness, whose evidence consisted in what she had heard. Her story, which had served as grounds for arresting and accusing the two boys, rested on one thing: that she had *heard* a voice through the half-open window of her second-floor room and recognized it as Marina's; furthermore, she claimed not only to have heard the voice but the words spoken: "Alik, take your hands off me! Sasha, you ought to be ashamed of yourself . . ." followed by laughter. Yet here she was standing right up against the judges' desk, almost touching it, leaning forward and mumbling, "Please say that again. I can't hear you."

"Have you been deaf for a long time?" Kirilov asked in some perplexity.

"Yes, a very long time. I can hardly hear, and I can't see anything at all."

"She's faking! She's not really as deaf as all that," Kostopravkina whispered loudly to the prosecutor.

Marchenkova did not react to this, but her eyes glittered malevolently behind thick lenses. She did in fact give the impression that for some reason she was play-acting; we therefore began her examination with great caution.

"Where are you receiving treatment? How long have you been under treatment? With which doctors?"

We immediately sensed that we were on the right track. Questioned about her infirmities, she answered willingly and with an impressive knowledge of specialized medical terminology. She also added some details to her earlier testimony: "I remember the day because I wasn't working at the sanitarium. I had the day off and was doing some housework. I recognized Marina's voice, but I paid no attention to the conversation at the time. I thought it was just some kids passing by and fooling around. I only remembered it much later, a long time after Marina's death. That was why I mourned and wept at her grave—because I had heard those words, and if only I had interfered, nothing would have happened."

As soon as her examination was finished, we submitted an application to obtain from the sanitarium where she worked a schedule of Marchenkova's working days and rest days during the month of June. June 17 had not been a Sunday; therefore she might very well have been working on that day, and her story of the overheard conversation might relate to another day and have nothing to do with the events surrounding Marina's death. We also requested that the court obtain Marchenkova's medical history from the clinic where she was an outpatient. This application was particularly important; once in possession of her medical documents, we could submit them to experts in forensic medicine to answer the question whether Marchenkova was capable of hearing from her room a conversation on the street.

The prosecutor simply referred the application "to the court's ruling."

After the obligatory exchange of nods, Kirilov announced, "The court rules that the application be left open. It will decide on the need to obtain the requested documents after all witnesses have been called and examined."

This ruling is one that advocates often hear in court, and in the overwhelming majority of cases it is a camouflaged form of refusal; similar rulings had already been made in this case. In fact, several of our applications that were actually granted by the court were never fulfilled. We never received, for instance, the requested statements from the police stations at Zvenigorod and Golitsyno about the boys' detention in the remand cells, although the court did receive a certified report of the weather conditions. It had indeed rained, not only on June 16 but also on the three preceding days, and the Akatov sisters and their mother all confirmed that the boys' clothes and shoes had been dry and clean.

Examination of the supplementary witnesses requested by the defense, the six "official witnesses" who had accompanied Yusov and the boys to the scene of the crime, was set for March 25 and 26.

The first was a factory worker from the nearby village of Bakovka. He had never seen Alik and had not been along on Alik's visit to the site. He had seen Sasha for the first time on September 10, 1966, when Investigator Yusov invited him to go along to Izmalkovo. Neither the court nor the defense had any reason to doubt this witness's sincerity and objectivity, and since the prosecution had no questions to put to him, the court gave the right of first examination to me.

I asked whether his rights and duties had been explained to him before he undertook to assist the investigation as an official witness.

"Yes. Investigator Yusov explained to me that I must stay beside Sasha all the time, watch carefully as he pointed out the route, remember the way we went, and, above all, remember the spot Kabanov would point out as the place where the rape was committed and the point where the body was thrown into the water."

"Could you now retrace that route and indicate on this map the places that Kabanov pointed out?"

"Of course I could. I remember it all very well."

As the witness gave the first part of his evidence, I listened calmly: the volleyball court . . . the faucet where they washed their hands . . . the main street . . . the Akatovs' house . . . the Big House . . . Then gradually I felt not just nervousness but fear starting to grip me. It was as though my own fate were being decided.

"I remember," the witness went on, "that we stopped at the last house on the left-hand side of the street and recorded the name of the occupants. Just past the house we turned left and took a narrow footpath that goes right across the orchard. We walked along that path. Then Sasha stopped and said, 'Here,' and pointed to an apple tree. I well remember that it was the second apple tree from the end."

His answer contained one hint that suggested I was getting the right answer, the words "walked along." The apple tree to which Alik had pointed was at the very beginning of the path, right off the main street.

"Could you find that tree on the map?"

"Of course. The map was drawn in my presence. I remember it well."

The witness approached the clerk's table on which the map lay and pointed confidently. "There it is."

Where was he pointing? I asked the court's permission to come over to the desk to look.

"There's no need for you to do that, comrade advocate. Comrade secretary, please record the following: 'The court certifies that the witness pointed to the second apple tree from the end of the orchard furthest from the village and closest to the gully and fence dividing it from Ruslanova's property.' Have you written that?"

Satisfied with that entry, I continued my examination. "Was the time needed to walk that distance measured by a stopwatch and recorded?"

"No, it was not."

"Did you measure the distance to the orchard and the distance you walked along the path in the orchard?"

"While we were driving to Izmalkovo, Yusov said we would only measure the distance along the orchard path. But when we turned off the street onto the path, it turned out that no one had brought a tape measure. Yusov suggested that I pace the distance. I counted the number of paces from the start of the path to the point where Kabanov stopped and pointed to the apple tree, and I wrote the figure down on a piece of paper."

"Did you keep that piece of paper?"

"No, I handed it to Yusov then and there."

"How do you explain the fact that in the written record of that site visit that measurement was not included? You signed the record, didn't you?"

"I suggested to Yusov that we ought to include the figure in the record, but he said it was enough to say 'the second apple tree from the end of the orchard.' I genuinely thought that was enough, so I agreed to sign the record."

I had no more questions, nor did Yudovich or the prosecutor.

The second official witness was also a factory worker from Bakovka. Again I asked him the same questions, but this time I was less nervous in waiting for his answers, being now more certain that the reply I would get would not only be favorable but very important.

The evidence of the two witnesses corresponded exactly. Once again the clerk of the court wrote in the record: "Kabanov pointed to the second apple tree from the end of the orchard bordering the gully and Ruslanova's property."

I had no more questions, but Voloshina asked permission to cross-examine.

"Tell me, witness, have you ever met the relatives of the defendants before coming into this courtroom?"

"No, I have never met them."

"No one asked you to give exactly the testimony you have just given?"

"No. The subpoena was brought to my home yesterday and this morning I simply took the train into Moscow. No one spoke to me."

"And no one tried to influence you here in the courthouse, before the opening of the session?"

"Of course not. I've already told you that I know absolutely no one here. I've never seen any of them before."

"Have you told the truth, witness? You know, don't you, that the penalty for perjury can be up to five years' imprisonment? Do you realize that?"

"The court warned me I had to tell the truth. Even without that warning I would have said the same. Because that was what really happened."

Kirilov appeared not to be listening to these questions or the answers, while our two lay assessors wore their unalterable expressions of boredom. I cannot even remember whether they were men or women, old or young. Even in such a serious case as this, all they ever did was nod their heads to show agreement with Kirilov's opinion.

"Tell me, witness, did Yusov force Kabanov to describe the murder in your presence?" the prosecutor went on.

"No, he did not force him."

"In other words, Kabanov described it voluntarily?"

"Yusov did not compel him."

"Did he point out the route voluntarily?"

"Yusov said, 'Go the way you went on June 17,' and he walked from the volleyball court down the main street."

"Everyone else has already told us that Kabanov was calm when he described the rape and the murder. Tell me, witness, would you confirm that testimony?"

It is not allowed to put questions in that form. No witness may be told what testimony was given before his, but the court did not admonish the prosecutor.

"It is hard for me to say whether Kabanov was calm or not. He spoke calmly. Yet I remember being puzzled because he was not so much calm as somehow apathetic, as though he were describing something that had nothing to do with him at all. He didn't react to anything. Even when a crowd gathered and people shouted, 'Filthy brute! Murderer!' he remained as apathetic as ever."

The prosecutor finished her examination and the witnesses were just about to be released when I decided to ask a few more questions. This witness's last answers had interested me.

"Where was the record of the visit drawn up?"

"All the data were noted down on the spot. The final version was written at the police station in Bakovka."

"Which of the participants accompanied you on the ride out to Izmalkovo?"

"I was in the car with Yusov, Kabanov, a photographer, and another official witness."

"Did Yusov ask Kabanov any questions in the car?"

"No, Yusov said nothing. He looked very tired."

"And what about Kabanov? Did he ask Yusov anything?"

"He didn't ask a question, but he said to him, 'I wish I were going home.' "

"Did Yusov reply?"

"Yes. He said: 'Wait, not so fast.' "

"Do you remember that well?"

"Yes, very well. The conversation puzzled me a lot. I couldn't think of any explanation for it."

That was a day of rejoicing for us, as had been the day when Marchenkova was questioned.

There was no further evidence that might in any way support the prosecution's case. As before, it rested solely on the boys' confessions.

On March 29 the various experts gave their answers to the questions of the court and the two sides: "It is possible that rape took place . . ." "It is possible that the corpse may have drifted in the water . . ." "It is possible that the bruises found on the corpse were caused before death . . ." and so on and so on.

In closing the session that day, Kirilov announced, "The court will recess for two days. The next session will begin at 9:30 A.M. on April 1." Turning to the prosecutor and the defense counsel, he said, "Prepare all your supplementaries"—meaning affidavits, character evidence, and supplementary questions—"and after that we will hear the final speeches of the prosecution and the defense. No extra time for preparation of the speeches will be allowed."

We were staggered. So that was the answer to all our applications which the court had left open. It meant that on April 1 Kirilov would simply reject them all. The case was a series of yawning gaps which, as before, would be covered by the formula: "The defendants have admitted their guilt and the court sees no reason to doubt the reliability of their testimony."

We decided to combine all our requests into a single, comprehensive application, and simultaneously to request that the court call for expert medical evidence on Marchenkova. We decided to risk asking for this even without prior knowledge of her medical history, because an application calling for expert evidence must be discussed by the court in private and must be answered in written form, giving precise reasons for the court's ruling. Since the clerk had recorded that Marchenkova could not hear the court's questions, that she suffered, on her own admission, from a serious hearing defect, the court would be unable to find any convincing grounds for rejection.

In addition to our joint application, we had to discuss our final pleas for the defense: who was to speak first, and how to divide between us the arguments dealing with the basic issues in the case.

We behaved like a perfect gentleman and lady, each of us offering the other the choice of when to speak, but I insisted that Lev should begin. It was "his" case and he had invited me to participate, and in addition, the division of the material which he had proposed made it essential that he speak first.

We decided that Yudovich would give an analysis of all the facts connected with the scene of the crime, where Marina's sweater was found and where the body was found, along with all the possible versions of the murder—the "soldiers' version," the "Sadykov version," and the "Nazarov version." This very complex part of our joint defense strategy was made especially difficult by the plethora of minor, disconnected facts, every one of which would have to be subjected to separate analysis and grouped into categories that, taken together, would add up to an argument in support of our common aim.

My speech would be devoted to a psychological and factual analysis of the reasons for the boys' confessions; to the evidence relating to the time span involved, which determined whether or not the boys could have committed the crime; and to analyzing all the forms of expert evidence: medical (whether Alik and Sasha were both capable at the time of having sexual intercourse), forensic pathology (the state of the corpse), the specialist's report on Marina's clothes, and the hydrological study of the lake.

We had two days to prepare ourselves. The need to reassess and reflect on the case was very great. I myself also needed to find a means of distancing myself, standing aside to weigh up all the pros and cons dispassionately, without readily rejecting all the cons or confidently accepting all the pros. I must try to put myself in the judge's place.

I went home to play endless games of solitaire, smoke cigarette after cigarette, stand up, sit down, stand up again and pace around the room. My head was bursting with thoughts, but they flowed in a formless stream with no unifying element. Then I decided to try to stop thinking, to do things that would calm my nerves. With Lev Yudovich leading for the defense, there was no chance I would be speaking on April 1, and after that I would have a whole night ahead of me, an excellent time to prepare a speech. So those two recess days passed in domestic chores, which always give me a sense of achievement, and in listening to music. I was running no risk, even if the improbable suddenly occurred and I had to make my speech early, because I really knew that just below the threshold of consciousness my defense plea was long since ready, and that as soon as the courtroom atmosphere began to work on me, my arguments would fall into place. The closing stage of a trial, when prosecution and defense make their final speeches, invariably has this effect on me. All fatigue and ailments vanish, even toothache. I feel like an old circus horse, head drooping, standing in the dark outside the arena until he hears the stirring, brassy sounds of "The Entry of the Gladiators," throws up his head, and starts pawing the ground impatiently.

Lev, however, was completely ready on the morning of April 1. He showed me his notes, or rather his detailed outline—eighty pages of small, neat handwriting. He had also prepared our joint application to the court, since he was the one who would submit it.

The members of the court entered and the judge declared the session open. Lev was about to submit our application when Kirilov stopped him, exchanged nods with the assessors, and announced, "The court will retire for consideration of a ruling." We looked at each other in perplexity, and Voloshina's expression showed that she was equally mystified.

Finally I said to Lev, "April Fool."

He looked at me in astonishment.

"April Fool! The court has played a trick on you. Virtue, as is proper on All Fools Day, is punished, and sloth triumphs. They're referring the whole case for further investigation. What a good thing I didn't write my speech."

Two and a half hours later the court returned from the consulting room. Kirilov pronounced a ruling equivalent in length to a summing up and a verdict. In it were enumerated all the basic defects of the investigation, all the gross infringements of the law that Yusov had committed. It included an order to detain and interrogate the men who had been put in the remand cells with Alik and Sasha, and to reinterrogate the three soldiers, on the grounds that their testimony was contradictory and the reasons for the contradictions must be established. The court's ruling also repeated the maxim which we, the defense counsel, had so frequently used during the trial: "To establish that the defendants could have committed a crime is not proof that they, and no others, did commit it." Expert medical evidence was called for to determine the degree of Marchenkova's deafness, and the court mentioned the point we had made, that the two defendants had indicated different places at which the crime was allegedly committed.

The ruling was a crushing blow to the procuracy. Not only in length but in content too, it was tantamount to a verdict of acquittal on grounds of insufficient proof of guilt. The crucial difference, of course, was that Alik and Sasha would not be released from custody. That day marked a period of exactly seven months since the day of their arrest. The RSFSR procurator had sanctioned their detention for six months, but the extra month was not a breach of the law because time spent on trial does not count toward the total period of pretrial detention. (The USSR General Procurator could have extended the boys' detention another three months, but Yusov had not applied to him for such permission.)

A few minutes later the session was declared closed. The courtroom was still crowded. The witnesses had to have their subpoenas countersigned by the clerk of the court, as proof that they had been legitimately absent from work, and the boys' parents were asking for a meeting with their sons.

"No, no visits allowed until the further investigation is completed."

Lev was putting the eighty sheets of his defense speech back into his briefcase and I was already out in the corridor, in the place allocated to smokers.

Kirilov appeared, smiling with satisfaction. He saw me and came over briskly. "Well, Comrade Advocate Kaminskaya, I am very glad to have got acquainted with you, and it will be a pleasure to have you in my courtroom on future occasions. Now let me give you and Yudovich a word of advice: hand over this case to two other advocates."

"But why should we? Because your ruling referred to the advocates' possible attempts to exert improper influence on their clients?"

Kirilov gave no answer.

"Or are we the unfortunate scapegoats?"

"To some extent you may be right in that interpretation. At any rate, it would be better for you to drop this case. It will inevitably bring you trouble."

And he walked off without saying goodbye.

We stayed on the case and we never regretted it, although it did indeed bring us trouble. And I prefer to remember Judge Kirilov, not when he shouted, "I forbid you to look at Burov!" to my co-counsel, but as he was when he read his final ruling, calm, dignified, and judicial.

4. The Second Trial

T HE MOSCOW PROVINCIAL COURT set the procuracy a great many questions for reinvestigation, including a check on all Yusov's infringements of the rules of procedure. To whom would the procurator hand over the case? This question was answered soon and unambiguously: the new investigator, who was to scrutinize Yusov's work and evaluate it, was Yusov.

Although Lev and I could not predict with certainty that the procuracy would display such a blatant lack of objectivity, we nevertheless took certain precautions. Each of us explained to our clients that they had a right to challenge an investigator, and it was agreed that if Yusov were appointed, Alik and Sasha would state that they had no confidence in him and would firmly refuse to answer his questions.

The two boys had learned a lot during the past six weeks. They no longer felt bewildered and entirely helpless, and they had begun to have hope. They realized they would have to fight for that hope, and we were certain that they would be able to carry out our agreement, no matter what pressure might be applied to them.

The next few weeks were full of uncertainty. Our immediate objective was to get the boys released from custody on the grounds that their original arrest had been unlawful and that the case against them had shown insufficient evidence of guilt to justify their further detention.

As soon as the case was back at the procuracy, which took two months, we submitted a joint request to the chief of the investigation department for the release of the two boys, but we did not count on rapid success. We knew, though, that if we didn't start the fight for their release immediately, Alik and Sasha would not be freed when the six-month detention period expired, because by then Yusov would have obtained permission from the Procurator General to extend the period. To each successive level of the procurator's hierarchy we wrote request after request for the boys' release, to which we received the invariable reply that our request had been forwarded to the procuracy of Moscow Province for consideration in the light of the court record. From there came the answer: "Request not granted." Not only we but the boys' parents were writing letters. Others, it turned out, were also writing to the authorities, and not only about the boys' release.

One evening Lev called me to say that he had been summoned to the Ministry of Justice to explain his conduct; the reason was a complaint lodged by Kostopravkina. A summons of this kind always presages trouble. A summons to the ministry was a sign of the seriousness of the accusation and the gravity of the possible consequences.

Next day Lev called me again: "What the hell is going on? Why do they seem to think I eat nothing but pork?"

"Have Alik's parents killed their pig again?"

"I don't know. Kostopravkina claims that they have slaughtered their pig and I've eaten it."

"And what conclusion was reached after this interesting conversation?"

"I was advised to hand over the case to another advocate and told to give them a written explanation, which I did. I wrote that I never eat pork, it makes me throw up. I am not handing over Burov's defense to anyone. Anyway, why don't they write complaints about *you?* Why are you any better than I?"

"Indeed, why don't they? It's a case of sex discrimination!"

It was not a matter of which of us Kostropravkina treated better, but which of us she treated worse. But she did not see me as the chief enemy, and not just because Lev had been on the case from the very beginning. Lev's appearance proclaims forcefulness and strength: tall, fairly solidly built, with energetic features and a loud voice, he cannot avoid making an impression on people. I, on the other hand, am small, and in those days I was quite thin. My voice sounds loud only in court. During recesses I am usually silent. And I am a woman, which is a significant factor influencing the assessment of professional abilities by people of Kostopravkina's educational level. It was her low esteem for my ability which insured that the force of Kostopravkina's ill will was directed mainly against Lev Yudovich. The whole idiotic business about the pork fizzled out into nothing, and its only effect was to cause Lev some quite unnecessary harassment. The Ministry eventually rejected Kostopravkina's complaint on grounds of its absurdity.

Once more time was passing, the boys were still in prison, and we advocates knew absolutely nothing of what was happening in the investigating offices of the procuracy.

Investigator Yusov phoned me when he had finished his inquiries and was ready for defense counsel to study the new material. He was ingratiatingly polite with me at this meeting, but I refused to be drawn into conversation with him.

Then Sasha and I sat from morning till night reading the four volumes of supplementary evidence, and I copied out all the relevant passages.

Yusov had done a titanic job. He had reinterrogated the whole village, missing no one. He had collected all the gossip and all the rumors circulating in and around Izmalkovo. He had expended enormous efforts in attempts to prove, for instance, that the new raincoat bought by Nadya Akatova could not possibly have been paid for with her parents' money; this was backed up by a complete account of the earnings coming into the Akatov household. Then followed more "evidence" from Brodskaya: she was convinced that Nadya's raincoat had been bought with the Burovs' money, so that Nadya would testify in court in Alik's favor. Certain villagers had noticed another girl who had also given evidence that supported the boys' case, and they testified that she had clearly been drinking—not at her own expense, of course; she was not the sort who would ever spend her own money on vodka—so obviously the Burovs had supplied her with liquor.

And so it went for four volumes. The only new document Yusov had added was a statement from the District Police Department confirming that citizen Ivan Kuznetsov and citizen Victor Yermolaev had indeed been detained in the remand cells with Kabanov and Burov respectively, and that these individuals had been released after identification, with orders that they were to "quit the confines of the City and Province of Moscow." This was very important, as it confirmed the boys' testimony that adult prisoners had been placed in their cells, but Yusov had not tried to find these men.

Neither Alik nor Sasha gave testimony to Yusov. Both challenged him at their first session. In his own hand Sasha wrote their only statement in the new material: "I have no confidence in you because you deceived me. I confessed because you promised to release me. You knew that I was innocent. I will not answer any more of your questions."

From then on, neither Sasha nor Alik was called for questioning, but this did not prevent Yusov from finishing his work on the case, letting all the previous "proofs of guilt" stand unaltered in the indictment.

Once more we drafted a detailed application to the procuracy, based on these arguments: (1) The original investigation was biased and conducted unlawfully; (2) the defendants' confessions were obtained by unlawful means; (3) the supplementary investigation failed to carry out the ruling of the Moscow Provincial Court (here followed a point-by-point listing of the court's instructions). Our application concluded with three requests: (1) To carry out the instructions of the court; (2) to hand over the investigation to an objective investigator; (3) to release Burov and Kabanov from detention pending retrial. We did not have to wait long for a reply: "Application refused."

That was that. There was no one to appeal to, because the investigation was now concluded and the case was back in the jurisdiction of the Moscow Provincial Court.

The new school year began—the second year of schooling the boys had missed—and still the case was not given a retrial date. It might be a good sign. Perhaps the Provincial Court had refused to accept the case, or perhaps it had been remanded for still further investigation. Finally we learned in late September 1967 that the case would be heard in the Moscow City Court.

The provincial court and the city court are both at the same level of the judicial hierarchy. The difference between them is not in their competence but in the territory subject to their jurisdiction. Neither the complexity of a case, nor its scope, nor the gravity of the charge can cause a case to be transferred from one of these courts to the other, and in this instance the reason was quite different. The Moscow Provincial Court refused to retry the case of the two boys. Not one of its judges was prepared to pass a verdict of guilty, yet not one dared acquit them either, because they all knew the case was being monitored by the Central Committee of the Party, and especially because the activities of Alexandra Kostopravkina were by now well known to that court. It was Kostopravkina herself who gave the court its pretext for refusing to try the next phase of the case. Indignant at Kirilov's failure to convict, she and Berta Brodskaya began to aim their protests at others beside the advocates. One of them stated: "After the conclusion of the hearing, we ourselves saw in the courtroom how Burov's and Kabanov's parents handed the clerk of the court a large bundle wrapped in paper. This, of course, was a bribe to both judge and clerk, to insure that only evidence favorable to the accused was entered in the court record."

This complaint had no consequences for either Kirilov or the clerk, because it was obvious to the authorities that no one gives bribes in front of a crowd of people right in the courtroom. The real reason for the transfer of the case was that all the judges of the provincial court took the initiative in extending the complainant's suspicion to themselves, and in a letter to the Supreme Court stated that Kostopravkina had expressed lack of confidence in their entire bench. They clung to that protest as the anchor that would save them from a professional defeat, and thereby deprived themselves of the chance of achieving a professional triumph, the passing of a just verdict.

The Moscow City Court accepted the case without objections, and it happened that the judge in the second trial of Alik and Sasha was a woman member of the city court bench, Judge Kareva, and that the case was heard in a courtroom on the second floor of that courthouse.

I am fond of that courtroom. It was there that I made my first speech for the defense, there too that I obtained my first acquittal. I even had a kind of superstitious belief that this courtroom brought me luck, as schoolgirls believe in a lucky dress that helps them pass exams.

Once more Alik and Sasha were brought into the courtroom, to stand on the other side of the wooden barrier immediately behind our backs. Opposite us sat the same prosecutor, Voloshina. On the first public bench sat Alexandra Kostopravkina, and behind her the boys' parents. Beyond them, almost in the far corner of the courtroom, was a new spectator—Olga Chaikovskaya, a well-known journalist. Her courtroom articles often appeared in the *Literary Gazette* and *Izvestiya*. To this day, living in America, I still read her pieces about Soviet justice in the *Literary Gazette*.

I did not know Olga then, but I persuaded her to attend this trial because Lev and I had decided we must try to get it covered in the press. The presence of a reporter, we reasoned, would have some restraining effect on the court, and if the boys were acquitted, it didn't matter a jot to us whether an account of the trial was published in the newspapers or not. If, however, the court tried the case with a bias, if despite the facts it delivered a verdict of guilty, then a newspaper article criticizing the verdict might help us later in a higher court.

Just before the hearing began, Voloshina turned to Kostopravkina and asked, "Where is the people's prosecutor? Why isn't she here?"

At that moment the door opened and a woman entered who was to play a great and vital part in our case and thus in the fate of Alik and Sasha. Neither Lev nor I knew who she was, but our attention was caught by her charming, gentle smile, the bright and cheerful look in her eyes—a rare sight in a courtroom. She glanced around her, then briskly approached the prosecutor, whispered to her, and gave her a document. Then she sat down beside Voloshina and produced a notepad and pen. She clearly intended to stay.

The court entered and we all stood up, still not knowing who the newcomer was. The court verified the presence of the participants: the defendants were brought in; a nod to the prosecutor; a nod to advocates Kaminskaya and Yudovich. "The people's prosecutor?" A questioning look at Voloshina. "Not present?"

"Present," announced the unknown woman. "I'm the people's prosecutor. My name is Sarah Babyonisheva. I have been delegated by the Moscow writers' organization to attend this case in the capacity of people's prosecutor."

Her mandate was scrutinized. Counsel for the defense was also shown her papers. The obligatory supporting documents were missing, including the minutes of the meeting that had delegated her. We could have objected to her participation, but then the court would have summoned the original people's prosecutor, the teacher whom we knew only too well. And this woman was, after all, an intellectual, a writer. There was a chance that she might be genuinely interested in seeing that justice was done, and at least she might not be quite so bloodthirsty as the other woman. We therefore said, "No objections," and the clerk noted it in the record: "The court ruled that citizeness Babyonisheva be admitted to participation in the case of Burov and Kabanov in the capacity of people's prosecutor."

With that the hearing began. As before, it started with examination of Sasha, then of Alik.

Judge Kareva did not shout at them, she did not stare at them as they gave their testimony, nor did she admonish us if we turned our heads around. She listened calmly, her lips clamped together; when she questioned Sasha, she did not threaten him or exhort him to tell the truth.

When we proceeded to examine the witnesses, however, Kareva lost her restraint. For her the witnesses were clearly divided into two camps: the "good" witnesses who were against the boys, and the "bad" witnesses who were for them. To the first sort she spoke kindly and encouragingly; the second group she incessantly interrupted and reminded of the penalties for perjury. Yusov had by no means been wasting his time when he had collected all the gossip that had been circulating in Izmalkovo. We began to realize that we were faced by a judge who had decided on a verdict of guilty even before the start of the trial and was now steadily putting that decision into effect.

The Akatov family, the mother and her two daughters Nadya and Nina, came in for an especially hard time, as did Sasha's sister Lena, and Irochka, the girl from outside the village who with her mother had rented a room at the Akatovs that summer. It was understandable. These witnesses were testifying to the time at which the boys had reached the Akatovs' house, and the judge had no evidence to refute them. No one else had seen the boys or knew when they arrived at the house.

For hours on end Kareva kept them on the witness stand. Again and again she put the same questions to them, with the aim of wearing them down to the point of collapse. The older of the two sisters, Nadya, was now sixteen, the age of criminal responsibility for perjury, and every answer that she gave was interrupted by a reminder of this fact. She was questioned closely about her raincoat and the source of the money with which she had paid for it.

"But I'm working! I bought it with my first wages. Why don't you believe me? I don't have but one raincoat, and everyone in our village has one."

Again she was questioned about the time, and again she was warned against perjuring herself. Pale, Nadya could only stand there and repeat, "But I'm telling you the truth."

And so it went on all morning, until Kareva announced the lunch recess, adding, "We shall continue your examination after the recess."

All this time Chaikovskaya was sitting in the courtroom and taking notes. Our hope that the presence of a reporter would have a restraining effect was clearly unfounded.

Lev and I lodged frequent objections. Kareva would listen to them, staring at us coldly with her bright eyes, her lips pressed together even more firmly, but she did not interrupt us or cut us off. For a while her examination of the witnesses would become calmer and she would adhere more closely to the rules, but before long it would start all over again.

Nor did our applications to the court fare any better. We were refused permission to subpoena the police officers who had placed adults in the boys' cells and had connived to keep the boys in the remand cells beyond the lawful term. Yet it was vital to establish exactly why such breaches of regulations had occurred. Twice the court not only rejected our application to transcribe but even to listen to the tape recording of the confrontation between the two boys. Twice too we submitted in vain an application for the court to adjourn to Izmalkovo and inspect the scene of the crime, knowing what strong evidence of our clients' innocence would result from such a visit.

Earlier that summer, while the case was back at the procuracy, Lev and I drove out there several times. We walked along every inch of the banks of the Samarinsko-Izmalkovsky ponds. We clambered down the steep bank at the point where Alik and Sasha had allegedly thrown Marina's body into the water, and discovered that a large part of the route from the orchard to the bank was along a very wet and muddy path. I could not have walked along it in ordinary shoes. Most important, the high bank from which the body had allegedly been flung into the water was directly over a spit of sand that ran out quite far into the lake. Beyond that the water was so shallow that I paddled about in it quite freely in my rubber boots with no risk of getting wet. To throw the body of an almost fully grown fourteen-year-old girl out as far as the place where the water was deep enough for Marina's body to have sunk, I was convinced that the efforts of two grown men would have been insufficient.

We saw that the apple trees were right beside a well-trodden path, a difficult, almost impossible place to commit a rape. We discovered that the place where Marina's sweater, a button from her bathing shorts, and a button from a pair of male underpants had been found was totally hidden from view, protected from any outside observer by bushes and trees. We saw that by walking along the stone slabs at the top of an old ruined dam it was possible to reach, quite unobserved, the end of the lake where Marina's corpse was subsequently found floating.

Twice Voloshina objected to the proposal that the court go to Izmalkovo: "The evidence is clear enough. This proposal by the defense will only lead to an unwarranted lengthening of the trial." And twice Judge Kareva, after the ritual exchange of nods with her two assessors, rejected our application.

The court did grant some of our applications. The three soldiers, Sogrin, Zuyev, and Bazarov, were called and examined. In my view, their testimony should only have increased the suspicions which were aroused against them just after Marina's death.

They had left the volleyball court with the Akatov girls, somewhere between 10:30 and 10:40, about four or five minutes ahead of Marina, Alik, and Sasha. They had followed the path right across the orchard, then along the fence around Ruslanova's *dacha* (therefore past the spot where the sweater was found), and back to Marshal Budyonny's *dacha*.

They and the truck driver, Poleshchuk, had changed their evidence in the earlier investigations, and now they stuck to the second version, which, in the words of the Moscow City Court, "excluded the possibility of the soldiers having committed the crime." Nevertheless, the court was also given new evidence that totally undermined the soldiers' revision of their timetable that night.

Poleshchuk testified that he had not been alone while waiting for the soldiers. Before reaching Budyonny's *dacha* he had detoured to pick up his girl friend, and she had been with him in the cab of the truck until the three soldiers had arrived. On the trip back to their army unit, Poleshchuk had driven Galya home. At the request of the defense, this woman was traced and subpoenaed as a witness.

She remembered that summer evening clearly, because she had moved into a new apartment the next day. "That evening was the only time I rode with Poleshchuk in his truck, so I couldn't possibly confuse it with another day. I remember well that he drove to my place to pick me up at 10:00 P.M. and suggested I go with him to take a look at the *dachas* in the Generals' Village. I had never been there before. We reached the intersection of the Minsk Highway and drove for about twenty or thirty minutes. Then we went to look at the beautiful *dacha* that belonged to Marshal Budyonny and some others nearby. We got back to the truck at 10:50 P.M. I remember the time, because I looked at my watch. I was very worried, because it was already late. Then we had to wait a long time, and Poleshchuk was upset. He was afraid I would think he had arranged the delay, and he apologized. The soldiers didn't arrive until around 1:00 A.M. I know, because by the time I got home it was well after 1:00."

Kareva promptly asked Galya why she had decided to take a drive so late at night with a man, and why she had gone with him to look at other people's *dachas*.

"But I thought his friends were already there and we wouldn't be alone. We did nothing wrong, we just had a look and went away again."

"And do you often go for rides at night with strange men?"

There followed a lecture on her behavior.

Galya was pale, her eyes full of tears. "But it was you who traced me and ordered me to appear in court. You told me to tell everything I knew. Why are you attacking me like this? I have described everything exactly as it happened."

"No one is attacking you, witness. You are in court. The court is not attacking you, the court is making clear to you the nature of your behavior."

Olga Chaikovskaya made an entry in her notebook, as did our people's prosecutor, Sarah Babyonisheva.

During the first days of the trial, Sarah put many questions to Alik and Sasha, and their testimony clearly surprised her, but she believed Alexandra Kostopravkina. Sarah, after all, came into court convinced of the boys' guilt before she knew anything about the case; she came, as far as she was concerned, to accuse.

After a few days, however, I heard Sarah turn to Voloshina during a recess and say, "What a strange and terrible case this is."

"What's strange about it?" retorted Voloshina. "It's clearer than clear —they killed her, and now they're trying to wriggle out of it."

It was around this time that a change came over first the prosecutor's and then the court's attitude to Sarah Babyonisheva. They did not like the fact that this people's prosecutor was taking an unusually active part in the trial, that she did not try to intimidate or shame the witnesses but merely put her questions in a calm, neutral tone. Sitting side by side at the same table, Babyonisheva and Voloshina were a living example of the contrast between two kinds of people: the intelligentsia and the illiterate but smug, self-satisfied official. Sarah's behavior was incompatible with this court, and the court realized it; they stopped seeing her as an ally and began to suspect that she was their adversary.

Judge Kareva did not disallow any of her questions, but she made it all too plain that she regarded not only Sarah's questions but her mere presence at the trial as superfluous. Once, after one of our customary requests for the court to adjourn to the scene of the crime, to which the prosecutor lodged her usual objection, Kareva said, "And I assume the people's prosecutor supports this application?"

"Yes, I do. I think it's very important. I live in Peredelkino. I have been to the area in question many times . . ."

"Comrade people's prosecutor, I must make it clear to you that you are not a witness. We have heard your opinion on the defense application. Sit down."

Two days later, the original people's prosecutor appeared in the courtroom. Both the state's prosecutor and Kostopravkina asked the court to admit her in the capacity of second people's prosecutor. But the teacher's mandate was valid only for the provincial court and she had not obtained a new one. The court was bound to sustain our objection.

Kostopravkina harassed Sarah most of all. The mother's bitterness was increased by the fact that it was at her own request that the writers' organization had delegated a people's prosecutor, and she herself had implored Sarah to take part in the trial, which involved six weeks of unpaid work of a kind wholly foreign to her.

How ashamed we used to feel when we drove away from the courthouse in Lev's car while Sarah Babyonisheva and Olga Chaikovskaya had to walk to the subway, a journey of at least fifteen minutes on foot. We dared not offer them a ride. To have done so could have harmed our case and compromised Olga and Sarah.

Among the witnesses questioned by the Moscow City Court was Nazarov, the man who, before Alik and Sasha did so, confessed to raping and murdering Marina. His testimony was interesting, for it provided a refutation of the thesis "If he's confessed, he must be guilty."

Nazarov stood in the courtroom, escorted by guards from the prison where he was serving a sentence, and his very presence made everyone who believed a confession to be irrefutable evidence have second thoughts. He confessed, didn't he? So once he's confessed, he's guilty. In that case Alik and Sasha couldn't be guilty. But if Alik and Sasha were guilty, then Nazarov wasn't. That meant that confession alone was not enough; other proofs were needed.

Nazarov's testimony was also important to us as an answer to the question why people confess. The reasons, it turned out, were exactly the same as those that had made the boys confess falsely. When Nazarov said he was innocent, they did not believe him; he already had a previous conviction for rape. Every attempt to prove his innocence was rejected by the investigator as unworthy of serious attention. He held out for a long time, insisting that he hadn't done it. Then he broke down and confessed to something he had clearly not done. In his case too there were promises of a mitigation of his sentence and threats of execution by firing squad; but the main reason, in his own words, was hopelessness, the realization that whatever he said, they were not going to believe him.

There was a further important circumstance that could be brought out only by cross-examining Nazarov. The tape recording of his testimony abounded in factual detail about the circumstances of Marina's death. How did he know these details if he wasn't the murderer?

Nazarov confirmed that he had learned them all from the investigator himself. The only thing the investigator had been unable to tell him was the way the girl had been killed; at that time the conclusions of the medical experts were not yet available. Nazarov testified that he had stabbed her, wounding her several times, but the medical report revealed that the corpse showed no traces of knife wounds. Thus the experts categorically refuted Nazarov's testimony.

Nazarov's evidence corresponded to an astounding degree with the testimony of the two boys, who stated that they had learned the details of Marina's underwear from Yusov. Not only did Yusov describe it; he showed them photographs of the garments. But he had made the mistake of showing these photographs to the boys in the presence of the official witnesses; thanks to this, the boys' story was confirmed in court.

Finally there came the moment when the court agreed to grant our application for stenographic transcripts of the tape recordings of all the interrogations and of the confrontation between the two boys. They did not trust us to do this job ourselves, but ordered the Moscow provincial procuracy to do it.

In examining the transcripts we established twenty-six instances of divergence between the two versions, and each instance concerned facts ascribed to the boys but not mentioned in their testimony, those very details on the strength of which the indictment stated:

The guilt of Burov and Kabanov is confirmed by the fact that, in confessing themselves responsible for the rape and murder of Marina Kostopravkina, they described to the investigator such details as could only have been known to them through having committed the crime. Their guilt is also confirmed by the fact that, when questioned separately, they disclosed to the investigator factual details concerning the place and methods of the rape and murder that were identical.

We now had to make sure that the results of our scrutiny were officially acknowledged by the court and added to the materials in the case. Only then would we be entitled to mention them in our final pleas for the defense and, if necessary, incorporate them into our appeals to a higher court. There was only one way to do it: to force—literally force—the court to examine our findings point by point during the trial, and to record each point separately in the record: "The court certifies the following noncorrespondence . . ." followed by the full text of the cited passages in quotation marks. We foresaw that our application would arouse determined opposition. It therefore had to be introduced in such a way that the court would not at first suspect its real aim and significance.

Next day Yudovich brought into court a huge sheet of paper tabulated in three columns. The first column contained the text of the transcript on each of the twenty-six points, the second listed the text of the investigator's manuscript version of the same points, and the third showed the discrepancies between the two.

Lev thought I should be the one to submit our application to have these discrepancies certified by the court, and we decided I would begin my application with a request for the certification of several other documents —character references, depositions about the health of the boys' parents, and certain passages from statements by expert witnesses, to which I genuinely needed to refer in my final plea. Then, without proposing a separate application, I would ask the court to certify the textual divergences.

As soon as the session opened, I requested that the transcripts of the tape recordings be added to the materials in the case. The prosecutor supported my request and it was granted without question. From that moment the transcripts became "materials in the case" and I acquired the right to have the court certify the correctness of any passage from them.

A few trivial questions of judicial procedure were discussed, after which the court announced, "We will proceed to the supplementaries . . ."

Voloshina put a supplementary question.

Yudovich, too, listed his supplements, all of which the court confirmed.

At last it was my turn, and I began by putting the same question to both defendants: "Did Investigator Yusov ask you any more questions after you had finished recording your testimony on tape?"

Both boys answered: "No."

Kareva and Voloshina were pleased to hear this answer. They saw it as evidence that the rules of procedure had been observed. Everything that was said had been recorded on tape, nothing had been omitted. And for me it was important to have this point specified in the record, to rule out any chance of Yusov's falsifications of the manuscript version being explained away as a purely technical infringement of the rules governing tape-recorded evidence.

As prearranged, I began by requesting the court's confirmation of the wording of certain passages in the experts' reports and the dates of certain documents—everything, in fact, that was affected by the formal require- ment that only materials certified correct by the court may be cited in an advocate's final speech for the defense.

And then: "In the investigator's manuscript version of the confrontation between Burov and Kabanov, volume 3, page 129, there is the following passage . . ."

Judge Kareva: "Comrade secretary, record this: 'The court confirms the presence of following passage in the manuscript record of the confrontation in volume 3, page 129 . . .' "

Kaminskaya: "In the transcribed tape recording of the confrontation, the same point is dealt with as follows . . ." (another quotation).

I purposely quoted a passage in which there were no substantive varia- tions between the two versions.

Judge Kareva: "Comrade secretary, record this: 'The court con- firms . . .' "

The same happened with two more passages that showed only minor discrepancies.

Then: "I request confirmation of a passage in Volume 3, page 86. In the interrogation of Burov, manuscript version, it reads: "Marina pulled away her left hand and I held her tighter. Marina was still wearing her swimming shorts. Sasha took off her shorts.' "

Judge Kareva: "The court confirms . . ."

Kaminskaya: "I request confirmation that in the tape-recorded version that passage is missing. There is no mention of swimming shorts nor of anyone taking them off."

There followed a pause of the kind that in court is almost like an explo- sion.

Kareva: "Comrade advocate, what do you mean by this?"

Kaminskaya: "I mean, comrade president, that on page 86 of volume 3 there is a passage, whose wording you have just confirmed. I also mean to point out that in the transcribed tape recording no such passage exists. Please compare the two versions and confirm the correctness of my obser- vation, as the law requires."

Another pause, then Kareva, slowly: "Comrade secretary, the court confirms that the passage in question is missing from the transcript."

Kaminskaya: "I request confirmation that in the manuscript version of Kabanov's interrogation, on page 96 of Volume 3, the following is written: 'I threw Marina's sweater and it fell not far from the fence around Ruslanova's *dacha*.' " I then pointed out that in the transcribed tape recording the passage read: "I don't remember which of us removed Marina's sweater or where it was thrown."

Voloshina was on her feet and shouting, "That can't be right! No doubt there is a correction at the end of the manuscript!"

I remained calm. There was no such correction to be found in the manuscript record, a document the prosecutor herself had laid before the court.

Again Kareva had to say, "Comrade secretary, the court confirms . . ."

I cited the next pair of divergent passages, and this time it was Kareva who howled, "Comrade advocate, the court suggests that you offer your reasons for this lengthy application. Explain why you are making us do all this work!"

Kaminskaya: "Certainly, comrade president. My application is based on Article 294 of the Code of Criminal Procedure of the RSFSR. It requires me to ask you to certify all materials in the case that are of importance to the defense. Since the records of the investigator's questioning of my client and of his confrontations with his fellow accused are undoubtedly prime evidence, and since you have admitted the transcribed tape recording for inclusion with the materials in the case, I am therefore requesting that you certify the exact wording of certain passages from these documents."

Kareva: "Is that all you can say in support of your request?"

It was the first time I had seen Kareva looking like this. Her face was covered with red blotches; she had passed beyond irritation to fury. It had just dawned on her that she was helpless in the face of my tactics. To each of my applications she was forced to pronounce the words, "I confirm . . ."

I spoke calmly, with a voice in which, it seemed to me, there was even a trace of boredom. The only symptom of strain was an uncontrollable trembling in my knees, fortunately hidden by the advocates' rostrum. My knees were not shaking because I was afraid, but from the need to restrain my contempt for the judge, the objective and impartial judge "elected by the people."

Afterward, during the recess, Lev Yudovich and Olga Chaikovskaya told me that during the whole trial they had never before seen such a look on my face; I was, it seems, totally expressionless.

I continued for about an hour, at which point Kareva made another attempt to stop me. "Comrade advocate, according to the court's schedule we are supposed to conclude the judicial hearing today. We have listened to you for long enough. The court doesn't have the time to spend a whole day on matters of this kind."

"You are mistaken, comrade president. The court always has time to spend checking and confirming the materials in the case as the law prescribes. You know that you cannot deprive me of my rights as defense counsel just because of a shortage of time."

And on we went.

In due course came the lunch recess, during which I only paced up and down the corridor, smoking. After the recess I once more stood before the court and, dispassionately as before, continued to put my requests to the court. I was in the grip of an icy, unshakable calm.

About half an hour after the recess, Voloshina leaped to her feet and shouted that this was a mockery of the court; she demanded that I either stop or finally explain to the court the reason for all this and declare what aim I was pursuing in requiring certification of all these "minor" discrepancies.

In the same bored voice I replied, "The law unfortunately prevents me from satisfying the curiosity of the comrade prosecutor. I am not entitled to voice my views, conclusions, or comments until my final speech for the defense."

Again Kareva was obliged to say, "Continue," and so it went to the very end, until all twenty-six points on our list were in the court record.

Thus ended the judicial hearing in the Moscow City Court.

The closing speeches for prosecution and defense are the last stage of the trial. After that come the final statements allowed to the accused—and the verdict and the sentence. Defendants await the closing speeches with almost as much trepidation as they await their sentence. Most of them are firmly convinced that they will get whatever the prosecutor asks for, with the court perhaps knocking off a year or two. They have good grounds for this belief. Especially in controversial cases, the prosecutor often makes prior agreements with the judge as well as with his or her superiors in the procuracy.

In the case of Alik and Sasha, there was no reason to suspect any behind-the-scenes complicity between Kareva and Voloshina. Voloshina was completely unknown in the city court; she represented an "outside" procuracy with which this court had no professional contacts at all.

That Voloshina would ask the court to find the boys guilty none of us doubted. Both Alik and Sasha understood this, and so did their parents. Even so, we had more than a hunch—in fact we were nearly certain—that something unusual awaited us during the concluding phase of the speeches for the prosecution and the defense. And we were right.

I can still see before me Sarah's face, with her diffident smile, as the judge announced, "The people's prosecutor, Comrade Babyonisheva, will now speak in support of the prosecution."

Sarah stood up slowly, with a look of mingled perplexity and timorousness, and began in a low voice: "I came to this court with a feeling of profound sympathy with the grief of a mother who had suffered the tragic loss of her child. I came filled with horror at the crime which had been committed and with indignation at those responsible for Marina's death. I still harbor those feelings; I am still prepared, as I was then, to ask the court to punish those who murdered Marina. Today, however, I don't know who they are."

In the remainder of her speech Sarah gave an account of how, as she listened to Sasha's and Alik's testimony, she gradually lost that unshakable conviction with which she had entered the court after agreeing to act as people's prosecutor, and how she began to have doubts about the veracity of their confessions.

For the first time in this case it was not we, the defense advocates, who pronounced the phrases "Not proven" and "I ask the court to acquit." These were the words with which the people's prosecutor, Sarah Babyonisheva, ended her speech. Chance or Providence had so arranged things that the people's prosecutor was a totally honest person, gifted with the rare ability to cast aside prejudices, to weigh the pros and cons of an argument objectively and dispassionately. Lev and I felt certain that the very logic of the case was bound to lead such a person to the inevitable conclusion: "Not guilty."

I have never heard of a comparable instance in all the time the institution of people's prosecutor has been in existence. Nor have any of my colleagues ever heard of a similar clash between state's prosecutor and people's prosecutor, either before or after our case. I think I am right to say that no other people's prosecutor has ever demonstrated such courage and independence.

Apart from its wider significance, Sarah Babyonisheva's speech was also interesting for its analysis of the evidence, especially in the part that dealt with Marchenkova. On the many occasions when I pondered this old woman's evidence, I labeled her a hysterical woman, being unable to find a more exact description. When reading this professional mourner's evidence, Babyonisheva was able to discern in it the characteristics of the traditional ritual keening over a grave. As she recalled that testimony in her speech, reciting it in a slightly singsong voice, Sarah made us all perceive this. She was able to demonstrate that the verbal structure of Marchenkova's testimony corresponded precisely with the rules of that particular form of oral folk poetry. First regret for the departed, the mourner's inconsolable grief at her death; then a eulogy of her qualities: how clever she was, how beautiful; then she lamented the guilt of the survivors at failing to watch over her: "Forgive me, Marina, my little one, forgive me, an old woman. Absolve me. Why do I dream of you every night? I didn't take care of you, I didn't save you . . ."

Sarah said that the investigator had made this ritualized form of mourning, in which the only certain fact was the girl's death, into the cornerstone of the indictment; he had given the force of evidential testimony to a flight of literary fantasy.

I remember that Yudovich gave a brilliant speech for the defense; yet now I am quite unable to remember its specifics. I can recall my own speech only because I kept the stenographic record of it. I remember bits of Voloshina's speech, but only those passages that I quoted or responded to in my own speech. Yet shorthand transcripts of our speeches were the object of special study and discussion at sessions of the Criminological Society of the Moscow College of Advocates and were also studied at meetings arranged at our respective law offices.

But for all their individuality of style and delivery, these speeches, as is the rule in our profession, remained examples of traditional forensic oratory. Babyonisheva's speech was memorable because of its complete divorce from that tradition, its unfamiliarity to the court, and that too increased its emotional impact.

Voloshina's speech for the prosecution, as we expected, was a verbatim repetition of the indictment. Although she was forced to admit that Investigator Yusov had allowed certain infractions of the law while conducting his investigation, she concluded: "I am bound to admit that Burov and Kabanov were good boys. Nothing in their previous behavior suggests that they had any criminal tendencies. If they had not renounced their confessions and denied their guilt, they might have come into court with heads proudly held high. But they rejected their confessions. I consider their guilt proven and I ask the court to sentence them each, under Article 102 of the Criminal Code of the RSFSR, to ten years' deprivation of liberty."

It seemed to me that nothing could better express the psychological predilection for a "confession" than "they might have come into court with heads held proudly high"—words spoken about two people whom the prosecutor herself regarded as guilty of committing one of the gravest of all crimes.

The prosecution and defense speeches lasted for two days. I spoke on the second day, and the lunch recess was announced when I finished.

We were standing in a long line in the City Court canteen, among judges, prosecutors, and advocates. Some of them had listened to Lev's speech the previous day and to mine. Fellow lawyers praised us, which we enjoyed, but the praise of judges and prosecutors was more than pleasant. It gave us grounds for a certain amount of hope. If several judges admitted that our arguments were convincing, if they agreed that we had refuted the credibility of the boys' confessions, then surely Kareva too, despite her evident prejudice, would weigh the pros and cons carefully.

At the very moment when Lev and I were confiding these thoughts to each other, Judge Kareva came into the canteen, headed toward us, and said in a loud voice, "Comrade Kaminskaya, I must tell you that you made a remarkable speech today."

I was shattered. I knew Kareva would never have allowed herself to say such a thing before my colleagues and her own if she had not irrevocably decided to convict. At home that evening I repeated Kareva's praise to my husband without comment. His reaction was exactly the same. "That means it's all over," he said. "The boys are done for."

Three days later, on November 23, 1967, we stood in the courtroom of the Moscow City Court to hear verdict and sentence. That is the moment when the heart seems to stop, when we wait for the words for whose sake we have worked so many months, spent so many sleepless nights, given not just our intellectual powers and professional skill but a piece of our lives.

And so the words were spoken: "In the name of the Russian Socialist Federated Soviet Republic. The judicial bench of the criminal division of the Moscow City Court finds . . . Burov and Kabanov guilty as charged under Article 102 of the Criminal Code and sentences them each to a term of ten years' deprivation of liberty."

Although we were prepared now, those words nevertheless fell upon us as though unforeseen, like a crushing weight. It is always so when one is sure of the rightness of one's cause. However clearly you understand intellectually that the client is going to be convicted, hope persists quite irrationally up to the last minute.

No doubt like trial lawyers the world over, I always get an attack of nerves before making a speech for the defense. Like my colleagues, I want to make it a good speech; a sense of professional duty is involved here, as well as a touch of vanity. But that nervous excitement cannot compare in intensity with the feeling on the day the verdict is to be given. Whenever my colleagues asked me, "When do you feel more nervous, before or after a speech?" I always replied, "I get most nervous of all when I'm waiting for the sentence to be pronounced and while it is being read out."

Often I would come home from a day in court so tired that I could hardly talk. I would eat dinner in silence, and then, without reading or watching television, go to my room. After a verdict of guilty, what I felt was not simply tiredness but exhaustion: a feeling of such total weakness that it was difficult to raise an arm or put one foot in front of the other.

When Sasha and Alik were convicted, I could not sleep all night. I lay awake thinking, "I hate this job. It would be better to be a janitor or a housemaid, anything, rather than take part in this disgusting farce." At that moment I really hated my profession.

Kareva did more than hand down a verdict of guilty. She gave a separate judicial decision stating that Sasha had renounced his confession of guilt under the influence of Advocate Kozopolyanskaya. Kareva found nothing prejudicial in any of Yusov's illegalities. She not only failed to reprimand Yusov by name but avoided all mention of the irregularities that had been established in her court: the unlawful arrests, the excessive period of detention in the remand cells, the placing of adults into the cells with minors. Nor was there any word about the falsified additions to the written transcript of the boys' interrogations, which she herself had confirmed. In contrast, Kareva reprimanded Kozopolyanskaya not because her allegedly improper behavior had been proved (it had not), but because in convicting the boys Kareva was obliged to indicate a reason for their change of testimony. The reprimand was needed to justify her verdict. A reprimand of Yusov would have invalidated it.

5. The Appeals Court

DEPRESSED AS WE WERE at the monstrously unjust verdict, we could not give way to despair. We had to force ourselves to hope; there was still the Supreme Court.

The evening of the day after the boys were sentenced, I was to meet Sasha's parents, Georgii and Klavdia Kabanov. I was filled with a profound sense of guilt and shame. Klavdia and Georgii came to my office with an enormous bunch of roses. Once again I was amazed at Klavdia's innate nobility and tact. "Thank you," she said. "I shall never forget all you have done for us," and she offered the words of comfort I had meant to offer her. "It's not the end, Dina Isaakovna," she said. "The Supreme Court *cannot* uphold the verdict. We know you and Yudovich will see that justice is done. Sasha will be free, believe me."

Next day, Sasha repeated almost the same words in the visiting room at Prison No. 1; he spoke of gratitude, of unshakable conviction that all would be well.

The Kabanovs' faith in Soviet justice was greater than mine. They knew less about it than I did. Unlike them, I could never bring myself to say, "It cannot be . . ." I could only say, "I hope . . ."

The new year, 1968, began. Sasha and Alik had been in jail sixteen months. In all that time they had had only one meeting with their parents, the day after they were sentenced. Now that the case was on appeal, they had no right even to meet with their lawyers. Alik and Sasha would know nothing of what was happening until their case was heard by the Supreme

Court of the RSFSR. Then it would be straight to the labor camps, if the verdict was upheld, or more prison if the verdict was overturned and the case remanded for retrial. Simple humanity required that their time of isolation be kept to a minimum, but an advocate could do nothing to hasten the appeals process; it was a routine that could not be altered.

Finally we were informed that the appeal would be heard at 10:00 A.M. on April 9.

We knew the personalities on the bench that morning, because the same judges review all appeals from the Moscow City Court. The chairman was M. Romanov, one of the best Supreme Court judges, and the rapporteur was Judge Karasev, whose questioning attitude in presenting a summary of the case to his fellow judges I appreciated. The public seats were filled, many of them with lawyers. They had heard what a controversial and interesting case this was.

Karasev took more than an hour to deliver his report on the case. He listed the grounds for the conviction and gave a very detailed exposé of the arguments in our appeals. Both of us asked for acquittal rather than a retrial. Lev's appeal, very long and circumstantial, ran to nearly fifty pages; mine was thirty, with five basic arguments: (1) In all the materials in the case, including the reports of the experts, there are no objective proofs of Kabanov's guilt; (2) none of the witnesses' testimony incriminates Kabanov in the rape and murder of Marina; (3) the verdict of guilty is based solely on Burov's and Kabanov's self-incrimination, which they withdrew before the case came to trial; (4) in confessing themselves guilty, Burov and Kabanov gave contradictory testimony; (5) the case materials themselves contain incontrovertible proofs of Kabanov's innocence, including what has to have been the real time scheme of the crime, the absence of mud on the boys' clothing, and the boys' behavior afterward.

My appeal ended: "On the basis of the above, I consider that Kabanov was convicted by the Moscow City Court for a crime he did not commit; that the materials in the case not only do not support a verdict of guilty but wholly disprove it. I therefore request the bench of the Criminal Division of the Supreme Court of the RSFSR to revoke the verdict of the Moscow City Court on Kabanov and to declare the case closed."

In a court of appeal the advocate cannot make new arguments but may supplement the text of the appeal with closer argumentation of particular sections. Although we had submitted very detailed appeals, there were many such supplementary contributions to be made.

When the rapporteur finished his summary, we gave our speeches. We were listened to with attention and an interest which, it seemed to me, never flagged. Babyonisheva's supporting arguments met with equal interest.

Then came the turn of the senior prosecutor, representing the highest level of the procuracy of the Republic, who said in essence: The case has been heard fully enough, and the guilt of the accused is proved incontrovertibly by their own confessions. Their guilt is also proved by the testimony of Marchenkova and numerous other witnesses, who made it clear that Burov and Kabanov were absent for not less than thirty-five or forty minutes. That time was quite sufficient to commit the rape and murder of Marina.

The court listened as attentively and courteously as before, then retired to confer.

After hours of waiting, we stood up for the third time as the court reappeared. Romanov was holding two small sheets of paper. That was too little for a ruling that the verdict be set aside. Lev and I looked at each other in despair.

"The court hereby states the grounds for its ruling . . ."

We exchanged glances. If our appeal were being disallowed, there would be no need for a lengthy statement. And then:

Under Article 339 of the Code of Criminal Procedure, the bench rules that the verdict passed on Burov and Kabanov on September 23, 1967, by the Moscow City Court, be set aside; that the case be remanded to the same court for reexamination, starting with a new preliminary investigation . . . that the measures of detention applied to Burov and Kabanov remain in force.

Hope again! Although Alik and Sasha faced many more months in prison, at least the verdict had been set aside, at least the court had admitted that the boys were wrongly convicted.

Three days later, when we got the full text of the ruling, Yudovich and I saw that our arguments had been incorporated into it: the verdict rested only on self-incrimination and the case lacked all objective proof of guilt. The ruling cited Yusov's misconduct with verbatim quotations from our appeals, and there was a passage, "The testimony of witness Marchenkova arouses grave doubts," followed again by quotations from us.

It was victory, a reward for all our labors. Yet Sasha and Alik could not know of the turn in their fortunes until an investigator called them in for further questioning prior to the new trial. Their parents and their counsel still could not see them.

The case sat in the Supreme Court for another six weeks. This was not negligence, but was simply because the court offices had no duplicating machines; all the documents had to be copied by typists.

At last, on May 29, I learned that the case had been sent back to the procuracy, and on the same day Yudovich and I sent a formal request to Gusev, Procurator of Moscow Province, for the immediate release of Burov and Kabanov. There was no reply to that or to our requests to see Gusev, or even to our request that the case be taken away from Investigator Yusov and given to a new investigator. A wall of silence went up. We learned from their parents that none of the Izmalkovo witnesses had been summoned to the procuracy; it looked as if no one was dealing with the case at all.

Three months later, on August 17, Lev and I were handed a phone message: Procurator Gusev would see us at ten o'clock next morning.

Exactly on time, Lev and I found ourselves in Gusev's office in the procuracy building. A tall, good-looking man sat behind an enormous antique desk. He did not get up, but merely nodded, which could have meant "good morning" or "sit down." Without waiting for a spoken invitation I sat down in an armchair beside the desk, while Lev took a seat alongside me. Gusev did not give us the chance to say a word: "I know why you wanted to see me. I have decided to grant your requests. Further investigation of your case will be conducted by Investigator Gorbachev of this procuracy. I have also decided to satisfy your request for the release of Burov and Kabanov from custody. They will be home in a few days. You may tell their parents." Another nod, and we were out of the room.

We ran down the staircase and outside to Pushkin Boulevard, the favorite of all Muscovites, flanked with old linden trees, where the benches are full of old people and lovers—and where we now stood, radiant and laughing. Our boys were getting out, our boys were going to be free!

There was no question of work on such a day. It was a moment for celebration. There was only one obligation we could not put off: we had to tell the boys' parents, to bring our joyful news to them. We could not telephone—nobody in Izmalkovo had a phone—and we couldn't go there because if the village saw us going into the Burovs' or the Kabanovs' house, there would be a new wave of gossip. We decided to go to my home, collect my son, Dmitry, drive him to the nearest point on the highway, and wait there while he walked to the Kabanovs'.

Two hours later we were in my apartment. We sat around the table, drank vodka, and ate whatever was in the house. Lev proposed the traditional toast: "To our profession!" We loved our profession—that day!

The telephone rang. When I picked it up, the only sound in the earpiece was uncontrollable sobbing, and I began to cry with Sasha's mother.

On August 20, 1968, after twenty-three months and twenty days, the boys came home.

The reinvestigation of their case lasted for seven months. Again we knew nothing of what was happening. This time it was in the office of a different investigator, although in the same procuracy of Moscow Province.

One day as I was sitting at a little desk on the fourth floor of the Supreme Court building, Karasev, the appeals court rapporteur, appeared.

"Well, Comrade Kaminskaya, still working on your case, are you?" he inquired, half jokingly, seeing that I was copying the text of the ruling.

"I can't deprive myself of the pleasure of having the full text of this ruling in my files."

"I'm not satisfied with it," said Karasev, and in answer to my questioning look he went on: "The case should have been closed. There's nothing more to investigate. But we decided to give the procuracy the chance to make another try. Then they can quietly let the case drop themselves. That way there'll be fewer complaints and less fuss."

Yudovich and I, however, did not think the procuracy would drop the case. There were too many illegalities, not only by Yusov but by the head of the investigatory branch of the procuracy and by Gusev himself, who had sanctioned the boys' improper arrests and unlawful detention. Not to protect Yusov—they would have cheerfully thrown him to the wolves—but to protect the entire provincial procuracy, they would do their utmost to get another conviction as the only way of covering up all their breaches of procedural law.

In March 1969, Investigator Gorbachev summoned the boys and their counsel to his office to tell us his investigation was complete. We were now permitted to acquaint ourselves with the new dossier, after which it would be sent to the court. By now it consisted of ten fat volumes, each three hundred to five hundred pages.

We began with Volume 9, which contained the documents added since the Supreme Court ruling, and at once encountered a surprise. While we had been submitting pleas for the boys' release and waiting in vain for answers, the case had been reheard in the Supreme Court of the RSFSR, this time by its Presidium, headed by Lev Smirnov, who was later to become chairman of the Supreme Court of the USSR. Only now, in March 1969, was defense counsel informed that as long ago as June 1968 the Deputy Procurator of the RSFSR, Kravtsov, had protested the Supreme Court ruling and asked that it be set aside and the verdict of the Moscow City Court be reinstated.

The law does not require that advocates be notified of the date for the hearing of a protest, but the procuracy had concealed the fact that a protest had been entered at all and so prevented us from submitting written objections to it.

Fortunately, the Presidium had rejected Kravtsov's protest. In addition, the ruling we were now reading sharply criticized the procuracy's breaches of law and its deplorable standards of investigation.

The second surprise was that after its protest was rejected, the procuracy, in the person of Investigator Gorbachev, had found our boys' cellmates. It turned out they had never left Moscow Province, but had been in Odintsovo all the time. More astonishing, Kuznetsov was not called Kuznetsov at all, but Skvortsov, and had been arrested by the Odintsovo police under that name. And Yermolaev was not Yermolaev but Dementiev.

Why should the Odintsovo police have issued a forgery? The actual identity of these men was a matter of complete indifference to them. It was expedient to conceal their real names only if those adults had been put in the cells for a special purpose and on Yusov's orders.

Skvortsov and Dementiev themselves had very little to say. They didn't know why they had been arrested in 1967—they thought it was some kind of routine checkup—nor why they had been held for a week. They had both been released on September 7, the day after Sasha and Alik confessed, and had not been made to sign an order banning them from the province. They had indeed been in cells with the boys, but they now had only the vaguest recollection of the boys themselves and of what they had talked about. No one, so they claimed, had instructed them to persuade the boys to confess.

A third surprise was that Gorbachev had visited the orchard with each of the six official witnesses whom Yusov had taken to the scene of the crime with Alik and Sasha. Each witness had pointed to the place in the orchard under the apple tree to which Burov and Kabanov had pointed, and each had pointed to exactly the same spot. All the necessary measurements were made then and there and all were absolutely identical. The statements of Alik and Sasha, which made it clear that they had pointed to different places, were refuted by the results of these measurements.

This was even more amazing since two of these witnesses had testified in the first trial and had fully confirmed the boys' testimony.

I showed Lev the extracts I had copied from all the documents on Gorbachev's visits. All six accounts had the same date and the same time. It was clear, therefore, that there had been only one trip and one measurement. This in itself was no guarantee that cross-examining these witnesses would produce truthful replies; it was only the first little thread to pull at in hopes of extracting the truth. We agreed that we would not request the examination of the official witnesses just yet. No one else was likely to suspect the existence of this new piece of falsification, and it would have shock value in court.

There was another significant change. When Gorbachev questioned her, Marchenkova had claimed that she had given false testimony earlier because she was afraid of Burov's parents. She told him that not only had she heard Marina's voice, but she had actually seen Marina and the boys. To anyone who had seen Marchenkova feeling her way in a well-lighted courtroom this claim was laughable. We would have to ask again that Marchenkova's medical records be obtained.

Having submitted that application, Yudovich and I, with Sasha and Alik, signed the document stating that we had fully acquainted ourselves with the materials in the case and began the long wait for the third trial. It might be a month or two, it might be four. We rejoiced again that the boys were out of prison; this wait would not be so hard on them.

Two months later, on April 28, we learned that the boys had been arrested again.

The warrant was signed by Gusev, the procurator of Moscow Province —later to become deputy procurator general of the USSR and then deputy chairman of the Supreme Court of the USSR—the man who had so magnanimously released Alik and Sasha six months before.

The investigation was completed. There was no reason to fear that the boys might abscond; during the six months they had been at liberty they had behaved impeccably. I could find only one explanation for this latest illegality. It was psychological blackmail, not only against the defendants but primarily against the court. Gusev was saying, "We are not going to back off. We shall fight for our position with all the force and authority we can command." No doubt it was a matter of indifference to Gusev whether Alik and Sasha were free or in prison. Their arrest was a weapon, and he used it without the slightest pity.

Again the months passed, months in which we had no right to see our boys—who had by now grown up and could not properly be called boys. They celebrated their legal coming of age back in Prison No. 1.

Yudovich and I were frantic. We petitioned the Supreme Court of the RSFSR to try the case itself, on grounds of its extreme complexity, and to our astonishment the petition was granted.

6. The Third Trial

THE THIRD TRIAL in the case of the State versus Burov and Kabanov began in September 1969 before the Supreme Court of the Russian Republic.

Lev and I went into this trial with an awareness of deep personal responsibility. It was our last chance to win this case: "The verdict of the Supreme Court is final and is not subject to appeal."

Once again there was the solid wooden barrier behind which the "boys" stood, flanked by armed soldiers. Having been allowed to see Sasha after the trial was scheduled, I had noticed how thin and pale he was. When I first visited him, he greeted me with, "Well, here I am back in jail. Will I ever get out of this place?"

Sasha understood that hope was not yet lost, but after the delights of freedom this second arrest had shattered him. That was why I visited him, though there was nothing new to discuss. Over the past two and a half years everything possible had been examined from every possible angle.

When Alik came into the courtroom, it was the first time I had seen him since his arrest. He had lost his front teeth. Lev said, "His teeth fell out—he's exhausted and very undernourished." Indeed, Alik was even thinner and paler than Sasha.

Presiding over the bench was Judge I. Petukhov. When he entered the courtroom to open the hearing, accompanied by the two people's assessors, I was seeing him for the first time. It was also my first encounter with Koshkin, deputy procurator of Moscow Province, who had replaced Voloshina as prosecutor. By appointing his first deputy to conduct the prosecution, Gusev was further demonstrating his determination to put up a stiff fight.

Sarah Babyonisheva was not at the prosecution desk. No people's prosecutor was taking part in this trial. I looked around the courtroom and saw the boys' parents and Alexandra Kostopravkina.

The judicial manner of Judge Kirilov in the first trial had been notable for its rudeness. Judge Kareva had exhibited an irrepressible bias. The distinctive feature of Judge Petukhov's behavior was his imperturbability. He listened calmly to our numerous applications and calmly heard the prosecutor's objections to them. Then, with equal calm, in a voice that was if anything a little too low, he would announce his ruling: "Sustained" or "Overruled."

Most of our important applications were granted. Odintsovo's deputy police chief and chief criminal investigation officer were called as witnesses, and the register of detainees in the remand cells for August and September 1966 was ordered to be produced. It was important for us to have documentary evidence of the names under which Skvortsov (a.k.a. Kuznetsov) and Dementiev (a.k.a. Yermolaev) had been detained. Marchenkova's medical history was also ordered up, along with her work schedule for June 1965. Our application for the court to adjourn to the scene of the crime was rejected as "not expedient," but the official witnesses would be called.

Petukhov's calm transmitted itself to all the participants in the trial. Prosecutor Koshkin did not shout at Alik and Sasha when they pleaded not guilty, nor did he show indignation when witnesses gave evidence that ran counter to his case.

Alexandra Kostopravkina also restrained her animosity, although this did not occur spontaneously. When Lev Yudovich began to cross-examine her, she refused to look at him and announced: "I refuse to answer Yudovich and Kaminskaya. They are being paid money to shield the real murderers. They are not true Soviet advocates; Soviet advocates do not act like that." Kostopravkina stood with arms akimbo, in her familiar pose of contempt.

Judge Petukhov answered her: "First of all, witness, put your arms down. You are talking to the Supreme Court. You cannot stand like that in court. Now listen to me carefully. If you want us to listen to you, if you want to tell us of what you know, you must answer the questions of all the participants in this trial. The comrade advocates are conscientiously carrying out their duty, which is to defend their clients. That is why they are here. We need their help just as much as we need the help of the comrade prosecutor. We greatly respect your grief, we remember how your daughter died; but we must ask you, too, to remember that in order to get to the truth of this matter we have work to do, and we must work calmly and reasonably . . ."

Kostopravkina accepted those rules. She realized that this court would not allow her to break them.

For the two months the trial lasted only twice did I notice signs of irritation on Judge Petukhov's face, and only because I was purposely watching him at times that were of great significance to the defense. Even then his voice remained as quiet and even as ever.

On the first occasion it concerned the examination of the official witnesses. Early that morning, before the day's session, Petukhov met me in the corridor and said, "This is going to be a hard day for you. The prosecution regards the evidence of the official witnesses as very important proof."

I said nothing in reply. Yudovich and I had firmly decided that the falsification we had discovered should be a surprise even to the judge.

Now the first of these witnesses, the official witness who had accompanied Alik Burov on the visit to the site, took the stand. He described briefly how Investigator Gorbachev had suggested he go with him to Izmalkovo again. The investigator had asked him to indicate the spot—the apple tree—to which Alik had pointed on September 7, 1966.

"I recognized it at once and pointed it out to the investigator. We measured the distance and noted it in the record."

Neither the court nor the prosecutor had any questions.

"Tell me, witness, who went with you to Izmalkovo?" I asked.

"I went there with Investigator Gorbachev."

"How did you get there?"

"We went by car."

"Do you remember the kind of car and its color?"

"Yes, it was a blue minibus."

"Was anyone besides you and the investigator in the car?"

"Only the driver."

"And at Izmalkovo, when you pointed out the apple tree and took the measurements, was anyone else present?"

"No. Only the investigator and me."

"Can you recall the date and time of that trip?"

"I remember the date well—it was March 2, 1969—and the time by my watch was entered in the record."

"I have no more questions for this witness. I ask the court to verify the facts. The record of that site visit is on page 52, Volume 10; it shows the date as March 2, the time of arrival as 10:15 A.M., the time of return to Odintsovo as 12:00 noon."

Although Petukhov was looking at me with his permanently impassive expression, I felt certain that he was disappointed. Why was I asking all these questions? What was I getting at?

Along came the second witness who had originally accompanied Alik. He told the same story. Neither judge nor prosecutor had any questions. I repeated all my questions. The answers corresponded exactly with those of the first official witness.

"No contradictions," observed the prosecutor.

"Indeed there are no contradictions. I ask the court to remember that the prosecutor was the first to make that comment. I now request the court to verify the date and time shown in the record of that visit, page 53, Volume 10."

Petukhov read out, "March 2. Time of arrival: 10:15 A.M.; time of return to Odintsovo: 12:00 noon."

When the third witness began his testimony, I saw Petukhov, unprompted, turning over the next page of the dossier. Then I noticed his normally pale face turn red. A minute later he himself, in his quiet voice, put "my" questions to the witness and listened calmly to the answers.

"Yes, only the investigator and I went . . . There was no one else with us . . . We drove in a blue minibus."

The examination of the other official witnesses proceeded in the same way. There was no need to explain to Petukhov that the records were falsifications, that all these witnesses were lying.

When the examination of the sixth and last official witness was finished, Petukhov addressed them all: "Witnesses, I should remind you that you can be held criminally responsible for perjuring yourselves. I am not threatening you. I am inviting you now to give the court truthful testimony. I am asking you to tell the truth."

And one by one they told what had really happened. All of them had gathered at the Odintsovo police station on March 2, where Investigator Gorbachev explained to them that a technical error had occurred in compiling the records of the previous site visits. It was therefore necessary for them all to go there again, and to make a joint effort to find the actual spot which Burov and Kabanov had pointed out. On arrival at Izmalkovo, they had all argued and pointed to different places, so the investigator had decided to take a vote on it and to name the spot that had a majority of votes. The vote was thus decided by the four witnesses who had accompanied Burov. The two who had visited the site with Kabanov were in a minority, but they too had signed the record. On the day before their appearance in court, they were once more assembled at the Odintsovo police station, where they were told, "Since you have each signed a separate record of the visit, when you come to court you must say that you were alone with the investigator and no one else was with you."

The next witness was Brodskaya, who asked permission to give her evidence seated, saying that she was not well. The court allowed her to sit down, and a chair was brought in for her and placed midway between the desks of the prosecutor and the defense counsel. She planted herself on it firmly and confidently, still the very picture of a strong-minded woman who knew no hesitation, no uncertainty. In a loud voice, rapping out each word, she gave her familiar spiel: "I know they are the murderers. Certain dishonest people"—a glance in our direction—"got them to renounce their confessions. As an old Communist, I demand that you, a Soviet court, punish them without mercy!"

When Brodskaya had finished, Petukhov addressed her in his quiet voice. "Witness Brodskaya, we are listening to you. We are still waiting to hear your *evidence*. Tell the court what you know about the case."

"But I've told you. I know they're the murderers. I know they tormented and killed Marina. Every Soviet citizen knows that in our country only guilty people confess!" Then, forgetting that she was supposed to be sick, Brodskaya stood up and demanded conviction "in the name of all decent Soviet people."

I noticed that for the second time Petukhov's normally pale face was red around the cheekbones and his lips were clamped together. After an almost imperceptible pause, however, he said calmly, "The court has no more questions. Comrade prosecutor, have you any questions to put to this witness?" It may have been my imagination, but I had the impression that the word "witness" was spoken with a touch of sarcasm.

Probably the most sensational part of the whole trial was the examination of the deputy chief of the Criminal Investigation Branch of Moscow Province. This examination was conducted from beginning to end by Lev Yudovich, and it was a triumph.

However much the witness tried to evade direct answers and took refuge behind the need to preserve the secrecy of police methods, he was forced to admit that two adults, Skvortsov and Dementiev, had been put into the cells with Alik and Sasha, with instructions to do a particular job, that this was the reason why their real names had been concealed, and that he had set up this operation at the request of Investigator Yusov.

Skvortsov and Dementiev were examined that same day. They confirmed that they had been in a cell with Alik and Sasha respectively. They recognized them in the courtroom. Both categorically denied having tried to influence the boys in any way, and denied that they had been asked to do so.

We asked them whether they had described to the boys conditions in the labor camps or the methods used at 38 Petrovka. Both witnesses denied this too, but the one Sasha called Uncle Vanya admitted that he had previously been convicted of causing grievous bodily harm in a brawl, that he had been held at 38 Petrovka, and that he had served his sentence in a strict-regime labor camp.

After we finished, Judge Petukhov told him, "Witness, the court has a request. Please unbutton your shirt and pull up your undershirt."

Yudovich and I waited tensely.

Uncle Vanya looked at the judge with dismay, then unbuttoned his shirt and pulled up his undershirt, revealing a chest covered with tattooing and slashed diagonally from side to side by a huge purple scar.

Sasha had described just such a scar at the first trial. It was the scar Uncle Vanya had frightened him with when he described the brutality of the labor camps.

That day was a day of hope for us, and we had solid grounds.

As the trial moved toward its end, we received and read Marchenkova's medical history. The summary for 1965, the year of Marina's death, was: "Right eye, practically blind; left eye, 20 percent sight retained; cataracts in both eyes. Hearing below normal: left ear, reduced by 60 percent; right ear, reduced by 85 percent." The extract from Marchenkova's work schedule showed that June 17 had been a working day for her. Her memory of what she had seen and heard on a "free day" had nothing to do with Marina.

Not one witness had incriminated the boys. The girls, young women now, had stuck to their testimony and had not been bullied. All was going well, but the sense of unease would not go away. This case had brought us too many rebuffs and disappointments, and neither Lev nor I could sense the mood of this court, its attitude to the case.

At last the time came for the summations of the prosecution and the defense. Once more a prosecutor asked the court to find the boys guilty and sentence them to ten years deprivation of liberty. They were now guilty not only of Marina's death but of the destruction of another human being, Investigator Yusov. Yusov had fallen gravely ill and had a stroke. He was paralyzed and had lost the power of speech. He was waiting for a verdict that would rehabilitate his personal honor, the only thing left to him.

I did pity Yusov. He should have been made to pay for all the evil he had caused, but to be stricken dumb and motionless was a punishment I would not wish on anyone. Still, I also thought of his victims, the young men who had spent what should have been the most carefree and joyous years of their lives in prison. I thought of Klavdia and Georgii Kabanov, and of Alik's parents, who for three years had lived with unjust and undeserved grief. At an age when one accumulates the greatest store of knowledge, when one's tastes and attitudes to life are formed and one's basic moral principles are acquired, Sasha and Alik had also accumulated knowledge and experience. They had discovered the meaning of lying and perfidy, and prison had become the source of their practical experience. Their friends were their cellmates and their principles were molded by prison guards. Life was not going to be easy for them, even if they returned home now. After three years inside, it would be hard to recover their trust and confidence in people. And what if they did not return? What if they were sentenced to ten years, a term they would have to serve knowing they had been unjustly convicted?

But now it was time to speak for the defense, and we were speaking to a substantial audience. Besides our regular observers, many colleagues were there. Law students and young advocates came. Several of Lev's friends attended and for the first time in my career I let some of my friends come.

Lev spoke first and made a colossal impression. Everyone congratulated him, and deservedly so. A friend of mine kept shaking Lev's hand and saying, "Magnificent! A brilliant speech."

Then I came up to Lev. "You're a bandit, a highway robber," I said.

"Forgive me, Dina, my dear, I'm sorry. I didn't do it on purpose. I was simply carried away."

Of course that was exactly what had happened. Lev was carried away and forgot our plan to divide up the material. He had not only seized on all the points I was to argue in my speech; he had held forth on them in my wording, which had grown so familiar to him that they ceased to be someone else's words.

I was not only dismayed; I was in despair. Later, though, I was very grateful to Lev for having spared me from the need to repeat myself. Thanks to him, my speech acquired the inner drive that makes thoughts and words come by themselves, that gives a prepared speech, even one based on heartbreakingly familiar material, the urgency of impromptu delivery. I believe that was the best speech I ever gave.

After the brief "final words" of Alik and Sasha, in which they reasserted their innocence and asked to be acquitted, the court retired to consider its verdict.

Three days later, I again sat in the big courtroom of the Moscow Provincial Court at the same desk where, in the winter of 1967, I had first seen the huge photographs of Marina. No one else had arrived, and I was glad to be alone. It gave me time to conquer my usual attack of nerves.

Nine o'clock. Alik and Sasha were led in and the armed soldiers flanked the wooden barrier, more of them than usual because it was the day of the verdict.

Yudovich arrived. By now the public and the boys' parents were being allowed in.

Finally, "All rise. The Court is in session."

"In the name of the Russian Soviet Federated Socialist Republic . . ." The quiet voice of Petukhov seemed to go on forever before: "Having scrutinized the materials in the case, having heard the testimony of the witnesses, the speech of the prosecutor assuming the indictment to be proven, and the speeches of defense counsel requesting the acquittal of the accused, the Criminal Division of the Supreme Court of the RSFSR finds . . ."

I was standing quite still, but my hands were clenched into fists.

". . . the Supreme Court of the RSFSR finds . . ."

Suddenly the words acquired a solemn resonance, and Petukhov's voice became almost loud. I glanced quickly at Lev. His face was pale and tense.

". . . the charges against Burov and Kabanov not proven . . ."

I heard nothing more for a moment. For the first time I looked around the courtroom. The first person I noticed was the writer Sergei Smirnov; tears were pouring down his face. Then came a shriek, and from the far end of the courtroom Lenochka, Sasha's sister, ran straight toward the prisoners with outstretched arms.

The commander of the escort barred her way—it is not permitted to approach the prisoners. Breaking off his reading for a moment, Petukhov said, "Let her pass." Clasped in an embrace, without letting go of each other for a moment, they listened to the rest of the long document.

At last came the final, solemn words: "On the basis of the above conclusions and having regard to Articles 303, 310, 316, 317, and 319 of the Code of Criminal Procedure of the RSFSR, the Criminal Division of the Supreme Court of the RSFSR pronounces Oleg Burov and Alexander Kabanov, having been duly tried, to be acquitted of the charges; the measures of detention against Burov and Kabanov to be rescinded and they to be released immediately in the courtroom."

The officer commanding the escort gave the order: "Release the acquitted!" and the door was opened in the wooden barrier which for three years had fenced off Alik and Sasha from life.

Everyone was shouting, weeping, and laughing. Lev and I kissed each other. I felt the tears on his face and said, "Lev, it's indecent, you're crying."

"Do you know what you were doing as you listened to the verdict? Shall I show you?"

He intoned: ". . . the charges against Burov and Kabanov not proven . . ." and suddenly clasped his head in his hands. "Do you think it's decent for an advocate to clutch her head during the reading of the verdict?"

We laughed again, and then we were kissed by the parents, by Lenochka, by Sasha and Alik.

Dear Sasha, perhaps he was not an exceptional boy, but he was dear to me, no doubt in the way that one grows to love hopelessly sick people whom one has tended and cared for. When I left my homeland and took with me only my best-loved books and my favorite photographs, I took a photograph of Sasha, a photograph he sent me long after the trial. There he is, grown up, in army uniform and wearing the badge for excellence that is awarded to efficient soldiers, and written in the corner is his touching, funny inscription: "Dear Dina Isaakovna! I wish you great happiness in your personal life, work, and study. Yours, Sasha."

Who, having lived through all this, can say that the work of an advocate is painful and unrewarding? Surely it is the happiest job in the world.

There were other postscripts to the case. In successive issues the *Literary Gazette* published a two-part article by Olga Chaikovskaya, each part a full page in length (that is very long for an account of a criminal trial in the Soviet press). The article was entitled "The Confession."

Then one day, two or three months after the verdict, I met Judge Petukhov in a corridor of the Supreme Court building. We were delighted to see each other, as people are who have taken part together in something worthwhile, and who have cherished memories in common. Petukhov invited me into his office and we sat down to reminisce. I asked him, "Why did you refuse our application for the court to go out to Izmalkovo, which we considered so important? We thought it was essential for you to see the place for yourself."

Petukhov smiled. "You're right, it was important. So important that as soon as I began to study the case I went straight out there alone, while I was still unknown to any of the witnesses. I saw it all—the orchard, the lake, the spit of sand running out into the water, and the glade where Marina's sweater was found. I had my reasons for turning down your application as unnecessary."

As I listened to him I thought: What good fortune when justice is in the hands of a judge like this. Calm, clear-minded, and intelligent, with a genuine urge to discover the truth.

Years passed. Sasha completed his military service, married, and had a son. He still lived in Izmalkovo. Many of the people who had shouted, "Bastard! Murderer!" came to visit him and his family and were amazed at how they could have believed that Sasha, of all people, had raped and killed Marina.

More years, and one day I found myself sitting in the office of an investigator of the Moscow procuracy, a certain Pantiukhin. He had not summoned me as an advocate; this time I was a suspect. He wanted to know why I had given an account of the case of the two boys to a newspaper correspondent from an imperialist country, Peter Osnos of the *Washington Post*, and whether I was aware that my action could be interpreted as undermining the authority of the Soviet Union.

I replied sincerely that I was not aware of any such thing. There are bad investigators, bad state's prosecutors, and bad judges in every country. The outcome of this complex case was, in fact, a triumph for Soviet justice. The judicial system was ultimately able to break free of the hypnotic influence of a confession, to thrust aside the heavy weight of popular indignation, and to forget that the case was being followed with special attention by the Central Committee of the Communist Party of the Soviet Union. I told the investigator that I was truly proud to have been involved in a case in which justice had triumphed.

PART
THREE

1. The Case of Sinyavsky and Daniel

T HE FIRST DIRECTLY POLITICAL CASE in my career was one in which I did not take part, and my first defense plea in a political trial was a speech in defense of Yulii Daniel which I never delivered.

Now, as I write, the only materials at my disposal are my memory and a little square of yellowing paper with the following text printed on it:

Moscow Municipal College of Advocates
Registration Card Number 279   January 12, 1966
ORDER NUMBER 89
The Advocates' Office of the Leningradsky District
hereby authorizes Advocate Kaminskaya, D.I., to
conduct the defense in the criminal case of
Citizen Daniel, Y.M., at:
Investigatory Department of the Committee of State
Security (KGB) of the Council of Ministers of the USSR.
(Signed)
Head of Advocates' Office

This document certifies that I had signed an agreement to defend a client and that the fee had been paid to the office cashier. It represents the only legally authorized, official mandate to the defense counsel and establishes certain rights and obligations for both the advocate and the prosecuting investigator: for me, the right and duty to defend my client; for the investigator, the obligation to allow me to study all the materials in the case. To gain access to these materials I had to hand over the order to the investigator, who would then file it along with all the other documents.

Order Number 89, however, is still in my possession, because I was prevented from carrying out my agreement to defend Yulii Daniel.

A great deal has been written about the case of Andrei Sinyavsky and Yulii Daniel, the two writers condemned by a Soviet court to long terms of imprisonment. The *White Book* that Alexander Ginzburg bravely compiled, and for which he in turn was arrested, contains comments from Soviet and foreign sources and an almost complete transcript of the trial. Since the book has been translated into several foreign languages, I do not intend to write about the trial itself, but to describe how it was organized, what the defense counsel faced, and how the authorities dealt with counsel and defendants. Even in the Soviet Union these facts are known only to a very few people.

In addition to giving such eyewitness testimony, I want to describe the atmosphere in the Soviet Union during late 1965 and early 1966, the period between the arrest of Sinyavsky and Daniel and their sentencing to seven and five years respectively in strict-regime prison camps.

Recalling these events in the 1980s, I am more than ever convinced that they represented a crucial turning point, forcing many people to reassess their attitudes and their principles.

In the years after Stalin's death, and especially after the Twentieth Party Congress of 1956, there was increasing self-examination and self-awareness, a constant process that was painful for people of the older generation and even for my generation. Our understanding of such concepts as bravery, civic courage, and decency changed. Although this spiritual emancipation occurred slowly for most individuals, on the historical time scale of such a young state as the Soviet Union, it took place with headlong rapidity.

I remember the terrible, shameful days of the persecution of Pasternak, a truly great Russian poet, which was the result of the publication in the West in 1957 of his banned novel, *Doctor Zhivago*. Pasternak's Nobel Prize was the signal for the start of a campaign aimed at making him renounce the prize and publicly repent his "treason."

At that time official propaganda was all that was heard. Not a single voice in my country was raised in Pasternak's defense. This was not from a shortage of people who were deeply pained at this ruthless, disgusting form of persecution, or even because the majority of the Soviet population was still governed by fear. I believe that many people, and I was among them, simply could not conceive of the possibility of a free, voluntary public commitment according to the dictates of one's conscience. From youth until my years of maturity I had been conditioned to associate public life exclusively with participation in official demonstrations, meetings and gatherings organized by the Communist Party or the state. I was aware of only one legal form of protest: silence. Silence had become the yardstick of human courage and decency.

This, then, was the criterion by which we judged people's behavior during the "Pasternak period." Even Olga Ivinskaya, Pasternak's close and beloved companion for the last fourteen years of his life, continued to measure the courage and decency of her contemporaries by that same yardstick, silence and noninvolvement, when she wrote *A Prisoner of Time*, published in English translation in 1978. To my knowledge, the first open expression of genuine public feeling about the tragic fate of Pasternak as man and artist came at his funeral.

Pasternak died on May 30, 1960. Not one Soviet newspaper announced his death. It was not until June 2 that the *Literary Gazette* published a short statement recording the death of "Pasternak, Boris Leonidovich, writer, member of the Literary Fund of the USSR." Such traditional phrasing as "We report with profound regret . . ." was missing, and the time and place of his funeral were not mentioned. This, of course, was carefully organized by the Literary Fund on instructions from the KGB.

Nevertheless, on that day thousands of Muscovites traveled to the village of Peredelkino to accompany Pasternak on his last journey. They had passed on the information about time and place by telephone, and around the ticket offices at Moscow's Kiev Station and in the suburban trains on the line to Peredelkino brave souls posted homemade notices, written by hand on paper torn out of school notebooks, giving precise instructions on how to reach Pasternak's home.

I was reliably informed that the governing board of the Literary Fund was under orders to prevent the funeral from turning into a demonstration. A special bus carrying Pasternak's coffin and members of his family was to drive rapidly from the house to the cemetery, where the casket would be hastily buried. This plan failed because the coffin was carried all the way to the cemetery, a distance of about a mile, by volunteer pallbearers who took turns by tacit agreement and prevented any official personage from coming near the coffin.

Olga Ivinskaya had good reason to call her chapter on the funeral: "They Bore Him Not to His Interment but to His Coronation." The thousands came to pay their last respects to "their" poet, but what made the occasion so significant was that those who came were moved not only by a feeling of loss but by a feeling of solidarity, and by the wish, if only at that last tragic moment, to express their dissent from the official attitude of the Party and the state—and to express it, perhaps for the first time in their lives, by public action. Those thousands, most of them total strangers, felt spiritually close to one another. It was a new, hitherto unknown experience of a profound sense of community.

Five years passed between Pasternak's funeral and the arrest of Sinyavsky and Daniel. After their arrest it quickly became known from foreign radio broadcasts and by word of mouth that they had both sent some of their novels and short stories abroad to a foreign publisher. These books had been published in France under pseudonyms (Sinyavsky's pseudonym was Abram Tertz, while Daniel wrote under the name of Nikolai Arzhak). It also became known that the contents of these works were the cause of their authors' arrest and that they were charged with spreading anti-Soviet propaganda under Article 70 of the Criminal Code of the RSFSR.

Conversations at that time inevitably turned to the Sinyavsky-Daniel case. Some people said that by sending their writings abroad without official permission and by consenting to their publication by a foreign publisher, Sinyavsky and Daniel had betrayed the interests of liberal writers who were trying to get their works legally published in the USSR; that the result would be to tighten the screws of censorship even further and extinguish what was left of the "thaw." (Interestingly enough, exactly the same accusations were later made against Jewish emigrants, on the grounds that their departure was betraying the interests of those Jews who stayed behind, by destroying the last vestiges of the state's tolerance of Jews.) I cannot, however, recall a single person who either approved of or failed to condemn both the arrests and the indictments on criminal charges.

My husband, Konstantin Simis—who had been a member of the Moscow College of Advocates since Stalin's death in 1953 and would remain a practicing attorney until 1971—and I were at one. We fully approved of the two writers' action as a manifestation of personal freedom. We were also convinced of the legal right of an author to publish his work in any country without special permission, and of the juridical untenability of extending the concept of anti-Soviet agitation and propaganda to cover works of imaginative literature. At the same time we were fully aware of what a desperate risk Sinyavsky and Daniel had taken. It was clear to us that in arresting them the KGB was working in collusion with the highest political authorities and that this alone made their trial and conviction inevitable.

Even though we did not know Sinyavsky and Daniel, we were confident that both of them had taken this risk in the cause of the writer's freedom of artistic expression. We respected their action and greatly admired their courage. In conversation with me and with our friends, Konstantin frequently said that he would gladly undertake to defend either one of them, and although none of their relatives or friends approached us, as practicing advocates we would discuss the case as an exercise in forensic tactics, always from what we regarded as the legally unquestionable standpoint— the two writers were innocent of any criminal charge.

Exactly when did we first meet Larisa Bogoraz, Yulii Daniel's estranged wife, and Maria Rozanova, Andrei Sinyavsky's wife? Although my husband and I can recall the general order of events, and even specific conversations, exact dates have inevitably escaped our memories. Most likely that meeting was in early December 1965. We both remember the phone call from friends of ours, and the words of their invitation: "It would be wonderful if you could come over and see us—right away." Something about the way it was said made us forget our tiredness and our plans for the rest of the evening and run along the street looking for a taxi, to get there as quickly as possible and find out what was happening.

Without taking off our heavy coats we went straight through our friends' apartment and onto the balcony that overlooked one of the main streets of central Moscow—an amateurish way of trying to avoid any concealed "bugs" in the apartment.

"We need your help," said our host. "Larisa and Maria want your advice. They'll be here in a few minutes." He was clearly nervous, peering hard at the sidewalk below us and across the street to check whether there were any of those unmistakable figures, the plainclothes agents.

Soon we were sitting in a large room on a soft couch, with Larisa and Maria opposite us in deep armchairs. The stereo system was switched on to full capacity playing a record loudly. We were as safe as possible from bugging. As it turned out, what the two women wanted was not merely advice but our agreement to defend their husbands. We were not the first advocates they had approached, but the others had warned them that the most they could do would be to ask for leniency. We were the first they had heard of who were saying that publishing one's works abroad was not contrary to Soviet criminal law, that Sinyavsky's and Daniel's actions did not constitute an offense, and that the proper course was to enter a plea for acquittal.

My husband and I had to decide which of us should be counsel of record for Sinyavsky and Daniel, for although we had both agreed to defend them it was impossible for us to appear in court together. The Presidium of the College of Advocates regarded it as highly undesirable for a husband-and-wife team to work on the same case (even an "ordinary" case), and it was obvious to us that we would never be permitted to appear together in a political case. Apart from that, there was a further, no less important, consideration. Any lawyer who prepared a serious and conscientious defense and thus came into head-on conflict with the prosecution was likely to be disbarred as a consequence. I thought we should not run this risk simultaneously.

My husband was not on the "access" list for political trials, but we thought this obstacle could easily be overcome, since "access" was often granted on a one-time-only basis. We were convinced that my husband's application would not be opposed, in view of his excellent professional reputation. The chairman of the Presidium of the College of Advocates was our close friend Vasily Samsonov, and we were relying on his help. We also hoped that Samsonov himself would take on the defense of the second accused. He had experience in political trials, including the Krasnopevtsev case, which had created a great stir. Krasnopevtsev and other graduate students and young history teachers at Moscow University had researched the perversion of "genuine Marxism" in the Soviet Union and discussed their findings at clandestine meetings. All of them were tried in 1958 and sentenced to several years of imprisonment. We were confident that Samsonov's acceptance of the companion brief would guarantee a proper defense.

That evening we agreed that if Samsonov accepted, he would defend Sinyavsky, and Konstantin would defend Daniel.

I think we both realized that my husband was psychologically better prepared to undertake this defense. I was ready to do it, and I felt that refusal to appear in a case because it was "political" was out of the question. Konstantin, on the other hand, actively *wanted* the brief. Knowing his character and convictions, I was aware that a trial of this kind meant a greater risk for him than it would have for me. His reason for wanting to participate was not ambition, but a profound need to express, in the manner most naturally available to him, his attitude toward the state's arbitrary abuse of the law. I was certain that in this particular case he would conduct a better defense than I could. It was not that I considered him the better defense attorney. On the contrary, I think I have more of the defense lawyer's necessary gift of gab. It was the specific nature of this trial, which demanded not only legal skill but profound literary-critical analysis, that made Konstantin the better candidate.

Within a few days the problem of organizing the defense was resolved. Samsonov agreed to defend Sinyavsky and thought my husband would undoubtedly be granted one-time access to the court. Maria conducted all further discussions about Andrei Sinyavsky's defense directly with Samsonov.

Two or three weeks went by, and then one evening Samsonov came to our house and announced that the access procedure was running into serious difficulties, that somewhere at the top the case was being treated as extremely important, and that although Konstantin's request had not been definitely turned down, to insure Daniel's defense it was essential to have another advocate in reserve. I, of course, was to be that other advocate. We had discussed this possibility earlier with Larisa, Daniel's wife, and she had given it her unreserved approval.

In early January 1966 we learned that my husband had been refused access, and so I became Daniel's official defense attorney.

I heard Yulii Daniel's name for the first time when he was arrested. I did know Andrei Sinyavsky by name, and had read his brilliant preface to the one-volume edition of Pasternak's poetry and his literary criticism in the journal *Novy Mir*. But of his fiction I knew nothing, not even that he had written any. I feel sure that most people were about as informed—or ill informed—as I was. Neither of these two writers had published any of their fiction in the Soviet Union. The outburst of public indignation at the arrests was not caused by Sinyavsky's and Daniel's position in Soviet letters or admiration for their important talents, which I now regard as unquestionable, but because they had been indicted on criminal charges for the content of works of fiction and because the state was judging authors for remarks made by their imaginary characters. Having suddenly realized that dissent could be expressed by means other than silence, people started to speak and act.

On December 5, 1965, in Pushkin Square in Moscow, the first free, spontaneous demonstration since the start of Stalin's regime took place. On the eve of the Sinyavsky-Daniel trial, people were demanding that it be open to the public and freely reported; leaflets containing these demands were distributed.

In mid-December Larisa Bogoraz wrote to Leonid Brezhnev, General Secretary of the CPSU, to the Procurator General of the USSR, and to the editors of all the Soviet national newspapers declaring that to repress writers for their works of fiction was "an act of arbitrary violence. . . . I affirm this and will defend my opinion as firmly in open public discussion as I would in private conversation." She wrote another letter to the head of the KGB and to the Procurator General in which she reported threats made to her by a prosecution investigator. "I am not frightened by these or any other threats . . . I have nothing to fear and nothing to lose; I have never in my life valued material possessions and have learned to set no store by them, but my spiritual values will remain unchanged, no matter what the circumstances . . . I am not asking for concessions, allowances, or privileges. I demand only the observance of normal standards of humanity and legality."*

* This and the following quotations are taken from Alexander Ginzburg's *White Book*. The letters were circulated but never published in the Soviet Union.

Sinyavsky's wife also wrote to the Procurator General of the USSR and the head of the KGB: "It is quite possible that the result of this letter will be my arrest (I am constantly under that threat) . . . But even my natural human fear of such an act of repression cannot stop me . . . I affirm, and will henceforth affirm on any occasion, that there is nothing anti-Soviet in [Sinyavsky's works], that they are *belles-lettres* and nothing else. Some people may like Abram Tertz' prose and some may not, but differences of literary taste and opinion are not grounds for the arrest of a writer . . ."

Now, seventeen years later, both in the Soviet Union and, I think, in the West, we have acquired a certain familiarity with such letters, and we have lost the sense of shocked incredulity that they evoked at the time. That is a pity, for even now every such letter remains an act of high, desperate courage, a demonstration of the true fortitude of the human spirit; but when a silence that had been enforced from above for many decades was first broken, the impression made by these letters was staggering.

I am not sure that the wives' letters were the first. Scholars, artists, and writers also wrote. Signed with their authors' full names, these letters spread around Moscow with incredible rapidity, stimulating further letters, appeals, demands.

The case of Sinyavsky and Daniel was the starting point of the "defense of legality" movement, which called for open reporting and constitutional freedoms. The circle of people who joined it grew wider and wider. Those who refused out of fear to sign a letter or an appeal in defense of the two writers were criticized. The moral climate had changed, and self-respect increased. I cannot say that this activism sprang from a hope of effectively influencing the fate of Sinyavsky and Daniel. If there were any such optimists, they were few. The basic feeling was "I cannot remain silent," a realization that not to protest would be unworthy.

Scarcely a day passed without news of those who had spoken out in defense of Andrei Sinyavsky and Yulii Daniel. The newspapers of Washington, New York, Paris, Rome, and London, writers, artists, lawyers and scholars of practically every country in the world expressed indignation at the arrest of the two writers and concern for their fate. Appeals to help them were addressed to the Union of Soviet Writers, to the new Nobel Prize winner Mikhail Sholokhov, to Mme. Ekaterina Furtseva, the Minister of Culture, and to Aleksei Kosygin, Chairman of the USSR Council of Ministers.

Neither Sinyavsky nor Daniel knew anything about all this.

Years later, when I finally got to know Yulii Daniel after his return from prison camp, he often said how important it would have been for him and

Sinyavsky then, in the months just after their arrest, to know that they were not being condemned by public opinion, and that individuals had cast prudence aside to stand up in their defense. It would undoubtedly have given them great moral support.

The reason they heard nothing about the outcry is linked with the way their trial was organized. The prosecution was coming to the end of its investigations, and we defense attorneys were preparing for our first meetings with our clients. I had to discuss with Daniel such matters as the complex question of whom to call as expert witnesses on literary questions; which of the prosecution witnesses to cross-examine; which documents to lay before the court. Furthermore, information about the unofficial campaign of support was now more than a matter of moral support; it had become an essential element in the case for the defense.

In frequent meetings Vasily Samsonov and I discussed problems of joint concern to us. Samsonov knew that a political trial involved a certain degree of personal risk for an advocate. He said to me at the outset, "I've been chairman of the College Presidium for too long—I prefer to leave the post in a blaze of glory." He knew that once he had said in court, "I ask the court to acquit my client," he would no longer be chairman of the Moscow College of Advocates. But it did not occur to him then that we might be threatened with disbarment.

Our informal though intensive preparations for the case went ahead, and there were no signs of serious obstacles.

When Vasily phoned me one day, I felt no sense of alarm. "There are a few things I need to discuss with you," he said. "I have a bad cold and I'm in bed. Could you come over to my place and talk here?"

Vasily was indeed in bed. I sat at his bedside and he at once made a categorical statement. "Neither of us is going to plead this case. We must both decline our briefs."

Without giving me a chance to interrupt, he went on, "There's no question of either of us appearing in this case. This is not merely a put-up job. If you really want to know, it's going to be a carefully staged show trial. We won't be allowed to conduct a real defense at all. Because I don't want to disgrace my name, I'm withdrawing, and that's the only way out for you as well. I'm asking you for your own good to withdraw."

"We can't do that. You can't and I can't. We knew it involved a degree of risk; well, the risk turned out to be greater than you supposed, that's all. Can you really bear to admit to yourself that you turned coward, that you were afraid to carry out your professional duty as your conscience dictates? I will not refuse this brief."

It was a long, painful conversation, in which each of us tried to persuade the other and neither succeeded. I remember Vasily's wife saying to him, "What are you afraid of? Why're you making such a fuss about it? Dina will prepare the case; don't stand in her way. Then when the case comes to court she'll get 'sick,' or she'll say that she's busy on another case, and the whole business will sort itself out."

"You don't understand at all! Can't you see Dina would never do that?"

Again Vasily tried to convince me, saying how fond he was of my husband and me, how concerned for our well-being, how he couldn't allow me to sacrifice myself on behalf of people I didn't even know.

I am sure he was sincere in saying this. Vasily was afraid for me and at that moment chiefly motivated by friendship.

We parted in a state of indignation. I was angry at what I regarded as professional betrayal; he was angry at my ingratitude and my unwillingness to listen to "the voice of reason."

Next day the secretary of the Presidium of the Moscow College of Advocates telephoned to ask me to come over at once for an urgent meeting.

Samsonov was waiting for me in his office. He no longer tried to persuade me; he simply said, "We have been summoned to the Moscow Committee of the Party. You can still withdraw from defending Daniel. You prefer to come to the Committee? Very well. Please wait outside in the corridor. I won't keep you long, then we can go together."

After about fifteen minutes Samsonov came out of his office.

"Are you still here?"

"Of course. We're supposed to be going to the Moscow Party Committee."

"I shall go alone, you have no business there. I must warn you, though, that you will *not* be defending Daniel. We cannot allow you to put our whole profession in jeopardy."

I reminded Vasily that he couldn't stop me from defending Daniel because he had no such right, that only a decision of the full Presidium could take me off a case or deprive me of access.

"I haven't time for discussion. I only ask you to send both wives to see me today. I must allocate them two other advocates as a matter of urgency. Goodbye."

Our parting was forever. When we happened to meet in court or at conferences we exchanged nods and passed by without stopping. It is very painful to lose one's friends, and I know Vasily suffered deeply too. Once, several months after our final goodbye, he told a friend of his and ours that the break with us was "an unhealed wound." He also said that in time I would come to appreciate that he had saved me from professional disgrace if not disbarment. I was never able to appreciate it.

I would not condemn Vasily Samsonov if he had declined from the very beginning to defend Sinyavsky. Everyone has the right to make one's own decision in such matters. I condemn him because he betrayed our profession on two counts. First, as chairman of the College of Advocates he capitulated to the illegal demands of the Moscow Committee of the Party, which were: to conceal completely from the accused the degree of public interest in their case; to refrain, in his pleading for the defense, from criticizing the "expert" literary opinion called by the prosecution; and not to make a direct plea for acquittal in open court. Second, in acceding to these demands he weakened the chances of legally defending not merely some abstract "accused" but *his own client.*

I by no means wish to imply that over the years of our friendship I regarded Vasily as having shared my political views, but I was convinced that we did share a common view of our professional duty. When people told my husband and me that we ought to forgive him, that he was forced to act as he did, we could not agree. Personally there was nothing to forgive —Samsonov had not done us any harm. He had simply turned out not to be the man we thought he was. We had nothing more to say to him, and in consequence there was no reason for us to meet. I do not think he had any right to expect gratitude from me. The inflexible line he took in this affair was not dictated by concern for me but fear for his own position. It was he who accepted the instructions of the Moscow Committee of the CPSU to rig the defense in conformity with their demands.

As though to contradict everything I have just written, I continue to recall the happy days of our friendship—the times when the four of us were together in the blessed calm of the countryside at Zhukovka; our talks that lasted long into the night; the outings on holidays; and above all that atmosphere of friendly good will, almost family love, that characterized our relationship.

I have told this story primarily because I believe the greatest evils in these post-Stalin years are perpetrated not by villains and hatchetmen but by collaborators and appeasers. The psychiatrists, for instance, who subject sane people to torture by psychiatry are probably not sadists with an irresistible urge to make people suffer. They are simply in a position where they either obey orders or are fired. Judges are faced with the same choice. All of us—lawyers, judges, doctors—have chosen professions that give us the right to make decisions affecting the fate of our fellow human beings. And if we neglect our professional duty to the detriment of those who are dependent upon us, we should not be in the profession.

I write this with an undiminished feeling of pain and loss. For many years I considered Samsonov one of the best advocates of my generation, not only because of his forensic talent but because of his sense of personal responsibility. I pity him now because he became the victim of the system which either exacts total obedience from an individual or throws him out.

After that last interview, I immediately asked Maria and Larisa to come to my office, as Samsonov had instructed me. I told them what had been said and informed Larisa that I was not declining to defend Daniel but could not guarantee that I would be allowed to do so.

Never before or since have I seen Larisa and Maria in such a state of despair and dismay. They had no time left; their husbands had been deprived of defense counsel at the very last moment. Even if they could find other lawyers, the new counsel would be forced into a position where, in effect, he or she could not defend their client at all.

Next day I was at a routine administrative meeting of our advocates' office when Samsonov called me again. "The two ladies in question have just left me. I hope to God you'll never have to hear such things as they allowed themselves to say to me." And he hung up.

A day later I heard from Larisa that they had been obliged to accept two advocates recommended to them by Samsonov.

Sinyavsky and Daniel were tried in 1966. Both were sentenced to imprisonment, Sinyavsky for seven years and Daniel for five. After they served their sentences and came back to Moscow they became friends of ours. Sinyavsky emigrated in 1973 and is now a professor at the Sorbonne. He has published several books since he has been in France. Daniel is still in Moscow, and his writings are forbidden publication in the USSR. Despite the distances that separate us, we are all still very close friends.

Thus ends the story of how I did not defend Yulii Daniel, a story whose conclusion is recorded in Alexander Ginzburg's *White Book:* "Kaminskaya's candidature as defense attorney was rejected by the College of Advocates without explanation."

2. My First Political Case

> In conformity with the interests of the workers and with the aim of consolidating the socialist structure of society, the law guarantees to the citizens of the USSR
>
> (a) freedom of speech,
> (b) freedom of the press,
> (c) freedom of assembly,
> (d) freedom to hold street processions and demonstrations.
>
> These civil rights are secured by the availability to all workers and their organizations of printing presses, supplies of paper, public buildings, the streets, the means of communication, and other material requisites necessary for their implementation.
>
> —*The Constitution of the USSR, 1936, Article 125*

THE YEAR WAS 1978. Behind us was our departure from the Soviet Union; months of waiting for United States visas in Italy; our arrival in America; our first meetings with Americans; our introduction to a completely new, in many respects incomprehensible and unexpected, way of life.

That evening my husband and I were the guests of an American family. It was not simply a friendly invitation to dinner; we, who had been expelled from the Soviet Union, were being introduced to an American dissident, an American civil rights activist. As we sat at table, the three of us expressed opinions on matters of which we knew nothing. Our American friend knew nothing about the reality of life in the Soviet Union; we had only our first and very approximate conceptions of America. He asserted, and tried to convince us, that there was genuine freedom in the Soviet Union, that the USSR was a democratic country. The fact that people were arrested, convicted, and imprisoned for political crimes was, of course, a bad thing.

"But it doesn't happen only in the Soviet Union," he said. "Civil rights are infringed in America too, we have our political trials and we convict people unjustly too."

It was a long, stupid argument without the slightest hope of mutual understanding, for although we were apparently talking about the same thing, each of us invested that term "political crime" with the meaning that was peculiar to the social systems of our respective countries.

When I described the political trials in which I had taken part, our opponent listened to me with obvious disbelief. He could not believe me when I said that the only grounds for arrest and conviction might be an open and public expression of opinion, and that no matter which article of the Criminal Code was used to convict Soviet civil rights activists, they suffered years in prison, labor camp, and internal exile merely for using their constitutional right to express opinions about certain actions of the Soviet government. I was to encounter such disbelief often. People would suggest, "No doubt they were accused of something else as well. They can't have been tried just for that. . . ." Young American students and mature, experienced people shared this attitude.

Let us hear, therefore, investigators of the procuracy and the KGB, judges of the higher courts, members of the special Vigilante Squad formed by the Moscow Committee of the Young Communists' movement, the Komsomol. Let us hear these harsh voices of the representatives of the Soviet regime and of Soviet justice. Let them spell out the grounds of the indictment. Here are excerpts from the transcripts of a criminal case in which the charge of "gross violation of public order" was brought under Article 190/3 of the Criminal Code of the RSFSR. Article 190 was inserted into the Criminal Code by decree in September 1966. Part 3 reads as follows:

> The organization of and/or active participation in group activities which grossly violate public order; or which entail disobedience of the legitimate demands of representatives of the authorities; or which entail disruption of public transport or of the functioning of state institutions and enterprises . . . is punishable by imprisonment for a term of up to three years or by corrective labor for a period of up to one year or by a fine not exceeding 100 rubles.

Testimony of the Witnesses, Members of the Komsomol Vigilante Squad:
Record of the questioning of witness Malakhov.
January 26, 1967

I am a member of the Komsomol Vigilante Squad. On January 22 of this year we were informed of the need to keep order on Pushkin Square as some form of disturbance was expected there. We arrived at the Square between 5:30 and 5:40 P.M. Around 6:00 P.M. a group of young people, numbering about thirty, gathered in the vicinity of the Pushkin Monument. They were standing around the monument itself in a tight group. Soon three placards of white material appeared. On one placard was written: "Freedom for Dobrovolsky, Galanskov, Lashkova, and Radzievsky." We knew these were the names of individuals recently arrested by officials of the KGB. On the other two placards was written: "We demand the repeal of Articles 70 and 190 of the Criminal Code as unconstitutional." With the Squad commander, Dvoskin, I went up to the nearest placard, the one calling for the repeal of unconstitutional laws. It was held by a girl and a young man. I asked them to hand over the placard. They gave it up without resistance. This all occurred very quickly and quietly.

Record of the questioning of witness Kleimenov
January 26, 1967

I am an instructor of the City Committee of the Komsomol and leader of the Vigilante Squad of the Moscow Committee of the Komsomol. Together with members of the Komsomol Vigilante Squad on January 22 of this year I led a patrol to Pushkin Square. We were warned to appear on the square after 5:30 P.M. At approximately 5:45 P.M. the members of the Squad commenced observation, having been stationed at a number of points. Toward 6:00 P.M. a group of young people gathered in the square and approached the Pushkin Monument. They numbered around twenty. Several members of the group mounted the pedestal and, in silence, raised several anti-Soviet slogans above their heads. Seeing that the wording of the slogans was anti-Soviet, we rapidly surrounded the group and removed the slogans. One of the participants, whose name I now know was Khaustov, began to resist and would not give up his placard. A struggle developed. As I was tackling Khaustov, I heard a voice from the group on the pedestal shouting: "Don't resist! Vitka, don't resist!" Khaustov stopped resisting, and he was taken to the Squad headquarters on Sovietsky Square. In general the square was quiet. When we had already removed those arrested and the citizens had begun to disperse, a tall young man in the crowd shouted: "Down with the dictatorship." Our Squad members immediately arrested him and took him to headquarters. His name was Yevgenii Kushev. No further resistance was shown.

The same testimony was given by the other members of the Vigilante Squad and by several policemen. The investigator used this evidence as proof of the guilt of the four arrested demonstrators.

By the end of March 1967 the investigation of the case was in its closing stages. The witnesses, including the accused, their relatives, friends, and even acquaintances, had all been questioned. The investigator had only to draw up the indictment. Instead, the case was transferred to and accepted by the KGB.

Covering letter from Malkov, Procurator of the City of Moscow, dated April 8, 1967 (Vol. III, p. 1), to Lieutenant General Svetlichny, Commander, KGB, City and Province of Moscow:

In accordance with Article 126 of the RSFSR Code of Criminal Procedure, the attached case under Article 190/3 of the RSFSR Criminal Code is hereby transferred to you for further investigation.

This was a classic example of cynical disregard of the law, for Article 126 of the Code of Criminal Procedure does not give the Moscow Procurator the right to transfer the case to the KGB and it forbids the investigatory department of the KGB to undertake cases that come within the competence of the Procuracy.

The transfer to the KGB was an unquestionable sign that the case was considered unusually important, on a level with "especially dangerous state crimes." Meanwhile, the individuals arrested on January 22 remained in prison, without contact with their relatives, without privilege of correspondence, without help from their advocates. The months passed, with infrequent summons to the investigator, months in which they were subjected to the oppressive regime of the KGB's investigatory prison.

In August 1967 the investigation was completed and the indictment drawn up.

I defended one of these demonstrators, a young man who has since become famous—Vladimir Bukovsky.

I admitted everything: that he had organized the demonstration, that he had taken part in it, that he had painted the slogans on the placards and had later, on the square, silently raised one of them above his head. The only thing I did not admit was that this was a crime. Freedom to demonstrate was guaranteed by the Soviet Constitution, and there were no laws, instructions, or directives that forbade participation in privately organized demonstrations or regulated the way they were conducted. I therefore submitted a request to Investigator Smelov to close the case before trial on grounds of "absence of criminal content in the actions of my client."

The request was rejected and the trial opened in the Moscow City Court. I asked for his acquittal. The court, presided over by Judge Shapovalova, found Bukovsky guilty and sentenced him to the maximum punishment under Article 190/3, three years' imprisonment.

I appealed this verdict to the Supreme Court of the RSFSR: "While not contesting the factual circumstances of the case enumerated in the verdict, I consider that they do not provide grounds for finding my client guilty of a crime." I asked the Supreme Court to revoke the sentence and close the case.

The appeal was heard on November 16, 1967. The three judges wrote:

The defendant himself did not deny that he organized a number of people to assemble on the square with the aim of publicly announcing demands for the repeal of certain articles of the criminal law and the release of four of his acquaintances who had been arrested for anti-Soviet agitation and propaganda, for which purpose he prepared the texts of the slogans and himself painted the wording on one placard. Nor did he deny that he had taken an active part in the demonstration which he had organized. The court was justified in coming to the conclusion that a gross violation of public order was caused by these actions.

The verdict of the Moscow City Court was upheld, and the defendant served his full three-year term of imprisonment. Unable to help him in any way, I lost that particular fight against Soviet justice on the issue that citizens of the USSR had the right (as the Constitution says they have) to demonstrate and to express their opinions publicly.

I had met my client in May, in Lefortovo, the KGB's detention prison. I stood behind a large desk facing a young man, almost a boy. He was wearing a checked shirt with an open collar; his hair was cut in a prison crop. Something—perhaps a look in his eyes, the high forehead, a sense of inner strength—reminded me of photographs of the young Lenin.

I had agreed to defend him. He had not yet accepted me.

"Are you a member of the Communist Party?" he asked.

"No."

"Do you have access to political trials?"

"Yes, I have."

I was being interrogated by my own client, the person accused of organizing the demonstration at the Pushkin Monument in January. It was he who had held up the slogan demanding the repeal of unconstitutional laws. Since then his picture has appeared on the front pages of newspapers in America, Great Britain, France, and Italy; he has had the fully deserved honors of being the guest of the queen of England and of talking to the president of the United States. He was, according to the Soviet press, a student dropout, criminal, parasite, and hooligan, whom the Soviet government later exchanged for Luis Corvalan, secretary general of the Chilean Communist Party.

At the time of our meeting Bukovsky was twenty-four years old. He had graduated from high school and enrolled as a student in the Department of Biology of Moscow University, which he later left (either through expulsion or "at his own request," according to which version you believe). He was closely connected with a group of nonconformist young writers who called themselves SMOG, an acronym made from the Russian words for courage, thought, image, and profundity. He had neither a profession nor what is customarily called "a position in society."

The investigation of his case was finished. Our task was to study the materials together, to submit any necessary applications for witnesses or additional information, and then to await the trial. We said very little to each other, not because we were inhibited by the presence of the investigator but because we simply had nothing to talk about. What could I discuss with someone who began our acquaintance in a spirit of distrust—which he had every right to feel? He did not know me. In his eyes the fact that I had access obviously counted against me, and I made no effort to make him change his mind. The only thing I might offer to allay his distrust would be to say that I was prepared to plead for his acquittal, but for the moment I could not do that. I had not read the dossier of the case; I did not know what the witnesses had said nor what legal arguments were in the indictment.

I made the only comment that precisely corresponded to the truth: "For the time being let us leave the matter of my participation open. After I have studied the case, I'll tell you my conclusions and suggest the line I might take in court. I want you to realize that I'll only be guided by strictly legal considerations. If I think your actions have any genuinely criminal aspect, I will tell you, and you and I can part company. But if the material gives me a chance of claiming that no violation of public order took place, that the demonstration did not impede the normal flow of people and traffic, I shall of course be obliged to ask for your acquittal. For a lawyer there is no alternative."

So we sat down facing each other and started to work. I carefully transcribed the testimony of witnesses and accused, and the records of the numerous house searches. I kept my records of this case and managed to bring them with me out of the Soviet Union. What follows is a precise reconstruction.

Record of interrogation of suspect Bukovsky, January 26, 1967:

I do not consider myself guilty. I cannot understand why I am a suspect. I do not regard what happened on Pushkin Square on January 22 as a violation of public order. At 6:00 P.M. on January 22 I was on the pedestal of the Pushkin Monument. About fifty people had gathered around the monument; I refuse to give their names. The placards bearing the inscriptions "Freedom for Dobrovolsky, Galanskov, Lashkova, and Radzievsky" and "We demand the repeal of Article 70 and the new Decree as unconstitutional" were raised for approximately three minutes. I took part in the demonstration and subscribe fully to these demands. No violation of public order took place. We did not obstruct the normal working of public transport. After a few minutes some people appeared on the square; they wore no armbands or other distinguishing marks which might have indicated that they were representatives of authority. Without producing any identity documents, but uttering shouts and threats, they threw themselves at the demonstrators and began to wrench away the placards. I was holding the placard demanding revision of the laws. I refuse to answer all questions concerning the participation of other people in the demonstration.

Record of interrogation of Bukovsky, March 6, 1967:

I do not consider myself guilty. I regard Articles 70 and 190/1-3 as unconstitutional and oppressive. I consider that a demonstration is not a violation of public order but a right guaranteed by the constitution.

I have often thought, reading such transcripts, how much easier it is to be brave in court than under investigation. In a courtroom the presence of spectators, even the minimal freedom of speech that accompanies political trials in the Soviet Union, create an extra incentive to show courage. People are listening to you; what you say will become known to your friends and sympathizers. This is strong moral support, and in group trials, when your companions are beside you in the dock, the behavior of each is an example and a help to the others.

Bukovsky was alone with the investigator. He gave his testimony without the slightest hope that it would ever become known to the outside world. Nor, of course, could he have dreamed that twelve years later his advocate would have the blessed good fortune to make his remarkable testimony heard.

At the time, preparing to conduct a very difficult defense in my first political case, I transcribed almost automatically everything that might be of use to us; but as I read and weighed each page of his testimony, I became more and more astonished at Bukovsky's firmness, more and more aware of what a high price this young man, still on the threshold of life, was prepared to pay for the right to think and speak his own thoughts.

Not long ago, when an American friend asked about my first impressions of Bukovsky, I replied, "Oh, Lord, I fell in love with him at once!" How else could I feel toward a person for whom a moral concept had become a rule of his life? I respected him for his firmness in sticking to his beliefs; I respected him for the way he shielded his companions. In all his testimony he used only one personal pronoun: "I" . . . " "I organized . . . " "I instructed . . ." "I suggested the wording of the slogans . . ." Not once did he answer questions about the other participants, not once did he mention them by name. He held firm even when he realized that not only the investigator but the statements of his fellow defendants were ranged against him, and that one of them had stopped saying "I" and now spoke only of "he," meaning Bukovsky. Bukovsky himself movingly describes this isolation in his book *To Build a Castle:*

To be alone is a tremendous responsibility. Pinned up against a wall, a man realizes: "I am the people, I am the nation . . ." and nothing else. He cannot sacrifice his honor, cannot divide himself, he cannot break apart and still go on living. There is no line of retreat left to him; the instinct of self-preservation pushes him toward an extreme position, in which he prefers physical to spiritual death.

This sublime sense of personal responsibility, this organic inability to sacrifice one's spiritual freedom, is the foundation of conscious heroism. It creates a situation where heroism becomes the natural, the only possible form of behavior. It is not given to many, but it was given to Bukovsky as the inevitable consequence of the development of his naturally strong character. The ability to put up an inflexible moral resistance did not come to him at once; it came after learning the grim lessons of persecution by the KGB, of searches, interrogations, arrests, and prison life.

The others arrested with him were all much younger. Their opposition to the Soviet regime was more an emotional rejection of the pressure of censorship on artists and writers (two of them were aspiring poets) than an articulate political conviction. They agreed on impulse to join a demonstration protesting the arrest of their friends, and later began to doubt whether they had done the right thing. They went to the demonstration because it would be "awkward to refuse" or "embarrassing to go back on one's word." Their arrest gave them their first taste of prison, their first real confrontation with the might of the Soviet apparatus of oppression.

Record of questioning of suspect Yevgenii Kushev:

I fully admit myself guilty, under Article 190/3 of the Criminal Code of the RSFSR, of having taken part in a gathering which grossly violated public order in the city of Moscow . . . Bukovsky told me about the arrest of Lashkova and the others; he said that he was planning to go the next day with the "Smogists" to the Pushkin Monument. Bukovsky said there would be slogans calling for "Freedom for Dobrovolsky and the others," for the repeal of Articles 70 and 190/3 and "Down with arbitrary rule and dictatorship." Bukovsky suggested that I take part and I did not refuse.

I arrived at Pushkin Square when everyone had already started to disperse. This was at 6:10 P.M. I was told that the vigilante squad had arrested and removed several people. I felt embarrassed at having missed the demonstration, and that is why I decided to shout, "Down with dictatorship." Some people came up to me and led me away. Since then I have been under detention. I very much regret agreeing to Bukovsky's suggestion, especially as I do not share his views. I condemn my own behavior.

In Kushev's testimony there was nothing that might have damaged Bukovsky in the eyes of the court. Bukovsky himself had admitted that he was one of the organizers of the demonstration and Kushev was undoubtedly informed of what Bukovsky had said. The rest of Kushev's testimony was of no particular interest to me as Bukovsky's defense counsel. What he said about Vladimir referred mostly to their literary interests and to attempts to form a young writers' literary society to be called "The Avant-Garde." Questioned about Bukovsky's political views, Kushev replied, "He and I never discussed political topics." His testimony did not change; he maintained his admission of repentance and his regret at what had happened from the beginning of the investigation until its very end.

The testimony of Vadim Deloné, however, shows a different picture.

Record of questioning of suspect Deloné, March 6, 1967:

> In my view, no violation of public order took place. I regard Articles 70 and 190/3 as unconstitutional. I came to Pushkin Square to express my protest against those articles and against the arrest of my friends Dobrovolsky, Galanskov, and others. With Khaustov I held up the slogan "Freedom for Dobrovolsky, Galanskov, Lashkova and Radzievsky." Almost at once some people in civilian clothes came running up to us and began to wrench the placards away from us. I told them they should act more politely, and I handed over the placard without resistance.

What happened to Deloné after the investigation was transferred to the KGB? Why did the rest of his testimony sound so different? I have no doubt that the time will come when Vadim feels compelled to write about what broke his will, what made him suddenly begin to speak with a different voice, and also to tell what it was that helped him to regain courage.

When I first saw Deloné he was little more than a boy, good-looking, intelligent, and overwhelmed at the role he was made to play in the trial as the price of being set free. I hadn't the heart to blame him, even though his later statements created a very grim background to the charges against Bukovsky. Public opinion did not condemn him either, but the judgment of his own conscience proved stern and uncompromising. Subsequently, he rose to the heights of true courage with his impeccable behavior after his second arrest, for taking part in a demonstration protesting the Soviet invasion of Czechoslovakia. He earned back his self-respect with the courage he showed at that 1968 trial. Through prison, labor camp, and enforced emigration, Deloné has fully atoned for that past guilt.

On March 16, 1967, Deloné gave the investigator a "Statement of Sincere Repentance." This statement contained all the phrases with which people customarily deplore their own actions and behavior: regret for the past, promises for the future. It was written in strictly legal language, since investigators often suggest wording for such statements in hopes of gaining the accused's confidence.

In this case the investigators needed one of the accused to repent, because the authorities wanted a trial in which the defendants were visibly prostrate in defeat. In handing it over to what we called the "solid firm," the secret police, the authorities intended to intimidate the accused by emphasizing the gravity of the crime and the magnitude of its threat to Soviet society. When intimidation is not enough to produce such a statement, it is often supplemented by the promise of release. The investigator had to make the statement so watertight that Deloné could not renounce it and to clothe it in language that would allow the court to give a noncustodial sentence. When the investigator told Deloné that if he declared his sincere repentance the court would treat him lightly, he was not deceiving him. The court was bound to award the sort of sentence the KGB wanted.

How else is one to explain the appearance in Deloné's case material of a document known as a "Voluntary Plea of Guilty"? This too is a legal term; under Soviet law, a court is obliged to treat a "Voluntary Plea" as a mitigating circumstance.

One should not imagine, however, that in the case of the Pushkin Square demonstration someone actually turned up at the procuracy or the KGB and voluntarily surrendered himself to justice. This document was simply a means of giving a suitable form to the testimony of Vadim Deloné, who had already spent more than two months in custody and for that reason alone was unable to report "voluntarily" to the investigator.

Voluntary Plea of Guilty

> Bukovsky influenced me very strongly. Bukovsky considered that the only way to achieve anything was by demonstrations, otherwise we would simply be crushed by tanks. Bukovsky's plans, which were far-reaching, and were founded on his profound distaste, not to say hatred, of communism, were not to my liking at all. . . . I write this because if my case does not come to court or if I do not receive a prison sentence, I shall put all my efforts into an attempt to correct my errors and into warning others against making the same mistakes—and that will not be entirely without value.

This document initiated a new stage in the investigation. The KGB investigator somehow forgot that he had been instructed to look into a case of "group action." Everything was now clear: Bukovsky was the real culprit. From then on, all the questions put to Deloné were about Bukovsky's views, his beliefs, his role in the "democratic movement." The answers produced all the really serious testimony against Bukovsky.

Testimony of Deloné, May 31, 1967:

> Bukovsky is the leader of a young people's underground movement. Bukovsky is a politician with the considered belief that democratic change is impossible

under the existing political structure. He has drawn this conclusion from the following considerations:

1. Theoretically, there is a great difference between communism and fascism, yet in 1937 it was no different from fascism, as it used methods of mass terror. The same methods were used by the Communists in Hungary in 1956.
2. In our country there is no freedom of opinion or of speech. The suppression of these freedoms is the fault of the Communists.
3. The *apparat* of permanent Party officials has long since superseded the Party as a whole.
4. The one-party system inevitably leads to a "cult of the personality" [on the Stalin model]. The leadership of a totalitarian party and its ministries constitutes the "new class."

Bukovsky's dream is the creation of a multiparty system in our country.

I realized that his position was close to being anti-Soviet and it was clear to me that I could not follow him down that road.

It is hard to say whether at that stage the KGB's aim was simply to exert psychological pressure on Bukovsky, to reach some compromise with him—perhaps the mere threat of an indictment under Article 70 would induce him to show repentance in court?—or whether they really intended to charge him with anti-Soviet agitation and propaganda. What is certain is that they failed to intimidate or demoralize Bukovsky.

Testimony of Bukovsky, May 5, 1967:

I do not conceal my political convictions and I am accustomed to speaking about them quite openly. My views as an opponent of communism were formed around the period of 1960 and have not undergone any changes since then.

I oppose the monopoly rule of the Communist Party in the implementation of democratic freedoms. I consider that a democratic state and the rule of law will come into being only when our citizens are assured of democratic freedom. I do not intend to alter or to recant these beliefs.

This statement ended Bukovsky's talks with the KGB in 1967; they asked him nothing more.

I had never before had the passionate desire to help another human being combined with the sure knowledge that I faced a wall that could not be breached by logical argument or by quoting the law. Later, in every political trial, these feelings returned. Time did not weaken them nor lessen the pain they gave me.

I spent many days studying this case, so simple and straightforward in content and legal form, yet so unusual for Soviet conditions. It became clear to me that I would, as I had hoped, plead for Bukovsky's acquittal on grounds of the absence of a *corpus delicti*, and I told him this. He began to trust me and I became his defense counsel in his mind too. His trust grew when I did not follow the advice of colleagues to ask that Bukovsky be examined by forensic psychiatrists. In this my colleagues were functioning as a channel of communication: the initiative for this suggestion came, as I suspected, from the Investigatory Department of the KGB.

To have submitted such an application would have opened up a new and, in my colleagues' view, promising way of resolving the whole case. "Bukovsky will be sent for psychiatric assessment and the case will be suspended. This will mean that the hearing can be postponed until after the celebrations for the fiftieth anniversary of the Revolution, and consequently until the amnesty. [A major amnesty was expected in November in celebration of the fiftieth anniversary of the 1917 Revolution. The amnesty did occur for thousands of criminals, but no political prisoners were released.] Whatever the psychiatrists say, Bukovsky will win. If he is declared fit to plead, he, like our clients, will have a chance at amnesty, and if he is declared mentally ill, then enforced treatment in a psychiatric hospital is always better than trial and prison camp. . . ."

So ran their argument, and they were completely sincere. In those days few people suspected that psychiatry was to become one of the authorities' methods of combating dissidence, a method of exacting the most monstrous and inhumane form of revenge on those rash enough to oppose the system. The Bukovsky case was the first in my experience to arouse suspicions that something of the kind might be afoot.

Even before meeting Bukovsky I knew that he had in the past been subjected to psychiatric examination and even to enforced treatment in a special hospital, just as I knew about his childhood and family circumstances, his tastes, inclinations, and interests. His mother, Nina Bukovskaya, quickly came to trust me; she realized that I was not asking these questions out of mere curiosity but as part of my preparation. I, in my turn, was delighted to find that she was intelligent, observant, and remarkably objective. Nevertheless, when she told me that Vladimir had once been declared not legally responsible, had been sent for enforced treatment and held for a long time in a madhouse, although completely sane, merely because of his political views, I did not believe her.

Nina Bukovskaya knew perfectly well there was no hope that Vladimir would be released after the trial. I saw how much her unvarying calm and dignity cost her. But when we began to speak of Vladimir's time in the psychiatric hospital, she lost her self-control. I could see that she feared the mental hospital for her son far more than the prison camp. Even so I could not believe that a sane, healthy person had been purposely locked up in an asylum. Understandably, I felt that in this I could not be guided by her opinion alone or allow it to override the opinion of professionals. But when I met Vladimir, his clear mind, his capacity to think logically and express himself succinctly, his lack of nervousness or excitability, sharply contradicted my notion of a mentally ill person, which was based on rather more than the average layman's experience.

The psychiatrists' reports, which were in the dossier, increased my doubts. Starting in 1963, Vladimir had been twice subjected to outpatient examination at the Moscow Serbsky Institute, and he had spent two years as an inpatient, first in a special psychiatric hospital in Leningrad, then in a similar hospital in Lyublino, outside Moscow, later in the Stolbovaya psychiatric hospital. On March 1, 1967, during the investigation of our case he was examined again and pronounced legally responsible. Several doctors examined him this time, and there were two reports with mutually exclusive conclusions. In one report he was given a "tentative" and "inconclusive" diagnosis of "a sluggish form of schizophrenia"; conclusion: "not legally responsible." Another equally "tentative" and "inconclusive" diagnosis described him as having a "psychopathic development of the personality"; conclusion: "not suffering from mental illness, legally responsible for his actions."

I could not ascribe these contradictions to the complexity of the diagnostic problem, the vagueness of the clinical picture, or substantial changes in his condition, because both sets of experts had listed exactly the same symptoms. What I was faced with were medical documents in which independent political views and criticism of the Soviet system were openly treated as signs of mental illness. When I consulted two distinguished clinical psychiatrists with many years of hospital experience, they confirmed my suspicions about the dubious nature of those reports. Both consultants (even now I cannot mention them by name) quite independently came to exactly the same conclusions. They refused to give a specific opinion on the mental condition of someone they had not seen, but both confirmed that the symptoms described in the documents gave no grounds for declaring him mentally ill. One of them simply could not believe that I had shown him a word-for-word copy of the report. "Are you sure you transcribed the whole document? No doctor could possibly allow himself to diagnose mental illness on those symptoms alone. It would be monstrous!"

When my colleagues approached me with their suggestion, I had already covered the full distance from doubt to certainty. I was not obliged to insist on another examination, and the right of deciding whether to try to use the psychiatric contradictions to "mitigate" his eventual fate was Vladimir's, not mine. Only he should decide whether enforced hospital treatment would really be a preferable alternative. Vladimir, too, rejected that alternative. It was then, on his own admission, that he finally became convinced I was an "honest" advocate.

We had grown used to each other during the long hours we spent studying the case together; even so, we never achieved the same degree of easy coordination in our work that I later achieved with, for example, Pavel Litvinov and Larisa Bogoraz-Daniel. In part this may have had to do with our somewhat different aims at the forthcoming trial. My task was to defend him within the law, that is, to demonstrate his innocence by giving a legal analysis of Article 190/3 of the Criminal Code, of Article 125 of the Constitution, and of the materials in the case which related directly to the demonstration. Vladimir, on the other hand, saw the trial as a public forum that would enable him for the first time to express his views in public. Defending the legality of the demonstration was, to him, only a part of it. His preoccupation was to compress all his political views into the framework of his "last words" in court. I did not blame Vladimir for this or try to discourage him; I only wanted to help him by insuring that his speech was succinct, relevant, and not cluttered with unessential detail.

Strange as it may seem, the chief obstacle to our collaboration was his knowledge of Soviet law. He had used his time in pretrial detention to study the laws governing judicial procedure, and he came to our first meeting with a sense of having discovered America. His retentive memory had apparently absorbed all 420 articles of the Russian Code of Criminal Procedure. This, however, did not make him a lawyer; he had not acquired the ability to be selective. His knowledge was the knowledge of an amateur, convinced that he alone was in possession of all this treasure. During our talks in prison, while smothering me with citations of all the articles of the Code of Criminal Procedure that the investigators had disobeyed, he never once mentioned the one infringement that would have effective consequences in his case.

At the very start of the investigation, all material concerning one of its participants, Khaustov, was removed from the dossier and the charges against him were treated as a separate case. Both the procuracy investigator who gave orders for the Khaustov case to be handled separately, and the judge of the Moscow City Court who tried that case, committed a gross infringement of Soviet law. Article 26 of the Code of Criminal Procedure allows a case to be divided "only in cases of absolute necessity and provided that this does not prejudice the comprehensiveness, thoroughness, and objectivity of the investigation and trial of a case." This requirement had clearly been violated.

At Khaustov's trial, which preceded the trial of the other three, none of the other demonstrators were called as witnesses. Khaustov was convicted solely on a basis of the testimony of the Komsomol vigilantes, which could hardly be called comprehensive, thorough, or objective. The verdict not only established that active participation in the demonstration at the Pushkin Monument was a gross violation of public order and, consequently, a crime; it also listed the names of the active participants. Thus, separation of the Khaustov case substantially damaged the legitimate interests of the other accused, because their fate was predetermined by the verdict on Khaustov.

Even though Vladimir was unable to feel complete confidence in me during the investigatory stage, I sensed an unusual degree of such confidence in one of the investigators on Captain Smelov's team, who sat with us during our permitted meetings, observing us as we worked. Often, after Vladimir had been escorted back to his cell, the investigator and I were left alone in his office. I would read the dossier while he would simply sit there, stupefied with boredom. Then gradually he began to tell me about himself, about the job he had before he joined the KGB, about his wife, and his son, who was then seventeen.

Almost every one of these conversations eventually came around to a discussion of Vladimir's case. It was obvious that it greatly interested him, and that he was curious about my line of defense. Once he asked me a direct question: "What are you going to ask the court, Dina Isaakovna?"

"I shall ask for acquittal. The investigation has not proved that there was a violation of public order."

Looking very hard at me, he said, "You're in a difficult position, Dina Isaakovna," and fell silent.

Next day he took up the point again: "You say you are asking for an acquittal. But how can he be acquitted when he's an enemy? No persuasion has any effect on him. He has an inflexible character. Of course, you're his lawyer, you have to defend him, but all the same something has to be done about him."

A few days later: "You know, Dina Isaakovna, I think about that client of yours all the time. I can't help thinking—what have we done so wrong that a guy like that is against us? He's the kind you wouldn't have minded going on patrol with in the war. He'd never let you down. You've got to give it to him—he has courage."

He said this so sincerely, with such a genuine desire to grapple with the contradiction, that I believed he was not trying to trap me but was taking advantage of a rare opportunity (rare for a KGB man, that is) of talking to someone of whom he did not have to be suspicious. Vladimir Bukovsky also remembers that investigator. In his book he recalls a story the man told that corresponds almost word for word with one I heard from him. It was a story about the war, an incident in which his comrades fought to the death rather than surrender, after which the German commander gave orders for them to be buried with full military honors. "So they buried these men who had been their enemies—but brave enemies. Now your Bukovsky—although he's an enemy too, I respect him for his courage." He used the word "enemy" whenever he talked about Vladimir, and he used it like a kind of incantation to quiet his conscience.

I usually listened to him in silence, without starting a conversation or objecting to what he said. He was the investigator, I the advocate. It was not for me to discuss with him the virtues or failings of the man whom he was accusing and I defending. When he told me that story, however, I did not remain silent.

"Well," I said, "let us regard your remarks about Bukovsky's courage as the equivalent of the full military honors to accompany the funeral you're preparing for him."

The investigator did not reply, and he started no more conversations with me until the last day of the investigation. That evening I stayed very late at the prison. I had already made an exhaustive study of all the materials in the case, but I stayed late to read the photocopy of Milovan Djilas' book *The New Class*, which had been confiscated during a search of Vladimir's apartment. I might never get the chance again. I felt embarrassed that I was delaying our investigator, who was not allowed to leave until I did. I was nervous, mentally cursing Vladimir for the appallingly bad quality of the photocopy.

"Go ahead and read," he said suddenly. "I've just read it myself. I can wait. I'm in no hurry."

As we said goodbye that night, he gave me a very heartfelt handshake and wished me well.

Out on the street it was already quite dark. I was walking along the narrow, deserted street flanking the long wall that shuts off Lefortovo Prison from the outside world, when I suddenly heard rapid footsteps behind me.

"I just wanted to say a few more words to you, Dina Isaakovna. I think you have taken on a very hard task. I can't wish you success—you and I both know that Bukovsky's fate has already been decided. We are forced to isolate him. I've told you about my son. I love him very much. I very much want him to be happy, to have a good life. But I would like him to have the same human qualities as Bukovsky."

"I fear that a happy life is incompatible with those particular human qualities. Goodbye, I wish you well, too," I replied.

Bukovsky wrote that this investigator left the KGB. I would like to think he did. He had a very good job before joining the secret police—he was a schoolteacher.

I cannot recall a single trial that I have found routine, still less boring, but the trial of Vladimir Bukovsky was strange in every way.

In *To Build a Castle* Bukovsky says,

> I looked forward to that trial as if it were a holiday, when for at least once in my life there was an opportunity of uttering my views aloud. . . . There was nothing solemn or tragic about the trial—just the usual red tape, official gobbledygook and indifference.

For myself, the peculiarity of the occasion became more and more evident the closer I came to the Moscow City Courthouse—the plainclothesmen standing conspicuously still among the crowds hurrying along the streets around Leningrad Station, the unusual number of cars parked around the courthouse. Instead of "Good morning, comrade advocate," with which the policeman at the courthouse door always greeted me, I was met with a brusque "Where are you going?" as a plainclothesman barred my way. He scrutinized my advocate's pass.

"Are you Bukovsky's defense counsel? OK, you can go in."

At 9:50 the bell rang to warn us of the imminent start of the working day. In a moment the daily crowd of visitors waiting on the street would pour into the building, filling the staircases, corridors, and courtrooms. I could already hear the sound of voices down below.

The corridor where I stood, outside the courtroom, remained empty. I had never seen it like this—no members of the public, no advocates, no court officials. Later I found out that for our trial the whole floor had been completely cleared. Other trials had been transferred elsewhere, clerks and information offices had been moved to other rooms. All this was to insure that no outsiders should reach this corridor, lest the uninitiated discover that a political case was being heard, that people were being tried for having staged a peaceful demonstration.

Vladimir sat behind me in the courtroom. Every time I turned around I could see his pale, calm face and his smile. He was in perfect control, and I knew it was the calm of a determined man. He was only waiting for the moment when the judge would say, "Defendant Bukovsky, the court invites you to testify in response to the indictment." Then he would say everything he thought about Soviet "democracy," communism, and totalitarianism. That was his aim, his self-appointed task, and no one was going to stop him. It was part of Vladimir's plan that the judge and the prosecutor should interrupt him, for then he would be able to expose the ways in which they had broken the law and demand that these infringements be entered in the trial record. I, on the other hand, wanted the hearing to proceed calmly, lest the court limit my scope for eliciting from the witnesses all the points of law I considered necessary.

Vladimir's objective was to prove that Article 190/3 of the Criminal Code was unconstitutional, therefore unlawful. I was going to insist that this article did not conflict with the constitution. It was a demagogic tactic but the only way I could oppose the indictment.

No court in the Soviet Union is empowered to declare a law unconstitutional. The courts have no right to criticize the law; their sole obligation is to administer it. Therefore no advocate may ask a court to do what the law does not allow the courts to do; I could and must affirm in court, however, that even after the enactment of Article 190/3, citizens of the Soviet Union had the right to exercise the political freedoms guaranteed to them by the Constitution; that the automatic equation of a protest demonstration with gross violation of public order was absolutely impermissible.

This assertion was entirely based upon the law. Neither in the text of Article 190 of the Criminal Code nor in the commentaries on it is the word "demonstration" ever used. As far as I was concerned, therefore, this was not simply the adoption of a well-founded defense position in an admittedly hopeless case; it was a part of my struggle against arbitrary and lawless rule, my contribution to the cause of justice and the fight to make the Soviet state observe its own laws.

I would like to jump ahead slightly to describe a little incident that occurred when Bukovsky was testifying during the trial. When organizing the demonstration, he told the judge, he had been absolutely certain that it would be dispersed and that the demonstrators would have no more than a few minutes at their disposal.

The judge asked him, "In that case, why did you undertake this whole pointless business?"

"I did not think our demonstration was pointless and now I am certain it wasn't. The people on the street will remember that they witnessed a free demonstration. They will remember that this forgotten method of voicing a protest still exists. And you, citizen judge, will not forget either this case or us. Later, you too will think about the people who went out to give public expression to their opinions and whom you tried for doing so. Therefore our demonstration was by no means entirely pointless."

I recall the intentness with which the judge listened to Vladimir, her long, hard stare, a pause, and then: "Go on, Bukovsky, we are listening to you . . ."

Knowing that the case was decided in advance, I did not regard my position as senseless either, just as I have never thought it senseless to keep up the struggle for legality, however many defeats one may suffer. I never again appeared in a case tried by Judge Shapovalova—she became a member of the Supreme Court of the RSFSR and no longer heard cases in the lower courts—but we often met in the corridors of the courthouse, and whenever she saw me at a distance she would slow her pace and make a point of greeting me cordially. Shapovalova interrupted Vladimir when he drew parallels between Spain, then still under Fascist rule, and the Soviet Union. She interrupted him whenever he spoke of the arbitrary behavior of the Soviet authorities. I know no other judge, however, who would have allowed him to say half as much as he did. Shapovalova became fully aware of the legal absurdity of the indictment, and my client and I both made a definite contribution to that awareness. I feel certain that, as Bukovsky predicted, she has not forgotten that case.

The actual start of the trial was delayed to await the arrival of the famous psychiatric specialist Dr. Daniel Lunts, who had been called by the prosecution to testify to the mental condition of Vladimir Bukovsky. (In Soviet law, expert witnesses must attend all sessions of any trial in which they testify.)

At last Dr. Lunts arrived: short in stature, carefully dressed, spectacles in heavy tortoise-shell frames, black hair, graying at the temples, smoothly brushed back. In the years since then he has been called a "KGB colonel in a white coat," but he looked like a civilian intellectual—and indeed, he comes from a distinguished family. Later, Lunts achieved distinction of a sad and shameful kind, when he—a scientist, a doctor with years of professional experience—became the man through whose hands the KGB punished dissidents with torture by psychiatry.

The trial could begin.

The clerk of the court gave permission to admit the public. Immediately our small courtroom was filled to bursting with a very unusual kind of "public." They all knew each other, talked and laughed loudly—a sort of KGB-Komsomol Rent-a-Crowd. They were sent to keep other people out, the people who for three days from morning till evening stood in the street outside the courthouse waiting for every scrap of news about the defendants. Later this practice of packing the courtroom became normal for political trials. In time I could tell the difference between those I had seen before and those who were doing their first stint as extras in this crowd scene. In this way the authorities tried to insure that "open" trials were effectively closed, to prevent any leakage of genuine information about what was happening. Even so, someone always managed to hide a tape recorder in a purse or a jacket pocket, or secretly take shorthand notes, so that after each trial an almost verbatim transcript of the court proceedings was circulated around Moscow in typescript and eventually published in the West.

Behind the defense desk I sat with my fellow counsels. Though professional colleagues, in this case our respective defense positions were in opposition. Deloné was defended by Advocate Melamed, Kushev by Advocate Alsky. For them, as for me, it was their first political trial.

Every Soviet advocate, indeed every person who understands the real facts of life under the Soviet regime, is well aware of the difference, in a political case, between saying: "My client did not do this; his guilt has not been proved, therefore he should be acquitted," and saying: "Yes, he did this and it has been proved that he did, but it was not a crime."

The first assertion is absolutely apolitical and therefore safe for an advocate to make. The second, even though it may be strictly based in the law, is always in opposition to the Party's ideological aims, and for that reason it goes beyond the framework of a legal defense plea and takes on a political nature.

If my colleagues had been able to dispute the fact that Deloné and Kushev had taken part in the demonstration, they would have pleaded for their acquittal without the slightest hesitation. They would have said the magic words, "I ask the court to acquit," and they would have earned international fame as brave and upright advocates. Unfortunately, such a plea was excluded in our case. Participation in the demonstration was proved beyond doubt. The other advocates decided they could not defend that action, which meant they would not defend the individual's right to take part in a peaceful protest. Because both of them were Party members, it was far more difficult for them to conduct an ideological argument in court than it was for me.

I regretted even more that the Khaustov case had already been tried, that I did not have a like-minded colleague such as Sophia Kallistratova at my side. I was sure she and I would have the same ideas about a proper defense, and indeed, when I later heard a tape recording of the Khaustov trial, I learned that although Kallistratova had admitted Khaustov's guilt in resisting the vigilantes, like me—and *before me*—she had insisted that participation in a demonstration did not constitute a crime and requested acquittal under Article 190/3.

My present defense colleagues' work was made significantly easier by the fact that the prosecutor admitted that Deloné and Kushev had played a secondary role. The indictment stated that they had neither initiated nor organized the demonstration, and the KGB regarded their participation as less active than Bukovsky's and Khaustov's. For Melamed and Alsky the examination of witnesses on the facts of the case had to be subordinated to the aim of making this secondary role seem even less significant, and to prove to the court that the degree of Deloné's and Kushev's activity was scarcely distinguishable from the actions of the other demonstrators, who had not been charged or brought to trial although the authorities knew who they were. While conceding that taking part in the demonstration was criminal per se, the two advocates had to convince the court that it would be unjust to punish their clients by a prison sentence. A request of this nature was all the more justified since the sanctions envisaged by Article 190/3 included, apart from imprisonment, such punishments as fines or corrective labor without confinement in a labor camp.

Were my colleagues right in accepting the indictment on the basis of Deloné's and Kushev's plea of guilty? Were they under obligation to pursue the line their clients had—not so freely—chosen? Was this effective in achieving the specific aim, the best defense of the client, which faces every advocate, no matter whether the case is criminal or political?

Soviet law gives no clear answers to these questions. Proceeding from its general provisions and established practice, the client's position is binding on defense counsel only when the client affirms that he did not commit the acts of which he is accused. In court, an advocate is not obliged to admit as proven any facts which his client denies. In cases where the accused pleads guilty, an advocate may differ from his client on the defense to be adopted. If an advocate sees that the prosecution case rests on a confession unsupported by other incontestable proofs of guilt, and that the confession runs counter to the objective facts, then he has not only the right but the obligation to ask the court for acquittal "on grounds of insufficient evidence." I had learned this well in the Case of the Two Boys.

The latter course is not purely academic. Soviet judicial practice knows of cases (although they are very rare) in which the court, accepting this form of defense, has acquitted the defendant.

In my view, in cases where the defense does not contest the facts, where the objections to the prosecution case are limited to an interpretation of the law and a legal analysis of the indictment, the advocate is absolutely free in the choice of defense and should not feel bound by the fact that his client has pleaded guilty. Lacking legal knowledge, the defendant may mistakenly regard his actions as criminal even when the law does not do so.

Our case was an example of precisely this situation.

It is much harder to answer the question whether my colleagues' line of defense was tactically effective. Did it, for instance, have more chance of success—because it was more realistic—than a plea for acquittal doomed in advance to failure? If the question concerned an ordinary criminal case, I would say, "Yes and no." An advocate has a much better chance in court if he asks for leniency rather than acquittal (complete acquittal being a relatively rare verdict in Soviet justice). In my experience of criminal trials, however, I have found that even if an advocate cannot get an acquittal, he will usually achieve an equal degree of mitigation of his client's sentence. Realizing the weakness of the prosecution case but not daring to acquit, the judge will give the mildest possible sentence in compensation.

This consideration gave me the moral right never to adopt a compromise position in court. And for precisely the same reason I did not think my colleagues' compromise position in this trial was justified by a genuine desire to improve the lot of their clients. For in a political trial as in an ordinary criminal one, an advocate should choose a line of defense firmly based in ethical considerations. He cannot let himself be guided by the fact that the verdict has been decided in advance; he must defend according to the law and the facts, otherwise he inevitably becomes an accomplice in the state's manipulation of the judiciary.

Thus I wrote down my plan of defense: (1) The citizen's right to demonstrate is guaranteed by the Soviet Constitution; (2) as the organizer of the demonstration in Pushkin Square, Bukovsky took every possible precaution to see that none of its participants violated public order; (3) as a participant, Bukovsky himself did not violate public order; (4) the intervention of the Komsomol Vigilante Squad and the dispersal of the peaceful demonstration were provoked solely by the content of the slogans; (5) such intervention cannot be counted lawful, since the content of the slogans was not criminal within the meaning of Article 190/3 of the RSFSR Criminal Code; (6) conclusion: ask for acquittal.

This argumentation also determined the nature of the questions I proposed to put to the witnesses. It was important for me to elicit from the Komsomol witnesses indisputable confirmation that the demonstration was not accompanied by noisy and unseemly behavior, that the intervention of the Vigilante Squad was induced purely by the slogans, which the squad members regarded as anti-Soviet and illegal. This was particularly important because Article 190/3 includes a prohibition against spreading slanderous inventions defaming the Soviet state and social system. The fact that this charge was not made is an example of the inconsequentiality and internal inconsistency of the prosecution, and that mistake gave the defense a chance to contest the substance of the indictment, the right to assert that it was not the actions of the demonstrators that were illegal but those of the vigilantes, who dispersed the demonstration without legal grounds for doing so.

The trial of Deloné, Kushev, and Bukovsky lasted three days. On the first day, after the indictment was read, the judge asked the obligatory questions of each defendant separately: "Do you understand the charges?" "Do you plead guilty or not guilty?"

Vadim Deloné and Vladimir Bukovsky answered in exactly the same words they had used when replying to the investigator.

Vadim: "I understand the charges and I plead guilty."

Vladimir: "I do not understand the charges. I plead not guilty."

Only Kushev's answer was unexpected: "I understand the charge. All the actions with which I am charged are correctly described in the indictment. But I don't think I violated public order. I did not disturb the peace nor did I interrupt the normal working of public transport."

Alsky looked at his client reproachfully and imploringly. That reply signaled a change of position. Kushev was not saying "I plead not guilty," but he was not saying "I am guilty" either. The reply put the advocate in the position of having to answer the question himself, and deprived him of the natural "cover" that a guilty plea would have given him.

The first to testify was Vadim Deloné. He spoke very calmly, with captivating, even artistic, sincerity. The court listened attentively, without interruptions, allowing him to say everything he wanted to about the events of January 22, 1967, about the reasons he joined the demonstration, and about his subsequent doubts whether he had done the right thing. He did not say in court that his participation was due to Bukovsky's influence nor mention Vladimir's political views and beliefs. Deloné must have known that he was running the risk of losing the mitigation of sentence he had been promised, and that this fundamental change in his testimony might have serious consequences, but by now he had somehow acquired courage and self-confidence. Here are excerpts from Vadim's testimony:

> I consider that the demonstration itself was not a violation of public order. . . . Vladimir in no way forced me to go to the demonstration. I made the decision myself. . . . When Vladimir asked me whether I agreed with the wording of the slogans, I replied that I did agree. I knew that the Soviet Union had signed the UN Declaration of Human Rights and that the Soviet Constitution grants the right to demonstrate. . . . Bukovsky spoke to us constantly about the orderly conduct of the demonstration. He instructed us not to resist. On the square, it was he who shouted to Khaustov to stop resisting and hand over the placard.

Here is the testimony of Yevgenii Kushev:

> I was very upset by the arrest of Galanskov and Dobrovolsky. I do not think their ideas are anti-Soviet. Furthermore, I believe that ideas should be fought with ideas, not with imprisonment. . . . Vladimir warned everyone not to resist, to hand over the placards at the first demand, and to disperse. There was no violation of public order by the demonstrators.

Kushev told the court that he felt bound to take part in the demonstration on the strength of the friendship that linked him to Galanskov and Dobrovolsky: "The main factor in my decision was our friendship. At the time, I was not concerned with legal questions. I did not believe that my friends were capable of doing anything dishonorable, still less criminal, therefore I could not remain on the sidelines as a spectator."

When the prosecutor, Mironov, asked Yevgenii whether he was aware that the demonstration itself was illegal, Kushev replied, "I cannot accept that. I do not regard the demonstration as illegal. Our constitution permits demonstrations. A demonstration is a natural and legitimate way of expressing one's feelings as a citizen."

Judge Shapovalova, a beautiful and intelligent woman, did not put a single question to Vadim or Yevgenii; she never interrupted them, nor did she point out that during the preliminary investigation they had expressed quite different attitudes toward their participation in the demonstration. This was not the indifference of someone who has already made up her mind, but an example of her characteristic sense of judicial propriety and professionalism. She had a solid reputation as an experienced and reasonable judge, and she tried not to alter her customary calm manner of conducting the trial, even when hearing the testimony of the principal accused, Vladimir Bukovsky: "I have already told the court that I plead not guilty. What is more, I do not understand what I am charged with. I am being tried for something that cannot be regarded as a crime in a single democratic state, and should not be treated as a crime in a country such as the Soviet Union . . ."

He went on to say that in the Soviet Union freedom of speech effectively did not exist, that in 1961 his friends Osipov, Kuznetsov, and Bokshtein had been convicted for nothing more than circulating a manuscript journal, and that the Osipov-Kuznetsov case was not unique: there had been many such cases in the Soviet Union, including the recent case of the writers Sinyavsky and Daniel.

Up to now, Judge Shapovalova had listened to Bukovsky's testimony with a calm and inscrutable expression, as though nothing unusual was happening, as though this were not the first time that such remarks as ". . . atmosphere of unfreedom in the Soviet Union . . . constitutionally guaranteed rights of the citizen are not being observed . . ." were being heard in this courtroom. But when the names of Sinyavsky and Daniel were mentioned, the judge interrupted Vladimir for the first and last time in the whole of his lengthy and very aggressive testimony.

"Bukovsky, the court is trying the case of the events of January 22. I would ask you to confine your remarks to the charges made against you. We are not here empowered to discuss the case of Sinyavsky and Daniel."

Equally calmly, with the same inscrutable expression, she listened to Bukovsky's protest against her remarks, against her interrupting his testimony and preventing him from explaining the motivation of his acts.

"Secretary, please enter Bukovsky's statement in the trial record. Bukovsky, you may continue your testimony relating to the charges against you."

All the rest of Bukovsky's testimony was equally sharp in tone, full of the same uncompromisingly blunt references to his attitude to "any form of totalitarianism," his refusal to countenance any suppression of democratic rights. All these remarks were logically connected either with the objective of the demonstration or with the way the demonstration was dispersed, and Judge Shapovalova did not interrupt him.

The testimony of all the witnesses called by the defense fully confirmed that the demonstrators had raised their placards in silence and that their actions had not involved any violation of public order. This was also confirmed by the members of the Vigilante Squad who had dispersed the demonstration. They all told the court that their intervention was caused only by the wording of the slogans.

The psychiatric expert, Dr. Daniel Lunts, also gave his conclusions: "Bukovsky is not mentally ill and is to be considered legally responsible for his actions. The diagnosis of Bukovsky as suffering from a 'sluggish form of schizophrenia' was erroneous."

After two days of testimony, the trial was approaching its end, and we advocates conferred again. My two colleagues had now come to realize that it would be improper to agree completely with the prosecution case by admitting that their clients' actions had constituted a gross violation of public order. We came to a joint decision that they would devote the major part of their respective speeches to character studies of their clients and analyses of the circumstances that had led them to take part in the demonstration. Both would affirm that the prosecution had not established a single fact proving that Deloné and Kushev were guilty of gross violation of public order, and they would say that a detailed legal analysis of everything that had occurred on Pushkin Square would be given, on behalf of the defense as a whole, by Advocate Kaminskaya as counsel for the principal accused. Thus was resolved the dispute between us that dated from the time when we had begun our study of the case before trial.

On September 1, 1967, Mironov summed up the prosecution's case. These were the main arguments on which the state based its request for a guilty verdict:

> An analysis of the materials in the case enables me to affirm that the defendants committed a crime that represents a great peril for the Soviet state. The crime they have committed is very rare in our country, and therein lies its particular danger. . . .
>
> Having learned of the arrest of their friends, Bukovsky and Khaustov organized a demonstration protesting both that arrest and the laws under which it was made. They expressed their disagreement by circumventing the existing rules, and it is in this that I see their violation of public order. . . .
>
> Their slogans demanded the release of the arrestees and the repeal of certain Soviet laws. I consider that qualifying their violation of public order as "gross"

is justified by the audacity of these slogans. The defendants allowed themselves to make a public attack on our laws and on the state security forces. Their actions were aimed at undermining the authority of our laws and the authority of the KGB. Therein lies the great social and political danger of the defendants' actions. . . .

All three were active participants in a crime and I request this Soviet court to find them all guilty.

The prosecutor asked the court to sentence the defendants to imprisonment: Bukovsky for three years, the maximum, Deloné and Kushev for shorter terms.

Next to speak was Melamed, counsel for Deloné. He devoted his speech, as we had agreed, to a description of Vadim's character, an account of his upbringing, and an analysis of the motives that caused him to join the demonstration. Melamed also insisted that Deloné had not violated public order and therefore, being charged under Article 190/3 of the Criminal Code, he should be acquitted. Even so, I consider that he, and Kushev's council after him, violated our agreement and destroyed our hard-won unity.

I could not understand, for instance, why Melamed invented the formulas he used throughout his defense speech: "not a criminal but an illegal act . . ." and "not a criminal but a socially dangerous act . . ." How could a lawyer describe a citizen's exercise of his constitutional rights as "socially dangerous," or speak of the "illegality" of a demonstration, when not one rule of either criminal or administrative law had been infringed?

Advocate Alsky did not mention social danger or illegality. He simply announced that he concurred with the legal interpretation just given to the court by his colleague. Alsky also felt obliged to devote a part of his defense plea to Kushev's Christian beliefs and the influence which one of the witnesses, Anatoly Levitin-Krasnov, had exerted on his religious outlook. There can be little doubt that his frequent meetings and talks with Levitin-Krasnov had led Kushev to accept Russian Orthodox Christianity. Alsky, as a member of the Communist Party and an atheist, could not reconcile himself to this, and betrayed it by asking "that Levitin-Krasnov be kept away from such witnesses as Lyudmila Katz, Voskresensky, and other young men and girls. It is inhuman to entice unstable youths into religion."

Melamed too felt the need to refer to Kushev's baptism, to explain that Levitin-Krasnov was his godfather, and to assure the court that "what Levitin-Krasnov did to Kushev was really terrible."

Melamed and Alsky concluded their speeches in similar terms: "The evidence in the case has not proved that my client violated public order. I therefore ask that he be acquitted of the charge under Article 190/3. If, however, the court will not agree with me, and maintains that there was a violation of public order, then I request the court to choose a sentence that does not involve imprisonment."

The only difference was that Melamed asked the court "not to destroy the creative potential of this gifted young man, Deloné," while Alsky begged them to "spare the budding signs of repentance and change that Kushev has begun to show during the months he has been in prison."

I cannot say that my colleagues' refusal to support the position I had proposed was motivated purely by fear for themselves. My position was also unacceptable to them because of a kind of psychological barrier. In our lifetime (Melamed, the oldest of us, was fifty-five at the time) there had not been one spontaneous demonstration, not one meeting or procession unsanctioned by Party authorities. The demonstration Bukovsky organized simply went outside the framework of what their minds could admit as permissible. They sincerely thought it wrong to concede that the demonstration was legal—years of stereotyped thinking created too strong a barrier to the idea. Since they considered the demonstration of January 22 alien as well as pointless, they were certainly not prepared to risk their position to defend it.

To admit that the demonstration of January 22 might be considered unlawful was a compromise, but a compromise that in no way jeopardized Deloné and Kushev. I do not blame Melamed and Alsky for adopting that standpoint, but it put me in the position of arguing not only against the prosecution but also against my fellow defense counsel.

I told the court that I was very much aware of the complexity of the task that faced me. I would, I said, refrain from following my colleagues' example of dwelling on the difficulties that my client had experienced and that would have entitled me to request a mitigation of his sentence. "An advocate cannot ask for leniency toward someone who is innocent, and the only request I have to make to the court is that Bukovsky be acquitted."

I went on to say that I could not concur with the assertion, made by both the prosecutor and my fellow advocates, that the constitutional right to demonstrate could be curtailed. Therefore it was impermissible to call the January 22 demonstration "unlawful" or "socially dangerous." The testimony of all the witnesses enabled me to affirm that the demonstration was not accompanied by any noise or unseemly behavior, the demonstrators had not hindered the working of any institution or organization and had not interrupted the free movement of traffic. The vigilantes had approached the demonstrators only when the placards were raised. The wording of the slogans was the cause of their intervention; it was in the content of the slogans that the prosecutor, too, perceived a violation of public order. The placards had not defamed anyone and contained no incitement to commit a crime. As for criticism of the KGB, this, like the criticism of any governmental body, was the right of every citizen under the Constitution. A demand for the repeal of certain laws and the release of prisoners did not constitute a criminal act.

I objected to the prosecutor's contention that although spontaneous demonstrations were not forbidden in our country, this demonstration had been organized "by circumventing the established rules." "What rules are these?" I asked. "If they are not laid down in the criminal code, then their infringement should not be punished under the criminal law. But I know of no such rules. And the prosecutor has not named them either." The natural conclusion of my analysis of the case was a plea for Bukovsky's acquittal in view of absence of a *corpus delicti*.

Later, when I had more experience in political trials, I still believed this approach was correct. I have never condemned myself for not defending Bukovsky's political views and for not identifying myself with his attitudes to the Soviet regime, although I agreed with some of them. That is the boundary which no advocate should overstep if he or she does not want to change places with the accused. In time, however, I took a different view of my first "political" defense speech. Defending Bukovsky against the charge of gross violation of public order in no way obliged the advocate to analyze his political convictions. Having rightly refused to defend his views, I should also have refused to discuss them. Instead, I had described them as "not serious," and had thereby implied to the court that I did not share them.

However much I subsequently tried to rationalize this, my conscience defeated me. If the battle with conscience had related to myself alone, I might be able to say, "I was wrong," and leave it at that. But this was a widespread sin, committed not only by me but by other advocates whose courage has never been in doubt. The real reason for such unethical behavior needs to be explained.

In Soviet advocacy there has long been an unwritten rule that a defense lawyer appearing in a case with political implications should not only condemn views held by his client which the state regards as harmful but should also announce his or her own "civic position," declare personal loyalty to official political doctrine. When I dissociated myself from Bukovsky's views, I was not only motivated by self-preservation, which played a part, but was, and mainly, adhering unthinkingly to the established pattern of behavior. Some time was to pass and my attitudes had to undergo considerable evolution before I came to ask myself, Why should I announce my "civic position" in my defense speech? Why should I declare my "loyalty"?

Someone else is on trial; my political views should be of no interest to the court. Why should lawyers have to pronounce these ritual condemnations of their clients' views? I could only answer that it was for reasons of self-preservation.

In subsequent political trials, too, I failed to cross that boundary. I did not express solidarity with my clients' attitudes to the Soviet system. On some occasions this did not trouble my conscience, because I genuinely did not share their views. At other times, it was the result of a conscious compromise. But when I defended Larisa Bogoraz-Daniel and Pavel Litvinov in 1968, in the case of the Red Square demonstration, and Anatoly Marchenko that same year, and when I defended Mustafa Djamilev and Ilya Gabay in 1970, I broke with this tradition and I never criticized my clients' political views. (In 1971 I was given the first reprimand of my career. The Presidium of the College of Advocates admonished me for failing to state my "civic position" when giving my speech in defense of Gabay; but particular mention will be made of this later.)

After defense counsel spoke, each of the accused had the right to give his "last word," his final speech to the court. In an ordinary criminal case the last words are usually brief—a few expressions of repentance and a plea for leniency, or assertions of innocence and a request for acquittal.

For those accused of a political crime, especially when they contest the indictment, the "last word" is the most important phase of the trial. In it they have the right to say whatever they consider important or relevant to their defense, including statements about their motivations. At this stage no one may put questions to them, interrupt them, or set a time limit. The judge may stop the defendant only if he "touches on matters unrelated to the case" (Article 297 of the RSFSR Code of Criminal Procedure).

I greatly admired the "last words" of Vadim Deloné. While listening to him I was once again struck by his verbal artistry and his ability to speak with such captivating sincerity that every word affected the mind and heart of the listener. It was an excellent defense speech, delivered with tact, restraint, and dignity: "I will not give a legal assessment of my actions. It is not for me but for you to decide whether I transgressed the law or not. One thing I can say, however: When I took part in the demonstration, it never once occurred to me that I was committing a crime."

Deloné made very skillful use of the prosecutor's speech. Mironov had "cited the example of people who, thrilled by the latest launch of Soviet cosmonauts into space, want to share their delight with others and go out on to the street waving a homemade placard with some such slogan as 'Hurrah! Our boys are in space!' Well, we wanted to share our grief: our friends had been arrested and we wanted to share our concern at their fate." He also said he regarded his participation in the demonstration as a mistake, not because he admitted it to be unlawful but because he thought a demonstration was not the best method of expressing his point of view.

"When I went to Pushkin Square, I did not think I was doing anything illegal, and I still believe that we did not break any laws," Yevgenii Kushev began. "My chief motive was friendship, and it was for that reason that I went to the square."

He also said that religion was the private business of each individual, and he could not understand why in this trial so many passionate and unjust remarks had been made about his conversion to Christianity.

Everyone in the courtroom listened attentively to Vadim and Yevgenii, but everyone realized that the main speech was yet to come, that the climax would be Bukovsky's last words. And so it was: it was the "main" speech in explosive force, in its fearless choice of words, in its frank refusal to take account of the limiting effects of what prisoners are normally permitted to say. For all its unconventionality and unexpectedness in a Soviet court, Bukovsky's "last word" was firmly within the tradition of political trials in prerevolutionary Russia, where it was customary to exploit the courtroom as a rostrum from which to proclaim and defend one's beliefs. Contesting the indictment was merely a pretext for him, and there were moments when it seemed to me that Vladimir had simply forgotten about it, that he had forgotten, too, the prospect that awaited him and the consequences his speech might bring upon him.

Why does the Soviet Constitution contain a guarantee of the freedom of street processions and demonstrations? Why was this article included? For May Day and the anniversary of the Revolution? But there was no need for an article of the Constitution to legitimize demonstrations organized by the state—it is obvious that no one is going to disperse those demonstrations. We don't need the freedom to be "for" something if there is no freedom to be "against" it. We know that the protest demonstration is a mighty weapon in the hands of the workers; it is their inalienable right in all democratic countries. Where is that right denied? In front of me is a copy of *Pravda* for August 19, 1967. A trial was held in Madrid of the participants in a May Day demonstration. They were charged under a new law, recently promulgated in Spain, which prescribed prison sentences of from eighteen months to three years for May Day demonstrators. I note the touching unanimity between the legislation of Fascist Spain and the Soviet Union . . .

Freedom of speech and a free press is primarily the freedom to criticize; no one is ever forbidden to praise the government. If you include articles on freedom of speech and freedom of the press in the Constitution, then you must tolerate criticism. What do they call countries where it is forbidden to criticize the government and protest actions? Capitalist, perhaps? No; we know that in bourgeois countries there are legal Communist parties whose aim is the subversion of the capitalist system . . .

Bukovsky concluded:

There are such concepts as honor and civic courage. You are judges and you are presumed to possess these qualities. If you really are persons of honor and civic courage, you will give the only possible verdict in this case—a verdict of acquittal . . .

I am absolutely unrepentant at having organized this demonstration. I think it achieved its object, and when I am free again I will organize more demonstrations.

That speech, on September 1, 1967, in the Moscow City Court, was a momentous event. I believe this was the first time since the start of Stalin's reign of terror that such merciless criticism of the Soviet system was uttered at an open court hearing in the USSR. For the first time a man spoke whom the judge could not stop, who was not cowed by the prosecutor's interruption: "A new crime is being committed here."

Late that evening, sentence was pronounced. Deloné and Kushev were found guilty, given suspended sentences, and released. Vladimir was sentenced to the maximum punishment.

This sentence was dictated to the court by the highest Party authorities; it was, of course, also approved by the KGB. But it was Judge Shapovalova who signed the verdict, in full awareness of its legal untenability. If we agree that there is such a thing as personal responsibility, that in circumstances of the state's oppression of the individual conformism is not an adequate excuse, then she bears the responsibility for the years of imprisonment to which Vladimir Bukovsky was subjected.

After the trial came more sessions with my client in Lefortovo, as we discussed our appeal to the Supreme Court.

When the appeal was heard, I spoke alone (my colleagues, satisfied with their verdicts, had not appealed). In my remarks to the court I expressed the same thoughts as in my defense speech, except that their exposition was different; the speech was less emotional, more like a bare architectural construct. I concluded: "I consider that Bukovsky was wrongly convicted: he did not commit a crime and he did not break a single Soviet law. Your ruling will not only decide the fate of the appellant; it will also be an answer to the question: Does the freedom to demonstrate, guaranteed by our Constitution, really exist in the Soviet Union?"

None of the members of that high court reproved me, nor did the prosecutor make use of his right of reply. The answer to my question, however, was no: the verdict was upheld.

Between that time and my departure from the Soviet Union I saw Vladimir only once more. It happened after his release from prison camp in 1970 and not long before he was rearrested and tried again.

I had already been deprived of access, and Vladimir came to ask me whether I would defend him again if he succeeded in getting permission for me to do so, and to know whether I would stand by that agreement even if I were pressured.

Recalling that conversation in his book, Vladimir wrote that he was sure of my consent because he felt certain I would not refuse him "even on her deathbed." It is hard for me to judge how I would behave "on my deathbed," but I can say firmly that in normal circumstances nothing could have kept me from defending him. Even so, I could not. Neither Vladimir's phenomenal persistence nor his long hunger strike had any effect on the authorities. Vladimir's mother made a request to the chairman of the Moscow College of Advocates. The reply was: "Your request cannot be granted. Advocate Kaminskaya does not have access to cases of this nature, according to the list confirmed by the KGB."

After Vladimir served his second sentence, he was no sooner released than he was arrested again and sentenced to more years of prison and labor camp. After each visit to him in prison, his mother would bring me greetings from him and even congratulations on birthdays and holidays; he had not forgotten his first advocate. During those years I gave Nina Bukovskaya all the legal help I could, and I first heard from her that the Soviet Union was conducting lengthy negotiations for the exchange of Vladimir.

Every weekend we went with our friends Yulii Daniel and his wife Irina to our rented *dacha* outside Moscow, where we were completely cut off from our usual life—no newspapers, no radio. Instead there was only the glorious winter forest, cross-country skiing, long talks every afternoon at lunch, a meal that extended imperceptibly into dinner. One weekend in December 1976 the Daniels had brought their transistor radio with them. We sat together around the table in our little dining room and listened to the Voice of America. Through the crackle of static and some indistinguishable music came the voice of the announcer: "The aircraft with Vladimir Bukovsky on board has landed at . . ." The rest was blotted out by a solid roar of static. Only then, excitedly interrupting each other, piecing together every word that we had been able to hear, did we realize that the long-awaited exchange had taken place and Vladimir was free.

For the first time in many years Bukovsky's name was omitted from the traditional private toast of Moscow intellectuals—no matter what the first toast, the second is to all those "inside." That evening we drank *every* toast to him—to his freedom, to his future, to the hope that fame would not spoil him.

One of us, I think it was I, said, "There's another who has gone. Another one we shall never see again."

Winter, pouring rain. My husband and I, with three companions, had squeezed ourselves by some miracle into a tiny car, and we were driving along a road in the dark.

The man beside me spoke: "Dina Isaakovna, it is really quite incredible that you and I, of all people, are together in this car for no other purpose than a visit to friends. We only used to meet in Lefortovo."

The time: December 1977. The place: the road from London to Brighton. *Dramatis personae:* Vladimir Bukovsky and myself.

3. The Red Square Demonstration— Case No. 41074/56-685

My dear,

Don't curse us, as everyone else is now cursing us. Each one of us made the decision independently, because it had become impossible to live and breathe . . . I can't even think about the Czechs or hear their appeals on the radio without doing something, without shouting aloud.

—Larisa Bogoraz-Daniel,
August 25, 1968

I T WAS JUST AFTER the trial of Anatoly Marchenko, the famous dissident and author of the book *My Testimony*, in which he described the prisons and labor camps of the Khrushchev era. Anatoly had been twenty-two when he was arrested in 1960 for trying to cross the border with Iran illegally. After serving a six-year prison sentence, he had moved to Moscow. Now, in August 1968, he was being tried for violation of the internal passport regulations, but that was only a pretext. The real reason for the criminal charge was the publication in the West of his book and his open letters in support of the new trend of democratization in Czechoslovakia and in protest against the Soviet press attack on the Prague experiment.

In this trial I was Marchenko's attorney. Many people came to the People's Court of Moscow's Oktyabr'sky District where the case was heard— Pavel Litvinov, Anatoly Yakobson, and others whose names I knew from their participation in the campaign for human rights in the Soviet Union.

Among those present was the person who was closest and dearest to Anatoly, and who later became his wife, Larisa Bogoraz-Daniel.

By an irony of fate, the trial was on August 21, 1968, the day it was disclosed that Soviet troops had invaded Czechoslovakia to "serve the cause of peace and progress," as *Pravda* put it. Everyone in the courtroom knew about the occupation except Anatoly. I was particularly asked not to say anything about it to him, because his friends were afraid of what his reaction might be.

After the verdict—Marchenko was sentenced to one year's imprisonment—the judge of the People's Court told me I could read the transcript of the trial on August 26 and then I would be given permission for a meeting with Anatoly in prison. I promised Larisa and Pavel Litvinov that I would be sure to see them beforehand, and we arranged to meet at 6:00 P.M. on August 25.

Larisa Bogoraz-Daniel and I had known each other ever since my unsuccessful attempt to defend her estranged husband, the writer Yulii Daniel. Our acquaintance continued because Larisa and her friends often asked me for legal consultations and advice. We also liked and respected each other, and soon became friends. I met Pavel Litvinov later, probably in 1967, when I began handling political cases. Pavel's parents were old friends of ours, and that set the informal tone of our relationship from the beginning. I liked his gentleness, tolerance, and personal courage, which I had observed during the trial of Yurii Galanskov, Alexander Ginzburg, and two others.

On January 11, 1968, just before the end of that trial, Pavel and Larisa wrote and sent for publication in the West an appeal addressed "To World Public Opinion." At that time, in Moscow and other cities, many people were writing or signing a great variety of letters of protest, which sharply criticized violations of "socialist legality" and demanded that the authorities observe "democratic norms." But Pavel's and Larisa's appeal differed notably from the majority of the letters being circulated. They did not address the authorities, the government, or the Communist Party, but each of us: "To everyone whose conscience is alive."

I remember listening to this appeal on a Western radio broadcast with some friends:

Citizens of our country!
This trial is a stain on the honor of our state and on the conscience of each one of us . . . Today not only the fate of the three defendants is in danger—this trial is no better than the notorious purge trials of the thirties, which ended for us in such shame and in so much blood that to this day we have not yet recovered from it . . .

We listened intently, afraid to miss a single word. It probably sounds strange or naïve that we put so much stress on words and ideas which to many Westerners seem natural and normal. But our generation had been born, grown up, and even grown old without ever being addressed in these terms, and the sound of words such as "conscience" and "honor" was especially solemn and moving.

The word "dissident" was then just beginning to acquire currency. It was then that I began to meet those individuals who have subsequently acquired worldwide celebrity as dissidents. They had in common an attitude of nonconformism and they commanded respect by their courage and readiness to sacrifice not only well-being but their freedom. Yet each of them was very different.

It sometimes seemed to me that certain dissidents were rather too attracted by the hazards in the political struggle. Talking to them I had a definite feeling that although they were fighting for the freedom to express their own opinions, they were insufficiently tolerant of the opinions and convictions of other people, and that they treated the fate of their sympathizers carelessly and with insufficient scruple. Once, returning home with my husband after one such conversation, I said to him, "You know, they are of course very worthy and courageous people, but I wonder what it would be like if by some chance they were to come to power. I don't think I would like it."

My relationship with Pavel and Larisa, however, and with many other dissidents, was not only based on the fact that we shared the same view of the Soviet system; I was attracted by the moral foundation of their convictions and by the methods which they and the movement (which later came to be called "defense of legality") used to spread their beliefs. By force of circumstance, several of the participants in this movement became my clients; by personal choice some of them became my friends.

I was glad to schedule a meeting with Pavel and Larisa, and I asked them to come, on August 25, 1968, to my home rather than to the law office.

It was a Sunday, and I cut short a walk in the country to be at home on time. I remember how annoyed I was when they failed to show up, without even calling to apologize.

Then through the noise and crackle of a Western broadcast we heard the news: "Today on Red Square in Moscow a small group of people tried to stage a demonstration protesting the Soviet occupation of Czechoslovakia."

I said at once, "It's Pavel and Larisa."

Nothing in our previous conversations had given me any grounds to make this assumption. I had the impression that Pavel and Larisa themselves did not regard public demonstrations as the best means of expressing disagreement or protest; instead, they felt that individual letters or written appeals to public opinion, which enabled them not only to protest but to argue their case in detail, were more appropriate for their purposes. I was aware, however, that they were deeply shocked by the occupation of Czechoslovakia, and, knowing them, I realized that they would not remain silent. The unique nature of the event determined the choice of a unique, untypical form of protest.

Next day, August 26, I was holding in my hand the note that is an epigraph to this chapter. It was a short note, addressed to me, which by some miracle Larisa had managed to write and send out while the KGB searched her apartment: "My dear, Don't curse us, as everyone else is now cursing us. Each one of us made the decision independently, because it had become impossible to live and breathe."

After my message came a few words for Anatoly Marchenko: ". . . Please forgive me and all of us for what happened today—I was simply not able to act otherwise. You know the feeling when you cannot breathe."

The note had been brought out by Alexander (Sania) Daniel, Larisa's son, who was then sixteen years old. His father had been sentenced in 1966 to five years' imprisonment and was in a prison camp. Now a similar fate awaited his mother. On the day of the demonstration Sania had been out of Moscow; he had returned that evening in the midst of the KGB's search of their apartment. He had thus been able to see his mother, take the note, and say goodbye to her before their separation.

That day I discovered the names of the other demonstrators: Konstantin Babitsky, Natalya Gorbanevskaya, Vadim Deloné, Vladimir Dremlyuga, and Viktor Fainberg.

I think it was that day or perhaps the next that I learned that Larisa wanted me to be her defense counsel. Soon afterward Pavel's mother asked me to defend him. Having checked with the investigator in charge of the case—a woman, Senior Investigator Akimova—to be sure there were no contradictions in the testimonies of Larisa and Pavel, I accepted the defense brief for both of them. I also learned that all the defendants were being charged with gross violation of public order and slander of the Soviet political and social system (Articles 190/1 and 190/3 of the Criminal Code of the RSFSR). This time the powers that be had not overlooked the slander section.

The state's investigation of the case was finished in the unbelievably short time of two weeks, and on September 14 the defense attorneys were able to begin studying the documents. Our team included Sophia Kallistratova, who to my special pleasure was defending Vadim Deloné; Nikolai Monakhov, defending Vladimir Dremlyuga; and Yurii Pozdeyev, for Konstantin Babitsky. The two other demonstrators, Fainberg and Gorbanev-skaya, did not stand trial. They were committed for psychiatric examination to the Serbsky Institute and found not responsible for their actions.

Also on September 14 I had my first meeting with my clients in the KGB's special prison for defendants under investigation—Lefortovo. I knew that Larisa and Pavel would be looking forward to this. They regarded me as both trusted advocate and friend. The opportunity to see and talk to them was also a bittersweet pleasure for me. For the first time in my life I was going into a prison to meet two people who were already dear to me, and of whom I was very proud.

My acquaintance with Investigator Galakhov began as soon as I arrived at Lefortovo Prison. He warned me that our work had to be done in the shortest possible time. "The authorities have decided to bring the case to court within the month. You are requested to organize your work so as not to cause us any delay. You can work as late as you need to, that has already been arranged with the administration."

According to Soviet law, the usual period for pretrial investigation of a straightforward criminal case is not supposed to exceed two months, but in practice the procuracy's investigators invariably get extensions. In this case, within two weeks the investigators had not only completed the interrogation of the seven arrested demonstrators and some thirty witnesses, but had arranged for six psychiatric examinations in the prison, one psychiatric examination at the Serbsky Institute (on Natalya Gorbanevskaya), and several expert forensic studies at a special research institute of criminology.

It was clear to me, as it was to other advocates with whom we discussed this case, that all this, especially the rapid completion of the formal reports and expert evidence, was being orchestrated by the KGB. To maintain direct surveillance over the procuracy's investigation, the KGB had arranged for all the defendants to be held in a prison that was outside the procuracy's jurisdiction, and where normally no prisoner would be admitted on the strength of an order signed only by the procurator. It was Lefortovo, the KGB's own investigative prison.

The demand that I finish my study of the case before the end of September was well within the bounds of possibility. If I worked on it every day I could read all the material, copy out the necessary extracts, and also have time to discuss defense tactics in detail with my clients.

The investigator, of course, would not allow the three of us to confer, as this would infringe the rigid rule that prisoners must always be isolated from each other. I asked that our meetings be scheduled so I could see each of my clients daily, for aside from practical considerations I wanted to keep them supplied with news of their families and friends and to be sure, too, of getting food to them every day. I knew quite well that Pavel and Larisa had not had enough to eat since the moment they were arrested.

My experience with investigators in previous political cases had shown me that while some of them agreed quickly and without trouble, others only after some persuasion, in the end they would all consent to turn a blind eye and let an advocate give the prisoners food in their presence. The only condition, which we always scrupulously observed, was that nothing could be taken back to the cells.

No objections were raised to my seeing one client before lunch, the other after lunch. I came to an arrangement with Galakhov that my clients would not be taken away for their meal and I would undertake to feed them myself, which saved us a great deal of working time.

Every day I brought with me two ample lunches prepared by Pavel's mother. Every morning I arrived at the prison bent under the weight of an enormous briefcase that my husband usually used for shopping. Galakhov would shake his head reproachfully and say, "Do you really enjoy lugging all that weight, Dina Isaakovna? Why don't you just bring them some sandwiches and a few apples? You're bringing real hot lunches—and for two people!" Every afternoon and evening I asked Pavel and Larisa what they wanted for lunch next day, and I studied their tastes so carefully that to this day if I were to be awakened in the middle of the night and asked, I would firmly reply, "Pavel prefers steak to anything else, and Larisa loves halva."

On September 14 I decided to see Larisa during the first half of the day. I was nervous, but when the guards led her into the room, Larisa looked relaxed, without a trace of anxiety or depression.

At this stage, my preparation for the defense was made considerably easier by the fact that this was my second case involving a demonstration (as far as I know, there had been no other such cases). I was therefore able to imagine in advance what the indictment would look like, but even so, I began by making a careful verbatim transcript of the charges against my clients.

The wording of the indictment against all the defendants except Larisa coincided word for word. It lacked any attempt at individual treatment, even though the law clearly demands that each indictment be directed *ad hominem:*

Investigation of the case has established the following:
Pavel Litvinov [or Vadim Deloné, or Konstantin Babitsky], being in disagreement with the policies of the Communist Party of the Soviet Union and the Soviet Government in extending fraternal help to the Czechoslovak people in

defense of their socialist achievements, approved by all working people of the Soviet Union, did enter into a criminal conspiracy with the other accused in the present case [here followed a list of names of the other defendants] with the aim of organizing a group protest against the temporary entry of the forces of five socialist countries into the territory of the Czechoslovak Socialist Republic.

Having prepared in advance banners with slogans containing knowingly false and slanderous fabrications defaming the Soviet state and social structure, namely: "Hands off Czechoslovakia"; "For your freedom and ours"; "Out with the occupiers"; "Free Dubček"; "Long live free and independent Czechoslovakia" [written in Czech]; on August 25 of this year he went to the Lobnoye Mesto ["Place of Execution"] on Red Square, where together with [again the list of names] he took an active part in group actions which grossly violated public order and the normal working of public transport, in that he unfurled the above-mentioned banners and shouted slogans similar in content to the texts on the banners, thereby committing crimes within the meaning of Articles 190/1 and 190/3 of the Criminal Code of the RSFSR.

If the wording of this charge had complied with Soviet law, it would have indicated exactly what in each particular slogan the investigator considered a "false and slanderous fabrication" and precisely who of the accused had "prepared" which banner—because the utterance of slanderous statements constitutes a separate crime (under Article 190/1)—and the precise texts of the slogans, and which of the accused had shouted them.

Knowing how the Moscow investigating authorities work, I can say with certainty that the wording of the charges was not the result of inexperience or carelessness. Counselor Akimova, the senior investigator of the Moscow City Procuracy, would not have permitted such obvious infringements of procedural law in any nonpolitical case. The wording is explicable, I think, on two grounds: first, the impossibility of framing the charges in precise conformity with the law when the actions in question did not, within the meaning of that same law, constitute a crime; second, the need to fulfill the demand of the Communist Party and the KGB that the demonstrators be arraigned on criminal charges. . . .

The investigators' dossier on the case comprised three thick volumes of documents. From the very first day, however, it was clear to me that for the defense the most important section was Volume 1, the testimony of the witnesses, along with the parts of the other volumes that recorded confrontations between witnesses and accused. Because the accused had refused to reply to most of the investigators' questions, these statements were very brief indeed. Larisa Bogoraz' most detailed statement was:

On August 25 I went to Red Square. I raised a banner protesting the entry of Soviet forces into Czechoslovakia. I refuse to answer the question which banner I held and which were held by my companions.

My actions did not violate public order or the movement of traffic, nor did they inconvenience those members of the public who were taking their Sunday walk.

The utterance of protest in itself does not violate public order. The slogans contained no slanderous fabrications, but expressed a critical attitude to one specific issue. I consider the charges made against us to be unfounded.

I refuse to collaborate in the process of investigation and will not answer any more questions.

Pavel Litvinov's testimony was equally brief, from his first answers on the day of his arrest to his last interrogation on September 12:

I refuse to testify. I regard my arrest by individuals in civilian clothes as an act of violence. Through this investigation I wish to lodge a complaint against the people who arrested us. One of them knocked out two of Viktor Fainberg's teeth, and I was punched twice. . . .

On Red Square I held up a slogan reading: "For your freedom and for ours." I personally did not shout anything. I refuse to say how and by whom the written slogans were prepared. I came to Red Square with the intention of demonstrating my negative attitude to the entry of Soviet forces into Czechoslovakia, which I succeeded in doing by holding up that slogan.

One of the reasons why we chose Red Square for the demonstration was the absence from it of vehicular traffic.

I refuse to answer any other questions.

Reading these statements I noted with pleasure not only Larisa's and Pavel's courage—which was no surprise to me—but their calm, restrained tone. The same restraint was evident in the more detailed testimony of two of the other demonstrators, Konstantin Babitsky and Vadim Deloné.

On the day after the demonstration, when I learned that Vadim Deloné was one of the participants, my first reaction was a feeling of great pity. Having already been convicted for taking part in the Pushkin Square demonstration, if he was once again convicted for a similar crime, he would not only be liable for the maximum sentence of three years but could also be made to serve the balance of his previous suspended sentence. Why hadn't his friends taken better care of him?

As it turned out, however, Vadim's appearance on Red Square had been a complete surprise to Pavel and Larisa. Intending to shield him, none of the other demonstrators had told Vadim about their plans. In my opinion, apart from the common cause, Vadim had another, profoundly personal motive that brought him to Red Square. Taking part in the demonstration was, I think, a form of self-rehabilitation. He had no need to rehabilitate himself in the eyes of other people; no one had blamed him for his testimony in the Bukovsky case. Everyone agreed that Vadim's behavior in court freed him from any possible reproach. I greatly respect that second motive of his and the high moral standards he had set for himself.

How Vadim Deloné found out about the demonstration is revealed in his statement:

I was told, by whom I will not say, that I should call up an acquaintance of mine on the morning of August 25. I went to see him that morning and from him I learned about the demonstration. He himself did not intend to go to Red Square.

After our arrest, in the police station, my companions told me that they had purposely not informed me about the demonstration. They had wanted to prevent me from taking part in order to protect me, knowing that I had already been given a suspended sentence [for a similar offense].

In this case the defendants' statements were much less striking than the uncompromising and politically harder-edged testimony of Vladimir Bukovsky. This was not because the Red Square demonstrators were any less courageous or less firm in their convictions. They were simply different. Their restrained tone was typical both of their individual characters and of an attitude to the investigation which each of them adopted independently, but which showed a remarkable unanimity.

Whereas Vladimir Bukovsky had said to the investigator, "I do not conceal my political views and I am accustomed to speak openly about them," the Red Square demonstrators refused to discuss their general views with the investigator, restricting themselves to giving their motives for the demonstration. Perhaps the only person whose cast of character might have spoiled the general tone of restraint was Vladimir Dremlyuga, yet he refused to give any testimony at all during the investigation and kept his fighting temperament in reserve for the courtroom.

On the day of the arrests, Konstantin Babitsky, a young scholar and author of several works on mathematical linguistics, said when questioned, "I went to Red Square today to protest our government's tragic mistake—the armed intervention in Czechoslovakian affairs." In his subsequent testimony he said he had no hesitation in characterizing the aims of the demonstration as "lofty," and this awareness of the moral worth of their actions was the unifying factor in the testimony of the accused and of their friends and relatives who witnessed the demonstration. Babitsky's wife, Tatyana Velikanova, for example:

On Sunday morning my husband told me that he had to go to the Lobnoye Mesto in Red Square at noon to take part in a protest against the sending of Soviet forces into Czechoslovakia. When I questioned him he replied that aside from himself others would also be taking part, but I did not ask him who they might be.

Investigator: Didn't you try to influence your husband, to dissuade him? You have three young children and you must have been aware of the consequences.

Witness: I did not try to dissuade him. If my husband felt that his conscience obliged him to take this action, to have tried to dissuade him would have been simply dishonorable.

A few days after the demonstration a friend of Larisa and of Yulii Daniel came to our home. On only one other occasion in our long years of friendship was I to see Anatoly Yakobson in such a state of unrestrained despair—the day we said goodbye before his expulsion from the Soviet Union. I shall always remember his tear-stained face, and how, through his sobs, he tried to recite some lines of Anna Akhmatova's poem of farewell to Leningrad, which he loved almost to the point of morbidity:

> *Our parting is not real*
> *For you and I cannot be parted:*
> *My shadow is upon your walls . . .*

After that parting I never saw Anatoly again. He really could not be parted from his country and he committed suicide in exile.

On that day in August 1968 Anatoly sat in my room, his face in his hefty boxer's hands, and through the sobs which shook his powerful frame he repeated over and over again, "I should have been with them. I should have been with them. I should have been with them. . . ."

Anatoly had been away from Moscow on August 25. The next day, when he heard about the demonstration and the arrest of his closest friends, this brilliant young literary critic wrote an open letter that is remarkable for its force and precision. Since then the manuscript original of that letter has become one of my saddest keepsakes. "Many people of humane and liberal temperament," Anatoly began, "while admitting the demonstration to have been a brave and noble act, believe at the same time that a public gesture which inevitably leads to the arrest and punishment of those taking part is unreasonable and inexpedient . . ."

I learned from him, and it was later confirmed by other friends of the demonstrators, that the plan to stage a protest was not supported by many who otherwise shared their views. Desperate attempts were made to dissuade them, because many thought from the beginning that it was "unreasonable and inexpedient."

Hence the reason for Larisa's note: "Don't curse us . . . forgive us . . ." which at first I had found incomprehensible.

Not long ago, here in America, I was talking to a good friend, also an émigré. He was one of those who, on August 24, had gone the rounds from apartment to apartment—from Babitsky to Larisa to Pavel—with the sole aim of trying to prevent the demonstration. His motive was entirely humane. Like the others, he was well aware of the only possible outcome of such an open protest. "I now realize that I was wrong," he said to me now. "I shouldn't have tried to make them change their minds. I should have been with them . . . It's hard to admit it, but I see now that I was simply being cowardly. That was why I let myself be persuaded that their project was senseless."

Anatoly Yakobson's letter went on to answer all those sympathizers who condemned the demonstration:

> It is impossible to measure a public act of this kind with the yardstick of conventional politics, where every action has to produce an immediate, quantifiable result, a material advantage.
>
> The August 25 demonstration was not an event in a political struggle but a manifestation of the moral struggle . . .
>
> We must proceed from the assumption that the truth is needed for its own sake alone and not as a means toward gaining something else; that our human dignity does not allow us to be reconciled with evil, even if we are powerless to avert that evil . . .
>
> The seven demonstrators unquestionably saved the honor of the entire Soviet people. It is impossible to overestimate the significance of the demonstration on Red Square.

With absolute justification, Anatoly called all the demonstrators "the heroes of August 25."

As I sat with one of those heroes in a room in Lefortovo, the investigator went out for a moment and Larisa and I were alone. She said to me, "Dina, my dear, tell him that we need to work together all day. Please, do it for my sake. Don't let me go."

Larisa was holding my hand and looking at me with eyes that were so beautiful and so full of genuine suffering that I was almost ready to give in to her. Her pain was absolutely real—the night before, she had begun to suffer from periostitis of the jaw, and she was still in agony. She squeezed my hand and repeated her plea in the hope that I would save her: she was afraid of going to the dentist.

Investigator Galakhov returned and patiently tried to persuade her.

"Now, Larisa Iosifovna," he said, "you're such a brave woman."

Larisa shook her head.

"No, really, I consider you the most courageous woman I've ever met— and you're afraid of going to the dentist. You ought to be ashamed of yourself."

Hypocritically—because I too have been terrified of dentists all my life —I said, "It won't hurt. You'll just have to put up with it for a little while and then you'll feel much better."

Larisa looked at me as if I were a traitor, and I couldn't help feeling guilty.

We never did persuade her to go to the dentist.

Every day I worked on this case I became more convinced that I was not the only one who had gained some valuable experience from the Bukovsky case. The investigatory authorities had learned a lot too. In the Bukovsky case, the KGB had assumed that the content of the slogans could be treated as a violation of public order *per se* and had not even tried to prove that the accused had committed any other crime. The authorities had been quite satisfied with the testimony of the Komsomol vigilantes that their "intervention" was justified by the "anti-Soviet" and "defamatory" nature of the slogans. Formally, the court accepted the investigators' interpretation and convicted under Article 190/3. But afterward the legal untenability of the indictment became obvious to the procuracy and the KGB. The authorities did not of course draw the correct conclusion from their previous mistake, that the right to demonstrate should be acknowledged. Instead they added the charge of preparing and spreading slanderous fabrications under the terms of Article 190/1 of the Criminal Code.

The investigatory authorities did not even try to prove this charge: they merely repeated the texts written on the banners. But the investigators tried to avoid the defense objections that the demonstration itself was being treated as a violation of public order. The prosecutors would not be satisfied with testimony that the wording of the banners was a violation of public order; they needed proof that the demonstration had been accompanied by disorderly behavior and had impeded the normal movement of traffic.

On this point the investigators had at their disposal, besides the testimony of the accused, that of three groups of witnesses.

In the first group were friends and relatives of the accused. The second group consisted of two objective witnesses whose testimony fully confirmed the accounts given by the accused and their friends. The third group included the actual prosecution witnesses, those whose testimony was used by the prosecution as proof of guilt.

Among the first group was Tatyana Velikanova, wife of Konstantin Babitsky:

I saw my husband, together with the other demonstrators, sitting around the Lobnoye Mesto and unfurling banners . . . Approximately two minutes later, two groups of men ran up and began to snatch the banners away. One of them— I remember his face well—kicked Fainberg in the teeth with his boot. Fainberg's mouth was bleeding profusely. None of my husband's companions stood up or reacted in any way to this provocative attack. At Litvinov's end of the row of demonstrators, someone else was being punched, I could not see who it was. A man kicked my husband in the hip. The violence did not come from the crowd of bystanders, but from the group of people who were obviously there for a purpose, although they wore no distinguishing armbands.

And Tatyana's friend Panova:

As I crossed Red Square to join Tatyana Velikanova I saw people sitting in a circle on the steps at the base of the Lobnoye Mesto and unfurling strips of white cloth on which slogans were written. It was noon. Almost at once men in plain-clothes converged on them at a run, coming from two directions, and began to beat up the people holding the banners and to take the banners away from them. It all happened very quickly. Babitsky was sitting next to a man with a battered, bloodstained face. None of the demonstrators so much as moved or spoke when their assailants began to beat them up.

Exactly the same testimony was given by the other friends and acquaintances of the demonstrators.

Among the second group of witnesses, those involved inadvertently, a woman named Yastreba stated:

My permanent place of residence is Chelyabinsk. I came to Moscow on vacation. On August 25 I went to Red Square at 11:50 A.M.—I simply wanted to look at the square and the Lenin Mausoleum. I saw this group approach the Lobnoye Mesto and sit down on the steps. Literally for a moment they raised their hands, holding banners painted with slogans . . . Almost at once several men ran up and took the banners away from them. The demonstrators did not even stand up—they remained seated. In the heat of the moment, an assailant struck one of the demonstrators over the head with a fairly heavy briefcase. People from the crowd tried to stop him, and I saw another assailant threaten the crowd with a swing of his arm. When the demonstrators were arrested they went quietly . . .

And the other, Leman, said:

On August 25 I was on Red Square. I saw a crowd at the Lobnoye Mesto and went over there. A seated man, wearing a green shirt, was kicked in the teeth. At that moment, a party of men started manhandling the demonstrators into some cars. Suddenly several men came running up to me and grabbed me by the arms. One of them said: "Is this the one?" Another replied: "No, it isn't." But the first man insisted: "Yes, it is." They twisted my arms behind my back, punched me on the neck, and pushed me into a car, in which I was driven to the 50th Precinct police station. I know none of the people who were arrested.

The Moscow procuracy carefully checked the circumstances of Leman's presence. It was established beyond doubt that none of the demonstrators knew him, that he was a witness purely by chance, and that his arrest was a mistake.

As to the numerous *prosecution witnesses*, with their voluminous and oddly similar testimony, these typical statements were the most damaging:

Witness Bogatyrov:

On August 25 I went to Red Square around noon to take a walk there. I saw a crowd around the Lobnoye Mesto. Someone there was shouting: "Free Dubček!" I ran over to the place. These citizens were already being put into some cars. It was a sickening sight. The arrestees were struggling, insulting the bystanders, shouting slogans—in other words they were behaving like out-and-out hooligans. One of the women called the crowd "pigs," shouted that she was being beaten up, although no one was beating her, and screamed. Someone gave me the banners that had been taken from the demonstrators. I did not read them but handed them over to the police. In the cars, the demonstrators continued shouting. At the police station I gave my name and address and left.

Similar testimony was given by Vasiliev, Ivanov, and Vesyolov.

Witness Davidovich:

I was passing through Moscow. My permanent place of residence is in the Komi Autonomous Soviet Socialist Republic. On August 25 I was in the GUM department store and went out into Red Square around noon. I saw a group of people moving across the square toward the Lobnoye Mesto. They sat down around the Red Square side of the Lobnoye Mesto and immediately unfurled banners reading, "Hands off Czechoslovakia," and another one in the Czech language. A crowd began to form. Some of the demonstrators began to make speeches. The citizens who had gathered around demanded their arrest. Some men in plainclothes began to push the members of this group into cars which had driven up. I helped them. No one beat them up.

Finally there was a document which read in full:

Report by Inspector Kuklin of the Moscow Traffic Control Division:
On August 25, while on patrol duty, I noticed a group of individuals on the thoroughfare around the Lobnoye Mesto. They were standing on the pavement holding banners and shouting. This group was impeding the free movement of traffic from the Spassky Gate of the Kremlin to Kuibyshev Street and in the reverse direction. The citizens did not respond to my demand to vacate the thoroughfare but continued to stand there and shout.

In my transcript I put an exclamation point in the margin.

I discussed this evidence with each of my clients. Pavel Litvinov said, "Dina Isaakovna, all that stuff is a pack of lies. We were sitting down all the time until they started throwing us into the cars. Not a single car drove across the square in the whole time we were there."

"My dear," said Larisa, "everybody knows none of that is true. Not one of us stood up for a second. We had decided in advance to stay seated and not to react to any provocation. Even when they punched us and kicked us, no one shouted or struggled."

I believed Pavel and Larisa unreservedly, because it was they who said it. In addition, from professional habit my memory fastened on certain details in the documents that enabled me to tell the court without hesitation: "This entire group of witnesses has given false testimony on a whole series of points that are essential for the prosecution case. The report of the inspector of the Traffic Control Division is a falsification."

In theory those star witnesses for the prosecution—Vesyolov, Ivanov, Bogatyrov, and Vasiliev—were also mere bystanders, as objective as Yastreba and Leman. But reading through the papers to double-check, I noticed something about these four and noted against each of their names: witness Vesyolov, official of military unit No. 1164; witness Bogatyrov, official of military unit No. 1164; witness Ivanov, official of military unit No. 1164; witness Vasiliev, official of military unit No. 1164.

How did it happen that they were all four in the same place at the same time? Why hadn't one of them said that he had arranged to meet his colleagues, or that he had to meet them by chance in Red Square? Why was it that the investigator, who had asked all the other witnesses to explain in detail everything connected with their arrival at Red Square, did not ask these witnesses any of the most obvious questions: Was their meeting pure coincidence or arranged in advance? Had they ever spent their Sundays together before? The investigator had not even asked them whether they knew each other. It was as if he was hoping that nobody would notice that all these witnesses, who gave such well-coordinated testimony against the accused, were in fact in the same military unit.

There was another detail. When filling out the questionnaire with the personal data of each witness, the investigator is not supposed to restrict himself to the mere indication of the number of the unit. He is supposed to indicate the witness's rank and the ministry to which his military unit is subordinate (Ministry of Defense, Ministry of Internal Affairs, the KGB). In the questionnaires for these witnesses, however, in the box headed "Rank Held," there was only the cryptic word "Official," meaningless in military terms and only explicable by the terminology of the KGB. There was no indication of the ministry to which "military unit No. 1164" was attached.

Davidovich had a law degree, had shown the investigator a Ministry of Internal Affairs identity card instead of the usual internal passport, and his place of work was simply military unit No. 6592. Adding to this the fact that his permanent place of residence and work was the Komi ASSR, a Soviet republic in which most of the strict-regime labor camps and prisons are concentrated, I had every reason to suppose that Davidovich was a senior official of the prison service. This by itself, of course, did not mean that he was telling lies, but I could no longer treat his testimony as that of an objective witness. There was also one detail, not directly related to the actions of the accused, which clearly indicated that Davidovich was either lying or knowingly concealing the reasons why he went to Red Square. Davidovich stated that he had walked out on the square from GUM, the biggest department store in Moscow, but GUM is always closed on Sunday. Even if Davidovich had, as he claimed, come to Red Square simply for a Sunday walk, he could not have gone into GUM.

It would be another matter if he had been taking part in "operational measures." GUM's main frontage gives onto Red Square, but its side entrance is on Kuibyshev Street, that is, on the "Government Highway," the route taken by official cars into the Kremlin and from the Kremlin to Old Square, headquarters of the Central Committee of the CPSU. There is a permanent police observation post on that side of the GUM building. If Davidovich was telling the truth when he claimed that he went into Red Square from GUM, he could only have done so as a member of an "operational measures" team, and my experience as an advocate left me in no doubt that the members of that team would give whatever testimony the KGB told them to give. Such notions as respect for justice or the citizen's duty to tell only the truth in court are not very widespread in the Soviet Union. These witnesses certainly had no need to worry about perjury. They knew that neither investigator nor judge would even try to catch them out in lies, no matter how obvious; that every word they spoke in court would be protected from criticism by the defense lawyers or the defendants.

I realized that this line of analysis, important as it was for our own assessment of such evidence, could not be used in court until I found firm confirmation that these witnesses had been subjected to improper influence. Equally, I had no doubt that however one may try to disguise a lie, it will sooner or later be revealed.

In the case of Traffic Inspector Kuklin, his damaging report was actually contradicted in his own statement to the investigator two days later:

On August 25 I was standing on duty at the corner of Kuibyshev Street. I noticed a group of eight to ten people walking toward the Lobnoye Mesto. I don't know why, but they caught my attention and I immediately ran toward the Lobnoye Mesto. When I reached the middle of the square, I noticed that the citizens seated around the Lobnoye Mesto were holding something in their raised hands . . . I did not approach the Lobnoye Mesto and therefore I did not see any slogans and heard no shouting . . . On the same day, at the end of my tour of duty, I wrote a report on this incident.

"I heard no shouting," he said on August 27.

"They were standing on the pavement holding banners and shouting

. . . The citizens did not respond to my demand to vacate the thoroughfare but continued to stand there and shout," he wrote in his report. And how could he have made a "demand" to the demonstrators if he "did not approach the Lobnoye Mesto"?

Kuklin was no ordinary witness; he was an inspector of the Traffic Police entrusted with one of the most responsible traffic-control posts in Moscow. All his attention was concentrated on the orderly movement of traffic. Naturally, his testimony would be of the greatest value in deciding whether the demonstration really had impeded the normal movement of traffic. In his report he had written, "This group was impeding the free movement of traffic from the Spassky Gate of the Kremlin to Kuibyshev Street and in the reverse direction." In the record of his questioning by the investigator, there was not a word about this. He did not volunteer and the investigator never asked whether traffic had been impeded and, if so, for how long.

All this might have aroused suspicion among the defense lawyers, but they would have remained only suspicions except for another helpful oversight. In questioning Inspector Kuklin on August 27, the investigator wrote down Kuklin's words: "On the same day [meaning *August 25*], at the end of my tour of duty, I wrote a report on this incident." Yet at the bottom of the report itself was written in Kuklin's hand, "*September 3, 1968.*"

A second, new report had replaced the first one, clearly because the contents of the first did not suit the investigators—and to such an extent did it not suit them that an official of the Moscow City Procuracy committed a criminal act by removing it from the dossier. Having made the substitution, it would have been no trouble to have the witness date his new report August 25, but the investigator forgot that Kuklin's testimony contained a giveaway: "*On the same day* . . . I wrote a report on this incident," and he thoughtlessly allowed the true date of the substituted report to stand.

People in the United States sometimes ask, "Why did you lawyers bother to track down all those contradictions in the evidence and plan so carefully for cross-examinations if the outcome of all these political trials was fixed in advance, if you knew that none of your arguments would influence the verdict?" The same question, phrased slightly differently, was also asked in the Soviet Union. People said, "Look, everyone knows they'll be convicted and given exactly the sentence decided by the KGB and the Party authorities. Why waste so much of your strength and nervous energy on a defense you know is doomed?"

It was during that period that one of the most famous of Moscow's "underground" poets wrote a song called "The Legal Waltz." He dedicated it to the advocates who defended in political trials:

The judge and the state's prosecutor
Just don't give a damn for the facts;
The trial's no more than a smokescreen:
The verdict's already intact.

The last two verses were addressed directly to the advocates:

When your client's on trial for "190,"
Your duty to him is quite clear:
Ask the court for a sentence that's lighter
Than the one he will certainly hear.

Why then do the advocates do it?
For excitement, the thrill of the fight?
Why bother to talk to a brick wall,
To right what cannot be put right?

Why indeed did we do it? If not for the excitement (that word strikes me as wrong), was it for the thrill of the fight? For some advocates their chief motivation was the urge to strip away the mask, to reveal to everyone what a tragic farce all these political trials were. For me, the unmasking was a consequence of my work, a result of the care with which I prepared each case, but not its motivation, never an aim per se. I never entertained the thought that because a case was doomed I could put anything less than my best efforts into the work.

My clients, too, studied the case with the utmost care. With each one of them I discussed in detail the testimony of the witnesses, explained to them the line I proposed to take in my defense, and taught them the correct way to ask and answer questions. All this was necessary because Soviet law grants the defendant the same rights of cross-questioning that defense counsel has, though they are not necessarily exercised in ordinary trials. I devoted particular attention to helping Larisa prepare for trial, because she intended to defend herself in court. She would thereby acquire all the procedural rights that the law grants to professional defense counsel, including the right of making a defense speech in addition to the defendant's own "last words."

As I have said, an advocate in a political trial has the customary obligation to condemn any unorthodox political views his client may hold, and to evaluate them from the "correct" standpoint. Only a very few advocates have ever abandoned that tradition. To go further, to declare sympathy with political views with which one agrees, is impossible if one wants to remain in the profession. Advocates are obliged consciously to restrict their remarks to the purely legal aspects of the defense. Neither then nor later did even the most uncompromising and morally demanding of the dissidents condemn us for this, yet even now I recall the keen sense of shame I felt when Larisa said, "I must make the defense speech myself. Someone must speak out publicly against the occupation of Czechoslovakia in the name of all the defendants. I think I can do this better than the others."

I knew Larisa could cope with this self-imposed task. She has an excellent ability to express her thoughts succinctly and the thread of her argument is always logical. Even so, I subjected every word of her proposed speech to the most careful, even niggling analysis. I told her over and over again, "Remember, they may forbid you to speak about your convictions, but no one can deprive you of the right to give the reasons why you went to Red Square. According to law, the court is obliged to establish the motives for all actions of which the defendant stands accused."

Larisa and I agreed that no one except one or two people close to her should know her intention in advance. It was important for her to retain the right to see me up to the start of the trial. We also agreed that after the trial I would again become her official defense attorney and would represent her in the appeal that was bound to follow.

Thus passed the short period of preparation for the trial. Every morning I would go to Lefortovo with the feeling that my two were looking forward to my visit, that I was needed. (The loss of this feeling has been hard to bear in my present calm, relatively unstressful life as an émigré.) Investigator Galakhov was a fairly lenient overseer. Bored by his enforced inactivity, he would often leave the office to have a chat with one of his fellow investigators, and in those free minutes alone we would sometimes stop talking about the case. Larisa and I talked about her son and about Anatoly Marchenko. Among other things, I told her about the extraordinary conversation I once had with the People's Court judge who tried Marchenko. He had made some extremely uncomplimentary remarks about Larisa, who had been a witness in the case, about Pavel, and about other friends of Anatoly's. In his opinion all these intellectuals were afraid to sign "open letters" about the Czechoslovak situation, and they were merely using Anatoly—"an ordinary Russian working-class lad"—as a screen. They were the ones responsible for his imprisonment, while themselves remaining in safety. Just after Pavel and Larisa were arrested, I had to go to the courthouse to give notice of appeal in Anatoly's case. The court secretary told me the judge wanted to see me urgently, and I went into the courtroom while he was hearing a criminal case. The same two people's assessors who had been on the bench during Marchenko's trial were sitting behind the judicial desk; one of the women noticed me, leaned over to the judge, and whispered. The judge unexpectedly interrupted a witness, announced a five-minute recess, and asked me to step into his office.

After a short pause, he said, "All of us"—he nodded toward the two assessors, who in turn nodded in agreement—"want to tell you we were unjust. We were wrong in our views about 'those people' and in what we said about them. If you have a chance to see them, please tell them this."

I agreed, and although the judge had named no names, I think I kept my promise when I passed on his remarks to Pavel and Larisa. Soon afterward, this judge resigned his post and withdrew his candidature for reelection.

By September 20, advocates and accused had completed their study of the case. On that day I submitted an application asking that the separation of Fainberg's case be revoked and an application that an extra charge against Larisa—that she had sent a "strike notice" to her office (for which she had promptly been fired)—be deleted from her indictment. Both applications were refused the same day. A similar application about Fainberg's case was made by the other advocates and also refused. Under no circumstances was the KGB going to allow Fainberg, with his missing and broken teeth, to appear in the courtroom.

> *Case No. 41074/56-68S*
> Compiled: September 20, 1968   SECRET
>   Copy No. 8
> Confirmed:
> September 23rd, 1968
> V. Koloskov
> Deputy Procurator of the City of Moscow . . .

> Typed in 15 copies
> Order No. 333/531
> September 23, 1968

The document, whose first and last lines are reproduced here, and whose secrecy is indicated by the classification and the limited number of copies, is the indictment in the criminal case of the demonstration on Red Square: Case No. 41074–68S. The S at the end of this number is another indication of secrecy. That letter alone, typed on the cover of each volume of the dossier, determines the special route by which the case by-passes all the regular channels, goes straight to the "Special Department" of the Moscow City Court, and is registered in a special card index of the court's "Special Chancery." All further progress of the case also moves by this special route, right up to and including the Supreme Court: "Special Chancery," "Special Registry," a "special" bench convened to hear the case.

Everyone concerned knew there was absolutely nothing secret about any of the materials in the case. The classification SECRET merely reveals what are called the "ears," the carefully hidden but still obtrusive ears of the KGB. The special chancery, the specially convened bench are also the telltale signs of the KGB. When the Soviet authorities declared for all the Western world to hear that the case of the Red Square demonstration was simply a normal criminal case, they were trying to conceal the real significance they themselves attached to it.

All the signs of KGB involvement were confirmed by the markings on this document. I was therefore not surprised at the lightning speed with which the case reached the court and a date was set for the hearing—no more than nine working days between the time it reached the Moscow City Court registry and the day named for the trial. Within those nine days a judge had to be appointed, a copy of the indictment given to each of the defendants (not less than three days before the start of the trial), and all the witnesses, some of them far from Moscow, subpoenaed. Finally, some token amount of time had to be allowed for the advocates to make their final study of the case and see their clients again. If the judge had been expected to conduct a fair trial, she would have had the hardest nine days—she had to study the three fat volumes of investigatory material, decide whether sufficient evidence had been collected to bring the accused to trial, and prepare to examine all those witnesses. That nine-day period was more than an exception: it was a uniquely short period, which demanded an equally unique efficiency from every component of the judicial system.

The courthouse staff managed to do everything on schedule. They even got postponements for all the other cases we defense lawyers were handling. Everything was subordinated to one aim—to get the trial over within a very short time, as ordained by some very high authority (I was later told that the order came from the Central Committee of the CPSU).

I had parted from Pavel Litvinov and Larisa Bogoraz on September 20. No more than a week had passed when I was again taking the familiar route to Lefortovo Prison, this time without the big briefcase and therefore without hot lunches for my two clients.

"What's happened? I wasn't expecting you so soon." With these words Pavel welcomed me. And only then, "Sorry, I didn't even say hello."

There was complete silence in our little office. Now and again we exchanged a few noncommittal remarks; all the rest of the time we were writing. Pavel was well aware that the meeting was bugged, and we conducted it in writing from beginning to end.

That morning I had arrived at the prison very early. I had hurried there in order not to have to wait in line, as the advocates usually do, and to get an office without delay. And indeed, in the reception area of the prison, where advocates write out their requests to see clients, I was alone.

The waiting began. From time to time I asked the duty officer when I would get an office, and he invariably replied, "You must wait, all the offices are occupied." Eventually he led me down a long, narrow corridor. Along the right-hand side were windows, to the left a row of doors leading into the offices set aside for meetings. All the doors were open, all the offices empty. I was the only visitor at that early hour. They allotted me the last office in the row, the smallest and most inconvenient of them all—it lacked even a bell to call the duty officer. When the meeting was over you had to go out into the corridor, shout through an old-fashioned megaphone, "Duty officer! Duty officer!" and keep on shouting while you wondered whether he had heard you. I asked permission to be able to use any one of the other offices —they had bells and more convenient desks. My escort answered firmly, "I can do nothing about it, comrade advocate. My orders are to give you this office and none other."

I could think of only one explanation for this refusal and for the long, pointless wait. I had come too early, and they had not yet had time to install the special microphones with which the KGB intended to eavesdrop on our consultations.

Nevertheless this time had been positively idyllic. We had worked in the old-fashioned, cell-like offices used for meetings between prisoners and their relatives in the presence of a guard, so that permanently installed bugging devices were unnecessary. Later we were given the use of some large, well-lighted offices on the second floor, with good desks and the inevitable special television set through which we could be observed. There even exchanging notes with one's client became dangerous.

Why should it have been dangerous? Even under the strict prison regulations, what could be criminal in consultations between advocate and client? Did I, for instance, bring forbidden things into or out of the prison?

I did. Nervous, terrified of being found out, I brought things. For those who smoked I brought cigarettes, which they smoked during the meeting and then put the rest into an empty pack of the same brand, which I had specially put in my purse, so that they could take them back to their cells. For nonsmokers I brought chocolate bars, which they ate in my presence piece by piece, after which I would stuff the wrapper back into my briefcase.

During our tête-à-tête meetings I would tell Pavel and Larisa about all the Western radio broadcasts concerning their forthcoming trial.

That was forbidden.

I gave them news of their families and friends, including the fact that Anatoly Marchenko's sentence had been confirmed on appeal and Anatoly himself had already been transferred to prison in the town of Solikamsk, far away in the Urals.

That too was forbidden.

I sometimes disguised and brought in letters from parents, wives, fian-
cées, and friends, letters full of tenderness and concern, expressions of
pride at their actions and admiration for their courage. Anyone who read
through my case notes carefully would have come across such letters:

> Testimony of Witness Vesyolov:
> On August 25 I went . . .
> My dearest friend,
>   To this day I cannot forgive myself for not having been in
> Moscow on your great and testing day. A great deal is being
> written and said about you. Everyone greatly honors you
> . . . May we meet again soon, no matter where fate may
> carry you. . . .

Letters were forbidden, so I was forced to go against my disciplined,
law-abiding nature and to employ the crude but effective camouflage of
slipping such letters in among the official papers that I *was* allowed to show
to my client. I was convinced that justice would not suffer, that the accused
needed to know that they were not forgotten, that people were thinking
about them, and that the demonstration had not been without effect.

From any advocate's point of view, Pavel and Larisa were model clients.
Highly intelligent, well educated, eminently skilled at putting their
thoughts into words, they had one overriding objective: to say truthfully
why they had gone to Red Square and what their motives had been. Each
of them quite independently decided upon his or her line of conduct in court,
which was, while refusing to answer a single question about the actions of
any of the others, to tell the complete truth about themselves. I did not
have to teach them *what* to say; all I needed to do was to adjust the phrasing
of their testimony to fit the requirements of procedural law.

Even so, we covered page after page with notes about how to answer
questions in court and how to ask them. This was a perfectly legitimate
subject of conversation between lawyer and client, but we crossed out
every line of these notes so that our arguments and tactics would not be
known in advance to the procuracy and the KGB, and hence to those witnesses whose perjuries we aimed to reveal in court.

My methods were not unique. Sophia Kallistratova once said, after a
meeting with Vadim Deloné, "It's a good thing, Dina, that I'm an elderly
lady. Otherwise I don't know what the prison guards would think of me. I
spent three hours with Vadim, and in all that time we didn't say a single
word aloud except hello and goodbye."

By now, being bugged was nothing new for me. Electronic eavesdropping had become a fact of everyday life for my whole family. I also knew
exactly when our apartment had been wired for sound. It happened toward

the end of October 1967, just after the trial of Vladimir Bukovsky, and just after I had finished studying the multivolume dossier in the case of Yurii Galanskov, Alexander Ginzburg, and others accused of anti-Soviet agitation and propaganda; the investigations for that case had taken a very long time, and their trial was yet to come.

One evening, after one of our rare courtroom successes in the Case of the Two Boys, we had a celebration at my home with Lev Yudovich and two other friends. Our conversation was interrupted by our son. Dmitry came into the room with an odd, worried smile and said to my husband, "Papa, I must talk to you for a moment, please come to my room."

My husband soon returned, looking no less worried and perplexed than our son. "I must warn you," he said, "that this whole conversation, every single word being said in this room, can be clearly heard in Dmitry's room. All you have to do is lift the telephone receiver."

We lived in a three-room apartment with two corridors. Dmitry and his wife had the room nearest the front door; we were in the room the farthest from it, with the two halls and the third room, my mother's, in between. There was no telephone in the room where we were. It was not even wired for a phone.

My first reaction was, "That's impossible!" I went to my son's room, lifted the receiver, and listened. I could hear the standard dial tone, and through it . . . Never before had I heard sound reproduced with such clarity—not just the human voice, but the sound of wine being poured, the faint tinkle of glass. Everything, magnified in volume, was coming to me through that earpiece. It was the clearest connection we had ever had.

Each of our guests in turn made the same journey from the dinner table to my son's room; everyone needed to be personally convinced. The guests agreed that the bugging device had to have been installed not only inside the telephone but somewhere in this room as well. If that was the case, then I had a very good idea of when it had been done and by whom. I at once connected it with a visit that had occurred the day before.

Among our acquaintances was a man we had often met at the theater, at previews of new movies, at the café of the old, elegant National Hotel. He had never been to our home, nor we to his. Several days before, this man had phoned to say that he urgently needed some legal advice. I suggested that he come to my office, but he was so insistent on advice from both my husband and me, that I invited him to our apartment. When he left, my husband and I had wondered for a long time just why he came, because the matter he discussed was thoroughly trivial. For several years this acquaintance had been tagged with the unpleasant reputation of being a secret informer for the KGB. My husband and I had never believed this, just as we refused to believe many such damning but unfounded rumors. Now, however, he seemed the only possible suspect.

We were neither frightened nor upset by the business with the telephone. We accepted it as a natural consequence of my work as a lawyer, and we decided that as far as we were concerned the bug did not exist. We had to be able to live, talk, and act freely in our own home, otherwise existence would be intolerable. (Later we realized it was impossible to keep to this decision, and we began to carry around those little notepads that are known in Moscow as "the dissident's companion," on which we wrote down everything that was not meant for the electronic ears.)

Next day, when I was alone at home, there came a ring at the doorbell. There in the hallway stood a tall stranger in a dark overcoat and a fur hat.

"I'm from the telephone exchange. I've come to test your phone."

"How kind," I said. "We didn't call for the repairman. Who told you to come here?"

"It's a new way of providing customer service—we go around checking all the phones in our sector. Have you any complaints about yours?"

I could not believe that Soviet customer service had attained such amazing heights of efficiency, yet I decided not to conceal the defect we had discovered in the bugging device. Having listened to my story about our sudden and fortunate ability to keep in touch with what was going on in the other rooms of our apartment, the repairman said hastily, "That's induction." Seeing my look of perplexity, he repeated in a confident voice: "It's caused by induction."

He had thoughtfully brought a new telephone instrument with which to replace our old one. As I saw him out, I offered him a tip, which is normal in the Soviet Union for anyone who carries out officially cost-free repairs. My repairman firmly refused it, rejecting the money indignantly. But he pocketed it when I said to him, "If you are really a repairman from the telephone exchange, then you ought to behave accordingly. They never refuse a tip."

After he had gone I called the service department of the exchange to try and find out who this man was. I told the supervisor that I wanted to express my gratitude to the repairman for his prompt and excellent work. They spent a long time checking their records, then called me back to say, "There must be some misunderstanding. We never sent a repairman to you."

After that, the word "induction" completely replaced the clumsy terms "electronic eavesdropping" or "telephone tapping" in our circle. Whenever somebody said, "My phone has induction," everyone knew what was meant.

Although our case was being tried by the Moscow City Court, the chosen venue was the courthouse of the People's Court of the Proletarsky District of Moscow. This is an old building, one side of which looks out over the River Yauza (a tributary of the Moscow River), and which faces a little backstreet. It is always quiet there—there are no big construction sites in the vicinity and the street is so narrow that it carries no through traffic. The trial was set to begin on October 9, 1968, at 9:00 A.M., an hour earlier than the regular start of the working day for the People's Courts and the City Court. Both the location and the hour were part of an attempt to keep away as many "undesirables" as possible, especially those loosely referred to as the "liberal intelligentsia," and, above all, foreign newspaper correspondents.

As soon as I reached the street corner I was surrounded by a dense crowd—familiar and unfamiliar faces, young and old. Some of them were concerned about the outcome of the trial, some came because the accused were dear to them, some wanted by their presence to express solidarity with the demonstrators. They would all have to stay outside; they would not be allowed into the courtroom. The courthouse, in effect, was blockaded: not only casual passers-by and these "undesirables," but even courthouse officials were being kept out. The staff of the People's Court of Proletarsky District was obliged to stop work throughout the hearing of our case.

With great difficulty I pushed my way through the crowd amid shouts of "Why don't they let us in?" "Why are those people being let in through the side door?" "We demand to be let in!" And those who recognized me added, "You must ask the court to let the public in!" The advocates would make this application, as we did at all political trials, and it would not have the slightest effect.

Then somebody yelled, "Let the advocate through!" My pass was checked and I was inside.

The third floor, where our case was to be tried, was empty. The doors of the courtrooms along one side of the corridor were all closed. Facing them was the door to the registry of criminal cases, where I heard voices. I went in.

There, grouped in a tight circle around the woman who was to try our case, Judge Lubentsova, were Judge Osetrov, chairman of the Moscow City Court bench, Funtov, the Deputy Procurator of Moscow, and several unknown senior officers of the KGB. A little to one side was Konstantin Apraksin, who had succeeded Samsonov as chairman of the Moscow College of Advocates. The bosses of the organizations concerned—the court, the procuracy, the KGB, and the advocates—had all gathered here to collaborate in stage-managing the work of this "independent" court. Clearly I had no business in this headquarters. I went back into the corridor to wait for our courtroom to be opened, and looked out the window as Sophia Kallistratova arrived and was surrounded, as I had been, by people talking urgently and insistently to her.

I had known Judge Valentina Lubentsova for many years, if an advocate can be said to know a judge in the Soviet Union. Although I had met her only in a professional context, we were on good terms. Lubentsova was always cordial to me, and her manner in court was invariably courteous. Although not distinguished for intelligence or education, she was an experienced judge—she had been on a People's Court bench before rising to the City Court—displaying a combination of reasonable severity and reasonable liberalism. I had often appeared before her in criminal cases and had never had occasion to regard her verdicts as blatantly unjust. Psychologically, Lubentsova was a totally Soviet person, who accepted the regime and was fundamentally satisfied with it. She was married to a colonel in the Soviet Army who worked in Moscow at the Ministry of Defense. They lived in a good, comfortable apartment building. I believe Lubentsova loved her work, or at least valued it highly. Her conformism was sincere. She believed whatever the Party told her, and however much the Party line changed, she accepted each zigzag as correct.

In 1968 the process of democratization in Czechoslovakia was the subject of lively and fairly frank argument at all levels (the only stratum of Soviet society in which I never mixed and whose views I cannot report was that of the Party *apparat*, the body of permanent, career Party officials). Many people genuinely supported the policy of the Soviet government. They believed that Czechoslovakia was beginning to restore capitalism, and that there was a real danger of an invasion of Czechoslovakia by West German forces. There were other arguments too, along the lines of "We shed our blood for them, they owe us their liberation from Fascism and now they're betraying us."

Although many people believed this, I am by no means certain that they were a majority. Equally often I met people who perceived the Prague Spring as an example offering the possibility of a freer life in our country too. Many people envied the Czechs, were thrilled by what they were doing, and took the incursion of Soviet forces into Czechoslovakia as a tragedy, a national disgrace.

Judge Lubentsova was one of those who believed Soviet propaganda and justified the Soviet invasion as reasonable and even necessary. In her eyes the demonstration on Red Square was criminal, even though formally it did not fall under a single article of the criminal law. To her the case was a classic example of the functioning of that "socialist approach to justice" by which every judge is legally bound to be guided (Article 16 of the Code of Criminal Procedure of the RSFSR). And the approach to justice of Soviet judges is above all "the reflection in their minds of the ideology of the Party and the state" (Commentary on Article 16). Lubentsova thought these defendants deserved to be punished. At the same time, her belief was somewhat generalized and was not reflected in her personal attitude to the defendants.

A few days before the trial I had a case in one of the People's Courts of Moscow. Describing the woman judge who was to try it, other advocates had said, "She is so compassionate. Though she doesn't like to acquit, she never gives heavy sentences." Knowing I was involved in the Red Square case, this compassionate judge said to me in corridor conversation, "If I had been in Red Square then, I would have gouged out their shameless eyes with my own hands, and with pleasure!" and her face expressed a matching hatred and cruelty. I said nothing in response, and I was equally silent when a young court clerk bravely said to her, "How can you talk like that? It makes me ashamed just to listen to you." I held my peace because I felt that if I opened my mouth I would be unable to keep within the necessary bounds of civility. And indeed what point was there in arguing with her? There was no hope of mutual comprehension. I remember other judges too, who expressed themselves about the case. After the trial, when Larisa, Pavel, and Konstantin Babitsky had been sentenced to long years of internal exile, some of them criticized the "softness" of the sentence. "They shouldn't have been sent into exile, but to a prison camp, and a strict-regime camp, too, in among hardened criminals. Exile! That's no punishment for such scoundrels!"

I am convinced that Lubentsova did not harbor such feelings. In conversation with her before the trial, in her behavior in the courtroom, and during the many and fairly frank talks I had with her after the trial, I never detected a trace of contempt for the defendants or regret that she had handed down insufficiently severe sentences. As far as I know, this case was the first political trial in her judicial career. Put in a position where she was not allowed to decide anything herself, where she was ordered in advance to convict all the defendants under specified articles, she seemed to accept these conditions as natural for such an unusual case and in no way a derogation of her judicial dignity.

Dressed as always in a modest suit, Lubentsova sat behind the judge's desk showing no signs of agitation, displeasure, or irritation. She fulfilled her allotted role as director of this judicial performance with professional

skill but, I thought, also without any genuine interest. Habitually interested in the question "Why?" she not only avoided putting that question
altogether but listened most reluctantly when the defendants explained the
motives and reasons for their actions. She vetoed important defense petitions with the categorical refusal: "The court sees no necessity for it."

And in a sense she was right. No matter what might be in the documents
the defense asked to be laid before the court, no matter what evidence
might be given by new witnesses, the defendants would be convicted as
planned. Every Soviet advocate can cite equally blatant examples of a judge
rejecting as unessential any evidence that potentially favors the accused
without even bothering to check the soundness of the corresponding aspects
of the prosecution's case. Yet Lubentsova was not that sort of judge; with
her this biased manner of conducting a trial, in which everything was subordinated to a predetermined decision, was an exception.

After the Red Square case, Lubentsova was often appointed to try
political cases, and I was told that she went on consistently ruling out all
contentious evidence that might favor the accused. At first this was not
reflected in her handling of ordinary criminal trials, but the habit of flouting
the law, acquired while trying political cases, gradually began to assert
itself. People began to notice in her the hitherto uncharacteristic traits of a
soulless bureaucrat. Not only advocates but prosecutors and even court
clerks began saying, "Lubentsova is not the woman she was." After a few
years, people had forgotten the time when an advocate would say to his
client, "You're lucky, Lubentsova is going to try your case—she's a good
judge."

In the first few minutes of this trial I was even more nervous than usual.
For the moment I was defending Larisa Bogoraz and Pavel Litvinov, but
in a few minutes Larisa would announce to the court that she intended to
conduct her own defense. For the first time in my career a client would
decline my services, and although I knew Larisa would make this application with the utmost courtesy, I still could not help feeling a twinge of
wounded self-esteem as well as increased anxiety for her.

Several applications were submitted jointly by all the defendants and
their advocates. We first asked the court to include six new witnesses.
Soviet law does not recognize the concepts of "prosecution witnesses" and
"defense witnesses." The investigator lists in advance which witnesses will
be called to testify. The law requires that those who have been questioned
be called, whether their statements favored the defense or the prosecution.
Leman, Velikanova, Medvedovskaya, Bayeva, Rusakovskaya, and Panova
had been questioned at the preliminary investigation, and had testified in

support of the defendants. Yet the investigator did not include one of them in the list, and it was this omission we asked the judge to correct.

We also petitioned again that the case be remanded for further investigation in order to include in it the case of Viktor Fainberg; that it be remanded also for identification of the individuals who made the arrests and investigation of the legality of their actions.

The court granted Larisa's application to conduct her own defense. Our application to call extra witnesses was partly granted: Leman, Velikanova, and Medvedovskaya were called. All other applications were rejected.

After the indictment was read, the court proceeded to examine the defendants:

Vladimir Dremlyuga, aged twenty-eight. In 1958 he was expelled from the Komsomol for "breaking up a Soviet family, failure to pay his membership dues, and his mustache." (In those days a young man's mustache might easily be regarded as criminal, for mustaches were a manifestation of the corrupting influence of the West.) He was also expelled from Leningrad University, officially on the grounds of "behavior unworthy of a Soviet student." The real reason for his expulsion lay in the following story. Dremlyuga lived in a shared apartment. One of his neighbors was a former KGB official, of whom Dremlyuga was evidently not fond. Dremlyuga got one of his friends to send him a note, care of his ex-KGB neighbor, with the envelope addressed "To Captain Vladimir Dremlyuga, KGB." This childish prank was held to be "discreditable to the State Security forces" and resulted in his expulsion from the university. The official description of Dremlyuga's character also stated that he had been convicted of illegal resale of automobile tires, and that during the search of his room the police had confiscated an impressively long list of amorous conquests.

All that was in the documents. In my memory I can still see Vladimir's face, full of lively interest in everything going on around him; I remember his continual flow of jokes during the court's recess periods and his total absence of despondency or perplexity. I also vividly recall Vladimir, on the second day of the trial, saying to me as he pointed to a couple of really beautiful girls sitting in the courtroom, cousins of one of the defendants, "Don't you think that one is sweet? You don't really think the other one is prettier, do you? Do you know—I'm in love! Don't laugh, I really am in love with her."

Konstantin Babitsky, thirty-nine, had university degrees in both mathematics and linguistics. A research scholar, he had published twelve articles in learned journals. At the time of his arrest, three more of his scholarly works had just been accepted for publication. Babitsky was married and his three children ranged in age from fifteen to ten.

He habitually wore an expression of intense concentration and absorption in his thoughts. He answered questions and gave his testimony with dignity, and he told the court with profound conviction, "You see before you people whose views may differ somewhat from generally accepted attitudes, but who love their country and their people no less, and who therefore have a right to tolerance and respect."

Vadim Deloné, aged twenty-one years. "Unmarried; secondary education; no fixed occupation; one previous conviction."

After his first arrest and trial, Vadim left Moscow and studied at the University of Novosibirsk. There he wrote poetry, for which he was twice awarded prizes. In the summer of 1968 Vadim decided to return to Moscow. On August 12 he received a temporary residence permit. On August 25 he was arrested, still with eight working days left in the permit in which to get a job. In fact he had found one, although there had not been time for it to be officially registered. In spite of this, the investigator had written "no fixed occupation," a statement that would influence the court in determining his sentence.

I had not seen Vadim since September 1, 1967, when he had been released from custody. He had been a boy then, and I had pitied him. Now he was a calm, responsible man, certain of the rightness of what he had done. His style of testifying had changed too. The very structure of his testimony, the words he used, had become more austere; refinement of language and slight theatricality had been replaced by restraint and confidence. What he said sounded no less sincere than before. He had not lost anything—he had gained. And what he had gained was self-respect.

Pavel Litvinov, aged twenty-eight. "Higher education; profession, physicist; no fixed occupation; divorced; dependents, one son, eight years old."

The name Litvinov is widely known in the Soviet Union. Maxim Litvinov, Pavel's grandfather, was one of the most active members of the old, prerevolutionary Bolshevik Party and later became one of the most celebrated Soviet diplomats. For many years he was People's Commissar (Minister) of Foreign Affairs of the USSR; he represented the Soviet Union at the League of Nations and was Soviet ambassador to the USA.

After graduation Pavel worked as a teaching assistant at the Moscow Institute of Chemical Technology. He liked his students and they liked him. But when he became active in the "defense of legality" movement, he was dismissed, and the notoriety that came with his and Larisa's "Appeal to World Public Opinion," as well as direct pressure by the KGB, made it impossible to get another job. Even so, it was quite wrong to call him a man with "no fixed occupation." Working as a private tutor in physics, he earned a modest but independent livelihood.

For a year Pavel had lived under permanent surveillance by KGB agents, who never let him out of their sight. They kept watch around his home, waited for him to come out, shadowed him on the street, in buses, in the subway. They followed him in a specially equipped car if he took a taxi. This is not a secondhand description. I saw the surveillance whenever he came to the law office to see me.

Larisa Bogoraz, at thirty-nine the oldest of all the defendants; a professional scholar with a master's degree.

Larisa is my friend. I know her far better than the other accused. I love her for her gentleness and kindness, her devoted friendship, her readiness to help anyone in need. A person who is ill disposed toward her once said to me, "I agree that she's a brave woman, but she is a bad mother and a bad daughter. Shouldn't she have thought of her son and her old parents?"

Often ill and always terribly alone, Larisa wrote from her distant exile, "I think a great deal about Sanyushka, and I don't just think about him. I remember him and picture him in my mind's eye as he was then, when we were together. You know how it is: one always only remembers the good things. I love him very much, and now I love him with a special mixture of tenderness and pain . . ." And, "I have a big nonprofessional favor to ask of you, Dina, my dear. Do be kind and call up my parents now and again, simply to comfort them, distract them a bit, give them a chance to talk a little about me. I can never get rid of the thought of how hard it must be for them at the moment."

During those first hours of the trial, as I listened to the meager scraps of information the defendants gave about themselves, I thought, "How different they all are; they are not like each other in any way." Yet in the essential points of their testimony they all struck the same notes.

Vladimir Dremlyuga: "I decided to take part in the demonstration long ago, at the very beginning of August. I decided that if Soviet forces entered Czechoslovakia, I would protest . . . Throughout my conscious life I have wanted to be a man who could express his thoughts calmly and proudly. I know that my voice will sound a dissonant note against the background of general silence, which is officially described as 'total popular support for the Party and government.' I am glad there were other people who joined me in expressing their protest. If no such people had appeared, I would have gone to Red Square alone."

Konstantin Babitsky: "Believing that the entry of Soviet forces into Czechoslovakia would above all harm the prestige of the Soviet Union, I felt it necessary to make my convictions known to the government and my fellow citizens. For that reason I went to Red Square at noon on August 25. . . . I went to Red Square fully conscious of what I was doing and aware of the possible consequences."

Vadim Deloné: "On August 21 I heard of the entry of Soviet forces into Czechoslovakia and was indignant at this move by the government . . . It seemed to me that if I failed to express my protest, I would thereby be giving my tacit support to this action. . . . I was not ashamed, and am not ashamed now, of my actions and my participation in the protest against the incursion of Soviet forces into Czechoslovakia."

Pavel Litvinov: "On August 21 Soviet forces crossed the Czechoslovak frontier. I consider this action by the Soviet Government to be a gross violation of international law . . . The verdict of guilty that awaits me is obvious. I was aware long ago of what that verdict would be—even before I went to Red Square. Nevertheless, I went to the Square. For me, the question of whether to go or not to go did not arise."

Larisa Bogoraz: "My action was not impulsive. I acted after careful reflection in full awareness of the consequences of the deed . . . It was the meetings, the radio bulletins and the press reports of universal popular support that drove me to say: 'I am against it, I don't agree.' If I had not done this, I would have felt myself responsible for the government's actions."

If one put these extracts into a single unbroken sequence, I doubt whether anyone could say which remarks belonged to Dremlyuga the Komsomol dropout, and which to Konstantin Babitsky the serious scholar; which to the youthful student Vadim Deloné, and which to Larisa Daniel, the mature, educated woman. The common moral foundation of their exploit somehow equalized these very different people by giving them a unity of viewpoint and a shared style of conduct in court.

The case of the demonstration on Red Square was my third political trial. In the first two the KGB succeeded in setting some of the accused against the others. In the Red Square case, despite the different levels of maturity and education of the participants, I could not attribute superiority in courage, steadfastness, or integrity to any one over any other. Among the defendants there were no leaders and no led. None of them gave way to doubt or repentance; each was prepared to share the fate of the others. This made the trial of the Red Square demonstrators very special in the history of Soviet political prosecutions.

On the first day the court sat from 9:00 A.M. to 7:30 P.M. The second day was no easier: 10:00 A.M. to 10:45 P.M.—almost thirteen hours of intensive work in an overfilled, unventilated courtroom. Every two or two and a half hours there was a ten-minute recess. For Sophia Kallistratova and me the recess meant the longed-for chance for a cigarette, but often there was not even a moment for that. The recess was a time in which the court allowed us to talk to our clients, a time when the defendants' relatives surrounded us. "How did it go?" "What impression did the witness make?" Innumerable, identical, unanswerable questions.

At the lunch break the court and our opponents were whisked away for lunch while we hastily ate our dry sandwiches in the courtroom. As in most of Moscow's courthouses there was no canteen. We did not pity ourselves when we thought of our clients, because during the trial, no matter what time the hearing was to begin, they were escorted out of their cells at 6:00 A.M., missing breakfast. For lunch they ate bread too, but it was black and stale. Sometimes they had a bit of sausage, if they had managed to save some from their parcels, those five kilograms they could receive once a month.

After a day like this, I would get home tired and hungry. As soon as I arrived, the phone calls began. It was impossible to count how many there were that first evening. Close friends would say, "Dina, my dear, I know you're very tired, just tell me in a few words—how is it going?" My acquaintances: "Dina Isaakovna, forgive me for disturbing you, I know how tired you must be. But in just a few words—how is it going?" And friends of my friends and friends of my clients: "How was it? How did the first day go?"

Later, night after night, when everyone else was asleep, I would sit in the kitchen, drinking black coffee, smoking, playing solitaire. Mentally I was back in the courtroom, seeing the faces of the witnesses and even hearing their voices, in an out-of-sequence rerun of the shots from today's film that had touched me on the raw.

"Witness, tell the court where you work and what your duties are."

"I disallow that question. The witness need not answer it." Thus Judge Lubentsova disallowed the question which in normal trials begins the examination of witnesses.

The same question was put in turn to witnesses Dolgov and Ivanov, of Military Unit No. 1164.

"Witness Dolgov, when you were in Red Square on August 25 did you see any of your acquaintances or professional colleagues?"

"No."

"Have you any acquaintances among the witnesses called to testify in this court?"

"No."

"Do you know Ivanov?"

"No."

"Do you know Vesyolov, Bogatyryov, or Vasiliev?"

"No."

He stood before the court with his head slightly turned toward us. He knew that the judge, the prosecutor, and the advocates were perfectly aware that he was lying, but he was quite unperturbed. Every time he said "No" he smiled at the advocates in a way that was almost disarming in its blatant effrontery. The smile said, "You don't have to believe me if you don't want to. But there's nothing you can do about it." And Judge Lubentsova said nothing.

"Witness Ivanov, do you know witness Dolgov?"

"Of course. We work together."

"And does witness Dolgov know you?"

"Of course. I know him and he knows me."

"Do you also know witness Vasiliev?"

"Yes."

"And witness Bogatyryov?"

"Yes, I know him too."

"Did you see these acquaintances of yours on Red Square on August 25?"

"No. I saw none of them."

Dolgov's smile was now saying: "Even before questioning Ivanov you knew I was lying. But he isn't telling the truth either. He will never say he saw me on the square, and the others won't admit it either. No need to worry."

Lubentsova was skilled at cross-examination. She loved the drama of tense courtroom situations in which by a series of questions she would force a witness to renounce a falsehood and tell the truth. Now she listened calmly to these mutually exclusive sets of answers and did not turn on the witness with her usual: "How are we to reconcile your testimony with that given by witness Ivanov?" "Which of you is telling the court the truth, witness? Which one of you are we to believe?"

For the defense counsel and the accused it was important to prove that Dolgov and Ivanov were lying, at least in this part of their evidence, in order to undermine confidence in the rest of their testimony. We needed to be able to say to the court that they were untrustworthy witnesses and that it was impossible to base the prosecution case on their testimony. But the fight to achieve this also had more far-reaching grounds than tactical advantage.

The defense was striving to prove that Dolgov, Vesyolov, Ivanov, and the others were officials of the KGB or the Ministry of Internal Affairs (that is, the police). The procuracy and the judge were trying zealously to conceal it. That a witness works for the KGB or the police by no means discredits his testimony. In most criminal cases the verdicts rest wholly or mainly on evidence given by uniformed policemen or plainclothes officials of the Criminal Investigation Department. Nothing, it would seem, prevented the witnesses from saying to the court, "Yes, we are officials of the KGB (or police officers). We saw that public order was being violated in Red Square and we arrested the offenders." Or even more truthfully they could have said, "We carried out the arrests on the direct orders of our superior officers in the KGB," and they could have named those officers, the people whose identity the defense lawyers had tried to elicit by a pretrial application and a second application to the court.

To have admitted all that, however, would have been tantamount to admitting that the Soviet state, as represented by its security forces, regarded a peaceful demonstration by silent, seated people as a crime. The state did not want to acknowledge this openly, preferring to lay the apparent responsibility, with its criminally violent method of dispersing the demonstration, upon "ordinary Soviet citizens." The authorities were trying both to protect themselves against tiresome accusations from the West that the Soviet state was violating the constitutional rights of its citizens and, at the same time, to make the dispersal of the demonstration by "ordinary citizens" seem an example of the "Soviet people's unanimous approval of the policy of the Communist Party and Soviet government." The state demanded that the court convict the demonstrators in such a way that no one could say, "They were convicted for demonstrating." The whole prosecution case was subordinated to that task, and the trial was conducted with that objective.

The contradictions in the testimony of Dolgov and Ivanov occurred because the two men were not well rehearsed. The organizers could not allow this to happen again, and a way out of this awkwardness—a crude, radical, but absolutely watertight solution—was found without delay.

The examination of the remaining KGB witnesses was set for October 10. Throughout that day, as we examined other witnesses, we were aware that the examination of Vesyolov, Vasiliev, and Bogatyryov lay ahead of us. We had prepared for this, discussing our tactics carefully. At last came the moment when only these three were left.

With an almost simultaneous movement we advocates turned the pages of our dossiers to the written records of the pretrial interrogation of these witnesses. Then we heard the calm voice of Judge Lubentsova: "The court informs the prosecution and the defense that witnesses Vesyolov, Bogatyryov, and Vasiliev have been unexpectedly called away from Moscow on official business. The court proposes to discuss with the two sides the question of completing the trial in the absence of these witnesses."

No official of any Soviet organization has the right to prevent a witness from appearing in court. No one would have taken the responsibility of sending three witnesses away on an official mission without special permission to do so. I had to assume that this was engineered by the KGB officers I had seen earlier, when I walked into that "staff conference." It also had to be assumed that this decision had been agreed upon with the officials of the court, for otherwise, being empowered to order the immediate appearance of the witnesses, the judge would have declared it impossible to conclude the trial in their absence.

The defense insisted on asking that these witnesses be called. If it had been an ordinary trial, the court would undoubtedly have granted the application, because incomplete presentation of trial evidence constitutes grounds for quashing the verdict and having the case retried. In the case of the Red Square trial Lubentsova had no fear of this happening; she knew that the Supreme Court of the RSFSR would in any case confirm a verdict of guilty and would overrule any defense objections.

Other contentious problems were solved with equal simplicity and speed.

On August 25 Police Officer Strebkov had been on duty at Red Square in a patrol car. He had arrested Konstantin Babitsky and driven him to the police station. When counsel for the defense discussed the materials in the case before the trial, it did not occur to us that Strebkov would be a favorable witness. We could not have hoped that a police officer would tell the truth. His trial evidence that the demonstration caused no disturbance to traffic was completely unexpected by anyone:

> On August 25 I was carrying out patrol duty on Red Square in a Volga car. At noon I received orders to proceed immediately to the Lobnoye Mesto. That day was one of those on which the public is allowed access to the Lenin Mausoleum and therefore the square was completely closed to normal vehicular traffic. Government cars are allowed to cross Red Square, but that is in another part of the square. The citizens who were arrested and the crowd which had gathered around them were standing well away to one side. If any vehicles had driven out of the Kremlin, the way would have been clear. The crowd would not have obstructed them.

Many other witnesses had given similar evidence at the pretrial investigation. Strebkov, however, was a specialist who by the nature of his work was fully acquainted with the traffic regulations for Red Square. The most valuable passage in his testimony was his statement, which carried the authority of an expert: "Not only was there no obstruction of traffic, but there could not have been."

Now we had to wait for the examination of Kuklin, who was called for the next day, October 10. By cross-examining these two witnesses we would totally refute Kuklin's report, the court's best evidence that the defendants had impeded traffic.

But once again there was an efficient, illegal way out of this dangerous situation. Despite our strenuous objections, the court released Strebkov from any further appearance.

The next day, Kuklin was examined by the advocates and the defendants:

Q. When did you write and hand in your report on the events on Red Square of August 25?
A. The same day, August 25.
Q. Please state more precisely the time at which it was written.
A. In the evening, after my tour of duty.
Q. How do you explain the fact that the report is dated September 3, and not August 25?
A. That is the date of the second report.
Q. Why did you write two reports about the same set of events?
A. The first report was incomplete.
Q. Where is the first report?
A. I don't know. I gave it to my superior officer. Later I was told he had passed it on to the investigator.
Q. Did you write the second report on your own initiative or did someone else suggest that you should do so?
A. My superior officer told me that I had to add something more to the first report to make it complete.
Q. What were you told to add to the first report?
A. That the most important factor in this case was the obstruction of traffic.
Q. When were you told of the need to supplement your first report?
A. I wrote the second report as soon as I was told to, that is, on September 3.

The transcript contains an added note: "At the request of the defense, the court confirms that the interrogation of witness Kuklin at the preliminary investigation is dated September 27, 1968."

Kuklin's testimony had totally discredited the statement in his September 3 report: "This group was impeding the free movement of traffic." In these circumstances, both the defense and the judge should have called for the original document, the report Kuklin wrote from his own observation on August 25. Under Soviet law, all such primary documentation must be included in the case materials. This guarantees to the court and to the two sides the opportunity to make an independent analysis of the contents of such documents. In "economic" cases (fraud, embezzlement, illegal trading, and the like) these documents include invoices, receipts, orders, estimates; in cases of bodily harm or murder, they include medical histories, test results, autopsy reports, pathologists' reports. In our case, Kuklin's first report was such a primary document. Again, however, the court ruled:

"The application of the defense to produce Inspector Kuklin's report of August 25 is refused, as the court sees no necessity for it."

Because the court was quite deliberately and consistently favoring the prosecution case, there remained only one method of defense: to subject the prosecution evidence to scrutiny and criticism.

The most important element of my own technique for analyzing testimony is to "forget"—to forget the witness's outward appearance and tone of voice; to forget everything that constitutes the emotional impact of a piece of testimony, everything that arouses sympathy or antipathy. This is the way I stop myself from giving overhasty credence to the testimony of a favorable witness and from overhasty rejection of the evidence of "enemies."

So it was in this case. I forced myself to overcome my distaste for the prosecution witnesses, to forget the openly mocking tone in which Dolgov replied to my questions, to forget the features of witness Davidovich, whose scarred face made him look like a sadistic gangster. Forgetting enabled me to see that there was nothing really damaging in the evidence given by these pillars of the prosecution.

The force of their statements derived not from facts but from opinions: "The behavior of these individuals was disgraceful," "They behaved in a provocative manner," "Like all the other citizens present, I was indignant at their rude and insolent behavior." Yet the court's duty is to evaluate testimony on the strength of the facts conveyed by the witness. And whether the court does or not, I must mentally cleanse the evidence of everything irrelevant, retaining only what directly answers the questions at hand—in this case, whether the defendants violated public order and whether the normal movement of traffic was obstructed.

Courtroom testimony of witness Dolgov: "I saw all the members of this group. They were holding banners in their hands. A crowd was gathering. The people around the group were growing indignant and shouting insults at them. When I arrested them, I was not aware of any of them putting up a resistance. Some cars drove up to the Lobnoye Mesto, into which the arrestees were put."

Courtroom testimony of witness Ivanov: "I saw a crowd on Red Square. I ran over to the Lobnoye Mesto. A crowd of about thirty people had gathered around them. The people were angry and indignant. I helped to put Dremlyuga into a car. He resisted by refusing to move."

Courtroom testimony of witness Davidovich: "They were seated around the Lobnoye Mesto and holding up slogans of a provocative character. For two or three minutes they addressed the crowd with speeches as if they were at a political meeting. One of the seated people said he was ashamed of our government. I helped to put one of them into a car, and he resisted."

There was another prosecution witness, whose objectivity the prosecutor was sure to stress; he was not an "official of military unit No. 1164," and he was not a policeman, but simply one of those who were genuinely indignant at the demonstration. Courtroom testimony of witness Fedoseyev: "They were sitting around the Lobnoye Mesto waving provocative slogans. Some cars drove up and they were made to sit in them. One of the arrested men [Fainberg] had a bloodstained face. As he was being put into a car, he shouted: 'Down with the government of tyrants!' Apart from that, another one said he was ashamed of our government. I heard nothing more. The people sitting down said nothing in response to the indignant remarks of the crowd."

This was the testimony of the most hostile witnesses, in its worst possible form for the defendants, in the form in which it lay before the members of the court as they passed sentence. On the other hand, much of what these witnesses said under cross-examination was not recorded. This was no chance omission. As the transcript is being made, the judge not only supervises the clerk's recording of testimony but also checks the whole record, giving instructions on what is to be added or deleted. Sometimes on the judge's orders the clerk will rewrite whole pages of the transcript.

In our case, all links to the KGB were deleted from the transcript.

Like most lawyers, I kept my own, unofficial record of trial proceedings. In my private record I noted the following:

Strebkov: "At the police station to which I drove citizen Babitsky, I saw the citizen who brought in the banner with the words 'Hands off Czechoslovakia.' He introduced himself as an official of the KGB. I saw him on Red Square on August 25." Davidovich: "Officials of an operational group of the KGB took part in making the arrests. They were all in civilian clothes. One of them showed his identity card."

Neither of these two pieces of testimony was officially recorded. In addition, the transcript contained conscious distortions of other testimony. Whenever a witness stated confidently that there was no traffic in Red Square that Sunday, the transcript read, "I did not see any cars passing, but there was a large crowd, and I might have failed to notice the traffic." "I did not hear them saying anything, but it was noisy, and they might have been speaking when I was not aware of it," replaced "The defendants said nothing."

Such falsifications of the record greatly degraded the value to us of testimony from the more objective witnesses. Despite this, however, I came to the firm conclusion that the testimony of the prosecution witnesses, even in the form in which it was recorded in the transcript, did not in fact add up to proof that the defendants had committed a crime.

My method of preparing for the defense—the method of alienation or standing aside—has not turned me into an unfeeling robot in court. I have always listened with trust and sympathy to testimony that favored my client, I have always felt inwardly indignant as I listened to the prosecution witnesses; afterward, however, by an effort of will I could forget who was "friend" and who was "foe," and squeeze out of their testimony, drop by drop, facts and only facts. This difficult process of categorizing and separating out sense data gives very short-lived results. After that, the emotional and factual material usually merges back into a whole. But I don't believe there will ever come a time when I forget either what Babitsky's wife, Tatyana Velikanova, said at this trial or how she said it: "They did not react even when people started beating them up. They just sat there without raising their heads. They did not resist when they were kicked. It was as though they were not there, as though they were in another world . . . I was amazed to see how my husband and his companions were able to restrain themselves and not show resistance."

At this point I lowered my head so that no one would notice my emotion as I listened to her story, the story of a woman whose husband was beaten up before her eyes, yet who was able to hold back from intervening and defending him. She was consciously fulfilling her self-imposed role as an impartial eye-witness, so that at the trial, which she knew to be inevitable, she could tell the truth. As she spoke, even the hostile noise from those officially planted members of the public quieted down, and there was a silence in which her dignified words rang out clearly, unaffected by fear, unchanged from her statement to the investigator: "I did not think I had the right to try and dissuade him. He acted in accordance with his conscience and his beliefs."

The prosecutor had not, of course, intended to produce this effect. A copy of Tatyana Velikanova's interrogation lay in front of him and he was mechanically asking the same questions. The effect produced by Tatyana's answer was so unexpected and incomprehensible to him that he was momentarily reduced to silence, and her statement remained in the record. Even now I can find practically nothing else to say about that prosecutor, except that he had an unpleasant, grating voice and possessed the unusual name of Drel, (a Russianized form of the English word "drill" and meaning "hand drill" or "brace"). After the trial, when colleagues asked about it, I had plenty to say about the defendants, the members of the court, and the advocates, but nothing at all about the prosecutor. He never asked a new, relevant question, merely repeating the questions the investigator had asked before him.

And so the long, high-pressure days of the trial sped by until October

10, when, at the end of the lunch break but before the public was back in the courtroom, I was standing alone in the empty corridor. Nikolai Osetrov, chairman of the Moscow City Court bench, came out of the office in which the headquarters staff was in session and headed toward the judges' little consultation room. He stopped, hesitated, and then came up to me:

"It's a good thing the hearing hasn't recommenced," he said. "I want to warn you and ask you to tell the other advocates that the final speeches for the prosecution and the defense will be heard today." Then, as though anticipating my objections, he added, "We cannot put it off."

A whole series of witnesses remained to be examined, after which the defense intended to submit several supplementary applications. Apart from that, we all needed time to prepare our speeches. Nevertheless, "The hearing will be finished today. The court will declare a short recess that will give you a reasonable amount of time to prepare. I think you advocates should find two hours quite sufficient. Don't argue, comrade advocate," Osetrov added sternly, and strode off to give the new orders to the judge.

The next person to give me this news was Apraksin, head of the Moscow College of Advocates. Emerging from headquarters just after Osetrov had gone, he did not know that it was no longer news to me. As I listened to him I thought, Don't they both realize this is indecent? Has the habit of condoning Party interference become so ingrained that they don't even bother to conceal it?

Apraksin also told me that a stenographic record of the defense speeches would be made, and that shorthand writers had already been assigned. "Be careful," he said. "Think carefully about every word, every phrase. You bear a responsibility to the whole college."

To prepare a complete transcript of the defense speeches in a trial is very unusual. Ordinarily only summaries of prosecutors' and defense attorneys' speeches are entered in the trial records. In this case, I was not surprised to learn of the complete transcript. I had known that the defense attorneys were being watched attentively by the Party leadership.

When I reproached Apraksin for not warning the advocates earlier, he admitted frankly that he had only just heard about it himself. Clearly the decision to accelerate the trial was even more of a surprise to Lubentsova, Osetrov, and Apraksin than it was to us.

The hearing resumed; it consisted mainly of the rapid process of refusing all our applications, after which the first phase of the trial was declared closed and the recess was called.

We advocates seated ourselves in various corners of the courtroom; one sat writing at a table, another perched on a bench and stacked his papers on a window ledge. I paced up and down the corridor. Osetrov was right in part. Mentally we had long ago prepared the main lines of our defense speeches. At the kitchen table, like me, or lying sleepless in bed, each of us had been silently testing our arguments and thinking over our wording, so that we would not let the speech run away with us beyond the bounds of the political censorship.

The prosecutor in a case of this kind had an extremely simple job if he chose to make a demagogic, propagandist speech, and an extremely difficult, not to say impossible, one if he tried to make a serious legal analysis of the evidence. Our prosecutor did not attempt the second course. In accusing the defendants, in the name of the state, of violating public order and defaming the social system, he spoke of "subversive activities of international imperialism and, first and foremost, of the USA"; of international imperialism's "campaign of anti-Soviet propaganda in connection with the Soviet Union's rendering of fraternal aid to Czechoslovakia." Bourgeois propaganda was spreading "slanders directed against the Soviet Union." A significant proportion of the speech was devoted to stressing that during the Second World War the Soviet Army had liberated Czechoslovakia from the fascist aggressors, and that slogans such as "Long live free and independent Czechoslovakia" or "For your freedom and for ours" were an outrage to the memory of the Soviet soldiers who died in those battles.

The prosecutor accomplished his duty to prove the charges in two sentences: "There is no need to prove that the slogans on these banners were of an obviously defamatory nature . . ." and: "The Soviet press has explained to all citizens the progressive nature of the Soviet government's actions and it is impossible not to be aware of this . . ." He also said that the term "demonstration" was a misnomer. He acknowledged that the Constitution guaranteed Soviet citizens the freedom to demonstrate, but he insisted (and in this he was absolutely right) that the Party and Soviet government recognized as "demonstrations" only those organized and sanctioned by the authorities.

This whole farrago of demagogic phrases and political slogans would have been normal at a political meeting. In court, even in a political case, one expects something more. Lubentsova was visibly disappointed. She listened to the "legal" part of the prosecutor's speech with an expression of unconcealed contempt, annoyed, no doubt, that she herself would be obliged to rectify his scandalous mistakes, which included mixing up Articles 190/1 and 190/3.

Finally the prosecutor proposed the sentences that should be awarded. Everyone froze into stillness, since the state was now speaking through the obedient mouth of Prosecutor Drel.

After listing all the "moral defects" of the defendants, to whom the

Soviet state had given "everything" and who, instead of trusting the Soviet press and Soviet radio, had "drawn their mendacious information from murky foreign sources," he went on: "Taking into consideration that Litvinov, Babitsky, and Bogoraz have no previous criminal convictions . . . I ask the court, in awarding sentence, to apply Article 43 of the Criminal Code of the RSFSR . . ."

Turning my head very slightly, I saw Larisa's eyes opened wide in astonishment and heard a deep sigh from someone in the courtroom. The advocates exchanged looks of perplexity, as for a fraction of a second each of us thought, Why Article 43, which entitles the court to give a less severe punishment than Article 190? What less punishment could there be than the minimum in Article 190, a fine of up to 100 rubles?

But the prosecutor was continuing: ". . . Litvinov, Pavel Mikhailovich, five years; Bogoraz, Larisa Iosifovna, four years; Babitsky, Konstantin Iosifovich, three years . . . of internal exile. Taking their previous convictions into account, I ask the court to sentence Dremlyuga, Vladimir Alexandrovich, and Deloné, Vadim Nikolaevich, to three years' deprivation of liberty each."

I was unable to make sense of this extraordinary proposal, hitherto unknown in Soviet law, whereby a request for mitigation of sentence was combined with an increase of the sentence to the maximum permitted under the "mitigating" article. Yet even as I heard Lubentsova say, "The court gives the floor to Advocate Kaminskaya to speak in defense of the defendant Litvinov," and as I stood up and slowly pushed away the notes which I never need when actually making a speech, I could not stop thinking: Internal exile for Larisa, Pavel, and Konstantin! Why, that's almost happiness!

Rereading the defense summations convinces me once again that it is impossible to do justice to a courtroom speech outside the courtroom. What a pity! Ours were excellent examples of forensic oratory. In this trial, the advocates as much as the defendants were united by a magnificent sense of solidarity, by readiness to help one another and an unqualified respect for our clients. Our aims were "lofty" too, and our speeches reflected this. Each of us found convincing arguments for refuting the indictment, and I believe I can say that thanks to the combined efforts of the defense, the legal untenability of the prosecution case was proved up to the hilt.

Describing my own speech is difficult. To praise oneself is immodest, to chastise oneself unpleasant. No doubt the speech contained both virtues and shortcomings. I spoke first, and that alone put me under an obligation to speak for the defense as a whole, so I concentrated primarily on a legal analysis of the prosecution case. The hardest task was to restrain myself. I fully shared the views of the defendants; like them, I regarded the incursion into Czechoslovakia as aggression. When I learned about the entry of Soviet forces into Czechoslovakia, I too had felt that one must shout, "Shame!" They had been able to do it; I had not. Thus in making my defense plea I felt an overwhelming need to express my own attitude. I had never before felt this need, or rather its pressure on me, with such force. When preparing my speech, I totally excluded the possibility of allowing this to show, in however concealed or camouflaged a form. The impetus to do so came from the prosecutor's speech.

His ceaseless repetition of a theme I found particularly detestable— "We shed our blood for them, while they . . ."; "We brought them their freedom, but they . . ."—aroused my urge to protest. As if the reward for freedom should be slavery! As if the way of showing gratitude for it had to be acceptance of oppression!

I answered the prosecutor as follows:

> I fully associate myself with that part of the prosecutor's speech in which he spoke of the great services rendered by the Soviet people and the Soviet Army. In those hard years of the Great Patriotic War, our people and our soldiers had every right to raise the slogan: "For your freedom and for ours" . . . I personally consider that the slogan "For your freedom and for ours" can never, under any circumstances, be regarded as defamatory. I shall always continue to say, "For your freedom and for ours," because I think the greatest human happiness is the good fortune to live in a free country . . .

That passage was appreciated by some of those who heard it in a way that is impossible to convey in writing. There was a long pause after the words: "In those hard years of the Great Patriotic War, our people and our soldiers had every right to raise the slogan: 'For your freedom and for ours' . . ." It was a pause I had not planned or anticipated. My voice suddenly broke off because of inner stress I experienced at that moment, and my hearers understood me even though the thought was not spelled out in full. Indeed, my fellow advocates and the defendants told me so at the time. Even a member of the KGB's "public" heard my message.

After all the speeches for the defense, the session was declared closed until next morning, and I stood leaning on the barrier that divided the accused from the rest of the courtroom, watching the people go out. A man among them, whom I had noticed before, was looking at me with a hatred that was, no doubt, as irrepressible as my own emotions had been.

As he drew level with me, he stopped and said very clearly: "Ah, you . . . shit!"

Larisa cried, "How dare you! How dare you insult an advocate that way!"

One of the other defendants called on the chief guard to arrest this man.

Someone demanded that he be given a summons. I was neither annoyed nor offended. The man had obviously taken my meaning.

There were others, too. That evening—or rather that night, because it was eleven o'clock before the session finished—two men came up to me. They were reporters from two Moscow newspapers, specially assigned to cover this trial. They gave me their names, which I still remember, just as I have remembered what they said to me, because it was so strange to hear it coming from Soviet journalists. "This is not the first political trial we've covered. We've been at all the other trials in which you defended. No doubt you blame us for writing about them. That's why we wanted to tell you that we aren't going to write about this trial. You won't see any pieces in the papers under our names. We realize what kind of people the defendants are."

Many years later, when my husband and I were leaving the Soviet Union, one of these journalists sent word to us. After a serious heart attack he had been in a hospital ward with an advocate we knew well, and had learned that I was disbarred and about to leave the country. When my friend left the hospital he immediately telephoned. "He was so insistent that I pass on to you his gratitude and respect, that I'm doing so on my first day back home."

The third day of the trial was taken up by the "last words" of the accused, after which the court retired to consider its verdict.

The only people left in the courtroom were the defendants, the guards, and the advocates. By now the guards were treating us considerably more liberally than before, and we talked to our clients almost without restriction. The conversation was no longer about legal matters—all professional topics had been exhausted. Later, when the time came to lodge appeals, we would again be talking (or rather exchanging written notes) professionally; again there would be the journeys to Lefortovo, the waiting for an obviously empty office to become available, the chance for Pavel to read between the lines of my Notice of Appeal: "Pavel my dear, we all love you and send you our best wishes and greetings."

But on that final day of the trial the lawyers clustered around the wooden barrier and laughed with the people who over those three days had become our closest friends. I was now smiling tenderly not only at Larisa and Pavel but also at Konstantin Babitsky, whom I had never seen before the trial and whose acquaintance I didn't manage to sustain afterward. I particularly remember a lively argument about some special kind of cake, unknown to me, which Vadim Deloné insisted I must try at once. I also remember that, disregarding the guard's halfhearted "Comrade advocate, you mustn't talk to him, he's not your client," I congratulated Vadim on the magnificent delivery of his "last words," and how especially handsome, even radiantly handsome he looked when he said, "I know that for five minutes of freedom in Red Square I may have to pay with years of imprisonment."

All the defendants had spoken their "last words" splendidly. It was in these, more than in the testimony I have quoted above, that each of them best expressed their individuality. Now as then I could not say who was the best. Personally, I had the greatest identification with the words Babitsky addressed to the court: "I respect the law and I believe in the exemplary role of judicial decisions. I call upon you to reflect on what instructive effect a verdict of guilty will have and what the effect of an acquittal will be. What ethical lessons do you want to instill? Respect and tolerance for other people's views, or hatred and the urge to suppress and humiliate any person who thinks differently?"

During that recess I had another conversation with Apraksin, an illustration of the variety of problems our behind-the-scenes headquarters staff had to solve. It happened that when Apraksin entered the courtroom, none of the other advocates were there. He called me aside and said in a low voice that the defendants could not hear, "It went off OK. The people 'up there' (he pointed at the ceiling) were not too pleased with your speeches, but there won't be any unpleasant consequences. So you can consider yourselves in the clear." Interestingly, this extremely rapid reaction to our speeches by the Party's top brass meant that our speeches had not only been taken down in shorthand but transmitted direct to the Central Committee building by concealed microphones.

Apraksin went on in a louder voice, "Don't leave the courthouse immediately after the verdict. You'll all be taken home by car—we know how tired you must be."

"Why today and not yesterday, when the session lasted till nearly midnight?" I asked. "And in exactly what cars are they proposing to drive us home?"

"Cars have already been ordered for each one of you, so you won't even have to wait."

His persuasiveness was wasted; I had already made up my mind. "I will not ride in one of *their* cars." In answer to Apraksin's look of astonishment I added, "We are defense counsel. We are separate from *them*, and it would be indecent to drive away in KGB cars."

My colleagues, who were coming back into the courtroom at that moment, also refused to accept the KGB's kind offer. Apraksin went out, but returned only a few minutes later.

"Perhaps you're right," he said. "Maybe it's better if you don't go in these cars. But whatever happens, you must wait awhile in the courthouse before leaving." Again he dropped his voice. "Leave the courtroom one by one, not in a group, and go out by the back door, so that the foreign journalists won't see you. And no interviews—remember, no interviews."

"In the name of the Russian Soviet Federated Socialist Republic. On October 11, 1968 . . ."

How stupid that those words still had such a solemn ring to my ears; how stupid that I still expected something from this court, which had made no independent judgments and never could. My colleagues and I sat waiting, keyed up with tension, as though it were a real court, as though there might be some hope, yet also knowing that in a few minutes I would be suffering the full bitterness of disappointment.

After the verdict, sentences were pronounced: Litvinov, five years' internal exile; Bogoraz, four years; Babitsky, three years; Dremlyuga and Deloné, imprisonment. All exactly as expected.

The verdict read by Judge Lubentsova corresponded precisely to the obligations the Party authorities had laid upon the court. The word "demonstration" was never once mentioned. Every scrap of evidence favoring the accused, every argument put up by the defense was ruthlessly ignored. And although Lubentsova used all her skill to eliminate the prosecutor's clumsy attribution of the charges to the wrong articles of the law, her efforts did not make the verdict any more convincing than the original indictment.

This failed attempt to give the verdict at least the appearance of legal respectability was a function of Lubentsova's characteristic professionalism, like her attitude to the advocates and our defense tactics. Thanks to her ingrained "socialist sense of justice" she regarded dissidence as a crime, but she also realized that it is an advocate's job to defend, and she therefore looked upon our work as the legitimate discharge of our professional duty. She showed no irritation or hostility. Indeed, after the verdict she invited all the defense counsel into her consultation room to thank us for our "conscientious and professionally irreproachable participation in this difficult case."

We went out through the main door, as we had decided to do, and were surrounded by the same people who had been standing on the street from morning till late at night for three days. Among them were the foreign journalists, who had kept the same three-day vigil on the street. We were handed bouquets of flowers by people who apologized for their not being big enough or beautiful enough, explaining that the much finer bouquets they originally bought had been stolen.

Only my first political trial, the Bukovsky case, was not accompanied by crowds outside the courthouse. Beginning with my second case, the trial of

Ginzburg and Galanskov, coming to the courthouse had become a tradition not only for friends and relatives of the defendants but for a wide circle of sympathizers. The bouquets also became a traditional sign of gratitude. The Red Square trial, however, brought the greatest number of people I have ever seen outside a courthouse.

Afterward, I heard from many eye-witnesses about what was happening on the street while the trial was in session. Besides KGB plainclothesmen and other security officials, many of whom were already known by sight, there were many workmen from a nearby factory assigned to play the role of the "indignant public." To help them act their parts successfully, they were supplied with free food and vodka at tables set up in a neighboring courtyard.

These drunken, unruly hooligans—men and women—worked in shifts, but there was no difference in the insolence and aggression with which they harassed those whom they unerringly recognized as supporters of the defendants. Policemen and KGB agents listened unmoved to their unprintable abuse, threats of revenge, and anti-Semitic remarks without the slightest attempt to make these "members of the public" see reason or stop the disorder. The flowers for the advocates, bought with voluntary contributions, were stolen by some of this mob, who had (under the eyes of the police) smashed the doors of a car to get them. The people I talked with remembered vividly how these people trampled the flowers into the asphalt so that not a single living petal remained whole. The bouquets we received were bought at the last minute with money raised by passing the hat a second time. Holding them, we were photographed by those foreign journalists whom our masters had tried to prevent us from meeting.

A few days later, Apraksin summoned me to express his displeasure: "I asked you not to go out by the main door and you should have taken account of my request. Now photographs of you holding flowers will be all over the bourgeois newspapers and there will be trouble again."

"And you think, do you, that it would have been more suitable if they published photographs of the advocates scuttling away out of a side door?" I asked. "Personally I don't care for pictures of my back view."

For a few precious days we renewed our meetings in Lefortovo. The appeal was lodged and the Supreme Court confirmed the verdict.

Then I began to get letters from distant Usugli (about 4,500 miles from Moscow), where Pavel was living in exile, and from Larisa in far-off Chuna, which is about 3,500 miles from Moscow. Pavel and Larisa reminisced about our long conversations at Lefortovo in their letters from exile: "That September-October wasn't such a bad time after all, was it? . . . The halva is nothing but a memory, because I can't eat it any more, alas; on these various deportations I have acquired some sort of disease . . ." wrote Larisa. And, "Darling, only a short note for now. I just wanted to talk to you—about nothing really. Just like then, in September."

"My dear lady lawyer! (My neighbor at Lefortovo used to say, 'There's your lady lawyer coming to visit you again.') Thank you for the trial, thank you for the conversations at Lefortovo. Remember?" Pavel Litvinov began his letter.

Yes, I remember. The funny and the sad. The important and the irrelevant. Even the absurdest details are stuck in my mind forever. I remember long talks in unexpected places with Maya Rusakovskaya, which inevitably ended with her asking me to take a letter to Pavel. I stuck these letters inside my file folder and when I was left alone with him he read them surreptitiously. They are still among my case notes, old letters of fourteen years ago that invariably began, "Pavlik, my dearest . . ." After his conviction Maya followed Pavel into exile. There they married, there their daughter was born and named Larisa. Later still, when Larisa and Anatoly Marchenko had a son, they named him Pavel. The bond that had grown between us will never, I think, be broken.

The people who went out to Red Square on August 25, 1968, are now scattered all over the world. Natalya Gorbanevskaya and Vadim Deloné are in France, Viktor Fainberg is in England, Pavel Litvinov and Vladimir Dremlyuga are in America. Larisa Bogoraz is living in Moscow. Her husband, Anatoly Marchenko, was charged with anti-Soviet propaganda and sentenced in 1981 to ten years' imprisonment and five years' internal exile. He is in prison today. Konstantin Babitsky lives in a village in Kostroma Province, where he works as a carpenter. On November 1, 1979, I learned that Tatyana Velikanova had been arrested. After Konstantin's arrest and conviction, Tatyana became an active member of the "defense of legality" movement. She was one of the founders of the Initiative Group for the Defense of Human Rights in the USSR, and in 1974 she and two others publicly announced their responsibility for resuming distribution of the samizdat journal Chronicle of Current Events, despite knowing that the KGB pursued with particular ferocity anyone connected with this journal. She had followed her conscience, her sense of civic duty and human dignity. Tatyana has the kind of moral fearlessness that enables a person to disregard personal well-being for the sake of a high cause. To have tried to dissuade her from taking this chosen path would also have been dishonorable, as well as futile. In August 1980, Tatyana Velikanova was tried and sentenced to four years of imprisonment and five years of internal exile.

Whenever I met these honored friends subsequently, after their release from exile or prison camp—some in Moscow, some in Paris, some in New York—it struck me again what different people they all were, how different their attitudes to many aspects of life. Some of them have grown even dearer and closer to me, others have drifted away. We have argued over many things, but even in the saddest moments of serious disagreements I have always reminded myself, "Remember, this is a person who went to demonstrate in Red Square."

My respect for their exploit has not diminished with the years and will never be erased from my memory.

4. He Sought Neither
Riches nor Fame

L ATE IN THE EVENING of March 27, 1979, I received a telephone call
from an old friend of mine from Moscow days. She had emigrated from
the Soviet Union to the United States several years before, and was due in
Washington that day. She was calling from the airport.

"Have you heard the news?" I shouted, interrupting her explanations
and excuses for getting in so late. "Have you heard? Alik is in New York!
Do you hear me? Alik is in New York!"

Twenty minutes later I was kissing her tear-stained face and telling her
about the prisoner exchange that had taken place that day. Its unexpectedness had overwhelmed us all: two Soviet spies for five prisoners of conscience.

My friend Lyudmila Alexeyeva, the overseas representative of the Moscow Helsinki Group, was probably the only person in America who had not
heard the news. In the hours since the first announcement, when my phone
was ringing incessantly, Lyudmila had been stranded in a remote American
airport waiting for an interminably postponed flight. For her, Alexander
Ginzburg was a comrade in the shared struggle for human rights in the
Soviet Union. For me, Alik's name is linked with memories of the most
difficult, the most painful of all the political cases in which I took part.
Rejoicing for Alik and for all the others who had gained their freedom that
day, I could not help thinking of that far-off year 1967; the office in Lefortovo Prison; the figure of my client, twisted into an extraordinary attitude,
his knees clasped by his hands and pressed to his chin so that the man

seemed to be folded double; his unfailing kindness and sweetness; and the smile with which he tried to hide his suffering.

That was how—at the moment of a sharp spasm of pain from a duodenal ulcer—I first saw my client Yurii Galanskov, the friend and "accomplice" of Alexander Ginzburg, and that was how I remembered him.

I first heard of Yurii Galanskov at the beginning of the 1960s, when a group of young poets, on their own initiative and without official permission, started holding poetry readings in Mayakovsky Square around the statue of Vladimir Mayakovsky. At once everyone began to talk about these readings. They were unique and, for that reason alone, dangerous. Yurii was known as one of the organizers and an indispensable participant. At that time there was no talk of nonconformism as a perceptible current in Soviet cultural and social life. Terms such as "nonconformist artist," "nonconformist poet" came into general use considerably later.

Even then, however, there were writers, artists, and composers whose methods and approaches to their art differed from the conventional state-imposed formula of "socialist realism." In countries with genuinely democratic and pluralist traditions, artistic nonconformity is not likely to bring the artist into conflict with the state. In the Soviet Union, such conflict is inevitable, although it is not necessarily evident on the surface. Much more frequently, I believe, the artist consciously or unconsciously exercises self-censorship over his public work and restricts the area of conflict to his private, most creative work.

I would call Galanskov a nonconformist person whose sphere was not so much poetry as the whole of life. Everything happening in the world affected him in the most immediate manner. He perceived every injustice as a disaster signal, a call for his instant help. Yurii had an innate drive to act only according to his conscience, and in this his reason had no control over his feelings. The combination of these character traits with great independence of judgment meant that from an early age Galanskov was conscious of and opposed to the structure of the Soviet regime and to the atmosphere of lies and social injustice. His awareness made him into an active opponent of that regime.

Yurii was born in 1939 into a family of very humble origins. His mother was a domestic worker, his father a lathe operator. From childhood he lived in poverty, yet he never found it oppressive. He seemed able to do without even the most essential possessions and sums of money. He always found someone who needed the things or the money more than he did. To use such words as "good" and "unselfish" in describing Yurii Galanskov's character one must use them in the most extreme, exaggerated sense. The expression "he's so generous, he'd give you the shirt off his back" applied to

Yurii in its most literal meaning. I don't know whether he was a religious man, but his spiritual purity, his gentleness, and his love of people (especially children) corresponds in my mind to the moral image I have of a true Christian.

After Yurii's conviction and imprisonment I never saw him again. In November 1972, five years and ten months after his arrest, he died in one of the strict-regime camps of the Mordovian region. For all those years, during which he was seldom free of agonizing pain and was slowly dying of hard labor, a chronic ulcer, and legalized starvation, he wrote from the labor camp letter after letter full of love and tender concern for others. Unfortunately, according to camp regulations Yurii was restricted to writing no more than two letters a month.

"Hello, everybody! Hugs, kisses, handshakes to everybody! Dear Mother, dear Father, Timofey Sergeyevich, my two Alenkas,* one of whom is Lena, I constantly think of you, of all my friends and acquaintances. When I go to bed I say, 'Good night, Mother, good night, Lenochka,' and I say 'good night' to everybody I love and respect. Many don't suspect that I carry them in my heart every day."

"Mother dear, I'm not cold, I'm dressed warmly, the stomach doesn't hurt too much, just a little. Don't worry and watch your health. Write more often. I love your letters."

"I got an atropin injection now, and I feel better . . . Mother, dearest, please don't worry . . ."

"Now I'm working, sewing mittens. At about ten o'clock I happened to look out the window. Dear God! I put on a hat, wrapped a scarf around my neck, and ran out. Pink, snow-covered roofs under a golden, sunny sky. I felt so happy. I saw violet smoke rise from the chimneys. In the west the sky had a lilac hue. What sunsets we had early in January—the sky was raspberry-colored! On Christmas Eve I thought of our friends and relatives, of all those dear to us."

"Mother, please bake some tarts (with apples, if you can) and take them to Katya and Mitya.† As many as you can, a whole pan full. Get them some candy, good candy, and small tangerines. Mother, when Katya and Mitya come to see you you must feed them. All right?"

"Hello, Mother, Father, and Lenochka . . . For three or four days I was in the infirmary, and early in September they rushed me to the hospital. Now that I'm in the hospital my health is somewhat better. If it stays like that in camp, I could live . . . Here's the latest: they'll release me tomorrow

* Alena—Yurii's wife, Olga Timofeyeva, and Lena, his sister.
† Small children of Yurii's friends.

—September 25 . . . So be it! If the pain isn't going to be too bad in camp, I could live there, too."

"Mother, you must trim a little Christmas tree for little Yura.* Of course he doesn't understand anything yet, but he'll enjoy it just the same. He'll smile, wave his little arms . . ."

And again from the hospital: "It's night. It's dark. I can hardly see the words. I'm writing by the glimmer of a streetlight through the window, using as support a book by Leopold Stokowski, *Music for All*. It's a nice book. I also have a book of poems by Baudelaire . . . I could grab only these two. Without books it's so boring. It's so boring to be alone, without the fellows. Only Misha Sado comes to see me at night. I would make him some coffee, but I have no coffee. I gave my ration to Yurka Ivanov, he'll have a hard time without coffee in Saransk." †

For himself Yurii asked only for books—poetry, psychology, biology, genetics, demography, logic—and more vitamin pills: "Buy them for me as often as you can. They're cheap." Reading all his letters, one could easily get the impression that his pain was bearable, that life, as he put it, "goes on its usual way, despite circumstances—as indeed, it should."

> To: The International Red Cross
> Commission for Human Rights
>
> APPEAL
> I was arrested on January 19, 1967. This is my sixth year in prison. I suffer from duodenal ulcer. I am able to eat only a small portion of the prison food, so that I am permanently undernourished. At the same time, due to the rules of the 'strict regime' prison camp I am effectively unable to receive the food I need from my family and relatives. As I am in permanent, extreme pain, I do not sleep enough. I have now been short of food and short of sleep for over five years, added to which I have had to do hard physical labor for eight hours a day. Every day I live in agony, every day is a struggle against pain and sickness. I have been fighting for my life for five years. . . .

Yuri was still writing his loving, thoughtful, totally uncomplaining letters to his family. The people who shared his family letters in 1972 were reassured—there remained, after all, only two years until his release. Yurii knew there was no hope; he knew what awaited him, and he spelled it out in the last lines of his appeal:

* The son of Yurii's sister Lena, born after Yurii was convicted and named in his honor.
† The letters are quoted from the book *Y. Galanskov: Poet i chelovek*. Possev Verlag, Frankfurt-am-Main, 1973.

The remaining two years of my sentence will kill me. I cannot remain silent, for not only my health but my life is threatened.

Yurii Galanskov
February 1972

On November 4, 1972, Yurii was killed. The people who held Galanskov's life in their hands have no right to say that he died of his illness.

The deputy chairman of the Moscow City Court bench, Lev Mironov, who on orders from higher authority sentenced Yurii to seven years of strict-regime prison camp, knew that this sick man could not survive. He knew that he was condemning Yurii to death in the camps. The camp administrators who ordered Galanskov to carry out the normal stint of forced labor knew that they were demanding the impossible. The camp doctors, who refused to certify him as unfit for work or to prescribe a special diet and medicines for him, knew they were refusing him the means of staying alive.

In June 1971, Galanskov's parents submitted an appeal for clemency to the Presidium of the Supreme Soviet of the RSFSR. They wrote of the sharp deterioration of his health, of how "when we go to visit him in the camp we can see the agony he is suffering. He cannot eat, cannot even talk to us. If he is not released at once, we fear that Yurii will not survive the two years to the end of his sentence and he will die in the camp."

The Presidium of the Supreme Soviet refused to consider the appeal of Ekaterina and Timofei Galanskov.

Seven political prisoners who were in the camp with Galanskov sent an appeal to Roman Rudenko, Procurator General of the USSR, eight months before Yurii's death. They wrote that Galanskov was not receiving competent medical attention and that he was not released from hard physical labor even during acute crises of his illness. "Frequently," they wrote, "he is unable to sleep for several nights in a row due to his terrible pain, and he is unable to eat for days at a time. What is more, he does not get the necessary medication." They concluded by predicting Galanskov's premature death. He was "slowly perishing before our eyes."

When the Procurator General received that letter, in March 1972, it would still have been possible to save Yurii. This was not done. He was killed slowly, methodically, and deliberately. He was thirty-three years old.

He was my client in a case involving criminal charges against him and Alexander Ginzburg, Alexei Dobrovolsky, and Vera Lashkova. They were accused of anti-Soviet activity (Article 70 of the Criminal Code of the RSFSR), but unlike the other political cases I have described, this case was based on separate actions of each of the four defendants. Each was charged with a separate offense, not always connected with the activities of the other accused.

Alexander Ginzburg was charged with compiling and sending for publication in the West a collection of materials known as the *White Book* on the 1966 trial of the two Soviet writers Andrei Sinyavsky and Yulii Daniel. Alexei Dobrovolsky's offense was keeping at his home and distributing among his friends anti-Soviet brochures and attempting to duplicate a series of *samizdat* works. Yurii Galanskov was accused of editing an uncensored literary journal entitled *Phoenix 66*, which included articles of an anti-Soviet nature. Vera Lashkova was charged with having typed for Ginzburg and Galanskov the materials that made up the *White Book* and *Phoenix 66*.

In addition—and this was the principal charge against them—it was alleged that Ginzburg and Galanskov maintained illegal links with an émigré political organization based in West Germany, the Narodno-Trudovoy Soyuz, or National Labor Union. The NTS openly called for the overthrow of the Soviet regime and its replacement by a new political and economic system founded on the principles of a political doctrine known as "solidarism."

Galanskov, like my other clients in political cases, was a convinced opponent of violence. His weapons in the struggle to democratize Soviet society were always words; the method of his struggle the open expression of ideas. His targets were oppression and social injustice. Not one of the charges accused him of committing acts that were immoral or dishonorable. I can assert that with certainty, even though Yurii was found guilty not only of an "especially grave crime against the state"—anti-Soviet activity —but of the illegal sale of foreign currency, a criminal act that is generally motivated by pure greed. Furthermore, I make this assertion despite the fact that the Galanskov case was the only political trial in which I did not ask the court for the complete acquittal of my client.

When I referred to this case as the most painful of all my political cases, I was alluding to the contradiction between "He has not done anything bad, harmful or immoral" and "He broke the law."

As I studied the case, I envied my friend and colleague Boris Zolotukhin, who was defending Alexander Ginzburg. Ginzburg's whole behavior under investigation and in court, the consistency and logic of his testimony, provided invaluable material for argument, particularly in relation to the central episode of the charges against him. Just as I had said to the court, "Yes, Bukovsky did this, but it is not a crime," so Ginzburg's advocate could say, "In this trial it is my privilege to defend an innocent man."

As Galanskov's defense counsel I did not have this privilege. I could say the word "acquit," and without serious risk to myself, in connection with the gravest charge against Galanskov—his links with NTS, its alleged supply to him of coding equipment, and the duplication and distribution of anti-Soviet literature. I was able to affirm that this charge was not proven, but I could not echo Galanskov's own words by saying, "Yes, he sold dollars, but that is not a crime, because the law forbidding the sale of foreign currency is an unjust law."

I could say in court that Galanskov's editing of *Phoenix 66* did not per se infringe Soviet law; I could also, to some extent, argue with the prosecution's characterization of articles in it as anti-Soviet. But I had no right to contest the anti-Soviet nature of one of the articles—Sinyavsky's essay "What Is Socialist Realism?"—or to maintain that its publication in Galanskov's symposium did not break the law. The Supreme Court of the RSFSR had ruled in the Sinyavsky case that the essay was anti-Soviet, and for the Moscow City Court, a verdict of the Supreme Court has the automatic force of law. As a lawyer I was bound by this ruling.

I sought a way out of the situation when I was preparing for the trial, and reflected on it as I mentally tested the correctness of my position. For years afterward this question gave me no peace, and I am still wracked by the impossibility of finding a solution which would reconcile my outlook as a professional lawyer with my conscience. My colleagues too believed an advocate could not ignore the law, and that in consequence I was not entitled to request a complete acquittal for Galanskov. The majority thought I should offer Galanskov a choice: he could either plead guilty on the counts that were incontestable or conduct his own defense. My colleagues argued, very reasonably, that when a defendant does not plead guilty, the standpoint of the advocate who refuses to plead for acquittal would always be perceived as a betrayal.

"Don't you see, the layman will never take account of the limitations imposed on someone who is a lawyer rather than a speaker at a political meeting? No one has the right to require us to submit to such undeserved humiliation. You must make it clear to Galanskov that once he has admitted doing these things, then the only logical conclusion is to plead guilty. You will not be acting against your conscience if you persuade him to enter a plea of guilty, just as Dobrovolsky and Lashkova have done."

Of course I worried about my reputation. I was far from indifferent to the way my position would be judged by all the people who were following this case carefully, and I would have felt much happier if Galanskov had pleaded guilty, thereby admitting the correct legal status of the acts which he did not deny having committed. I agreed that the logical conclusion in a conflict between a defendant who denies guilt and an advocate who cannot contest his client's guilt is the withdrawal of the advocate's services. I felt it impossible, however, to face Galanskov with the choice of either pleading guilty or conducting his own defense. I also knew I could not persuade him to change his position. Yurii had asked me to defend him, and he had agreed, fully aware of my proposed line of defense.

What makes a case interesting? For spectators or readers, interest is determined, as a rule, by the story-line or plot. For a lawyer, it lies in the problems a case poses—problems that may be social or profoundly personal, but that are always, ultimately, psychological or moral.

In political trials the advocate confronts a great many wide-ranging problems—social, moral, psychological, and legal. Argument about the facts, however, and the consequent analysis of the evidence, is generally of secondary significance. Our clients' activity is deliberately open and its legality can be proved, whether the proof is disregarded or not. Vladimir Bukovsky and Pavel Litvinov—and indeed all the other defendants in those cases, no matter how they pleaded—admitted taking part in the demonstrations.

The case of Galanskov, Ginzburg, Dobrovolsky, and Lashkova presented the defense with the problems common to all political trials. In addition, however, it involved a bitter fight between prosecution and defense over the facts themselves. This contest was all the more complicated because it was established that one of the accused had—if not in full then certainly in part—undoubtedly committed the acts that the KGB held to be criminal. The main argument was: "Who?" Was it Galanskov, as the KGB maintained, or was it Dobrovolsky, as all the objective evidence indicated?

When I began to write about the Galanskov case, I intended to discuss it in the light I see it in today, now that time has distanced me from the event and brought to light new facts that have caused me to reassess the case. Yet with each page I wrote, I felt more of the emotions and anxieties of those days returning to me, and it became impossible to put these feelings aside. I decided to write as if the intervening years had not passed, without second thoughts. I therefore mentally returned to September 1967, when Yurii and I were studying the case in Lefortovo Prison, when Dobrovolsky was, to me, enemy No. 1.

Pity for Dobrovolsky's ruined life came later. At the time I regarded him with contempt, seeing him as a liar and a traitor. Unable to dissociate my feelings from the evil he caused to Yurii Galanskov, I perceived Dobrovolsky as a personal enemy.

In mid-January 1967, the KGB received separate visits from two citizens, Tsvetkov and Golovanov, who worked in one of Moscow's design and planning offices. Their work involved copying documents, plans, drawings, and so forth on a special copying machine. In their separate statements to the KGB, Golovanov and Tsvetkov said that at the request of their friend Radzievsky they had agreed, for a small payment, to do some moonlighting on the official copying machine in their institution. Radzievsky had brought them a folder containing a number of sheets of typescript. Having read the material, however, and realizing that it was anti-Soviet in nature, each of them independently decided to take the typewritten sheets to the KGB. As a result, Radzievsky was arrested and interrogated. He confirmed the testimony of Tsvetkov and Golovanov, and stated that he had been given the material by his friend Alexei Dobrovolsky. He himself had not read it, and did not know that in carrying out Dobrovolsky's request he was handling anti-Soviet texts.

On the same day, January 17, and at the same time, squads of KGB officials searched the apartments of Dobrovolsky, Galanskov, Ginzburg, and Lashkova.

At Ginzburg's and Galanskov's homes they found and confiscated various typewritten letters and appeals to the public, and one copy each of the typewritten collection of articles and other material known as *Phoenix 66*. Lashkova was arrested that day, Galanskov and Dobrovolsky on January 19.

Dobrovolsky, of course, had been mentioned by Radzievsky; Galanskov was picked up because his signature was on one of the documents the copiers had handed to the KGB. The real reason for the searches, however, was that the KGB had been shadowing all these people for a long time and were only looking for an excuse to pounce. The KGB knew that Alexander Ginzburg had compiled a large collection of documents on the Sinyavsky-Daniel case. Ginzburg had made no secret of this; he had even sent a copy of the collection, complete with his name and address, to the KGB, as a means of stressing the legality of this exercise. The KGB also knew that Galanskov edited *Phoenix 66*, and that their friend Vera Lashkova had typed the materials for both the collection and the journal.

It is hard to say with certainty why, given so much information, the KGB did not arrest them earlier. Presumably it was restrained by the very real threat that new trials would only increase the fiercely critical reaction the Sinyavsky-Daniel trial had evoked abroad. A trial of Ginzburg solely for compiling the *White Book* would demonstrate to the whole world, perhaps even more strongly than the Sinyavsky-Daniel trial, the lack of freedom in the Soviet Union. The *White Book* is a compilation virtually devoid of editorial text or comment. It contains a stenographic transcript of the Sinyavsky-Daniel trial, comments on the trial from the Soviet and foreign press, and letters from individuals or organizations addressed to the Soviet leaders, the Union of Writers, the judiciary, and the procuracy of the USSR. Its aim is stated in the few words of a very brief preface by its editor: "Let the voice of public opinion neither be silent nor weaken until the return to our midst of those who cared more for the fate of their country than for their own fate—Andrei Sinyavsky and Yulii Daniel."

To try a person for this one sentence was impossible, even in the "flexible" conditions of Soviet justice. If Ginzburg had put into his collection only protests and letters condemning the trial, it might have been possible to agree with the KGB's claim that the collection was propagandistic (although even then there would have been nothing criminal in Ginzburg's actions). But with amazing conscientiousness and objectivity Ginzburg included all the most vicious attacks on Sinyavsky and Daniel from Soviet newspapers, the letters from indignant and infuriated writers, scholars and "ordinary Soviet citizens" that proliferated in the pages of the Soviet press at the time. This collection provided no ground for charging its compiler with anti-Soviet propaganda or defamation of the Soviet political and social system.

The KGB therefore sought other ways of bringing a criminal charge against Ginzburg; they looked for any pretext that would let them throw the book at him. And this pretext was found. It was the copy of Galanskov's *Phoenix 66* found in Ginzburg's apartment. As the first step in drawing Ginzburg into the net, the investigation set out to find proof that *Phoenix 66* was not in Ginzburg's possession by accident, that he had taken an active part in compiling this journal. That could be made much more incriminating than compiling the *White Book*.

Ginzburg was arrested January 23.

The first interrogations of the prisoners added very little to the KGB's information. Galanskov at once admitted that he was the compiler and editor of *Phoenix 66*, but he maintained that Ginzburg had had nothing to do with the work on the journal and that he, Galanskov, had taken no part in compiling the *White Book*. Galanskov also stated that he had left a copy of *Phoenix 66* in Ginzburg's apartment the last time he was there before the search. Galanskov frequently dropped in on Ginzburg, sometimes leaving things for him when he was not at home. Ginzburg had not been home this time and could not have known that a copy of *Phoenix 66* had been left. Ginzburg also denied any involvement with the journal. Lashkova affirmed that the materials she had typed for Galanskov and Ginzburg had been quite separate, and that she had never heard from either of them that they had collaborated on the two works.

It is hard to say what the outcome of this trial would have been if all the defendants had stuck to these statements, if no one had given the investigators the material they needed to stage a sensational trial. Even without that material, of course, the investigators would not have simply closed the case. Having already failed to stop them by warnings and threats of suppression, the authorities would not have let these four go unpunished. If they had had only the evidence found in the first searches, together with the defendants' original testimony, the investigators might, however, have limited the indictment to charges of defaming the Soviet system and been satisfied with prison sentences of up to three years (as provided for "defamation")—instead of up to seven years (as provided for the more serious crime of "anti-Soviet propaganda")—served in "general-regime" instead of "strict-regime" camps.

The principal, and at first the only, source of this priceless information was Alexei Dobrovolsky. In his testimony at the pretrial investigation he said a great deal about himself, about his childhood, about the formation of his personal philosophy and his attitude to the Soviet regime. Alexei had lost his father at a very early age and was brought up by his mother, an engineer by profession and a Stalinist by conviction. He grew up in an atmosphere of admiration for Stalin and everything connected with him. For Alexei, as for many others, Khrushchev's 1956 denunciation of Stalin was a profound personal shock, and such was the strength and sincerity of his previous faith that he found it extremely difficult to come to terms with that trauma. For making a speech in defense of Stalin and against the campaign denouncing his "cult of personality," Dobrovolsky was expelled from the Komsomol. Such was the first outcome of his disagreement with the Party's "general line." During the investigation, and later at the trial, Dobrovolsky himself said that he had given long and painful thought to the political problems that interested him. "Obviously," he said, "the task was beyond my powers. I drew incorrect conclusions from the denunciation of Stalin, and gradually became an opponent of the Soviet regime."

When Dobrovolsky was nineteen, he was arrested and convicted for anti-Soviet activity: "I did not plead guilty. I believed at the time that I was wrongly convicted. The years I spent in the prison camp did not change my view of the Soviet system, but added to it a feeling of personal resentment."

After his release, Dobrovolsky was arrested twice more for anti-Soviet activity. On the first occasion the case against him was dropped; the second time, he was declared not legally responsible and hospitalized for compulsory psychiatric treatment.

There was a great deal in Dobrovolsky's behavior that made no sense to me. He was not my client, so I had no personal contact with him, but I cannot regard his testimony to the investigator, or his stories about himself as recorded by the KGB interrogators, as absolutely trustworthy. I am convinced that these pieces of testimony, which impressed some people as being sincere, were really motivated by his very strong sense of self-preservation. The coloring he gave to his actions was dictated, in my view, not by repentance but by fear. Many people thought the dominant trait in his cast of mind and outlook on life was his psychological instability, that the violent changes from fanatical Stalinist to anti-Soviet activist, followed by another switch that even took him to monarchism, was the result of psychopathological aberrations. This was also used to explain an even more profound change, from deification of Stalin to membership in the Russian Orthodox Church.

Dobrovolsky was examined by several psychiatrists, who all agreed that he exhibited certain deviations from the normal. He was diagnosed variously as a psychopath and a schizophrenic. Allowing for the caution with which I regard the conclusions of Soviet forensic psychiatrists, I do think Dobrovolsky genuinely had some form of mental illness. I also believe this affected his character and his behavior, coarsening and intensifying certain inherent character traits. His inflated sense of his own ego went beyond the immodesty that normal people quite frequently exhibit. His distrust grew into suspiciousness, his natural thrift into greed. It is possible that a morbid craving for self-assertion pushed him into greater political activism, or was at least an extra stimulus.

The people I knew who detected mental illness in Dobrovolsky's political changes did not form that opinion as a result of his first and cardinal change, from Stalinism to anti-Sovietism. What struck them as so unnatural was his espousal of monarchist convictions. Whether or not Dobrovolsky really was a monarchist is moot. He himself never said he was. The only evidence of these views was a portrait of the last Russian czar, Nicholas II, which hung in his room, and the statements of certain witnesses. By the 1980s, "monarchist," as applied to a certain group of dissidents, had become more familiar, and no one would call such views a sign of mental abnormality. At the time of the trial, however, whenever I mentioned Dobrovolsky's alleged monarchism people said, "What? Is he absolutely crazy?" I nevertheless believe that both the switch from Stalinism to monarchism and his conversion to Christianity were perfectly explicable by the kind of indoctrination to which Dobrovolsky was subjected from childhood and which was in the very marrow of his bones.

To Dobrovolsky, Stalin was an idol, almost a deity. He saw him as the incarnation of wisdom and strength in his ability to govern a huge country single-handed. Dobrovolsky's disillusionment with Stalin did not, however, turn him into an opponent of autocratic rule. The idea of the country's transformation into an absolute monarchy certainly did not contradict the political theories so instilled in him that they became part of his total outlook. He was simply never weaned away from the principle of concentrating power in the hands of one man. I also think that Dobrovolsky always was essentially a religious man. His early object of belief was a pseudoreligion, but when he became disillusioned with it, he did not lose his need for a faith, and his interest in Christian religion and philosophy sprang from an inner compulsion to believe in something authentic and sublime.

His arrest in our case was an intolerable ordeal for Dobrovolsky. He had suffered too many traumas already. When I first saw him, briefly and by chance, in Lefortovo in September 1967, he was a crushed and demoralized but also a fanatically purposeful man. The price he might have to pay for saving himself was of no concern to him: part of the price was his "repentance," the condemnation of his own views; the chief price, with which he hoped to buy his salvation, was his testimony against Galanskov and Ginzburg. He was prepared to give any evidence the investigators wanted. Some of what he said may even have been true, but to a far greater degree he invented and lied with a sort of passionate ecstasy. A note of passion, indeed, was characteristic of all his testimony, whether he was confessing himself guilty and repenting or denying his guilt.

His first reaction to his arrest was to deny everything: "Radzievsky is slandering me. He is lying shamelessly; I never gave him anything." Next day, January 20: "Radzievsky is concealing the identity of the person who really gave him those materials. He is shamelessly slandering me. Galanskov did not give them to me and I didn't give them to Radzievsky."

Interrogation followed interrogation, and in every one he repeated, "He is slandering me . . . he is lying shamelessly . . . he is trying to incriminate an innocent person."

Between interrogations Dobrovolsky wrote lengthy statements addressed to the investigator. Besides begging the investigator to believe him, he suggested various ways that his noninvolvement in the handling of these materials might be verified: "You can easily convince yourself of this if you check the fingerprints which were undoubtedly left on the folder and the sheets of typescript inside it."

By the time I read the transcripts of his interrogations and Dobrovolsky's handwritten statements, I knew that Dobrovolsky had indeed given the material to Radzievsky. Dobrovolsky himself had admitted it. I did not blame him for these lies. While intellectually aware that every lie is immoral, I laid the responsibility for it at the door of those who put people in prison for a single attempt to photocopy an article criticizing official policy.

Dobrovolsky's last recorded interrogation in the initial stage of the investigation was on January 28. After that came a long break, during which he and Galanskov were sent for psychiatric examinations at the Serbsky Institute. The link with the investigator, however, was not broken. On February 15, Dobrovolsky wrote him:

> Reflecting on our conversation of yesterday, I am prepared to provide the investigatory authorities with the missing copies of the journal *Phoenix 66* . . . There is no time to be lost, because it is always possible that a copy may be sent abroad. . . . If you agree to release me, if only for a few days, I will be able to render this assistance to the investigation.

That statement marked the beginning of what I can only call Dobrovolsky's collaboration with the KGB. In all his subsequent statements and answers to questions, the center of gravity shifted to other people; Dobrovolsky no longer confined himself to saying, "I am not guilty." He said, "Others are guilty." Handwritten statement, March 13:

> I have been trying to convince you that I gave nothing to Radzievsky, not even the open letter to Sholokhov. I have suggested that you check the fingerprints on that letter. I have also suggested other methods. You have refused to make use of them. You are continuing to hold me in detention on the evidence of one person only—Radzievsky. His testimony is false. Galanskov gave him the letter to Mikhail Sholokhov and all the other materials. Radzievsky tried to incriminate me, because he knew that I was once diagnosed as a "schizophrenic" and he thought I would therefore not be arrested. I am absolutely innocent and have never had anything to do with these materials.

March 22:

> In my confession of March 13 I was insufficiently frank with you. I concealed the fact that Galanskov handed over the materials in my presence. I saw them. It was in January 1967, in the evening, near the Lermontov Monument. The testimony I am now giving you is truthful . . .

These statements were preceded by several letters from the hospital which Dobrovolsky tried unsuccessfully to smuggle to Galanskov and to members of his own family.

"Yurii!" he wrote. "I implore you to take all the blame on yourself. I simply cannot go to prison now, you know that. . . ."

"Yurii! I can't stand it, you must take the rap . . . I beg you to do this. . . ."

And in every letter it was "I beg you," never once "You should" or "You ought to." Never once did he use arguments of the kind that might persuade a genuinely guilty person to save an innocent one. There was no such tone as "You are guilty, not I, therefore you must bear the consequences."

Dobrovolsky claimed innocence only when writing to others. To his wife and mother he swore that he was an "innocent victim," and called upon what he held "most sacred"—God—to be his witness. This letter was distinguished from the others by its elevated style and high-flown phraseology, in which the writer seemed to be carried away almost to the point of ecstasy, of religious supplication. Did he swear by God to arouse the pity of those who already pitied him anyway, and to persuade his own mother and his devoted wife of the truth of a lie, or did he expect the letter to be intercepted, as it was, and hope to convince the investigator, to whom he would be justified in dissembling and whom he had reason to fear?

If Dobrovolsky had not subsequently admitted that it was he in fact who had handed over all the materials, then that letter, apparently not destined for the investigator, would have served as a serious psychological argument in his defense. Nor is it impossible that at the moment when he wrote the letter, Dobrovolsky had just such an aim in mind. This is borne out not only by the style of the letter but by the fact that Dobrovolsky must have known it had practically no chance of reaching its addressees. The Serbsky Institute is not a hospital; only those accused of crimes are sent there for examination, and they are held under guard. It is organized on lines that make it virtually a prison, and staff as well as doctors are carefully screened.

Dobrovolsky's aim in writing to Galanskov was obvious; no differences of interpretation are possible. These letters were laconic, his request expressed briefly and clearly: Take all the blame. Yurii did receive these letters and turned them over to his investigator. By the time they began, more than the handing over of materials for photocopying to Radzievsky was at stake. Dobrovolsky's apartment had been searched a second time and the KGB had found an encoding device, special carbon paper for coded writing, anti-Soviet literature from the NTS-controlled publishing house, Possev, and a fairly large sum of money. Dobrovolsky was interrogated about these finds on March 24:

> In July or August 1966 I received a package from abroad. Its contents included an encoding card, leaflets with anti-Soviet texts and foreign carbon paper specially made for coded writing. Later, before the November holidays, I received a second package. It contained books. At the end of December I received a third parcel, in which were more books published by the Possev publishing house and a letter from the NTS.
>
> Between the second and the third package, Vera Lashkova, at my request, wrote a letter to the NTS, using the cryptographic material already sent to me. In the letter I confirmed receipt of the packages . . .

Four days later he said:

> Galanskov was linked with the NTS. He told me so himself quite plainly. In August he brought me an encoding device and some leaflets, which he asked me

to have copied and sent out to certain addresses in the Soviet Union and abroad. At first I agreed, then changed my mind and refused. That was how the encoder and the leaflets happened to be at my apartment. Galanskov said he maintained permanent contact with the West. He gave me, for me and my friends, anti-Soviet books published by the NTS. I gave Lashkova the coded letter to the NTS on Galanskov's instructions. It was from him, too, that I obtained the special cryptographic paper.

In December 1966 I saw some dollars at Galanskov's apartment—he said he received financial help from abroad. In October 1966 Galanskov met a foreigner. It was through this foreigner that he passed a copy of the *White Book* to the West.

The rest of Dobrovolsky's testimony (and there was a great deal) brought no change, only additions to the basic statement of March 28, which not only provided the necessary evidence against Galanskov but also implicated Ginzburg, whom Dobrovolsky hardly knew: "I heard that it was Alexander Ginzburg who put Galanskov in touch with the foreigners. . . . I heard that Ginzburg edited *Phoenix 66* jointly with Galanskov . . ." He could produce no facts to support his assertions, and no corroborating witness. Yet these remarks were sufficient for additional charges against Ginzburg.

Ginzburg never said a word that might have been used, even indirectly, against Yurii Galanskov in the investigation or the trial. Nor was the testimony of the third defendant, Vera Lashkova, of any use as proof of Galanskov's guilt on the main count that my defense contested. Numerous witnesses were questioned and none of them supported Dobrovolsky either. Even so, he was not the only person who incriminated Galanskov. There was one other man whose testimony, perhaps in greater degree than Dobrovolsky's, provided the investigators with the necessary incriminating evidence. That man was Galanskov himself.

From the day of his arrest on January 19 until May 6, all of Galanskov's statements can be summed up in a few words: "I wrote the letter to Sholokhov. I was the compiler and editor of the journal *Phoenix 66*. I consider that I acted within the law and therefore do not regard myself as guilty."

At his interrogations on May 6, which, excluding the lunch break, lasted from 12:40 P.M. till 8:30 P.M., he confirmed all Dobrovolsky's accusations— meetings with NTS representatives who came to Moscow, acquisition from them of an encoder, copying paper, money, and literature, correspondence with the NTS conducted with the aid of a numerical code, transmission to the West through these representatives of the *White Book* and *Phoenix 66*.

All this, in more detail, was in the extensive transcript of an interrogation on May 17, entitled "A Sincere Confession."

Only a few days passed, however, before Galanskov began to make some alterations to this "sincere confession":

I don't know who handed over the *White Book*. I took no part in this. [May 31]

I wrote the coded letter for the foreign woman known as Nadya, but I did not send it off; instead, I burned it. In this undelivered letter I wrote about relations between the young poets who belong to the [unofficial literary group known as] "Smogists." [June 8.]

I know nothing about the handing over of the *White Book*. I did not give the encoder, the journal *Possev*, and the NTS books to Dobrovolsky. [June 12.]

I had no NTS books. I received neither books nor parcels from the NTS. I totally refute Dobrovolsky's testimony. [June 13.]

All the evidence about my meetings with NTS representatives and receiving coding materials and literature from them is sheer fabrication. I wanted to save Dobrovolsky, who has been begging me to do so for a long time. [June 16.]

All my testimony, beginning with May 6, was pure invention. I was consciously and falsely incriminating myself, in response to the requests, not to say entreaties, of Dobrovolsky. [June 19.]

If only that had been the end of it; if only the defense had been able to maintain in court that Galanskov's confession was temporary, that he had retracted his false testimony during the pretrial investigation and had explained the motives that drove him to tell these lies! Instead, in a series of interrogations on July 21, July 26, July 28, and July 31, Galanskov made such statements as "I met the NTS representatives. . . . I received the coding materials, literature, and money from them. . . . I gave it all to Dobrovolsky. . . . I instructed Dobrovolsky to write the coded letter. . . ." And on August 12, the transcript of that day's interrogation specifically stated: "Defendant Galanskov expressed the wish to write his testimony in his own hand." The handwritten statement read:

In late summer or early fall I had a succession of meetings with four foreigners, from whom I received packages containing NTS materials and books. All these foreigners identified themselves as members of an organization based abroad— the "Committee for Cooperation with SMOG." In November a foreigner named Henry arrived in Moscow; he represented some organization of lawyers. From him I received 260 dollars and 300 rubles in Soviet currency. It was through him that I sent the *White Book* to the West. In January came a foreign woman called Nadya. She gave me the cryptographic paper, a numerical code, and the addresses to which I should send letters destined for the NTS. Nadya was the intermediary who took my journal *Phoenix 66*.

Again, if only even this new "confession" had been all!

The pretrial investigation was completed September 21, and three days before that Yurii again changed his testimony. This time he did not deny meeting the foreigners but denied that they were from the NTS. He did not deny that he had written a coded letter but denied that it had been addressed to the NTS. He admitted having met a foreigner called Henry in November but denied having given him the *White Book*. He admitted having met a foreign woman called Nadya but denied having given her *Phoenix 66*. He admitted participation in the resale of dollars but said he had received them from Dobrovolsky, whom he had wanted to help. He ended this day's testimony: "In admitting to everything of which Dobrovolsky accused me, I wanted to get him out of trouble, considering that I was in any case responsible for editing *Phoenix 66* and writing the 'Open Letter to Sholokhov.' "

If we add to these statements the fact that Yurii viewed the forthcoming trial as a farce and thought open mockery of the court would be the most appropriate conduct for him, I think it will be apparent that my job was going to be extremely hard. For Yurii was a difficult client; he agreed with all my reasoning and listened carefully to my advice; indeed, he was exceptionally grateful for every sign of attention and sympathy I was able to show him. He was, however, physically utterly exhausted and morally distressed. He tried to conceal his weakness and self-reproach behind a display of bravado and sarcastic rudeness to the investigators. He laughed at them when what he wanted to do was scream with pain. Not wanting hostile, alien people to see how sick he was, he aroused their irritation because he could not bear to arouse their pity.

On October 12, 1967, a few days before the expiration of the maximum permitted term of pretrial detention of the accused, we finished our joint study of all nineteen volumes of the investigatory material and I said goodbye to Yurii until the trial. I would spend the next few days trying to make sense of the vast amount of documentation that needed to be analyzed and systematized. My fellow defense counsel and I waited impatiently for the moment when the case would be handed over to the court and we would have the chance, without guards and clients, to reread the more important passages of the evidence and discuss defense tactics among ourselves. But time passed, and no one told us the trial date.

Finally, early in December, we were told that the case would be heard in the Moscow City Court by Judge Lev Mironov and that the trial would open at 10:00 A.M. on the morning of December 11. The news was doubly unwelcome. This was not enough notice for us and the prospect of a trial presided over by Mironov was not pleasant.

I have always been wary of advocates' opinions of judges, because we tend to praise judges when our cases end favorably and to curse them when the judgment goes against us. That is far from being a reliable and is certainly not an absolute criterion. Even so, Mironov of all people! Colleagues who had encountered him in the people's courts, before his elevation to the City Court, were almost unanimous in abusing him, and too often the word they used was "sadist." His treatment of advocates was disdainful, but his behavior toward defendants was hostile and insulting. In our case I don't think these attitudes had much to do with its subject matter. Mironov simply derived pleasure from the opportunity to humiliate people, to display his power over those who were defenseless and dependent on him, whether they were defendants or witnesses.

My first acquaintance with Mironov's judicial style came even before the trial. One morning, as the court's working day was beginning, a little procession proceeded along the third-floor corridor of the Moscow City Court building: first, showing the way, came Valentina Osina, a secretary of the "special registry"; behind her was one of my colleagues, Vladimir Shveisky, carrying a pile of volumes of case material on his outstretched arms; I was the last in the cortège, and I too had a great stack of volumes in brown binders, each stamped "The Case of Ginzburg, Galanskov, and Others." Suddenly I heard a loud voice. Peering out from behind my load I saw a tall, solidly built man leaning heavily on a stick. He had just climbed up the steep staircase to the third floor and had not had time to catch his breath.

"How dare you try to make a fool of me!" he said loudly to Valentina. "How many times must I climb up here and down again to get a simple piece of information? I want to know when the Ginzburg trial is due to begin. Why don't you answer me?"

"I've already told you that I know nothing about that case. There is no such case in our registry," Valentina replied, looking desperately around at us and trying to check whether the man could read the title on the top volumes of our stacks: "The Case of Ginzburg . . ."

The stranger turned to Shveisky. "Vladimir Yakovlevich, can you perhaps tell me what's going on here?"

Shveisky had no time to reply before Valentina butted in. "I can give you some advice," she said. "Go and see Comrade Mironov. If that case really has come to the Moscow City Court, Mironov will undoubtedly know about it." Then to us, "This way, please, comrade advocates. I'll show you where you'll be working."

I realized the full absurdity of this situation when I discovered later that the man who had stopped us was an indirect client of Shveisky's in this very case. He was the famous General Pyotr Grigorenko, who had asked Shveisky to defend Dobrovolsky. Realizing that the secretary had behaved in accordance with Mironov's orders, Shveisky was embarrassed and perhaps even afraid to tell the truth to his client. Mironov would undoubtedly refuse to see Grigorenko, for the judge knew him as one of the most striking figures in the dissident movement.

In 1961, Pyotr Grigorenko—general, professor at the Frunze Military Academy, holder of countless orders and medals, a long-standing and convinced Communist—spoke out at a Party conference in strong criticism of Nikita Khrushchev. At the time, Grigorenko got away with a severe reprimand from the Party authorities, demotion in the service, and transfer to an obscure post in Soviet Asia. But there he publicly criticized the policies of the Party and the government, until finally he was expelled from the Party and dishonorably discharged from the army.

A judge, of course, is not obliged to receive visitors and answer their questions, but Mironov forbade his staff to answer any questions about this case, even from relatives of the accused. Almost in tears, Valentina Osina tried to justify herself to the indignant Shveisky: "What can I do?" she said. "I'd be glad to tell them the truth. Do you think I like making people run up and down stairs to find out about a case that's been on my desk for weeks? Those are Mironov's orders."

At the time, I tried to find some reasonable explanation for these instructions and was unable to do so. Mironov must have been aware that as soon as the advocates knew the date of the trial, it would be impossible to keep it a secret. We would certainly tell our clients and their families at once. Mironov's order was simply a way of hurting and humiliating friends and relatives of the accused, people already tormented by anxiety and distress.

The main thing that worried the advocates at the time, however, was not Mironov's evil nature but the impossibility of completing our preparations for the defense in the time available.

Studying the case each day in the KGB prison, we had of course tried to copy as much as possible into our own files, but it was impossible to transcribe nineteen volumes. At home, reading our notes, each of us spotted questions that needed amplification or further study. Filling these gaps in the few days left to us was all the more impossible because we had to spend at least two days with our clients and, after a six-week break in contact, prepare them for the trial. We decided not to wait until the start of the trial but to submit at once two separate applications signed by all the defense counsel. The first asked that the trial be postponed for five or six days, the second that the case be heard in open court. With no justification except the letter "S" for "Secret" on the cover of the dossier, Mironov had decided to hear the case in closed session, and this illegal decision was in no way justified by the subject matter of the indictment. We were determined to object to it.

We submitted the applications to Mironov, and that same evening his secretary informed us that the first application was rejected. The second one would be considered later and the court's decision made known in due course. As soon as the trial began we would resubmit this application. Meanwhile, before we met our clients again, the most pressing need was to meet and hammer out jointly our general tactics on the principal and most serious count of the indictment—the defendants' receipt, possession, and distribution of NTS literature and their criminal links with the organization.

As described in the indictment, the NTS was an émigré organization whose specific aim was "the overthrow of the USSR's existing political system and the restoration of a bourgeois order by means of both ideological and armed struggle against the Communist government." The authorities viewed everything that originated from the NTS as anti-Soviet, so that distribution or even possession of such literature was a criminal offense. "The NTS is an overseas branch of the CIA. . . ." "The NTS is an espionage organization. . . ." automatically accompanied every mention of the organization in the Soviet press.

The first question facing us, then, was whether the NTS really was an anti-Soviet organization. Could the defense contest this?

Our knowledge of NTS political literature was limited to the brochures found in Dobrovolsky's apartment and thus included among the documents in the case. Even that small amount of material, however, was enough to bring us to the inescapable conclusion that the prosecution's claim could not be disputed—and not because to have done so would have been dangerous or tactically unwise, but because the NTS really was anti-Soviet. Its aim was not the democratization and liberalization of the Soviet regime within the framework of the existing political structure, but the substitution of that structure by a fundamentally new political regime based on different moral and social principles. The authors of the brochure "Solidarism—The Idea of the Future" and the other publications we read started from the viewpoint that the Soviet Union was a totalitarian state which by its nature was incapable of evolving into a state governed by the rule of law; it could therefore never insure genuine harmony between the individual and society, the liberty of the governed, or the safeguarding of human rights. The writers of these brochures subjected all the political ideas underlying the Soviet state to telling criticism and summoned their readers to fight the existing system and establish a new regime by methods ranging from ideological propaganda to revolution and the violent overthrow of Soviet power.

We advocates all agreed that the defense could not dispute the anti-Soviet character of this literature. Distribution of such literature was prohibited by law, and a lawyer was bound to admit that a client who broke this law was guilty. We agreed too that we could accept the prosecution's claim on this point only after analyzing each brochure, and that we categorically rejected the statement: "Everything published by the NTS is anti-Soviet."

In court Yurii Galanskov denied ever having received, read, or distributed NTS literature; thus I had the right and duty to maintain that this section of the indictment against him was unproven. Lashkova and Dobrovolsky did not deny that they had read these brochures and given them to other people to read, and their counsel, in asking that the charges be reframed, were doing the only thing on their behalf that an advocate could do within the law.

The second issue on which, despite the clashes among our clients, we advocates wanted to adopt a common stand concerned the degree of criminality imputed to the literary and journalistic writings that Galanskov had included in *Phoenix 66* and Ginzburg had put in the *White Book*. This was a difficult and crucial part of our preparation. Again and again we read and reread these works, discussing every dubious sentence. The dispute that each of us conducted with the prosecution in court was to a great extent the result of our joint, collective labors and unanimous conclusions, reached only after long arguments and the emergence of new ideas, some of which came to us during the trial itself.

The defense lawyers in this trial were colleagues with whom I was connected by years of professional collaboration and, I am sure, mutual respect. Each of them was a true professional, a highly qualified and talented lawyer. Semyon Ariya, Vladimir Shveisky, and I were all of the same generation, probably even of the same age. Boris Zolotukhin was considerably younger, probably no more than thirty-five or thirty-six years old. He had come into advocacy after previously working for the Moscow City Procuracy, where he had already earned a reputation as an excellent forensic orator, a well-trained lawyer, and an upright, independent-minded man. I am sure that in time Boris would have become a brilliant advocate. Nature had endowed him with talent combined with a personality that imposed high standards on himself and perpetual dissatisfaction with his own performance. The Ginzburg-Galanskov trial was Zolotukhin's first political case. It was also his last. At the time of this trial I was already aware that I had no colleague who was a better, more devoted, and dearer friend than Boris Zolotukhin, but I had no idea how stark his future would be.

In those early December days we four worked from morning to night on our preparations, and we kept finding problem after problem that demanded new solutions. Suddenly, while we were sweating away at it, Mironov let us know that the hearing would be postponed after all; our application had been granted.

For the first few minutes we were delighted, interrupting each other to ask the secretary, "When will it begin? How long is the postponement?"

"I don't know, comrade advocates. You will be informed later of the new date. No need to rush your work now, you have plenty of time."

When we were alone and the euphoria had subsided, we began asking each other, "What does this mean? Why has Mironov decided to postpone the trial? Why hasn't he named a new date?" If Mironov had postponed the trial for four or five days, we would have been equally surprised: as a rule, political trials were never postponed, however pressingly the defense might request it. But now the starting date had been postponed for an indefinite and, apparently, lengthy period. Clearly this had not been done for the advocates' sake. We could only guess wildly at the reason. The only thing of which we felt certain was that something ominous was afoot behind the scenes, that somewhere, outside the courthouse, new decisions were being made which needed time to put into effect, and that our application was being used as a pretext. We figured out the most likely explanation only later, on the basis of things that happened during the trial.

At least we had some time. We finished our preparatory work. Each of us was able to have several client meetings. December passed and the new year came in. On January 4, 1968, a phone message came to our law offices: the Galanskov trial was set for 10:00 A.M. on January 8.

On the third floor of the Moscow City Courthouse there are several judges' offices and one courtroom, the largest in the building. It takes up almost the whole floor and is most often used for conferences of the judges from all over the city. For that reason there is no special, barred-off area for the accused. When the City Court hears cases with a great many defendants (twenty or thirty people), this courtroom is used. Here the accused do not sit at one side, as in most courtrooms, but directly in front of the judge and people's assessors. They have wooden benches, two people to a bench, with backs, armrests, and room for notepads or papers.

When we came into this courtroom on January 8, we did not recognize it. The benches had been removed, half the room was empty of seats, and four small, uncomfortable chairs had been placed—well apart from each other—in front of the judge's desk. Behind them was a large open space, and the few rows of chairs for the public were lined up near the back wall.

Soon these rows were occupied by people who had been specially invited —a few officials from the Supreme Court of the RSFSR and from the procuracy, a few officially picked journalists, and several KGB investigating officers. One of the invited guests was a well-known movie director who openly boasted of his friendly relations with the top brass of the KGB. He used to insist that Yurii Andropov, head of the KGB, was a kind, good-natured man who was distressed almost to the point of tears every time he ordered an arrest. In addition there were some people from the Moscow City Committee of the Communist Party. A very few places were left free, clearly reserved so that later, at the request of the defense, close relatives of the defendants could be seated. There was no room for friends or any genuine "public." Only parents and wives of the defendants were allowed in the courtroom.

The prisoners were brought in.

For the first time I saw Vera Lashkova. She seemed little more than a girl: very slim and delicate, a tiny head on a thin neck, hair scraped back and held with a rubber band. She and Ginzburg sat on the two chairs in front, nearest to the judge; beside each of them was a guard armed with a submachine gun. In the second row were Galanskov and Dobrovolsky, similarly guarded.

In the few minutes before the trial opened we were able to talk to our clients and give them some final advice. I asked the guard commander for a bench for the defendants instead of those narrow little chairs, at least for the ailing Yurii Galanskov. But Yurii himself intervened: "I don't need anything from them. I'll sit here like the others." And there he sat for the five days of the trial, doubled up with pain, bending forward or trying to raise his knees as high as possible, without a word of complaint.

The psychology of an advocate must seem odd. During the early stage of my acquaintance with this case, my initial doubts disappeared day by day, just as my conviction grew daily firmer that Dobrovolsky was lying. This feeling came partly from increasing familiarity with the documents and the objective evidence that supported this belief. But also, against my will, my mind willingly accepted everything that spoke in Yurii's favor.

The long interval of postponement gave me time to think through the methodology of my defense and analyze the documents collated by the investigators. As to defense tactics, I had doubts only about how to structure my dispute with the prosecution to make it as well-argued and convincing as possible. I would have had to conduct this dispute even if the material evidence had been found in Galanskov's possession rather than Dobrovolsky's, even if Yurii had changed his testimony ten times rather than three. It was my professional duty. My most serious doubts were caused by another matter.

In defending Yurii I was in the position of having to accuse another defendant, a man who had been through as much mental stress as Yurii. Of course every advocate encounters this problem fairly often in ordinary criminal cases, and it requires a great deal of skill and tact not to overstep the bounds of ethical conduct. One must not get so carried away in the heat of the contest as to jeopardize another's fate, not merely that of another defendant but of one's own client as well. An aggressive defense always evokes an aggressive reaction. It offers the prosecution in rebuttal and the court a chance to extract from one's defense speech new evidence and new arguments against both defendants.

I realized that I would not be able to avoid a clash with Dobrovolsky. Furthermore, I could not just assert that Dobrovolsky had falsely incriminated Yurii; I would have to say *why* he had told these lies. Therefore I would also have to say: "He's guilty and he's trying to save his own skin by saddling Galanskov with the guilt for acts which in reality he himself committed."

To take this line was justified by my professional duty to defend my client by all legal and professionally ethical means. Even so, I was still plagued by a certain inner disquiet.

Whenever I read and reread Yurii's illogical and inconsistent testimony, the question arose in my mind, "What if . . .? What if Dobrovolsky's incriminating testimony about Galanskov were not all lies?" Certain details in Dobrovolsky's statements were indirectly confirmed in the testimony of Vera Lashkova, whose behavior under investigation (and later in court) was rational and morally irreproachable. I could easily find perfectly plausible explanations for these details, and they did not per se incriminate Yurii; but they did raise certain doubts.

These doubts were not such as to allow me to change my basic line of defense on the incidents connected with the NTS, which in any case I would not have had the right to do, being bound by my client's position. Yet in terms of ethics, this position struck me as by no means unassailable.

And there was one more factor; in doubting the truth of his statements I was *not* also doubting the morality of Yurii's actions (or alleged actions). Even if I were to admit that he had done everything of which he was accused, in my view he would still not have deserved reproach. I could see nothing immoral in receiving, reading, and disseminating literature from any publishing house anywhere and expounding ideas of whatever nature. I could see nothing immoral in writing coded letters, since only their *content* (which did not figure in the accusation) can be immoral, not the method of writing them. The state itself, by its total police surveillance and illegal interception of private correspondence, drives its citizens to adopt such methods. Nor could I condemn anyone's connection with the NTS, provided that connection did not lead him to commit improper acts.

In political trials the moral dimension of the defense takes on particular significance, and this inevitably affects the methods and tactics of defense counsel. These methods are hard to specify, but they exist. It was not by

chance that in the case of the Red Square demonstration none of the advocates based their defense on such usual arguments as the lesser degree of
their clients' involvement compared with that of the other defendants; none
of them tried to prove who had initiated the demonstration or who had
written the slogans. On that occasion, all the advocates respected their
clients' highly moral stand of equal and collective responsibility.

In this new case the clash between two defendants did not excuse me
from observing the highest ethical standards. As soon as I began to have
doubts about these subtle degrees of involvement, my zeal to expose Dobrovolsky began to seem rather less justifiable, my condemnation of his
behavior less than wholly deserved. When I entered the courtroom I was
determined to keep the sense of aloofness that would enable me to be
impartial and objective.

After the reading of the indictments, the court proceeded to examine
the first defendant, Alexei Dobrovolsky. And I found that minute by minute, with every sentence and every mention of Yurii Galanskov's name I
could feel my emotional, partisan attitude returning.

> Galanskov said he was meeting some foreigners, from whom he received litera-
> ture, coding materials, and money. . . . The literature these people brought to
> Galanskov was published by the NTS. . . . Galanskov transmitted the *White
> Book* to the West through the foreigner called Henry. . . . Galanskov received
> money in Soviet and foreign currency from Henry. . . . Galanskov said he had
> sent out *Phoenix 66* through Nadya, who worked for the [émigré] journal *Grani*.
> . . . Galanskov gave me encoding materials and some anti-Soviet leaflets to be
> copied. . . . Galanskov said he kept up a correspondence with the NTS by coded
> letters written with a special kind of carbon paper. . . . It was from Galanskov
> that I received the 2000 rubles that were found when my apartment was
> searched . . . the money Henry gave to Galanskov was meant to help Galan-
> skov's activities. . . . Galanskov instructed me in the principles the NTS prop-
> agated. . . ."

Such were the answers Dobrovolsky gave to Terekhov, the prosecutor.
Such were the reasons why, from the first day of the trial, Dobrovolsky
again became my enemy No. 1. I no longer remembered that he was exhausted and distressed by his arrest and detention, and by the prospect of
a long prison sentence, although I never for a moment forgot this where
Galanskov was concerned. My usual sympathy for any person in trouble
had disappeared.

If threats of a new and very long sentence had induced Dobrovolsky to
choose repentance as his only possible method of defense, if he had publicly
recanted and condemned his own views as anti-Soviet and therefore criminal, I would scarcely have regarded him as a hero but I would not have
thought him a traitor. Dobrovolsky, however, defended himself by ruth-

lessly betraying his companions: Galanskov, whom he regarded as his friend; and Ginzburg, whom he hardly knew and of whose views and actions he was almost totally ignorant. If Dobrovolsky's testimony about Galanskov was to some degree explicable by their joint involvement in some of the incidents cited, so that in talking of himself he could hardly have helped mentioning Galanskov, his testimony about Ginzburg cannot possibly be explained on these grounds. Yet the charge of involvement with the NTS rested entirely on Dobrovolsky's hearsay evidence: "I heard that Ginzburg had long-standing connections with foreign organizations. . . . I was told that foreigners often came to see Ginzburg. . . . I guessed that Ginzburg was planning to send the *White Book* out to the West. . . ."

Similar in its effect was this passage from Dobrovolsky's examination by the prosecutor:

> *Prosecutor:* Were they expecting Henry to come so that they could hand over the *White Book* for transmission abroad?
> *Dobrovolsky:* Yes.
> *P.:* Did they [Ginzburg and Galanskov] hand it over in secret?
> *D.:* Yes.
> *P.:* So they did it secretly because the book contained anti-Soviet documents, did they?
> *D.:* Yes, it contained anti-Soviet documents.
> *P.:* Were they afraid of being caught?
> *D.:* Yes.
> *P.:* And so for that reason they concealed their links with the NTS?
> *D.:* Yes.

The prosecutor's phrasing of the questions is also noteworthy. He did not so much ask questions as supply a set of ready-made answers. Dobrovolsky had no need to provide the court with facts, all he had to do was to agree with the prosecutor. Such "leading" is forbidden by Soviet procedural law. Terekhov knew this; he was after all Senior Deputy to the Procurator General of the USSR. It was equally well known to Judge Mironov, who never once interrupted the prosecutor.

I think this method was chosen because both Terekhov and Mironov knew that Dobrovolsky was completely uninformed about the facts in the charges against Ginzburg, and that unaided, without prompting, he could not have given the required testimony. They had correctly judged his willingness to give the prosecution any possible help, and they were sure he would gladly say yes whenever necessary. His sole aim was to retain the support of the KGB and consequently assure the court's leniency toward him.

If my task had been limited to undermining confidence in Dobrovolsky by proving that he had changed his testimony several times, this would have been comparatively easy to achieve. A similar task faced Zolotukhin and he handled it magnificently, making Dobrovolsky admit that he had never witnessed a single meeting between Ginzburg and representatives of NTS and had never heard Ginzburg mention any such meetings, and thus establishing that Dobrovolsky knew neither the names of the foreigners Ginzburg had allegedly met nor the places and times at which the meetings were supposed to have taken place. The unreliability of Dobrovolsky's testimony about Ginzburg became glaringly obvious.

My situation was different. Dobrovolsky's testimony about Galanskov was entirely specific and concrete. He named the names of people Galanskov had met; he named the places and times of the meetings. Furthermore, Galanskov himself did not deny a whole series of facts which the investigators learned from Dobrovolsky's testimony, though he gave them a different interpretation.

Trying as always to reason as the judge might reason, I said to myself, "Dobrovolsky's testimony about Galanskov may be lies, prompted by his desire to avert the blow from himself, when he says that all the incriminating materials found in his possession belonged to Galanskov, and that not he but Galanskov was connected with the NTS. But this testimony may also be true. They both met the same foreigners. Both of them were seen to have dollars (though Galanskov says these dollars were Dobrovolsky's, whereas Dobrovolsky says they belonged to Galanskov). Dobrovolsky said that Galanskov sent his *Phoenix 66* abroad through an NTS emissary; Galanskov denied this. But extracts from *Phoenix 66* were published in the NTS journal *Grani* in West Germany, so that Dobrovolsky's testimony has, to some degree, been confirmed."

The most objective judge, in conditions of complete independence, would have been faced with a difficult choice between these mutually exclusive versions, given by two defendants equally interested in maintaining their own standpoint. And I was not certain that even in such ideal conditions the dispute would be decided in Galanskov's favor.

What would I achieve if I proved to the court that Dobrovolsky had at first concealed his participation in the attempt, through Radzievsky, to have the literary materials copied, and that then, having admitted this, he had insisted that he had only been carrying out Galanskov's instruction? To this my inner opponent would quite reasonably object: "This sort of behavior by a defendant is frequently encountered. It only shows that Dobrovolsky was trying to evade responsibility and conceal his part in this episode; but once having admitted to it, it does not mean that he was necessarily giving false evidence about Galanskov's role in the incident." And that essential figure, my inner devil's advocate, would add: "Don't forget that in

Dobrovolsky's latest testimony there is a good deal of logic and common sense. After all, the materials Dobrovolsky tried to get duplicated had been included by Galanskov in *Phoenix 66;* as compiler and editor he was interested in insuring the maximum possible distribution of his journal, therefore he had a motive for getting this material copied. But what reason had Dobrovolsky for wanting it copied?"

I realized that until I could find a reasonable answer to that question, until I could show the court that Dobrovolsky had his own interest, independent of Galanskov, for having these writings copied, I had practically nothing to put up against Dobrovolsky's testimony. There was very little likelihood that my examination of Dobrovolsky would produce any new information. Even so, I tried to probe in a direction which—if it revealed anything—would subsequently enable me to affirm that Dobrovolsky had his own reasons for meeting the foreigners, his own reasons for having the literary materials copied:

Kaminskaya: Who was the first foreigner you met?
Dobrovolsky: A French journalist called Gabriel.
K.: When did that meeting take place?
D.: In August 1966.
K.: What did you talk about?
D.: Literature.
K.: Can you be more precise? Did you discuss a particular literary group?
D.: Yes, we talked about the "Smogists."
K.: Did you make any requests to that foreigner?
D.: Yes, I did. Right now I can't remember exactly . . . but I did ask him something. [Pause] I gave him an article I had written, to take abroad. I wanted it published.
K.: Did you ever happen to talk about that article to any other foreigner?
D.: Yes. I talked about it to Henry. He told me it had been published.
K.: What else did he say to you about that article? Did he, perhaps, tell you his opinion of it?
D.: Yes. He offered me moral encouragement.
K.: Was that all he said about the article?
D.: No. He said I would be getting a fee for it.
K.: Did Galanskov have anything to do with this article of yours and did he send it abroad?
D.: No. I met Gabriel alone.
K.: Were there any other occasions . . .

At this point I was interrupted by a sharp remark from the judge: "Stick closer to the point, comrade advocate."

I put a new question:

K.: Did the discussion of your article with Henry take place at your first meeting with him, or later?
D.: I talked about my article during my second meeting with Henry.

K.: Who else was present at that meeting?
D.: No one. There were only the two of us.

Again the judge interrupted. "Comrade advocate, I forbid you to put these questions. Dobrovolsky is not accused of transmitting material for publication abroad. Don't object, comrade advocate; I will disallow all such questions in future."

It was true that Dobrovolsky was not charged with this offense, but according to Article 280 of the Code of Criminal Procedure the judge may disallow only questions "that have no bearing on the case." The meeting with Henry was a specific episode in the indictments against both Galanskov and Dobrovolsky, and I had the undoubted right to elucidate all the circumstances of that meeting. I could do nothing but lodge an objection against the judge's ruling and then submit to it.

Judge Mironov disallowed my questions because he sensed the purpose behind them and realized that they were threatening the basic structure of the prosecution case, that Dobrovolsky had been a mere helper, drawn into crime by Galanskov. Any indication that Dobrovolsky had an autonomous interest in meeting foreigners, any hint of independent financial transactions between Dobrovolsky and Henry, assumed to be a representative of the NTS, would undermine the plausibility of this structure.

Another excerpt shows that Mironov's reason for removing my question from the record was not its irrelevance. Witness Yepifanov, an acquaintance of Galanskov and Ginzburg, was being cross-examined.

Prosecutor: What do you know about Galanskov's meetings with the Swede?
Galanskov: I protest against this question.
Judge: Defendant Galanskov, I forbid you to interfere in the cross-examination.
Kaminskaya: Comrade chairman, I request that the prosecutor's question be stricken from the record. The indictment says nothing about a meeting of Galanskov with the Swede, therefore the question goes beyond the scope of this court examination.
Zolotukhin: Comrade chairman, you have turned down many of our questions but you have never stricken from the record questions by the prosecutor which obviously exceed the scope of this court examination.
Mironov: Comrade prosecutor, continue with your questions.
Prosecutor: Witness, answer my question.
Witness: I know nothing about the meetings of Galanskov with the Swede.

Mironov was not simply a partial judge; he prevented the advocates from conducting an effective defense by disallowing important and legitimate questions and rejecting essential applications. Since neither money nor valuables had been found when Galanskov's apartment was searched, one of the charges against him rested on Dobrovolsky's assertion that Galanskov had given him the money for safekeeping. Yet during the pretrial investigation Dobrovolsky's wife had applied three times to the KGB demanding the return of the money confiscated during the search. She wrote that it consisted partly of joint savings from wages and partly of sums her husband had borrowed from his friends in religious circles. This contradicted Dobrovolsky's testimony and required clarification. On the second day of the trial I was handed a short letter from General Grigorenko in which he stated that he knew the source of the money in Dobrovolsky's apartment and was prepared to testify. I applied for him to be called as a witness. The court refused to hear his evidence on the ground that he was a patient at a psychiatric clinic.

Several hours later the prosecution was examining a witness named Basilova, wife of the poet Gubanov. Gubanov had stated that Ginzburg used to bring foreigners to their home. Ginzburg denied this. The prosecutor wished to use this testimony to prove that Ginzburg maintained connections with foreigners.

Prosecutor: In his testimony your husband, Gubanov, said . . .

Basilova: I wish to make a statement.

Judge: I will not allow it.

Basilova: I shall make my statement all the same. I wish to know what right the KGB has to reduce a man by various forms of persecution to a state where he is legally irresponsible and then interrogate him in that state. What is more, they have used the testimony of a mentally sick man as evidence in this court.

Judge: That is defamation of the KGB. You will answer for your slanderous remarks.

Basilova: That is not slander. My husband's condition was certified by a doctor.

Judge: Commandant, remove this witness.

Zolotukhin: I have some questions to ask the witness.

Judge: Very well, you may do so.

Zolotukhin: Your husband is a patient in a psychiatric clinic, isn't he?

Basilova: Yes.

Zolotukhin: How long has he been there?

Basilova: Six years.

Zolotukhin: With what diagnosis?

Basilova: Schizophrenia.

Zolotukhin then drew the court's attention to the medical certificates in the case materials which showed that witness Gubanov was suffering, and had suffered for several years, from a grave mental disorder.

Zolotukhin: Advocate Kaminskaya's application was rejected because Grigorenko, according to the certificate from a psychiatric clinic, is a sick man. Why, therefore, is the testimony of Gubanov—an obviously sick man, hospitalized several times for schizophrenia—accorded such great importance that it is accepted as the sole and sufficient evidence of Ginzburg's guilt on one of the counts of the indictment?

Zolotukhin asked the court to expunge Gubanov's interrogation from the record. The court heard him out, but stated in a written ruling that it did not find sufficient grounds for removing Gubanov's testimony. The court did not examine Gubanov, whose mental state obviously excluded any possibility of public questioning. Yet in its verdict the court referred to his pretrial testimony as proof of Ginzburg's guilt.

Almost every trial produces something unexpected, surprises that sometimes might have been foreseen and sometimes are unpredictable bombshells which require an advocate to respond instantly and correctly.

January 10, 1968, the third day of the trial: it was 10:00 A.M. and the day's session had just begun.

The prosecutor submitted an application to the court: "I request the court to call as a witness citizen Brox-Sokolov, who may be able to give valuable testimony in the present case."

Who on earth was Brox-Sokolov? There was no mention of his name in the pretrial investigation material, and no witness or defendant had mentioned him in the courtroom.

The prosecutor explained that Brox-Sokolov was a citizen of Venezuela who had come to the Soviet Union as a tourist and had been arrested by the KGB in December 1967. The investigation of his case was not yet complete, but he had already given certain testimony that was relevant to the present trial.

To be able to respond to this application and give the court our opinion on it, the advocates needed above all to be able to study the testimony that Brox-Sokolov had given to the authorities. Our request for this material was fully in accordance with procedural law; such applications were always granted.

Again prosecutor Terekhov rose to make a statement: "I should inform the court that the case of Brox-Sokolov is of special importance to the state, and therefore the materials in his case cannot be publicly released."

But if Brox-Sokolov's testimony was so secret that it could not be shown to us, all of whom were cleared for access to secret documents and allowed to defend cases involving state secrets, how could this witness be examined in open court? Clearly not all his testimony was quite so secret as the prosecutor claimed. (Incidentally, Brox-Sokolov was tried six months later in the Moscow City Court. He was tried in open court, in the presence of press and public, and the case was reported in Soviet newspapers. There were no state secrets in his case, and the court, after finding him guilty of anti-Soviet propaganda, "in consideration of his sincere repentance" ordered him released from custody right there in the courtroom.)

We submitted a new application, this time asking access only to that part of Brox-Sokolov's testimony on which he would be examined in our trial. This, surely, the court could not refuse. Mironov listened, leaning against the high back of his judicial chair; having heard our objections, he gave a barely discernible nod to the two assessors on his left and right and then without changing his pose except to intensify the grimace of squeamish disgust which never left his face throughout the trial, dictated to the clerk of the court: "The prosecutor's applications granted. Citizen Brox-Sokolov to be summoned to this court for examination in the capacity of a witness. The request of defense counsel to study the records of Brox-Sokolov's investigation is refused."

Throughout the day, while the witnesses were being examined, while attention was strained to the limit, I could not get rid of the thought of this unknown Venezuelan citizen, whose testimony we were due to hear. During the recesses, talking to our clients, each of us tried to discover who this mysterious Brox-Sokolov might be and what connection he might possibly have with our case. He had come to the Soviet Union one year *after* our clients were arrested, and none of them had ever heard of him before.

At 7:00 P.M. came the piercing sound of the bell announcing the end of the working day, the noise of departing footsteps, then silence. Our trial went on, as witness after witness was examined.

Almost all the witnesses whom the prosecution called were friends or acquaintances of the defendants, sympathetic to them. Whereas Mironov listened benevolently to the testimony of Tsvetkov and Golovanov, the photocopier informants, the behavior he allowed in the courtroom when friends and relatives of the accused were examined was indescribable; there was hardly a break in the laughter and the insults shouted from the public benches.

The spectators laughed when witnesses characterized Galanskov as kind and unselfish or Ginzburg as a talented young man. They laughed, too, when witnesses talked about themselves, as if it were funny when, asked his profession, a man replied, "I am a poet," or, "I am a writer on religious matters." The laughter was incessant throughout the tragic testimony of the witness Basilova.

Mironov obviously approved of this reaction from the "public." The judge himself did not laugh at the witnesses; he used his powers to taunt them. According to law, witnesses, once examined, must remain in the courtroom and are not allowed to leave until the end of the hearing. Judge Mironov, however, forbade any of the defendants' friends to stay in court.

Whenever he curtly dismissed a witness, the court usher (specially appointed by the KGB to keep order during our trial) had already opened the door into the corridor, so that the witness could not stay in the courtroom for a single extra minute.

When the examination of one of Ginzburg's acquaintances, Vinogradov, was finished, Mironov pronounced the familiar: "Witness, you are free to go." Vinogradov, however, asked to stay in the courtroom: "You must allow it. According to Article 283 I have to stay here."

"Under that same Article 283 you will immediately leave the courtroom. Commandant, conduct the witness out." Mironov's response evoked the special approval of the Party elite in the audience.

Examining witnesses is a very difficult part of the advocate's work. One must listen and find time to make notes, and one must sense the witness's mood and state of mind instantly, because this determines what one can usefully ask him. That day and evening, however, I was distracted by the ceaseless nagging thought: Who is this Brox-Sokolov? When will he appear? And still witness succeeded witness, so that there was not even time to realize how tired I was after these ten hours of almost uninterrupted work.

Now a young woman was on the witness stand—black hair, dark eyes, dressed in black, too, with a large black scarf patterned with bright red roses around her shoulders. This was Aïda Topeshkina, a long-standing acquaintance of Yurii Galanskov and a friend of his wife. Again there was laughter in the courtroom. How funny it was to hear that Galanskov was "poor as a church mouse," that he had invariably helped the witness at difficult moments in her life; it was also amusing that he loved children.

The people in the public seats were not always the same. Each day of the trial some new faces appeared in place of those I had seen earlier, but the new people were as raucous as the others. During one of the recesses we were standing in the hallway outside the courtroom. Beside us was an enormous window, almost as high as the wall itself, looking out onto Kalanchevskaya Street. There was a crowd in front of the courthouse—overcoat collars turned up, the women in woolen scarves. They had been standing for hours in the merciless cold of deep winter. At that moment I heard a voice behind me: "What wouldn't I give for a machine gun right now! I'd let that bunch down there have it point-blank." This produced a burst of laughter. It was a group of spectators from the courtroom. These people not only found the trial a laughing matter; as soon as the mask slipped for a moment, they revealed themselves for what they were: Fascists.

I often think about this scene. People standing in the cold, freezing, not leaving, just standing. This is indeed a demonstration, one without slogans and placards, without bands and banners, but a genuine demonstration of solidarity.

Oh, how small the circle of these revolutionaries.
That's why it's easy to surround them in the yard . . .

wrote a famous Moscow songwriter in a song he dedicated to this trial.

We thought at the time that it was a big crowd out there, but perhaps it wasn't that large after all. Just a few special people whose names appeared in letters of protest, in appeals to world public opinion. They join these silent demonstrations, trial after trial, until they themselves are taken to the courtroom, not as spectators or witnesses but as defendants. How many of them have walked this road from demonstrations of solidarity to the defendants' cage . . .

Whenever political cases were being tried, I always noticed the plain-clothes KGB men lurking among and around the crowd outside. They were watching the demonstrators, photographing them, trying to provoke them, in the hope of intimidating people and suppressing this tradition of silent moral support. It ought to have been easy to harass them into dispersing, yet year after year the crowd never grew smaller and the tradition was kept up. On that day, as we looked out the third-floor window at the people standing below, it was easy enough to distinguish who were sympathizers and who were KGB agents. Although both sets of people were equally frozen in the subzero cold, both sorts hunched themselves into their coat collars and stamped their feet in the same way; even at that distance there was no mistaking who was who.

The recess ended, and it was time for us to return to the courtroom.

When Aïda Topeshkina had answered the last question that was put to her, she wanted either to add something to her testimony or to make some kind of statement. "We're not interested in your statement. You may go," snapped Mironov. From the audience came shouts of: "Off you go! Get out! . . . You should be looking after your kids! You ought to be ashamed of yourself!"

Mironov used rudeness to punish witnesses if they were recalcitrant, refused to be intimidated, or showed any independence. A witness who let fall even a single word of condemnation of the defendants was treated quite differently.

One of the witnesses was Ludmila Katz, whom I remembered as a witness in the Bukovsky trial. A young pretty girl closely acquainted with all four defendants, she confirmed that Dobrovolsky had given her books published by NTS:

Judge Mironov: Dobrovolsky gave you literature of an obviously anti-Soviet nature. How could you, a Soviet citizen, have anything more to do with him after that?
Witness Katz: At the time, I didn't know he would turn out to be such scum.

Mironov would naturally have preferred it if the witness had condemned Galanskov or Ginzburg rather than Dobrovolsky, but he was grateful even so. He smiled and permitted Katz—alone among all the witnesses—to stay in the courtroom. A few minutes later, however, Mironov realized he had misunderstood her condemnation. It was borne in upon him that in calling Dobrovolsky "scum" the witness had not been blaming him for giving her NTS books or telling her about the organization. She had condemned Dobrovolsky's treachery.

A recess was announced, after which Katz was not allowed back into the courtroom. Mironov personally took care of that.

Another witness was now on the stand, and again Mironov made no attempt to stop the shouts of abuse, gave no admonitions to observe the obligatory rule of silence in court. He was not following a directive from higher authority or incapable of conducting a trial properly. He simply enjoyed watching the defendants being taunted, their friends derided.

Then silence fell. Even the noisiest spectators shut up. People seemed to be holding their breath. The only sound was Mironov's voice.

"Witness, tell the court your name, age, and nationality."

"My name is Brox-Sokolov, Nikolai Borisovich. I am twenty-one years old and a citizen of Venezuela. I was born in West Germany, but I now live in France."

We listened to Brox-Sokolov's testimony with the utmost attention, waiting for the really important part of it, the evidence that would damn our clients, the evidence for which this witness had been brought from prison.

I am a student at the University of Grenoble in France. I speak Russian well enough to give my testimony without the help of an interpreter.

I came to the Soviet Union as a tourist. In November 1967 I met a girl in a café. She told me about some young Russian writers who had been arrested by the KGB, and asked me whether I would agree to give these writers some help during my trip—which involved mailing letters on their behalf in Moscow. This girl, Tamara Volkova, named the writers she wanted me to help: Galanskov, Ginzburg, and Dobrovolsky. During my meeting with Tamara she convinced me that these people were real writers, and I therefore agreed to give what help I could to people who had suffered for their artistic integrity. I learned from Tamara that she was a representative of NTS and that Slavinsky, who gave lectures at the university on underground literature, was an important figure in that organization.

In early December 1967 I met Tamara again. There was another man with her, who was also, I gathered, a representative of the NTS. By then I already knew the date of my departure for the Soviet Union, and we agreed that . . .

"Comrade advocates, stop talking. You are disturbing the court's work."

The judge had interrupted the witness's testimony to admonish us. Mironov was right. We were talking.

"Do you remember the date we applied for a postponement?" one of my colleagues asked me.

"I understand now why they granted it," said another.

"They were expecting him," I whispered in reply.

Were we right in our supposition? Only the KGB could give a precise answer, but we had solid grounds for our suspicions.

One could, of course, assume that the correspondence in time between the postponement and the date of Brox-Sokolov's arrival was pure coincidence; but the new starting date of the trial had not been set until Brox-Sokolov was arrested. The KGB was obviously expecting him; they already had information that a man with a special mission was coming to Moscow. On the day before he left France to travel to the Soviet Union, Brox-Sokolov met an NTS representative who gave him a body belt into which were sewn five letters, photographs of our defendants, special paper for coded writing, an enciphering device, and 3000 rubles in Soviet currency.

Brox-Sokolov was arrested on the third day of his stay in Moscow. He had not yet tried to carry out any of his instructions. The body belt was still unopened. His behavior during those three days was no different from the behavior of an ordinary tourist and could not have aroused suspicion. He had not set up any illegal contacts nor met any of the people who were under KGB surveillance. He was arrested in the open, in a park, in circumstances that were in no way compromising.

The decision to arrest a foreign citizen in this way undoubtedly meant that the KGB had information about Brox's mission. I would not be surprised if the KGB knew the exact contents of the body belt in advance. As soon as Brox was arrested, as soon as the belt was found and opened, as soon as the photographs of our defendants were lying on the investigator's desk, alongside the coding paper and ciphering instrument—identical with those found in Dobrovolsky's apartment—the new date was set for the trial.

If our supposition—our certainty—that the trial was postponed for this potential witness's arrival was correct, then it must be said that the elaborate operation did not do much to bring about the KGB's plan of "exposing" the defendants.

It did have a psychological effect. There was considerable emotional tension as we sat expecting some amazing revelation. But no revelation came. Although he blamed himself for having agreed to carry out the instructions of the NTS and condemned the NTS even more severely for having "abused my confidence and enticed me," Brox did not tell the court anything that would serve as proof of the defendants' guilt. The envelopes he was supposed to mail in Moscow turned out to contain nothing but short biographies of our clients accompanied by an appeal to strive for their release. The money and the encoding materials were to be given to a man who had no connection with the defendants, and so were useless as material evidence in our case.

All the information Brox gave the court about Galanskov, Ginzburg, and Dobrovolsky was drawn from the Grenoble lectures on illegal Soviet literature. It was obvious to everyone who heard Brox-Sokolov that a firm prosecution case could not be built on his testimony. There was, however, another aim, which to the KGB and the propaganda machine of the Communist Party was no less important than proving the defendants guilty: to compromise the NTS and its leaders, which would morally compromise Ginzburg, Galanskov, and Dobrovolsky.

To achieve this objective, much use was made of Brox-Sokolov's testimony. There was not a single newspaper article on the trial in which his evidence was not cited. Equally widely quoted were his opinions, such as his view of the "gentlemen of the NTS" and his disparaging comments about the defendants: "I thought they were writers. In France they were described as writers. But I see now they are not writers at all. They are being tried as criminals for having links with the NTS."

By January 11 the trial was approaching its final stages. All the witnesses except one had been examined, all the evidence scrutinized. Suddenly the prosecutor asked permission to submit a new application. In his hands was a sheet of heavy, expensive paper with a typewritten text, and he asked the court for permission to include among the materials in the case "a document of exceptional importance."

"It is clear from this document," said the prosecutor, "that the NTS is an agency of American intelligence; it figures in the budget of the CIA and is wholly financed by the latter."

One of us, without waiting for Mironov's ruling, asked the prosecutor, with more than a touch of irony, "Did the CIA give you that document?"

"No, comrade advocate," the prosecutor replied quite seriously. "This information has not come from the CIA but from the KGB. I earnestly request that it be added to the materials in the case."

We examined this unique document. At the top, a letterhead in large type: COMMITTEE FOR STATE SECURITY OF THE USSR. At the bottom, the huge seal of the KGB and a signature. Despite defense objections, this document was formally added to the materials in the case. The following is its full text:

The KGB is in possession of reliable data proving that, after the defeat of Hitlerite Germany, the NTS was entirely maintained first by the British and then by American intelligence. American intelligence annually remits to the NTS 200,000 dollars, intended principally to cover the cost of salaried employees of this organization and the prosecution of anti-Soviet activity.

Furthermore, the CIA also supplies the NTS with funds for specific anti-Soviet missions, including ideological propaganda campaigns against the USSR, and the training and dispatch of NTS emissaries and liaison personnel to the Soviet Union.

January 10, 1968.

> Committee of State Security
> of the
> Council of Ministers of the USSR
> Deputy Director of Administration
> [signed]   Olovyannikov

Now the remaining witness was called. As in the Bukovsky trial, we awaited the expert psychiatric evidence of Dr. Daniel Lunts.

Dobrovolsky had been an outpatient at a psychiatric clinic since 1955, and had several times been hospitalized for psychiatric treatment. In 1964 he had been sent to the Serbsky Institute for examination by forensic psychiatrists, and had been declared legally not responsible. In 1966 he underwent treatment for schizophrenia in a psychiatric hospital.

Galanskov, too, had been hospitalized more than once on psychiatric grounds. For a long time he was treated in Moscow's Sokolov Psychiatric Hospital. Among his papers in the case, apart from the usual medical certificates, was a special "Expert Consultants' Report" which pronounced the same diagnosis on Galanskov as on Dobrovolsky: schizophrenia.

This time, during the pretrial stage, a medical commission headed by Dr. Lunts had declared them both legally responsible, and he repeated this conclusion in court. If ever there was an obedient science, it is Soviet psychiatry.

My knowledge of psychiatry is limited to what an advocate needs to know. I studied forensic psychiatry in law school, then kept up to date with the specialized literature on the subject. I had, however, spent a lot of time in Galanskov's company, during which I had observed him closely and had, of course, formed my own opinion of his mental state. In my view, his character and thought were not so much marked by deviation from the normal in the medical sense as by deviation from standardized thinking. Yurii was absolutely lucid and alert, thoroughly well informed, and his

actions were completely logical. He was also an unusual personality; sometimes we even laughed together at his eccentricities, which were always
charming and likable. Never once, however, did I feel the slightest doubt
of his mental integrity and stability. I was forced to agree with Lunts's
conclusions, at least about my client.

The evidentiary stage of the trial was completed. Prosecution and defense speeches began on the same day.

What had these four days of judicial hearing provided for my defense of
Yurii Galanskov? What new elements had emerged from the testimony of
witnesses and defendants? Alas, my position remained as difficult as before.
It was still two men standing before the court and giving contradictory,
mutually exclusive testimony about the same events. Like all defendants,
both were keenly concerned about the outcome of the trial, but their relative positions were unequal: all the confidence of the court was placed in one
of them, Dobrovolsky.

Alexander Ginzburg's testimony in court was excellent on all counts of
the indictment against him. His statements were precise, concrete, and
convincing. Where the defense of Galanskov was concerned, however,
Ginzburg's evidence related only to one incident, their alleged collaboration
on the *White Book*. As before, Ginzburg affirmed that he had edited this
compilation alone, with no help from Galanskov.

Galanskov's testimony in court was lengthy and diffuse. He admitted
being the compiler and editor of the journal *Phoenix 66* but did not consider
this criminal. He categorically denied any links with NTS. He denied sending *Phoenix 66* or the *White Book* abroad, denied receiving any literature,
money, or encoding materials from the visiting foreigners. He explained
his pretrial testimony, in which he had admitted all these things, as follows:

> By taking all the responsibility on myself, I intended to save the others, includ-
> ing Dobrovolsky. But when I discovered what Dobrovolsky had been saying
> about me in his testimony, I was angry with him for telling such lies and so I
> withdrew my first testimony. The second time, I admitted everything of which
> Dobrovolsky had accused me, under pressure from the investigator.

In court Yurii gave an exact account of this pressure. The investigator
had said that unless Galanskov reverted to his previous testimony, not only
he but all the others would be more severely punished; all of them, it was
threatened, including Vera Lashkova, would be sentenced to forced labor
in the uranium mines. This passage of Galanskov's courtroom testimony
was not, however, recorded in the transcript of the trial.

Many of the witnesses had provided evidence that Yurii was an unselfish
and honorable young man. On the other hand, one of the most well-disposed

witnesses had described how on Yurii's instructions she had sold dollars (for which she paid with a long term of imprisonment), and had shown the court that Yurii must have known the dollars would be sold on the black market. "I feel certain," she said, "that Galanskov would have spent that money for some entirely noble, unselfish cause, and not on himself. But like everyone else in our country, he must have known that selling foreign currency was a crime."

My hardest task was not explaining away Dobrovolsky's evidence but dealing with that of Vera Lashkova.

At the pretrial stage, Vera had confirmed some of the facts contained in Dobrovolsky's version. She confirmed that in her presence Galanskov had given Dobrovolsky books published by NTS. She confirmed that at Galanskov's dictation she had typed a letter written in code, and that she had seen dollars in Galanskov's apartment. In court she added more detail, saying that although she had seen books handed over, she did not know what they were; that she assumed they were NTS publications because on the same day Dobrovolsky had given her some brochures published by NTS. Lashkova also testified in court that she had once seen a single dollar bill in Galanskov's apartment, but that she had also seen a much greater quantity of them in Dobrovolsky's possession. In her courtroom testimony Lashkova further confirmed that she had used security precautions when typing a letter for Galanskov—Yurii had brought her a pair of thin rubber gloves for this purpose—but she could not remember either the contents of that letter or the contents of the coded letter. In any case, both letters were about ordinary everyday matters, and she had no idea whether their texts had any concealed meaning.

During our talks in Lefortovo, Yurii had assured me that Vera was telling the truth. One of these letters was addressed to the committee of SMOG and contained information about Soviet "Smogist" poets, while the other was sent to Batshev, a fellow Smogist who was then serving a sentence of exile in Siberia. Yurii explained that he could not write to them in plain language because he knew all his letters were intercepted, and I accepted his explanation.

I realized that compared with Dobrovolsky's testimony, Yurii's explanations to the court would not sound very convincing, but we had nothing else to offer. Probably the most valuable piece of evidence in Galanskov's favor was Lashkova's testimony about Dobrovolsky's intention to edit a journal of his own on the lines of *Phoenix 66*, and although Vera slightly weakened her testimony by saying that these plans of Dobrovolsky's were somewhat vague, he had, in fact, already started collecting material, as several other witnesses confirmed.

Vera Lashkova did not betray Yurii in any way. Realizing that any other behavior would go against the grain of Vera's character, the two had agreed long before that if Vera was arrested she would tell the truth, and she did.

When I first saw Lashkova in court, in the difficult situation of someone accused of a serious crime, she impressed me as being a dignified and honorable person. The tone of her testimony, her lack of obsequiousness toward the judge and the prosecutor, and the consistency of her position all made one feel sympathy and respect for her.

I particularly remember the moment when her counsel, Semyon Ariya, was coming to the end of her examination. "Vera," he asked, "you have been under detention for a year. You have had time to think it all over and to reassess what you did. Do you now regret engaging in these activities?"

Vera was standing in front of the judge's desk, her head slightly toward us, and as Ariya spoke, her looks hardened into a stony expression. Then came a barely audible whisper: "Don't ask me that question."

Ariya's face flushed until it was crimson; even the top of his bald head turned red. It was a terrible moment for an advocate—to ask a question which his client did not want to answer and which was therefore likely to do her harm. Mironov was staring hard at Vera, and one of the lay assessors, a woman who until then had merely stared at the proceedings in glazed boredom, turned toward her with a look of interest. The voices in the courtroom had fallen silent; there was no line of retreat.

Again Ariya spoke, almost pleading with Lashkova in desperation. "But why, Vera? You and I have talked about this. You must understand—your fate is being decided at this moment. Answer my question. Do you now regret what you did in the past?"

That night, when I told the story at home, I said, "Vera stood there, thin and erect as a candle . . ."

That's how I remember her—a thin candle, with huge eyes in her small face. And I won't forget how she lifted her head, looked straight in front of her, and calmly said, "No. I don't regret."

That evening, after the courtroom session, each of the advocates worried about Vera. Before the trial an investigator had said to one of my colleagues, "In this case, Galanskov will get the longest sentence, seven years; Ginzburg will get less, five years; Dobrovolsky will get not more than two; and as for Lashkova, she'll get off with a year." Although this investigator was offering his own opinion, experience had taught us that the "opinion" of a KGB investigator tended to coincide with the "opinion" of the court. The trial began January 8, 1968. Vera had been arrested January 17, 1967. Now there were only a few days to go until the end of the period predicted by the investigator, and since pretrial detention time is deducted from a prisoner's sentence, Vera might go free in a few days—provided the court did not increase her sentence. But it was possible that her answer to that question would earn her extra punishment.

Each of us knew that the defendants' fate was not decided in court, that the KGB had judged the case long before it came to trial and the sentences had been fixed at the highest echelons of the Party. Yet if reduction of a preplanned sentence was almost impossible, an increase might well be approved. The incident between Vera and her advocate was cause for alarm.

When I reached the courtroom next morning, Ariya was already in conversation with Vera. I could see him trying to persuade her against her initial opposition; then she listened in silence to his lengthy arguments.

"We have agreed," Ariya told me, "that I will not ask her that question again, but that if the court or the prosecutor puts it to her, she will answer them in less categorical language."

Indeed, no sooner had the day's session opened than the woman assessor immediately addressed Vera: "I would like you to answer again the question put to you yesterday by your advocate. Do you regret what you did, or don't you? You must realize that a great deal depends on your answer. . . ."

Vera replied in these words: "I don't regret having helped some of the defendants as individuals. But if what I did was in any way harmful to the Soviet people, I regret that."

It is unlikely that the court interpreted this reply as repentance; indeed, I feel sure that had it been in Mironov's power, Vera would have paid dearly for it. Fortunately, however, it was now too late to change the high-level decision already made, and four days after the verdict Vera was set free.

On January 11, Terekhov delivered his speech for the prosecution, much of it taken up by a denunciation of the NTS—its "anti-Soviet espionage network" and its attempts "to subvert our state."

"Any link with this organization," said the prosecutor, "is a grave crime against the Soviet people."

Completely rejecting the courtroom testimony in which Galanskov denied his guilt, Terekhov built the case against him entirely on Dobrovolsky's evidence, to which he gave unquestioning credence. "Dobrovolsky was drawn into crime by Galanskov . . . Dobrovolsky did not play an active role. . . . Dobrovolsky repented and proved his repentance was genuine by his correct behavior under investigation and in court. . . ."

Galanskov, on the other hand, had maintained "direct and systematic links with the NTS. . . . Not only did Galanskov himself engage in anti-Soviet activities, he drew Lashkova and Dobrovolsky into them. . . . Galanskov, by deceiving the court in an attempt to avoid responsibility and well-deserved punishment, has shown the court that he has no intention of repenting. . . ."

The prosecutor's "suggested" punishments corresponded with the KGB investigator's prognosis: seven years for Galanskov, five for Ginzburg, two for Dobrovolsky, and one for Lashkova. From the "public" came an immediate burst of applause, mixed with shouts of "That's not enough! They should be given more!"

The defense speeches began after the lunch break.

All that day there had been more people in the courtroom than usual, some of them very familiar to us. They included all the senior judges of the Moscow City Court, headed by its chairman; several men in the uniform of the procuracy; and members of the Presidium of the College of Advocates. Other judges from around Moscow had come, and even some advocates were allowed in. All this heightened the electric charge in the atmosphere, familiar to anyone who has ever had to speak in court; I had felt this special kind of tension since I got up that morning.

Perhaps it was because of my self-absorption that at first I did not notice something else that was new in the courtroom; there was a change, an unfamiliar feature which I could not at first identify. Only later, when I noticed one of my colleagues staring fixedly at one spot on the opposite wall, did I observe the novelty. High up, on a level with the hanging light fixtures, certain objects of indeterminate shape had been fastened to the wall and carefully draped in black muslin, like the stuff some people drape over lamps and mirrors in a room where a corpse is lying.

The reason for this strange new decoration became clear to us during the recess. Overnight, the courtroom had been wired for sound. The speeches in the final stage of the trial were being relayed directly to the Central Committee of the CPSU. Our work was to be monitored not only by the senior members of the judiciary but also by the highest level of the Party.

In keeping with the tradition of giving the first word to the defendant who has turned state's evidence, Vladimir Shveisky led off with his speech for Dobrovolsky.

Defending Dobrovolsky was relatively easy. The charges against him were limited to those to which he had pleaded guilty, so that his defense was not obliged to contest any facts. There could be no dispute over the anti-Soviet content of the NTS brochures which Dobrovolsky had admitted distributing, nor over the framing of the charges under Article 70 (anti-Soviet activity); Dobrovolsky had admitted in court that his activities, like those he attributed to Galanskov and Ginzburg, "had been criminal and anti-Soviet in nature" and "committed with anti-Soviet intentions." All this predetermined the line that Shveisky adopted in his defense plea. Basically, his speech was devoted to a psychological analysis of the reasons that had brought Dobrovolsky to crime. Shveisky's dispute with the prosecution was restricted to denying the criminal character of one of the documents confiscated from Dobrovolsky, "A Description of Events in the Pochayev Monastery." (This argument, which Ariya and I also pursued, was the defense's only success; the court agreed with us.) The document, written and signed by the monks of the Pochayev Monastery, described the arbitrary harassment and physical indignities to which they had been subjected by the local authorities. At the time of our trial the accuracy of these facts had already been admitted by the Soviet government.

For me, Shveisky's speech was significant not so much for what he said as for what he did not say. I knew Vladimir Shveisky well. He was an ambitious man who was very jealous of his professional reputation. Fame for him was not some insubstantial recompense but the true reward for his labors, and he strove hard for it. This trial gave him an opportunity to make a notable speech that gave full play to his abilities. Knowing Shveisky's character and his polemical temperament, I can say with certainty that on this occasion he exercised great restraint by avoiding the more aggressive and potentially more effective tactic of attacking Galanskov. He did not accuse Galanskov of giving contradictory testimony and refrained from making him seem responsible for Dobrovolsky's misfortune. He defended Dobrovolsky as though his client were the sole defendant. Shveisky knew that the court could not step outside the bounds of the charges levelled against Dobrovolsky, therefore could not find him guilty of direct links with the NTS independently of Galanskov; thus while avoiding a contest with Galanskov, Shveisky at the same time did not betray Dobrovolsky's interest.

I don't think many advocates would have imposed such limitations on themselves. My only disagreement with Shveisky related to the legal interpretation he gave to Galanskov's "Open Letter" to Sholokhov.

A winner of the Nobel Prize for Literature, Mikhail Sholokhov is probably the most famous of the officially approved Soviet writers. I don't know how sincere he is in his protestations of loyalty to the Soviet state, but his name has long been associated with the most obscurantist and reactionary trends in Soviet public life. At the Twenty-third Congress of the Soviet Communist Party, in 1966, he had made a speech about the recent trial of the two writers Sinyavsky and Daniel, whose outcome had not pleased him. He regarded their sentences of seven and five years respectively in strict-regime camps as too lenient. He regretted that the days were gone when, as he put it, "people were not judged by the book but by a healthy sense of revolutionary justice," and when, for publishing their books abroad, Sinyavsky and Daniel might have been given any punishment "up to and including the firing squad." The "Open Letter" to Sholokhov was a reply to that speech. Shveisky called this letter "anti-Soviet." I could not agree with this description.

Semyon Ariya's speech in defense of Vera Lashkova was chiefly memorable for the clarity of its construction, the logic of his conclusions, and his brilliant legal analysis. There was absolutely no attempt to play to the gallery, and a complete absence of showy rhetoric. Some people may have found it excessively cool and dispassionate, but the professional lawyers who attended that session gave this speech a high rating.

Like Shveisky, Ariya did not deny that his client had committed a crime. He did, however, undertake an extremely precise yet bold definition of the limits of the concept of "anti-Soviet activity," and argued forcefully against too wide an interpretation of this law. Here Ariya's legal analysis acquired a distinctly political tinge; it was as though he were walking a tightrope— the merest wobble, the slightest loss of balance, and the limit of what it is permissible to say in a Soviet court would have been over-stepped. But he never once lost his balance; his exact, carefully considered wording enabled him to say just what was needed.

I found Ariya particularly convincing in his treatment of the charge against Lashkova of having transcribed documents for the *White Book*. Vera had typed a great many of the materials in the *White Book*, but only one of them, "A Letter to an Old Friend"—which was written by an anonymous author and contained strongly worded criticisms of Stalin—was regarded by the prosecution as anti-Soviet.

I don't know whether it was Zolotukhin (defending Ginzburg, the editor) or Ariya (defending Lashkova, the typist) who conceived the idea that allowed them to avoid the dangers of arguing about the contents of this document and at the same time to plead for an acquittal on this count. Both Zolotukhin and Ariya made effective use of this tactic in their speeches.

"It may be," said Ariya, "that 'A Letter to an Old Friend' contains elements of a criminal nature, but it is no part of the defense's task to analyze its content. Lashkova typed the *White Book* so that it could be circulated among a small group of responsible officials, and not for general distribution. The collation and transcription of any material for such a purpose cannot be said to be criminal."

On those counts in which Lashkova could not deny her involvement, he asserted that she had no anti-Soviet intent, and that in consequence her offense should be reduced from "anti-Soviet propaganda" to "defamation of the Soviet political and social system."

When Ariya finished his speech at 8:30 P.M., the long court day came to a close. Boris Zolotukhin's speech and mine were postponed until the next and final session, which was to begin at 8:30 A.M. January 12.

There followed a sleepless night for me caused less by the need to rehearse the argumentation of my speech (it was all prepared, considered, and systematically laid out in my mind) than by the thought of Yurii being sentenced to seven years. How could a sick man survive for so long in a prison camp? Lawyers get to know that feeling of responsibility for the defendant's fate, and also the feeling of compassion for that defendant. I think the line dividing true lawyers from hacks runs along those feelings. But when the feeling of responsibility is coupled with a sense of total impotence, when sympathy with the person awaiting punishment is coupled with the knowledge that this punishment is tantamount to a death sentence, it is almost impossible to bear.

So I paced around our small kitchen, trying not to disturb my family's sleep, and asked myself again: What had I overlooked? What had I left uncompleted? What essential point might I have forgotten? Why could I always detect a note of personal irritation at Yurii Galanskov in the manner of Terekhov, the otherwise calm and unemotional prosecutor? Why, when Yurii gave his testimony, was the look of disgust on Judge Mironov's face even more pronounced than usual? Since it is part of an advocate's job to instruct one's client how to behave in court so as to make a good impression, or at least so as not to annoy the court, did these reactions to Galanskov mean that I had failed in this?

But even if Yurii had not irritated the court; even if he had been able to suppress the urge to hide his weakness and self-reproach with displays of bravado and sarcasm; even if, when asked why he had written letters in code, he had not replied that he was practicing to take over Andropov's job as head of the KGB (and he gave many more such answers), he would have received seven years all the same. The only thing that might have helped him was "repentance"—and that I could not teach him.

My speech in defense of Yurii Galanskov was in two parts. The first part dealt with those counts that covered his links with the NTS. This relatively lengthy section was largely taken up with an analysis of Dobrovolsky's testimony, as the source of most of the prosecution's evidence against my client. It was the most emotional part of my speech, and I think I did—for that mythical impartial judge—demolish Dobrovolsky's testimony, in part by offering a psychological analysis of what had induced Galanskov to incriminate himself by falsely confessing to things that, in reality, he had not done. My line of argument in this, politically the gravest set of charges against Galanskov, did not expose me to any risk. It was a perfectly normal type of defense, a familiar dispute over the facts, and I was able to ask the court for an acquittal on all these counts without the slightest danger to myself.

When I made this speech I believed that Galanskov had no connection with the NTS. I now know that this was not so; after Yurii's death the NTS announced that he had been a member of their organization. Even knowing this, I have not changed my attitude to Galanskov. As before, the basic criterion for my opinion of him was not whether he had links with the NTS but whether those links led him to do anything cruel or dishonorable. Even the most severely moral judge could not have found anything immoral in the actions for which Yurii was put on trial. My belief in his goodness and altruism remained unshaken.

The attack on Dobrovolsky in court was a professional necessity. My personal attitude to his role in the case, however, has changed since then. He was in the disastrous position of being the person in whose possession the KGB found all the material evidence of connections with the NTS. It needed great steadfastness and courage to accept sole responsibility and not to give other names to the investigators. Dobrovolsky lacked both steadfastness and courage, but it is not for me, never having been deprived of freedom, to pass judgment on him, whose experience had already included prison, prison camp, and psychiatric hospitals.

"Dobrovolsky is a sick, broken man who deserves pity, not condemnation." Those words were written from prison camp, with a special request that they be made public, by the person who knew the truth of the situation from the very start. They are the words of Yurii Galanskov.

The second part of my speech was a much more complex task. I gave an analysis of the five articles, essays, and so on which, among other material, Galanskov had included in *Phoenix 66*, and which the prosecution had classed as anti-Soviet. In my speech I analyzed each of them in detail, and I argued that three out of the five were not criminal. This left two documents: Sinyavsky's essay "What Is Socialist Realism?" and the "Open Letter to Sholokhov." I liked Sinyavsky's essay very much; I was prepared to defend it, and I believe that despite certain passages in which, politically, Sinyavsky sailed very close to the wind, it might have been successfully defended. But that should have been done earlier, at the trial of Sinyavsky himself. Now I needed to find a wording that would save me from having to agree with the Supreme Court's opinion of this essay, and would stress that only the formal requirements of the law prevented me from disputing that opinion. I expressed this position in two sentences: "The verdict of the Supreme Court of the RSFSR in the case of the writers Sinyavsky and Daniel, which has the force of law, is binding on the Moscow City Court. This consideration saves me from the need to analyze this essay here."

It remained for me to comment on the final count of the indictment, to tell the court whether I agreed that the "Open Letter to Sholokhov" was an anti-Soviet document and that its author, Yurii Galanskov, had written and distributed it with anti-Soviet intent.

No other trial has ever brought me such doubts about the correctness of the defense I chose. Many times since then I have reread that letter, in which Yurii described the Soviet system as "a military-police machine, which to this day continues to stifle freedom in Russia," declared that "the regime has reduced the Soviet people to the level of cattle," and called "*Homo Sovieticus*" a "failure to the same degree that the Soviet system itself is a failure."

"Why should you feel these doubts, Madame ex-Soviet Advocate? Why distress yourself?" would be a normal Western reaction to Yurii's manifesto. Why shouldn't someone call his country's regime a military-police machine, say the Soviet system is a failure and that it stifles freedom? Americans, Englishmen, and Frenchmen regularly curse their governments; they shower their political systems with even more unflattering epithets than these, and calmly go on about their business without fear of consequences. But in the Soviet Union the expression of such opinions is a criminal offense, punishable according to law with five to seven years of imprisonment.

I could not claim that what Yurii had written was not meant to apply to the Soviet system as a whole, but only to a particular decision of the government, the line I was able to take in defending Pavel Litvinov. I could not say that the criticism was directed against certain specific, albeit highly placed, individuals. To defend Yurii against this charge, I chose the way of compromise.

My standpoint was not determined by fear for myself or by the fact that Shveisky and Ariya had already admitted the "Open Letter" to be either anti-Soviet or criminal. I made my decision alone—no one exerted any pressure or influence on me—and I made it only because a few isolated passages in this letter were, in Soviet law, criminal. That is why I told the court that if Galanskov had limited himself in this letter to criticism, no matter how sharp, of Sholokhov, I would have asked for this count to be removed from the indictment. I said that in spirit this letter was directed against Sholokhov's speech, which Galanskov regarded as vicious and inhuman, and not against the Soviet system; I said, too, that Galanskov was not alone in his opinions of Sholokhov's speech. Only a few generalized remarks and not the overall meaning of the letter deprived me of the chance to contest its criminal character. I asked the court to concede that in writing the letter Galanskov had no intention of undermining the Soviet government, and therefore to alter the charge from "anti-Soviet activity" to "defamation of the Soviet system."

Having described what I regard as the somewhat dubious part of my speech, I would also like to mention the passages which pleased me.

First, I think that I had the advantage over my colleagues who defended Sinyavsky and Daniel because I did not avoid analyzing the literary works in *Phoenix 66*. I argued that it was equally impermissible to identify an author with his literary heroes and to extend the working of the criminal law to a piece of fictional literature.

Second, I believe my genuine feelings of compassion for Yurii helped me find the right words when I said of him that he was motivated by the most honorable intentions. I am glad that some words from my speech, "He sought for himself neither riches nor fame," were later chosen as the title of a book about that strange, kind, and good man.

Boris Zolotukhin's speech was the last for the defense. In spite of our friendship we had never before worked together in a trial. To me, Boris's speech was the revelation of a new talent. Everything in it was carefully thought out and highly persuasive. It was notable for its moral level and for the boldness of its general conclusions. It was also one of the few forensic orations that lose nothing by being read, although perhaps I am helped by the fact that whenever I read it I can hear the familiar voice. I was watching the members of the court very closely to observe their reactions during Zolotukhin's speech, and I noted the obvious disapproval with which Mironov listened to Boris's references to Western responses to the Sinyavsky-Daniel trial. When Boris reminded the court that Louis Aragon, the French writer and French Communist Party Central Committee member, as well as the secretary of the British Communist Party, John Gollan, were among those who criticized the trial, Mironov's expression changed visibly. This was a very sore point for the Soviet Communist Party: for the first time these loyal friends had publicly condemned the actions of the Soviet government.

Mironov's expression of displeasure was still there when in the silent courtroom we listened intently as Zolotukhin said:

> Ginzburg regarded the verdict in the Sinyavsky-Daniel case as unjust. I want to put to you one general question: What should a citizen do if he holds such a view? He can react to it with apathy or it may arouse in him the need to communicate his opinion to others. A citizen may either look on indifferently as guards escort away an innocent man, or he may take some action on that man's behalf. I don't know which sort of behavior the court finds preferable. But I believe that the behavior of the person who is not content with indifference shows greater civic spirit.
>
> Ginzburg did everything he could to help Sinyavsky and Daniel.

Without literary analysis, Zolotukhin asked for Ginzburg's acquittal on the grounds that the compilation of a documentary collection intended to be read by the upper ranks of the Soviet leadership, regardless of the nature of its constituent documents, could not be regarded as anti-Soviet propaganda or anti-Soviet activity.

According to procedural law, after the defense speeches the judge offers the prosecutor the right of rebuttal. The prosecutor can object to defense counsel's arguments, rectify what he regards as misrepresentation of the verbal or documentary evidence, or point to political errors committed by the defense. Terekhov declined to avail himself of the right to reply.

That, and the fact that Mironov had not admonished any of the advocates or interrupted their speeches, were the first significant signals that defense counsel need not expect any personal vengeance for our efforts in this trial. During the ten-minute recess after Zolotukhin's speech, the prosecutor came over to our table. "I congratulate you, comrade advocates," he said. "That was an interesting defense, not just a routine job of work. You really did everything possible for your clients."

A few minutes later Apraksin, the head of the College of Advocates, said to us, "Well done. Everything is fine; there won't be any unpleasant consequences."

The anxiety I had felt during Ariya's and Zolotukhin's speeches was dispelled, and all of us were uplifted by a strange, ironic sense of triumph. We congratulated each other and listened with delight to the words of gratitude expressed by our clients and their relatives.

The accused said their brief "last words." Vera Lashkova, Yurii Galanskov, and Alexander Ginzburg did not ask the court for leniency and did not repent.

Yurii's request was: "I call upon the court to show restraint in its decisions affecting Dobrovolsky, Lashkova, and me. As for Ginzburg, his innocence is so obvious that no one can doubt what the court's decision should be in his case."

Alexander Ginzburg said that he knew he would be convicted because "no one indicted under Article 70 has ever been acquitted. You may imprison me, you may send me to a camp, but I know that no honest person will condemn me." As they heard him say, "I plead not guilty, being convinced that what I did was right," the "elite" of Soviet society on the public benches roared with laughter. Ginzburg's final words, "I ask the court to award me a sentence no less than that given to Yurii Galanskov," were drowned in noisy shouts of "Too little! They should give you more!"

The court retired and the defendants were led out. We were alone in the empty courtroom. Whatever we may have said, we could think of nothing but the impending verdict.

"Will they convict Alik?"

"They can't find Ginzburg guilty—that would be monstrous!"

We all realized that to hope for justice in a political trial was more than naïve, but the complete failure to prove Alexander Ginzburg's guilt was so obvious that even we, accustomed to arbitrary injustice, could not accept the possibility that he might be convicted. As to what awaited Yurii, I realized that if he got less than seven years, it would be a miracle. Even so, I hoped for that miracle: "If only they give him just five."

When my colleagues insisted, "It's no use to hope. Yurii will get seven years," I nodded in agreement, but in my heart I was angry with them for saying this, and I continued to await a miracle.

The sentences were read: Seven years' imprisonment for Galanskov, five for Ginzburg, two for Dobrovolsky, one for Lashkova.

From the body of the courtroom came shouts of "Not enough! Too little!"

If only in some small way, even by six months, Mironov had reduced the "predictions" of the KGB investigator, at least it would have been a little less obvious that the five days of the trial were a cruel farce. This was one more piece of evidence that, among the series of political trials in which I participated, the Ginzburg case takes first prize for cynical flouting of the law and shameless vindictiveness toward the defendants.

Once again we four advocates stood in the empty hallway of the Moscow City Courthouse, unable to summon up the courage to cross the threshold and go out on the street. The brief sense of triumph, the pleasure at a job conscientiously done, had evaporated as though it had never been. How could we face those families and friends? What could we say to them?

Depression and shame were all I could feel.

I will never forget the next few minutes, when I stepped out onto the street and saw the people frozen to the marrow in the terrible cold. They had not gone away after the trial was over but had waited there to offer us bouquets of red carnations.

Boris drove me home in silence, and at my door he gave me his bouquet. "That's for you," he said. Then, interrupting my attempts to refuse: "You must take it. Let's say it's your first present—after all, tomorrow, January 13, is your birthday."

We could say no more, weighed down by injustice, by anguish for the people we had tried to defend, and by a terrible feeling of helplessness.

5. The Bar on Trial

I MMEDIATELY AFTER the January 12 verdicts, three of the defense lawyers filed notice of appeal: Zolotukhin because he had asked for Ginzburg's acquittal; Ariya and I because we had asked for the attribution of our
client's offenses to be changed from Article 70 of the Criminal Code (anti-
Soviet activity) to Article 190/1 (defamation of the Soviet political and social
system).

For Semyon Ariya this meant a straightforward legal argument about
correct attribution, which did not affect Lashkova's release four days later.
For Boris and me the court of appeal was the place to renew the fight on
behalf of our clients—for release in Ginzburg's case, for a significant reduction of sentence in Galanskov's. We talked long and often about our appeals,
discussing the problems connected with them.

I cannot recall that either of us expressed worries or premonitions about
ourselves while we waited out the appeals process, although there were
certain grounds for anxiety.

Apraksin had told us at once that all had gone well and none of us would
find ourselves in trouble. Very soon, however, rumors began to circulate
around the College of Advocates that the top Party bosses were displeased
by Boris's mentioning the critical reactions to the Sinyavsky-Daniel trial of
distinguished Western Communists. But it seemed to me (and I think to
others) that the only consequence of this displeasure would be that the
Moscow Party Committee would not support Boris for reelection to the
College Presidium in the balloting due to be held shortly.

Among themselves advocates were saying that they would vote for Zolotukhin whether the Party supported him or not. With our system of genuinely secret balloting, Zolotukhin might not become chairman but we could almost certainly insure that he was voted onto the Presidium. A Party member, he had enjoyed Party support up to now and had been the most likely candidate for chairman, if not at this election then at the next.

Then the rumors stopped. Judge Mironov, who was supposed to react to any politically incorrect pronouncements, had listened to the whole of Zolotukhin's defense speech without saying a word and no disciplinary action had been initiated against Boris for incorrect conduct of the defense. I thought that if a judge like Mironov, who so cordially detests advocates, has not found a pretext to admonish him, then Boris has nothing to worry about.

January and February passed, and the first days of March. We finished studying the transcript of the trial and submitted our detailed notices of appeal. We were waiting for our appeals to be heard by the Supreme Court when suddenly events began to move so rapidly that their chronological sequence began to blur. It started with an article in the French weekly *Le Nouvel Observateur*. The article claimed that great changes were taking place in the Soviet Union, that a welcome process of liberalization, of democratization was occurring in Soviet society. To illustrate his thesis the author quoted the passage from Zolotukhin's defense of Ginzburg that contrasted indifference to injustice with "civic spirit."

The author insisted that the mere fact that an advocate in a Soviet court was able to request acquittal for a defendant accused of a political crime, together with the fact that the defense was conducted by advocates chosen by the accused and not nominated by the state, was incontestable evidence of the democratization of the Soviet system. I don't suppose the author of those well-meaning lines realized that his article would incite a savage reprisal. I am sure he did not foresee this any more than we did when, along with a few of our friends, we had an opportunity to read the article.

After the publication, however, it was only a matter of days before we learned that the Party had instituted disciplinary proceedings against Boris, and that his "case" would be dealt with immediately by the Dzerzhinsky District Committee of the CPSU. Several advocates who were Party members told Zolotukhin that he should admit his error, show remorse, and publicly repudiate the *Nouvel Observateur* article by telling the Moscow newspapers that his speech was distorted. They assured Boris that if he did this, he would not be expelled from the Party.

I'm sure these advocates meant well. I am also certain that their advice was inspired by high Party authorities.

Zolotukhin did not accept this advice, and on March 21, 1968, he was expelled from the Party by a decision of the Dzerzhinsky District Committee. Simultaneously the Committee recommended to the Presidium of the College of Advocates that Boris be dismissed from his position in charge of the Dzerzhinsky District law office.

The absurdity and illegality of persecuting an advocate for doing his professional duty must be self-evident. No advocate in Moscow can have failed to realize this or to have been outraged by the injustice of this repressive act. But after Zolotukhin's expulsion, some people laid part of the blame for what had happened on my husband and me, because they felt that Boris's unyielding attitude was to some extent due to our influence. We, however, could not accept the honor. His refusal to admit the error of his chosen defense tactics, of whose rightness he was convinced, was not the result of outside influence but of Boris's innate integrity. He could not accept the offered compromise because he was a courageous and honorable man.

There are people who are honorable in intentions but whose good intentions are vitiated by weakness of character. Boris was strong enough to be honorable in both aim and action.

He had begun his career as a prosecutor in the procuracy, in other words in a considerably more respected branch of the legal profession. Boris came from a family whose social status undoubtedly contributed to his advancement. His parents were both Communist Party members. His father held a very high position, with the rank of minister, in the Soviet hierarchy and enjoyed all the privileges the state affords to the ruling elite. The Kremlin's restricted-access stores, government-owned vacation homes and health clinics—Boris knew such things at first hand, they were his milieu. He was born and raised in an atmosphere of absolute loyalty to the regime which had given his father everything, had made him, a country shepherd boy, into a minister.

To the best of my knowledge Boris's father loved him dearly and was glad to help him make a good career. But by the standards of the Soviet establishment his career did not work out—and never could have. Under Soviet conditions, people of independent character, people who are principled and honorable, do not make a career in public service, no matter what their attitude to the regime may be. His independence of mind and adherence to principle predetermined Boris's enforced resignation from the procuracy. Specializing in major cases of "economic" crime—embezzlement, illegal trading, black marketeering, currency offenses, and the like—he prosecuted his cases according to the facts and the law. During one such trial Boris came to the conclusion that the guilt of some of the accused was not proven.

"If as a result of a judicial hearing a prosecutor decides that the evidence presented in court does not support the charge raised against the defendant, he is obliged to withdraw the indictment." (Article 248, Code of Criminal Procedure of the RSFSR.)

Zolotukhin acted in accordance with this law. The governing body of the Moscow Procuracy demanded that he insist on the guilt of the defendants in question and press for their conviction. The case itself was too scandalous and the accused had been too long in detention before the trial; to drop it now would mean severe loss of face for the procuracy. Zolotukhin had the choice of obeying his superiors and asking the court to convict people he regarded as innocent, or resigning.

Zolotukhin made a speech in court in which he gave detailed arguments in support of his plea to acquit the defendants, and then left the procuracy. It was thus that he became an advocate and, some years later, the head of one of the law offices in the center of Moscow and a member of the Presidium of the College of Advocates.

The entire college was disturbed at Zolotukhin's expulsion from the Party. We all realized that the matter was one of great importance for every member of the College—that is, whether in a political trial, when a client's guilt was unproven, an advocate could ask for an acquittal, or whether the defense should merely ask for leniency and thereby betray the client.

Zolotukhin was greatly liked and respected in the college, but it was a realization of common danger that persuaded the college to give him open support during the first stages of the authorities' attack. When the disciplinary case against him was heard by the Dzerzhinsky District Party Committee and then, at the appeal stage, by the Moscow City Party Committee, the Party secretary of Boris's law office tried to prove the groundlessness of the accusations and gave him a brilliant character reference.

The advocates who had been in the Ginzburg-Galanskov trial also tried to help him. We decided to write to Viktor Grishin, the first secretary of the Moscow Committee of the Party. We did not tell Boris about this, but after long discussion and careful joint editing, a letter was composed that satisfied us all.

We wrote that each of us had more than twenty years' experience of trial work, including cases that involved crimes of special danger to the state. This experience, combined with our participation in the Ginzburg trial, enabled us to make an informed judgment on Zolotukhin's work on that case. We went on:

> The position chosen independently by each of the defense counsel was then discussed jointly by all of us in order to avoid any errors. The line of defense taken by Advocate Zolotukhin was admitted unanimously to be the only possible one for the defense of Ginzburg. Any one of us, any conscientious advocate,

would have been obliged in the circumstances to adopt the same position. To diverge from it by admitting Ginzburg's guilt would have meant, in practical terms, depriving him of a defense in this trial and thereby violating his rights guaranteed by Article III of the Constitution of the USSR. . . .

We do not know how Comrade Zolotukhin's defense speech was utilized by the bourgeois press. But if his words were not distorted, the exposition of Comrade Zolotukhin's speech can only increase the prestige of our country and of Soviet justice, since it has shown that a defendant can call upon the most highly qualified and skilled lawyers to defend him when he is on trial.

The three of us signed this letter, and it only remained to send it to its addressee. Then either Shveisky or Ariya showed it to Zolotukhin. They undoubtedly acted with the very best intentions—to get his agreement to the text and find out whether anything should be added. But they should not have done it. Knowing Boris, I could have told them beforehand that he would refuse to allow others to place themselves in jeopardy. And so it happened.

Having persuaded Shveisky and Ariya to drop the idea, Boris then telephoned and persuaded me as well, saying that it would be wrong for me, not a member of the Party, to send such a letter to the Party authorities. I blame myself for giving in to his persuasion. The only thing I can say in justification is that I did not understand the full danger of what was happening. As far as I was concerned, Boris's expulsion from the Communist Party was a crying injustice but not a disaster. Although I did not say so to Boris, I privately thought that he was well out of the Party, just as he could survive perfectly well without being head of a law office or a member of the College Presidium. The important thing was that he should remain an advocate, which I had no doubt he would do.

Even when Boris said that if he were disbarred I would have to take over Ginzburg's appeal in the Supreme Court, I did not take him seriously; I simply swore at him for entertaining such a thought. I thought that Mironov's failure to file a complaint against him was an absolute guarantee that the college authorities would not bring disciplinary action.

A few days or perhaps a week later I heard, not from Zolotukhin but from a member of the College Presidium, that the authorities were not going to stop at his expulsion from the Party. The Moscow Committee of the Party had demanded Zolotukhin's expulsion from the College of Advocates. Then I realized that this was not just a spot of trouble for Boris but a real disaster.

Boris was happy in our profession. He had told me so many times. He loved advocacy and was profoundly committed to it. Although I knew he was not threatened with starvation—in time he could find himself another job—I regarded his potential disbarment, denying him the work for which he had a genuine vocation, as nothing short of a catastrophe.

Our appeals against the verdict of the City Court in the Ginzburg-Galanskov case were heard on April 16. Knowing that neither Ginzburg nor his parents would object, I offered to take Boris's place in the defense of Ginzburg. Boris, however, refused my offer. He considered it his obligation to conduct the case to the end, even though he was well aware that by repeating arguments that had already been severely criticized by the authorities, he was running the risk of worsening the consequences for himself. His arguments before the Supreme Court were irreproachable in their clarity and persuasiveness. The inadequacy and injustice of the Moscow City Court's verdict were made plain.

The bench of the Supreme Court that heard our appeals included several familiar figures. Two of them were former City Court judges, before whom I had appeared innumerable times. Earlier, in trying usual criminal cases, they had been true judicial arbiters; now, as members of the special bench of the Supreme Court, they were not expected to judge: they just did as they were told.

The verdict of the Moscow City Court was upheld.

At the beginning of May, I learned that the matter of Boris's disbarment would be raised at a session of the College Presidium. According to the Statute on Advocacy, questions of enrollment in and exclusion from the profession are the prerogative of the elected body that governs the college, its Presidium. The Moscow Committee of the Communist Party had decided not to infringe this law directly, and had instructed the advocates themselves to deal with Zolotukhin.

I know for certain that before the Presidium session, the Moscow Party Committee representative called a preliminary meeting of the Presidium's "Party group" (that is, all its members who belonged to the Party) and warned them that anyone who disobeyed the directive of the Moscow Party Committee and dared to vote against Boris's expulsion would also be expelled from the Party. Therefore my first move was to try to persuade the members of the Presidium (fourteen or fifteen at the time) that if they all refused to vote for Boris's expulsion, the Party Committee would have to accept this.

My first attempt to persuade the Presidium members took place in the Butyrki Prison, where I had gone for a meeting with a client. I had climbed the steep stairs and was walking down a long corridor. Toward me along the corridor came another woman advocate, Lyubov Sokolova.

Lyubov Sokolova's name was known to every lawyer in Moscow. She was one of the most skilled and experienced advocates of her day, with a flawless professional reputation and the authority of a thoroughly upright person. When she saw me, she spoke first about the very subject I was about to bring up.

"Dina," she said, "this is an awful business, an absolute scandal. I haven't been able to sleep for thinking about Boris. I can't take part in this meeting; I won't come to the Presidium session. I'll say I'm sick, that I've had a touch of heart trouble again."

"Why?" I asked. "You *must* come. They're counting on you. If you vote against Boris's expulsion others will join you."

She was standing beside me, tall and thin, hair slightly tinged with gray, features that might have come from an antique Byzantine ikon—an ascetic face with beautiful elongated eyes: the strong face of a woman with a will of her own.

"You must be crazy," she replied. "Do you realize what you're saying?"

Lyubov Sokolova was probably the only member of the Presidium who had absolutely nothing to fear. She was not a Party member and she could hardly be threatened by any form of reprisal. Her fear was irrational; she told me so herself: "Don't try to persuade me, Dina. I understand everything. I'm an old woman and I have a secure pension. Was that what you were going to say to me? If only I knew why I'm afraid! I can't explain it. It's simply beyond my powers to grasp it. But I won't take part in this shameful business. At least I will not disgrace myself."

My second approach was also to a woman, also not a Party member. Advocate Maria Blagovolina was a friend of mine and of Zolotukhin's—a determined person, full of the joy of life, a tireless and magnificent raconteuse with whom we had spent countless enjoyable evenings. I always thought of her as "one of us."

"I'm not afraid for myself," she told me. "I have nothing to fear. What could they do to me? Well, suppose they expelled me from the college? I'm well aware that I'm not the world's greatest advocate, and anyway I'm due to retire on a pension soon. As for money, well, I needn't tell you that I have enough to see me to my grave and beyond." Maria's father had been the most distinguished professor of gynecology in all Moscow, and his services had been highly prized by the government. Lenin had issued a special decree allowing his family to keep in perpetuity their old prerevolutionary house in the center of Moscow.

"But, well, it's Seryozha, my son. You must understand, he is just starting his career. I haven't the right to cause him any trouble. So I won't come to the session of the Presidium, but more than that I cannot do."

And so it went—one after another, men and women, Party members and nonmembers. Only once during these conversations did I sense a hostile attitude toward Boris, a half-concealed condemnation of him for having put us all in a dangerous situation through his unyielding stand. This attitude emanated from another non-Party man, Ivan Parkinson, also an old advocate with an excellent reputation, who in addition possessed the special aura of a man who had served his term in Stalin's prison camps and had earned the respect of his fellow prisoners by his irreproachable behavior. I had the impression that Parkinson envied Zolotukhin his youth and talent as well as the rapidity with which he had earned recognition, respect, and affection among the members of our profession. Only later did I discover that his animosity was caused by another and more serious, but no less shameful reason.

All the others suffered agonies of indecision, realizing that they were being asked to take part in a base, unjust act of reprisal, and all of them could see only one way out—to abstain.

Once during this period of tension Ariya, Shveisky, and I met again to write another letter, this time to Konstantin Apraksin. This time we decided to write separately. One of the others, either Ariya or Shveisky, thought that a joint or "collective" letter was a form of protest of which the Party authorities disapproved, whereas they tended to react more favorably to individual letters as being the expression of the writer's personal opinion. And so it was agreed. I decided to take action independently, without telling Boris what I planned to do.

On May 31 I sent a letter to Apraksin, with a copy to all the other members of the Presidium. In it, in concise form, I laid out all the arguments of our first letter, adding the reminder that before his speech for Ginzburg, Zolotukhin had in my presence informed Apraksin and his deputy, Isaak Sklyarsky, of the position he intended to adopt in his defense plea, and that both of them had approved of Zolotukhin's line of defense.

Then I wrote a passage addressed to all members of the Presidium: "The expulsion of an advocate for doing his professional duty is unprecedented and puts a grave burden of personal responsibility on every member of the Presidium who supports such a measure," and I asked permission to address the session of the Presidium.

Two or three days later, Apraksin telephoned. My husband picked up the phone and had to listen to a string of accusations, reproaches, and threats against me. Apraksin begged my husband (they had been students together in law school) to try to persuade me, "before it's too late and while it's still possible to save her," to withdraw my letter. He announced that I was already in isolation, because Ariya and Shveisky had withdrawn their letters. Naturally my husband refused to do anything of the sort.

That evening, either Shveisky or Ariya—I have forgotten which—came to see us and said that on the previous day they had both been summoned to the District Committee of the Party and told to withdraw their letters to the Presidium immediately or lose their Party membership cards. As he told us this, we could see that he was painfully ashamed, that he realized he was betraying a comrade, but I could not blame him. As a Party member he was in a much more vulnerable position than I. When he had gone, I thought to myself for the nth time, thank God I'm not in the Party.

At this point Boris learned about the affair of the letters. He did not try to persuade me to withdraw my letter; he merely said, "You must realize you can't do anything to help me now. Everything is already decided." Neither of us knew then that I was not alone: Sophia Kallistratova, whom I had not been able to get in touch with, had on her own also written an extremely sharp protest to the Presidium.

The first session of the Presidium scheduled to vote on Boris's expulsion was canceled for lack of a quorum—the overwhelming majority of the Presidium members were "sick."

Once again the Presidium's Party group was convened. Again the representative of the Moscow Party Committee warned that each of them would be expelled if they either abstained or failed to obey the directive. A second session of the Presidium was set for June 13.

On June 13 my husband and I went to the Presidium building early, to talk to each member of the Presidium again. I remember how they entered with bowed heads, and how, talking to us, they would not look us in the eye. The only promise I could get from those I managed to speak to was that they would support my request to be allowed to address the session.

Presidium sessions are open to all advocates. Everyone has the right to attend and to speak. On that day almost the full complement of the Presidium was seated at the long T-shaped table covered with green cloth; the only absentee was Lyubov Sokolova. Apraksin announced that she had suffered a severe heart attack. There were only a few people in the public seats. This session had purposely been called for daytime, when nearly all advocates are in court. Besides my husband and me, there were only two or three advocates, friends of Boris and colleagues from his law office. In the seats nearest the head of the table was a row of strangers, people from the Moscow Party Committee.

Apraksin declared the session open and immediately addressed those of us who were sitting in the body of the hall: "Comrades, I must ask you to leave the hall. This is to be a closed session." Naturally this demand was not addressed to the representatives of the Party Committee.

Some of the audience got up to leave, but I asked Apraksin to explain the reason for such an unusual method of discussing the disciplinary case of

Zolotukhin. No doubt Apraksin had expected everyone to obey his order automatically. At all events, he was completely unprepared for my question, and said the first thing that came into his head: "We're discussing a defense plea made in a trial that was heard behind closed doors."

"You're mistaken," I said. "The case was heard openly and reported in all the papers. Besides, I took part in that trial. Even if there had been any secrets in it, I would know them already. Unlike the members of the Presidium, I am thoroughly familiar with the proceedings . . ."

Apraksin interrupted me: "Kindly leave the hall immediately," and then, his voice rising to a shout: "Do you want me to call the police?"

I made a last attempt. I addressed the Presidium members, calling them by name, asking them for only one thing—to allow me, a participant in the trial in question, to give a first-hand account of Zolotukhin's speech, which none of them had heard. But not one of them said a word, even those who only minutes before had promised their support. Not one would look at me. Only Boris Zolotukhin turned to me and said, "Please go. You can see what's happening here."

So we went out. I don't know how much time passed while we stood in the corridor near the doors into the hall. No doubt the session was fairly lengthy. Every member was made to speak; no one was allowed to remain silent.

Later, those same people vied with each other to report what had happened behind the closed doors, and each one reported that his remarks had been more restrained than those of his colleagues. One member had objected to disbarment on the grounds that since Zolotukhin was accused of political misdemeanors, it was premature to decide the issue of his continuance in the college because higher Party bodies had not yet exhausted all opportunities to discuss and review his case. The same member, Vladimir Petrov, abstained from voting on the motion for exclusion. He remained a member of the Party and was not punished for his stand.

Those who described the speeches to me were unanimous in naming the member who had spoken most aggressively against Boris, and whose accusations went even further than those of the Dzerzhinsky District Party Committee. This man was the non-Party advocate Ivan Parkinson. I learned only then that he had been recommended for the honorific title Honored Jurist of the Republic, and that the decree of the Presidium of the Supreme Soviet to that effect was to be published next day. Parkinson was afraid that if he didn't make a tough anti-Zolotukhin speech he would be deprived of this official honor. He preferred instead to lose forever his good name and his reputation as a decent man.

To this day I cannot fathom just why the authorities took such a relentless reprisal against Boris. I cannot accept the explanation of many Western commentators that it was because he asked the court to acquit Ginzburg. Both before and after him, advocates have made the same plea in complex political cases, and it has not brought them trouble. I think one factor was that this trial caused more national as well as international comment than the two previous cases in which advocates had called for acquittal, those of Khaustov and Bukovsky. Moreover, before the trial public opinion was concerned about all four defendants, but afterward it was Alexander Ginzburg who attracted most of the sympathy and indignation. Vera Lashkova had been set free and was no longer a cause for concern; no one cared much for Dobrovolsky, having heard about his treacherous role; far fewer people than before the trial signed letters in support of Yurii Galanskov, because of doubts about his possible links with the NTS. Many people preferred not to speak out openly in defense of someone who was connected with that organization.

Most of the letters in support of Ginzburg referred to Zolotukhin's speech as having "unquestionably proved his complete innocence." Among Party and government officials Zolotukhin's name had become associated with this wave of indignation; the article in Le Nouvel Observateur was the last straw. I believe the insistent demand for Zolotukhin's "recantation," and above all a public recantation in the press, was caused by the government's urgent need to provide a retort to Western public opinion, one that did not come from a Soviet hack journalist but from the very man whose moral authority had been praised.

There was another important reason. In his defense speech Zolotukhin, albeit in veiled terms, had expressed his personal approval of what Ginzburg had done: "I don't know which sort of behavior the court finds preferable. But I believe that the behavior of the person who is not content with indifference shows greater civic spirit." The authorities held it against Zolotukhin that he not only failed to condemn Ginzburg's "criminal actions" but in some measure declared his approval of them.

On June 13, by a resolution of the Presidium of the Moscow College of Advocates, Boris Zolotukhin was expelled from the college.

And what did we do when the pale but absolutely calm Boris emerged into the corridor first and said to us, "I am no longer an advocate"?

We went home with him, where we drank to his health. June 13 was his birthday.

PART
FOUR

1. The Last Trial

D URING THE NIGHT of November 16, 1976, I had a strange dream. I dreamed that I had awakened but was still in bed. In front of me was the glass-paneled double door leading into the next room of the *dacha*, where we were spending the weekend. There, sitting on the sofa, his hands resting on the small oval table, was a completely unknown man. He was wearing a heavy overcoat and a fur hat.

"I must be dreaming," I thought, and shut my eyes.

When I opened them again, there beyond the glass doors were two men, both sitting on the sofa, both in dark overcoats and fur hats. They were looking intently at me.

"I can't be dreaming," I thought. "I must ask them who they are."

I can still hear my voice asking, "Since you have come into my house, will you please tell me who you are?"

The reply was, "We have not come to see you. We have come on state business."

I woke up. It was early morning. I was lying in the room where, straight in front of my bed, was the glass-paneled double door dividing the bedroom from the living room. I got up and drew back the curtains which we always pulled across the glass doors at night and looked into the living room. It was dark and empty. The small table in front of the sofa had been moved against the wall. In its place was the long dining table, with dishes, glasses, and cutlery still not cleared away from dinner the night before.

We had stayed at the *dacha*, which we rented from fall to spring, with our friends Yulii and Irina Daniel. We had gone out to celebrate Yulii's birthday, November 15, even though it fell on a Monday and on Tuesday morning my husband had to be back at work at the institute. Over breakfast I told Konstantin about my dream. It would not leave my mind. It haunted me all the way to Moscow, retaining its vividness and reality.

In Moscow my husband and I parted; he went to work, I went home. With unusual clarity I remember the short walk home from the bus stop. I did not take my usual route but went along the opposite side of the street from our apartment house, and I was surprised at myself for changing my habit of years, which was always to cross the street at exactly the same spot. I looked up intently at the windows of our apartment, as though expecting to see something there. The windows were dark, as they should have been in an empty apartment. The downstairs hallway, too, was silent and empty. I went up in the elevator to the fifth floor and opened the door to the landing. I was greeted with, "Good morning, Dina Isaakovna. We've been waiting for you a long time."

Two men were standing outside our front door. One was middle-aged, the other younger. Both were in dark overcoats and fur hats.

I did not have to ask who they were or why they had come. My only thought was that there on my husband's desk, beside the radio, in the apartment into which they were both about to accompany me, lay the neatly stacked and corrected typescript of a book. My husband had been working on it for more than a year, and tomorrow we intended to wrap it up and send it off to the United States for publication under a pseudonym.*

In the meantime I had been surrounded by a solid ring of men who had suddenly come down from upstairs. In my hand was a small sheet of paper bearing the familiar word "Order." It was a warrant to search our apartment on suspicion of harboring literature of a defamatory and anti-Soviet nature. The order was dated November 15 and countersigned by the Deputy Procurator of Moscow, Yurii Stasenkov. "Yurochka has signed it," I said automatically, calling Stasenkov by the familiar form of his first name, which by right of my greater age I had first called him many years ago. At that time he had just graduated from law school and had started work in the procuracy of the Leningradsky District, near the law office where I worked.

We stood on the landing for a long time, as I refused to let them into the apartment until my husband came. I needed time to collect my thoughts.

---

* His book was published in the United States in 1982 under the title *USSR: The Corrupt Society* (Simon & Schuster, New York).

But chiefly I needed to see my husband, to find out what had happened to him and what he would say to the investigators about his manuscript, which a Soviet court would undoubtedly treat as criminal.

Then my husband came out of the elevator accompanied by two men. The face of one of them was familiar. "You must be mistaken, Dina Isaakovna," he said in reply to my remark that we had met before. "This is the first time I've ever seen you."

I knew this was not true. Once, out walking at the *dacha*, Irina and I encountered this man, and I said to her, "I think that man is tailing us." To which she replied, "God, how jumpy we all are. We meet a man who's taking a breath of fresh air and we immediately think we're being tailed. I'm not just saying that to you. I'm saying it to convince myself. I don't like the look of that man either."

My husband was calm, though paler than usual. As we walked into the apartment, he had time to whisper to me just one word, "Sorry." He was apologizing because, when we left for the *dacha*, I had asked him to hide the typescript and he had not done it. He thought no one would come into our apartment. There was only one day left before we sent it off and there was nothing to worry about.

The search lasted six or seven hours. At the end of it there was a pile of "defamatory and anti-Soviet books" on the floor: Solzhenitsyn's *Gulag Archipelago*, Pasternak's *Doctor Zhivago*, Sinyavsky's *In the Shadow of Gogol*, a great deal of fiction and poetry, picked out for one reason only: it had been published abroad. There was Nabokov, Akhmatova, Mandelstam —I can't remember them all. A heap of photographs taken out of our family albums was stacked on the table. The only ones they left were snapshots of us and our son in his childhood and pictures of our parents. All the rest, along with a camera I had been given as a birthday present, were confiscated. On the table too, tied up and sealed with sealing wax, lay the typescript of my husband's book.

In the evening, when the search was over, my husband and I were told to get our coats.

"Are you arresting us?" asked my husband. "We need to know what to put on."

"Wear whatever you always wear," the investigator said evasively.

We went out to the street. In front was my husband with his escort; I was a few feet behind him with mine. Several cars were parked outside the entrance. As my husband was getting into the first car, he shouted to me, "They're taking me to the *dacha*."

Jammed in between two investigators, I was put into the back seat of another car and we drove off. It was a great relief to see that all the cars were taking the familiar highway out of Moscow. We *were* going to the *dacha;* we would be together a little while longer.

When we arrived, my first thought was for the Daniels. Had they gone home yet? I could not bear to think that Yulii, who had already done five years in a strict-regime prison camp, would again be subjected to searches and interrogations. But there was no one at the *dacha;* they had gone. I immediately felt an extraordinary sense of relief. That night, however, we learned that Yulii and Irina had been arrested that morning on their way into Moscow, and had been detained until late in the evening at the Moscow procuracy, where the authorities were hoping in vain that the Daniels would provide some evidence against us. Then, when it was obvious that they would get nothing, they had released them.

The search was soon over. They confiscated one book, a work by the Russian philosopher Berdyaev, and then only because it was published abroad.

All the time I was anxiously wondering what would become of my husband. I had less fear for myself because I had guessed, overhearing various chance remarks, that they had really come for my husband's typescript, and that all the rest was merely supplementary material for an indictment against him.

As we drove back to Moscow in the dark, I did not know where we were going this time, or, worst of all, where they were taking my husband.

They took me to the Moscow procuracy. As we entered the reception hall I saw the familiar figure of the policeman guarding the entrance. For years I had walked in at that door and nodded carelessly to the man on duty, scarcely noticing him as I walked on into the building. This time everything was vividly imprinted on my memory: the policeman's astonished look as he recognized me; the empty waiting room long after the work day was over. Then the investigator led me into a large office with two desks in it—and silence. A silence broken only by a familiar, beloved coughing that could be heard through the wall. How happy I was to hear my husband's characteristic cough, which I could not have mistaken for any other. It meant that he was here and was not yet under arrest. I was still able to say calmly to the investigator, "You're wasting your time asking me these questions. I will not answer them. I don't intend to answer any of your questions now. It's ten o'clock at night. You came to search us at ten o'clock this morning. I'm tired and hungry."

Then came the hardest time, when for a while I lost my self-control. I was alone in the office. The investigator had gone out to ask his superior what to do about me, since I refused to answer any of his questions. I sat listening to the silence, straining to catch the slightest rustle, the sound of my husband's voice. But I couldn't hear anything. The reassuring coughing had stopped. Then came the loud, distinct sound of many feet in the corridor, a loud slamming of doors, and again—absolute silence.

"They've taken my husband away!"

I ran to the door, intending to rush out into the corridor—perhaps I might see him, say goodbye to him. The door was locked. I hammered on the door, and when the policeman came I demanded to be let out, although I knew this was useless. I don't know how much time passed, no doubt only a few minutes. Finally the door was opened.

"Where's my husband? You must tell me where my husband is!"

The investigator and I were standing in the open doorway of the office. There was no one in the hallway—even the policeman had disappeared. Suddenly the investigator turned around, walked away without a word, and flung open the door of the neighboring office. My husband was sitting there.

"O.K.?" I asked him with my eyes.

"O.K.," he replied wordlessly.

The door of the office was slammed shut, and then the investigator made a remark to me for which I shall always be grateful to him: "Don't worry, no one is going to separate you."

A few minutes later Konstantin and I went home. As we entered the apartment, the first thing that came into my mind was my dream, which in the whirlwind of events I had completely forgotten. Now it came rushing back to me, with all its real, concrete details and the all too prophetic words: "We have come on state business."

Throughout the year that separated the search of our apartment from the day we were forced to leave the Soviet Union, we lived a strange double life. One was our outward life, in which as usual I went to the office, received clients, gave legal advice, spoke in court; the other was a life in which we were summoned to the investigator for questioning—my husband often, I less frequently. Every morning before the regular interrogation, I put into his jacket pockets a spare handkerchief, a cake of soap, toothpaste and toothbrush; then an hour—two—three—went by and I was still waiting for the promised telephone call. Then at last: "Don't worry, I'm on my way home."

My friends did their best to see that on these days I was never left alone. God knows how my working women friends arranged things, but someone was always with me on the bad days, and we spent the long silent hours together.

Every time my husband went to be questioned, one of our friends followed him to the procuracy and waited in a nearby doorway to see whether he came out alone or was driven away under escort. It happened one day that my husband was questioned not in the city procuracy but in the district procuracy, which was on a nearby street. Our friend, whose devotion we so appreciated in those difficult months, followed my husband and waited for him on the first floor of the building. Suddenly she heard my husband's voice saying loudly, "What? Are you taking me to the city procuracy?" and saw him leave the building with the investigator. By the time she reached the street, they were no longer to be seen. She told me afterward that she ran all the way, because at first she got lost; then as she reached the city procuracy she saw a police van driving away. At this she telephoned me.

"Dina . . ." she said, and stopped.

"What happened?"

"I saw him led out by the investigator. Then I lost sight of them. Then a van drove away from the procuracy. You know the kind—a special van . . ."

"I understand," I said.

Again and again I dialed the investigator's number—it was always busy. Then the phone rang. It was my husband, calling from a subway station. The whole affair of his "arrest" had been an act, a purposely staged scene in the "theater of cruelty."

The care and devotion of our friends through these months was no surprise to us. We knew them well enough not to doubt them. What was really a surprise was the reaction of people who were not so close to us, people we regarded simply as acquaintances. We had never imagined that among them too we would find such unfailing readiness to help in every possible way. I never once had to ask for anything; people spontaneously offered their help. I often thought this was not just out of sympathy for my husband and me, but that it was an unmistakable sign of a change in the social climate of the country. There were those, of course, who were afraid to be seen in our company for fear of harm to them or their families, but there were not many, and I know that these few were ashamed of avoiding us and suffered for it.

For the whole of that year my husband and I lived as we had decided to on the day after the search, without in any way changing our way of living. As before, we went to the *dacha* on Friday evenings, we went to concerts and exhibitions, and, of course, we worked hard. When, however, we were alone and not in the bugged apartment but in the forest or on the street, our conversation invariably came back to November 16, the day of the search. How could it have happened? Why had they come to us?

We never talked about my husband's book at home. All our discussions took place on the street or at the *dacha*, where we felt safe from bugging.

Even when we found out that a bug had been installed in the *dacha*, and then that we were being followed whenever we went outdoors, the question still remained: "Why?" We racked our brains to recall what had happened over the past years in order to try to pin down the moment when real surveillance might have begun. The bugging of private homes in the USSR is so commonplace that we had not considered it a mark of special interest. What had evoked this new concern?

Starting from quite recent events, memory took us back farther and farther in time.

The first open, official warning that the authorities considered my professional activities politically harmful came in connection with my defense of Ilya Gabay and Mustafa Djamilev. Their trial took place in Tashkent, capital of the Uzbek Union Republic, in 1970. Before the start of the trial, when in September and October of 1969 I was studying the twenty volumes of investigatory material, I realized that I faced the most difficult kind of defense in a political case—a situation in which the facts are not in dispute and a legal argument inevitably shades off into politics.

The charges against Djamilev and Gabay were identical in type. Both were accused of preparing and distributing, mainly in Tashkent, "defamatory" documents: factual reports, open letters, public appeals. Neither denied coauthorship of these documents, but both asserted that the facts described in them were true, and therefore they refused to plead guilty.

There were thirty-five documents that the investigating authorities considered criminal in content. After painstaking analysis of each one I came to the conclusion that while they were sharply critical of certain aspects of official policy, none of them actually contained any "lying fabrications which denigrate the Soviet system." On October 8, 1969, I submitted to Berezovsky, the Uzbek Republic's investigator for specially important cases, a request to dismiss the case on the grounds of "lack of *corpus delicti* in the actions of Mustafa Djamilev and Ilya Gabay." The application was rejected.

Nevertheless, the documents were not lies. What the authorities had against them was that they were essentially truthful accounts of state mistreatment of one of the Soviet Union's minority peoples. The USSR is a multinational country, a federation of "union" and "autonomous" republics. One of the latter was the Crimean Autonomous Republic, in the southernmost part of Russia, in the Crimean Peninsula. The native population of this fertile, prosperous maritime region were the Crimean Tartars. During the Second World War, when most adult Tartar men were fighting in the ranks of the Soviet Army, the Crimean peninsula was occupied by German troops. Those who remained under the occupation were mostly women, children, the old, and the disabled. Soviet forces liberated the Crimea in April 1944. In May of that year the State Defense Committee of the USSR issued a secret decree accusing the Crimean Tartar people as a whole of collaboration with the Germans. As punishment the Crimean Tartars, down to the newest-born infant, were ordered deported from their ancient homeland. On the night of May 18, 1944, the villages of the Crimean Tartars were surrounded by units of the Soviet Army. In the course of that one night the entire Tartar population of the Crimea was herded into freight cars and shipped off to specially designated regions of Soviet Central Asia, which they were forbidden to leave on pain of arrest and trial. The horrors of the deportation and the conditions in which the deportees were forced to live are best described by a single appalling statistic: during the first eighteen months of exile, in Uzbekistan alone (the chief region of "special settlement" for the Crimean Tartars), 46.2 percent of the deportees died of starvation and disease.*

In the Crimea, all Tartar schools, theaters, newspapers, and libraries were closed, and all books published in the Tartar language were destroyed.

In 1956, after Stalin's death the Twentieth Congress admitted the illegality of this action, whose cruelty and injustice were obvious to everyone. In 1956, also, by a decree of the Presidium of the Supreme Soviet of the USSR, the Crimean Tartars were freed from open police surveillance, but the same decree forbade their return to the Crimea.

Since then there has arisen what I can only call a national Crimean Tartar movement to win the right for the Tartars to return to their homeland. At first this movement, for reasons of principle, remained quite apart from the general "defense of legality" movement in the Soviet Union, and the Tartars conducted their struggle by mass petitions addressed to the leaders of the Soviet state and the Communist Party. Every such petition began with an assurance of the Crimean Tartars' loyalty to the Soviet government and to the Communist Party, and to the Leninist principles of its nationalities policy.

The trials in the 1960s of the most active participants in this campaign were the Soviet authorities' only reaction to the just demands of this peaceful, hard-working, and long-suffering people. Gradually the logic of nonviolent struggle led the Crimean Tartars to realize the need for contact with participants in the larger democratic movement in defense of human rights. Thus they acquired, among other peoples of the Soviet Union, at first sympathizers and then active helpers and devoted friends, the first of

---

* *Tashkentsky protsess* ("The Tashkent Trial"). A documentary collection. Alexander Herzen Foundation, Amsterdam, 1976.

whom was the writer Alexei Kosterin. After Kosterin's death in 1968 the torch was picked up by another member of the Crimean Tartar defense campaign, General Pyotr Grigorenko.

In May 1969, in answer to a Crimean Tartar petition signed by two thousand people, Grigorenko was to speak as "People's Defense Counsel" at the trial of ten activists of the Crimean Tartar movement. Twenty days before the start of the trial, however, Grigorenko was tricked into going to Tashkent and arrested. Shortly afterward, Ilya Gabay and Mustafa Djamilev were arrested in connection with Grigorenko's activities. All three were charged with preparing and distributing documents about the plight of the Crimean Tartars and the campaign for their return to the Crimea. Grigorenko was subjected to a forensic psychiatric examination by a commission which came to the unanimous conclusion that Grigorenko was absolutely mentally healthy. This result did not suit the plans of the KGB, which did not want a public trial of a distinguished old general. He was ordered reexamined, this time by the Serbsky Institute in Moscow. Obedient to the KGB's instructions, the new panel of psychiatrists pronounced Grigorenko mentally ill. The charges against him were dropped, and he was locked up for several years in a "special" psychiatric hospital.

The Gabay-Djamilev case was not my first professional connection with the Crimean Tartars. I had been in Tashkent a year earlier to defend a Tartar activist and I had met his relatives, other activists, and sympathizers. I discovered then that the struggle of the Crimean Tartars was a truly *national* campaign. Old and young, men, women, and children, all literally lived for the idea of returning to their homeland. These people had achieved a high level of prosperity in Uzbekistan, but they were ready to abandon everything, to give up their orchards and vineyards without compensation, simply to be allowed to return to their own country. They were trying to get for their children a balanced spread of vocational training, so that after they return they will have Tartar doctors, Tartar teachers, Tartar engineers. "What do you want to be when you grow up?" I asked a ten-year-old. "I'll be a teacher in a Tartar school," he said. "When I'm grown up we'll be living at home."

Long afterward one of my visits to Tashkent coincided with a great celebration in honor of three convicted activists of the Crimean Tartar movement. This celebration symbolized for me all I had learned and felt about the Tartar people. I was invited to a reception for them. As we sat at long tables in a garden, I heard a remarkable story. On the day the three men were released from prison camp, a bus drove up to the camp gates carrying the welcoming party. The entire road from the gates to the bus was covered with flowers. As the gates opened and the three were let out, they were met by music, national music played by an amateur national orchestra. And all the way to Tashkent every Tartar village greeted them with flowers and festive tables set right out on the road.

Next day I was at a family party in the home of one of the released prisoners. Only a few people were present; I was the only non-Tartar guest. The released man's wife, mother of his two small children, said, "In our family there has been one other day as happy as this. That was when we gathered to celebrate my brother's return to freedom."

"Mustafa," said the oldest man at the table, "we're so happy that you're here with us today. But tell me, what are you planning to do tomorrow?"

And Mustafa replied, "As of tomorrow, I shall again take up the struggle for my people."

"I drink this glass," the wife went on, "as a pledge that my husband will prove worthy of my brother."

Mustafa Djamilev was her brother. He was born in the Crimea in 1943, during the Second World War. His father was mobilized into the Soviet Army, leaving his mother with four small children. Mustafa was not yet eight months old when the whole family was forcibly deported from the Crimea. His childhood was the grim regime of "special settlements," hunger and humiliation. Instead of fairy tales he listened to stories about the Crimea, about the former life in their homeland. His whole life was ruled by the dream of return. He grew up a fighter fanatically devoted to that dream.

When I first met Mustafa in the fall of 1969, in the Uzbek KGB prison, he was a fully mature man with a strong and purposeful will of his own. Life had not so much educated him as forged him. Beginning in 1966, he had been tried and convicted five times. He had sustained a ten-month hunger strike in protest against illegal repressions, resisting force-feedings as long as he humanly could. He gave himself no breathing space after each release from prison camp. He lived, and still lives, as though fulfilling a sworn oath to dedicate himself without respite to the struggle for his people.

My second client in this trial was Ilya Gabay, or, as everyone called him, Ilyusha. He was a humanist and a cultivated man. He lived in Moscow, where he taught Russian language and literature. Teaching children was his vocation and mission in life. Poetry was his other pleasure. Whenever I talked about Ilyusha with people who knew him, they invariably smiled; it gave them pleasure merely to talk about him and to tell of his kindness, gentleness, talent, and learning. There was nothing in Gabay's nature that was cruel, or even tough. He had an amazing capacity to understand people and, understanding them, to forgive. He was strict and unyielding only toward himself.

Even before his trial began I received many letters from various parts of the Soviet Union written by Ilya's former students and even acquaintances. Conspicuously absent from these letters were social and civil subjects, although letters defending those accused of political crimes are usually full of them. Instead, these were letters from people who were grateful for the good they had received, for the help and the moral support.

A letter came from a person who carries a heavy share of guilt toward Gabay. He had insulted Ilya unjustly and was then dropped by all their friends. He wrote about the time when he thought suicide was the only way out: "It was Ilya who with the clarity and nobility of his heart and rejection of any harshness forced me back into normal life, so that I was no longer ashamed of myself at every step." And from a person who had serious family trouble: "Ilya did everything so that my son would not experience any bitterness about what happened. And now Ilya is the greatest person in the world for this eight-year-old boy, who misses him terribly and thinks of him constantly, despite the forgetfulness of children. Children fall in love with him at first sight and remain his friends forever."

At one time Ilya worried about a boy he hardly knew who had been orphaned; at another Ilya's concern went to an old man, probably met on the street, who had come to Moscow to try to get his pension. Each letter tells a story of help, goodness, generosity.

I got to know Djamilev and Gabay in unusual circumstances. I had very little opportunity to make a personal judgment of their characters, and my opinion was largely influenced by the nobility and courage with which they both behaved under investigation and in court. The unique situation in which I saw them brought out their most fundamental traits. With Mustafa these were the qualities of a fighter: determination, consistency of purpose, decisiveness. Ilyusha was cast in a different mold: he was born to write poetry, to teach and educate children, to study.

An elderly woman wrote to me, "I love Ilyusha as if he were my own son. I cannot imagine anybody who would know him and not love him." I could not imagine that either. Even the special prosecutor, Berezovsky, an archcynic and a careerist, once said, "Your Gabay, he is such a good person. I'm sorry for him. Djamilev I understand. He is a Tartar, he fights for his people. But Gabay, what does he want? Why did a Jew get himself into this jam that doesn't concern him?" One of Ilya's poems gave an answer:

I would be glad if the pain of others
Dwelled within me and split my heart

As I was preparing his defense, Gabay's poems helped me understand his spiritual world and sort out the true motives for his actions. Unlike

Berezovsky, I did not need to ask why he, a Jew and a Russian intellectual, "got himself into this jam that doesn't concern him." I understood that the pain of the Crimean Tartars truly split Ilya's heart.

After the Tashkent trial, I saw Ilyusha only once more, in 1972, when he came to see me after his release from prison camp. He blamed himself very much for the fact that I had gotten into trouble as a result of his trial. We talked about his plans for the future and he told me he wanted very much to teach again but knew that a person convicted of a political offense would not be allowed to work in the Soviet school system.

Then there was a series of events which I can record only at second hand, from the accounts given by his wife and close friends. First, soon after our meeting came news of the arrest of Pyotr Yakir and Viktor Krasin, both part of the dissident movement. Yakir was Ilya Gabay's closest friend, a man whom he trusted implicitly and of whom he was very fond.

Yakir's youth from the age of fourteen had been spent in Stalin's prison camps. He had lived through the imprisonment of his mother and the execution of his father, Jonah Yakir, a four-star general and commander in chief of the Ukraine Military District who in 1937 was charged with high treason and executed as "an enemy of the people." Viktor Krasin had also been arrested before. Neither Yakir nor Viktor could withstand the threat of another, very long prison term. From them the KGB discovered the names of many of the people who were editing the *Chronicle of Current Events*, the *samizdat* news bulletin that records violations of human rights in the Soviet Union. The Central Committee of the CPSU had long ago ordered the KGB to destroy this underground bulletin, which was regarded as particularly subversive because of the accuracy and speed with which it gathered and distributed its news. Now, because of Yakir and Krasin, everyone connected with the *Chronicle* was threatened with arrest and trial on criminal charges.

It was a very difficult period for the dissident movement. Many people thought it had received its death blow, that it would be destroyed not only by the government but, chiefly, by the loss of its moral authority.

Ilya and his wife Galina, then expecting their second child, were among those named by Yakir, and Ilya was summoned for interrogation. To Ilya, who had never once betrayed a friend while under interrogation, the behavior of his friends was a cruel blow. What he found hardest to bear was that the treachery or weakness of these two had, in many people's eyes, compromised the whole movement. The cause for which he had endured imprisonment and lost his beloved profession had been degraded.

On September 5, 1973, the KGB staged a press conference in Moscow's Central House of Journalists, at which Yakir and Krasin were the chief figures. Ilya Gabay saw on the TV screen the friend who had been almost like a brother to him, looking cleaner, better shaved, and more tidily dressed than he had ever seen him. He heard Yakir talking about his connections with various Western organizations which, as he put it, "only pay lip service to the idea of human rights"; he talked, too, about the "degeneration of the 'defense of legality' movement." I was told that after this press conference Gabay sank into a total and irreversible depression. He could find no way out of his despair. During the morning of October 20, when his wife had dozed off after breast feeding their newborn daughter, Ilya threw himself off the balcony of their apartment. He was killed instantly. Ilya did not strike me as impulsive, still less hysterical or unbalanced. Only the most unrelenting sense of hopelessness can have brought him to that tragic end.

The Tashkent case was just beginning when I received a personal warning that was as prophetic as my dream of arrest, but absolutely real.

In September 1969, when I was planning a trip to Tashkent to study Ilya's and Mustafa's case, I suddenly felt reluctant to go. I love Tashkent, I knew I would be met and taken care of there and would be free for a while of domestic chores and worries. I was about to embark on an interesting case and I would be defending good, decent people. Nevertheless, it took considerable effort to overcome this feeling and go. Once in Tashkent, this strange unease disappeared, and I forgot it until I came back to Moscow.

A few days after my return, I was called in to see Nikolai Borovik, the head of my law office. We talked about the forthcoming trial of Gabay and Djamilev. I said that I had submitted an application for the case to be terminated, and if it failed I would enter a plea in court for their acquittal.

"You shouldn't go there," said Nikolai. "Hand over the defense of these two to some other advocate. That's my friendly advice—don't ignore it."

I knew this advice was coming from a man with information that came straight from the KGB. Everyone in the College of Advocates knew about Borovik's close links with the secret police, although it was only after his death, when the KGB wanted to give him a funeral with full military honors, that we discovered he had been a KGB lieutenant colonel. I had worked with Borovik since 1945 and was on good terms with him. I had no doubt that he genuinely wished to shield me from trouble.

"You have become a specialist in political cases," he said. "You just move on from one political trial to another. 'They' don't like that. And remember, it will be much easier for them to get even with you in Tashkent than in Moscow."

When my husband and I discussed Borovik's remarks, he agreed that this was a serious warning, but we both knew that I could not follow this friendly advice.

When the trial date was announced I had a vague, irrational presentiment that something unpleasant was awaiting me in Tashkent. I was relieved when bad weather delayed my flight for forty-eight hours, and I had a sense of doom when I eventually heard the announcement: "Please board the aircraft now for the Moscow-Tashkent flight."

It was January 12, 1970. I went straight from the airport to the courthouse, hoping I was in time for the start of the trial. I barely made it, and Judge Pisarenko greeted me with, "Comrade advocate, why do you defend so many of these people? And not because you're told to, but by their personal choice?" His remark expressed sincere perplexity, but it also contained a certain threat. The names of advocates who defended in political cases were never mentioned in the Soviet press. Judge Pisarenko must have heard of Bukovsky, Marchenko, Litvinov, and Galanskov, but the fact that he knew I had defended all these people meant that someone had specially told him so. In particular, I was put on my guard by the last part of his comment: ". . . not because you're told to, but by their personal choice." In other words, it is not the state, the KGB, or the College of Advocates that assigns you to defend these "renegades." *They* choose you, obviously sensing that you are an ally.

I did not allow the judge to see my suspicions, but that night, when I phoned my husband, I said, "Obviously the decision has been made—it's trouble for me."

The trial itself added a new dimension to the difficulties of political trials. Always before I had been exasperated at the illegal practice of keeping defendants' friends and sympathizers out of the courtroom and packing the public seats with selected representatives of officialdom. The atmosphere of hostility torments the defendants, and makes an adequate defense even harder. This time, down in Tashkent, there were no restrictions on public entry, and the courtroom was filled to overflowing with activists of the Crimean Tartar movement. The atmosphere was one of warm and noisy sympathy for the accused and solidarity with their cause.

Every word from the defendants was accompanied by a buzz of approval; every hostile remark from judge or prosecutor evoked an instant loud reaction. While Gabay was being examined the court managed to retain a certain semblance of judicial procedure, which was greatly helped by Ilya himself, a naturally quiet and reserved man. But what happened during the examination of Mustafa Djamilev did not even remotely resemble a trial in a court of law. Mustafa's passionate nature reached the spectators, while the response from the public made Mustafa even more emotional, more categorical in his statements, more ruthless in his arguments. Like any good political speaker he responded to contact with a live audience, and he spoke less to the court than to his grateful and excited listeners in the public seats. I say this without reproach, for Mustafa and his supporters had no moral obligation to respect this judicial travesty. Working in that atmosphere of fervent partisanship, however, became extremely difficult for me.

The court's unconcealed hostility toward me increased literally hour by hour throughout the trial. When it was my turn to examine, Judge Pisarenko invariably said, "Now we can be spared the noise for a while. Comrade advocate, please put your questions." And indeed, silence reigned as long as I was speaking, but whenever the judge intervened the noise broke out at once.

"Shame on you! You're afraid of the truth!"

"Why are these people on trial?"

It required a lot of professional experience and just plain tact to conduct a trial in these circumstances. Pisarenko was plainly not up to the task. I cannot comment on his professional experience, but I can say without hesitation that in all my career I had never come across such a stupid, incompetent, miserably educated judge. His legal training was nonexistent, and his general knowledge was that of a child in elementary school. During the examination of Tatyana Bayeva, an active participant in the human rights movement, she answered the question whether she was a member of the Komsomol by saying that, in her view, membership in the Komsomol was degrading.

"Degraded?" Judge Pisarenko asked.

"Not 'degraded,' degrading," Tatyana corrected him.

I thought the poor woman would be overwhelmed by a flood of threats and moralizing. She was slandering the progressive vanguard of Soviet youth! But Pisarenko just continued his examination. He did not know what the word meant.

More to the point than Pisarenko's ignorance of common foreign loan words was the fact that he did not understand the meaning of the arguments and explanations with which the defendants justified their actions. He sincerely could not conceive of the possibility of dissidence. In his simplistic, firmly held view, there existed, on the one hand, the beautiful, happy world of Soviet socialism, and on the other, the nasty, unhappy world of capitalism. In the latter, which was wicked and disgraceful, there lived some people who were wicked and others who were deluded. Newspapers in the capitalist world were published exclusively to attack and libel the Soviet system. Capitalist radio stations served the same purpose.

Pisarenko commented on the testimony given by the defendants: "Gabay, why do you think that article was published in an American magazine? With what object would this have been done?" "Can anything written in a bourgeois newspaper ever be objective?" "Can a capitalist newspaper ever be objective from the viewpoint of a Soviet citizen?"

There was unfeigned horror and revulsion on Pisarenko's face when Gabay replied, "It is perfectly possible for capitalist newspapers to be objective. What's more, where is it laid down that communists have a monopoly on the truth?"

With the same total conviction Pisarenko believed every word printed in Soviet newspapers. He was incapable of understanding that a normal person might doubt their accuracy or not share their view of events.

"Who gave you the right to draw your own conclusions?" he asked Gabay with absolute sincerity.

The reply, "I think every person has the right to think," caused Pisarenko to freeze in bewilderment for a moment and then to say reproachfully, "Gabay, Gabay, don't you really understand anything? How can you say such things?"

Every remark of this kind produced a roar of laughter in the courtroom, although I didn't find it at all funny. Only years later, rereading the transcript, could I smile and say, "God, what an idiot the man is!" At the time, however, I was appalled. In this weird trial, the entire dialogue was conducted on two independent planes; each person said his piece, but without the slightest hope of being understood.

At one point I thought the moment had come when I could make the judge realize that Soviet newspapers can be mistaken. It was on the second day of the trial, January 13; Pisarenko was reading Gabay one of his regular lectures: "Gabay, you said you didn't believe the statements in Soviet newspapers announcing that our forces entered Czechoslovakia at the request of the Czechoslovak people. How could you not believe that, Gabay? After all, our newspapers speak for the Central Committee of the Soviet Communist Party, so . . ."

I whispered softly so that only Ilya could hear me as I repeated certain words several times: "Enemies of the people, enemies of the people, doctors' plot, doctors' plot, January 13, 1953, January 13, 1953 . . ."

"In 1937," said Ilya, "our newspapers were daily reporting the 'unmasking' of enemies of the people. Later, the same newspapers wrote articles telling us that they were not enemies of the people at all, and had been rehabilitated. Today is January 13. I remember the articles that were published on January 13, 1953, about the doctors who had supposedly plotted to murder Soviet leaders by giving them the wrong medical treatment. Three years later the same newspapers wrote that the 'doctors' plot' was nothing but a fabrication. Which story am I to believe?"

I felt triumphant as I listened to Gabay's answer. I thought the mere mention of the newspaper articles of those years was sufficient response to the question whether a person had to believe every word printed in a Soviet newspaper. But my triumph was in vain. As usual, Pisarenko was sincerely amazed at Gabay's lack of logic and his failure to understand the simplest things.

"But, Gabay, you're contradicting yourself. You say yourself that the Soviet newspapers later published a denial. Correct? And was there a denial about Czechoslovakia? When they do print a denial, *then* you can say so."

At this trial the people's assessors were women. One of them had a flaming red face and invariably sat with her fat arms folded on her chest. The other one was wearing a green knit jacket. Of Pisarenko I remember only his tiny eyes which every day radiated more hatred, the philistine's deep hatred of everybody who is different. As I was looking at him I was thinking of Yulii Daniel's fantasy novel, *This Is Moscow Speaking*, in which the Soviet government proclaims an "open day for murder," a day when anybody can murder somebody. If Pisarenko, I thought, read in the paper that Soviet citizens had the right to commit murder on a certain day, he would not waver or doubt. He would grab an ax, if he could not get a gun, and slaughter all those intellectuals, all those dissidents, all the Crimean Tartars, and, of course, all the Jews.

As the trial went on, relations between judge and defendants were strained to breaking point. Despairing of his attempts to explain even the simplest points to the court, Mustafa Djamilev decided to decline my further services as his defense counsel, on the grounds that he could not allow himself to put his advocate in jeopardy; then he refused to answer any questions; finally he demanded to be taken out of the courtroom. He refused to participate in or even be present at what he rightly called "this shameful farce." Even Ilya began to lose his self-restraint.

As I stood up to speak, to object to the judge's method of examining a witness, I could feel the tension rising in every nerve. It cost me a colossal effort not to launch into a shouting match. At that moment the door of the courtroom opened and in walked a messenger carrying an enormous pile of telegrams. Slowly and calmly she marched down the long aisle, came up to me, and said, "Sign here, please." Then, equally calmly, she walked out of the courtroom.

"May I continue?" I asked the dumbfounded judge.

The surprise effect was so great that Pisarenko listened to the rest of my objection without interrupting me. During the recess he asked, "Are you celebrating something today? You seem to have received a lot of congratulations." And without waiting for my reply he added, "We'll give you something to celebrate, too."

I did have something to celebrate that day—it was my fiftieth birthday.

Friends and colleagues did not know what hotel I would be in, so the birthday telegrams were simply addressed to Advocate Kaminskaya, City Court, Tashkent.

I took Pisarenko's words as a direct warning to watch my step during my defense speech. I was not proposing to alter the line I had taken during the pretrial investigation—that there was nothing criminal in the actions of Djamilev and Gabay, and they should be acquitted. But for the first time in my life, I wrote out my speech in full beforehand, thus depriving myself of the opportunity to make a single impromptu remark. I had to weigh every word I would say in court. I knew I could not escape retribution that way, but I would not give the court any weapons to use against me.

At the start of my defense speech, Pisarenko interrupted me with the unusual request to speak as slowly as possible, so the clerk could record my speech word for word rather than in the usual summary form. Fortunately, my hours of burning the midnight oil paid off. My memory unfailingly produced the phrasing I had so carefully thought out, so that subsequently I did not need to ask to correct, deny, or retract any of it.

By the verdict of the court on January 19, 1970, Gabay and Djamilev were found guilty and sentenced to three years' imprisonment.

In my case, the court served me with a notice of disciplinary censure: "The contents of Advocate Kaminskaya's speech give grounds to believe that she is lacking in the qualities needed for the tasks which the government and Party authorities require a Soviet advocate to fulfill." This notice of censure, bypassing the Presidium of the Moscow College of Advocates, was sent directly to the Ministry of Justice "in order that the appropriate measures may be taken"—in other words, in order that I would be disbarred.

However, I was not expelled from the profession, and I am certain that the only person who saved me was Judge Pisarenko. I must therefore thank fate that the KGB's chosen instrument of my downfall was such a stupid man.

The disciplinary case against me, which the Ministry of Justice entrusted to the Presidium of the College of Advocates, took exactly a year to investigate. It was heard by the Presidium on January 19, 1971, the last day of the statutory twelve-month period in which an advocate can be called to account for a censure. On January 20 the writ would have become void. Once again, as when Zolotukhin was expelled, my colleagues and friends sat facing me across the long table.

I had been told in advance that a motion for my expulsion would be put to the Presidium but I would not be expelled. Several Presidium members were going to oppose the motion. "I'm ashamed enough at having taken part in the ousting of Zolotukhin," one of the deputy chairmen said to me. I knew that the inspectors appointed to study my case (the senior inspector, appointed by Apraksin, was ill disposed toward me) had not found a single faulty passage in my defense speech. I knew that a special objection to my censure had been lodged by one of the judges of the Supreme Court of Uzbekistan who had heard my appeal in the Gabay case, and such an objection was almost unique in Soviet judicial practice. I knew too that the president of the Supreme Court of Uzbekistan had requested the Presidium of that Supreme Court to withdraw the notice of censure, although on January 8, 1971, the day his request was to be heard, he withdrew it at the insistence of the KGB. All that undoubtedly helped me.

But these moves of support were made possible by Judge Pisarenko. He was so sincerely convinced that the freedom of speech guaranteed by the Soviet Constitution had nothing in common with a person's right to express his own opinions that he actually wrote in the notice of censure:

> Advocate Kaminskaya stated in open court that every person is allowed to think for himself, that beliefs and opinions cannot be grounds for prosecution under the criminal law, and on that she based her plea to acquit the defendants.

It was in this that Pisarenko saw my unfitness to be a Soviet advocate. The Presidium of the Moscow College of Advocates declared the censure unfounded, but "admonished" me instead for not declaring my "civic position" and not condemning the views of my clients.

Thus in the thirty-first year of my career in advocacy I received my first professional rebuke. From that day onward I was deprived of access to political cases.

My professional situation hardly changed after January 1971. Admittedly I was no longer an elected delegate to the advocates' electoral college, and I ceased to receive an annual bonus for "irreproachable and highly skilled work." Whenever I took a case outside Moscow, the College Presidium invariably asked whether the case had any political implications, and they had to be convinced that I was defending in an ordinary criminal case before they issued the necessary travel warrant.

None of that worried me very much. The only thing that really annoyed me was having to stop supervising trainee advocates. This was the only kind of volunteer work that I was never tempted to avoid, and it had given me great satisfaction. I was very fond of my interns and proud of their successes. In every other respect I suffered no restrictions. I was more than fully employed and earned more than before.

Although I no longer defended in political trials, people came to me for consultations and followed my recommendations as to the choice of an advocate. The number of people who consulted me increased year by year. My husband's advice and mine was sought by Jewish activists, nonconformist artists, and writers intending to publish their works abroad without official permission. As a result, our home and our whole life was under permanent surveillance by the KGB, although no open, official pressure was applied to us over those years.

In January 1973 our son Dimitry and his wife Natalya emigrated to the United States. We, however, firmly decided to stay put. Despite all the complications and burdens of life in an unfree society, our life was interesting and eventful. And the company of our friends even made it happy.

But the KGB had not forgotten about me, and its second warning was of a rather strange kind.

In 1975 Anatoly Marchenko was arrested again. After finishing his previous term of imprisonment, in September 1972, Marchenko had settled in Tarusa, a small country town in Kaluga Province. He was not allowed to live in Moscow, where his wife, Larisa Bogoraz, had a room. In May 1974, Marchenko was placed under the so-called administrative surveillance of the local police. The function of administrative surveillance is to monitor the behavior of people released from prison camp but who, in the view of the camp authorities or the police, "have not begun to improve." Administrative surveillance limits a person's freedom; one is forbidden to go out of doors in the evening, to go to the movies, to the theater, or to a restaurant, or to go outside one's home district without police permission.

Marchenko is by nature a very reserved, mature, and stable man. When he went to Tarusa he got a job and led a normal, quiet life, never disturbing public order. The Tarusa police had no complaints about him. The grounds for administrative surveillance were that he continued to carry on the fight for human rights in the USSR. The KGB officially warned Marchenko to cease all such activity and pressed him to emigrate from the Soviet Union. Marchenko's signature under the appeal protesting the expulsion of Solzhenitsyn in February 1974 was an answer to that warning. Administrative surveillance followed by a criminal charge of maliciously violating its restrictions were the KGB's method of reprisal.

Larisa and I discussed which of the Moscow advocates should undertake Anatoly's defense, now that the stage of pretrial investigation was coming to a close. We considered many names, then finally asked each other why I shouldn't take the case myself? There were no official obstacles to this, because the charges against Marchenko were not formally connected with his civil rights activities. Kaluga, where Anatoly was in prison, was no more than three hours away, so I did not need the Presidium's special travel permit. Larisa paid the office cashier the statutory fee of twenty rubles for my services, I filled out a registration card in which I truthfully stated that Marchenko was charged with violation of administrative surveillance, and the college issued me an "order to defend" without any complications.

On the day before the agreed date for going to Kaluga, I called Larisa and we arranged to go by the train that left Moscow at 7:00 A.M. and to meet in the third car from the front. As it happened, we met on the platform; the train had just come in and we got into the nearest car, which was not the third car. Two or three minutes after the train had pulled out of the station, Larisa suddenly gave me a sharp jab in the ribs. I looked up and at once saw the man who had attracted her attention. He was walking along the corridor, having apparently come from the next car, and he was staring hard at all the passengers. Seeing us, he quickly walked the remaining distance, and sat down opposite us.

He was an elderly man, well over sixty-five, with the purplish-red nose of an alcoholic and cheeks of the same color. He looked as if he suffered from hypertension as well. He was wearing an overcoat patterned in big black-and-white checks and a peaked cap of the same checkered material. Neither his age nor his striking appearance and dress would have led one to suspect him of being a man under orders to follow us. But he did not take his eyes off us for a second, as though afraid we might disappear and he would have to walk the length of the train again to find us.

"Perhaps he just likes our looks," Larisa whispered. I looked at her, tired and short of sleep, then thought what I must look like after getting up at 5:00 A.M. I replied firmly, "Don't flatter yourself."

When we got off the train in Kaluga we did everything we could to get rid of this man. Nothing worked. He stopped when we stopped, ran after us when we walked faster. It was both absurdly funny and pathetic to watch this old fellow dashing around the concourse of the Kaluga station when Larisa went to the ticket office and I went in the opposite direction to look at return schedules. We agreed that Larisa, who of course was not allowed to visit Anatoly, would wait for me at the prison for half an hour, in case my visit was unexpectedly canceled; otherwise we would meet back at the station to return home together on the train that left at 5:30 P.M. Our inseparable companion carefully eavesdropped on this conversation. On the way to the prison we lost sight of him. He was not lurking around the building waiting for us, either. I transferred to my briefcase the bottles of mineral water that Larisa had brought for Anatoly (who was on hunger strike and not taking any food) and we parted.

Nothing, however, worked out as we had agreed. The investigator had indeed changed her plans, and I was unable to study the case materials that day, but I could not get away at once either. She had decided to read out the indictment to Marchenko in my presence, since she was afraid that the sharp deterioration in Anatoly's hearing might later be exploited by the defense. Although the meeting was not long, as Marchenko refused to give any testimony, it still took more than an hour. We agreed with Anatoly that I would come again to study the case, and with that I left.

As I came out of the prison, bending under the weight of a briefcase full of the mineral water Anatoly had refused, to my delight I saw Larisa. She had decided to wait until noon. There were still several hours until the next Moscow train. We wandered around the beautiful old town of Kaluga, admiring the view of the river in full flood, which could be seen from almost every street, and not forgetting to look behind us for our "checkered man." He was nowhere to be seen. In any case we had nothing to hide from him, but it was a pleasure to feel free of that constant watching eye.

We reached the station twenty minutes before train time and sat down in the almost empty waiting room. The tail still had not shown up. The Kaluga station is a terminus, and the trains come in to the platform long before they are due to depart. We sat opposite a glass door leading onto the platform and waited for the train to come in. Ten minutes passed—still no train.

"That's funny," I said. "Maybe we should go out and take a look."

"You're behaving like a hick," said Larisa. "Our train's not going anywhere else. The platform's here, the tracks are here. All we have to do is wait."

When there were four minutes left before our scheduled departure, Larisa agreed to go out onto the platform. It was quite empty—except for the last car of our train standing at the far end, and the wooden bulletin board showing that the train was just about to leave for Moscow. How we ran! I never thought I had the strength to run so far so fast. Fortunately Larisa grabbed my heavy briefcase with the mineral water, otherwise I would have collapsed. We jumped aboard only seconds before the train pulled out and stood in the space at the end of the car, panting and unable to move.

"Look, there's someone else running," said Larisa.

I looked out. Running along the platform, almost bursting with exertion, was our checkered man. From purplish-red the color of his face had changed to pale lilac. He was breathless; but he made it.

"Steady, old fellow," said a kindhearted woman as he followed us into the car. "You'll kill yourself if you run like that at your age."

He stood there in the aisle, clutching the back of a seat, unable to move. The color slowly drained from his face, leaving it a deathly white. His eyes glittered with hatred. He was sure we had remained in the waiting room until the last minute in order to shake him off. Again we sat opposite each other, his glare riveted on us as he listened to every word we spoke—although we did not say much, since his presence killed all desire to talk or even to read.

When I told this story afterward, I would ask, "Why did they do it? What was the point? Why did they have to follow an advocate visiting a client, and not even for a meeting alone but in the presence of an investigator? What could the KGB learn that they didn't know already?" The replies were always the same. It was what is called "demonstrative surveillance," psychological pressure as a means of intimidation, of making people feel that every step is being watched by the KGB. To make sure that they notice they are being followed, an easily recognizable tail is used, someone who looks unusual and wears conspicuous clothes.

In my case, my friends thought, this demonstrative surveillance was also a kind of warning, a reminder that they had not forgotten about me. It was probably true, but this time too I disregarded the warning. Our family was still determined to behave as we thought fit.

Friends also told us repeatedly that surveillance amounted to more than a warning, that it was a clear signal of the authorities' desire to see us leave. It was not, however, clear to us. We did not want to emigrate, to abandon the lives we had built for ourselves, nor to leave the people who were dear to us. And since no officials told us we were unwelcome, we refused to understand the warnings directed at us.

I can only guess why the KGB gave us this choice between arrest and exile. It was often done during the years of détente. Arrests and political trials would provoke objectionable reactions in the West, so Soviet authorities preferred to force troublemakers to leave quietly. At the same time the authorities hoped the expulsions would help them crush the dissident movement.

We openly met a number of American and French newspaper correspondents whom we liked, and we discovered that it is not only Russians (as many Russians think) who can be faithful friends. We tried to help these visitors overcome the barrier of isolation that surrounded them, to show them the good things in Moscow, the things a country with long cultural traditions can be proud of. We guessed that our meetings were watched and photographed; later it turned out that some of them were even filmed by movie cameras.

We knew something of the overall motives, of course, but why did they have to keep a car, in the cold weather, parked across the street from our house and filled with trained cameramen to film my husband and me as we came out with Peter Osnos, the *Washington Post* correspondent, and got into his car to drive to his home for dinner? It was the only time we visited Peter and Susan during the day, and I remember it very well. On the previous evening they had invited us to their home to see their newborn son, which was why we were asked to come in the daytime and not in the evening. We took a present to congratulate the baby's mother, and when Peter came for us at the agreed time, my husband and I were immortalized on film clutching an enormous parcel.

Later, after we had emigrated, these shots were shown on Moscow television. The accompanying voice-over commentary announced, "These people are setting out on an espionage assignment with an American spy masquerading as a journalist." The KGB was perfectly aware of the absurdity of that commentary. Not once during our interrogations was either of us asked about that meeting. They were simply accumulating material which might later be useful as falsified evidence.

Often I am asked to name the principal, immediate cause of the KGB's pressure on us and the subsequent demand that we leave the Soviet Union. I never know how to answer that question, or which particular cause to single out.

Our whole life was the cause—my participation in political trials, the fact that we became legal advisers of all the dissidents—and the authorities got bored with answering questions about why Advocate Kaminskaya was not allowed to defend Bukovsky at his second trial or to defend such well-known civil rights activists as Sergei Kovalev and Anatoly Shcharansky. And then, not unimportant, there was our readiness to associate with foreign journalists.

In other words, we tried to act as though we were free people in a free country.

The third warning—the search of our home and the charges against my husband—was one we could not disregard. Now the authorities were doing everything they could to force us to get out. This was the purpose behind the whole theatrical performance: the search, the interrogations, the threats to arrest my husband. If we did not submit to this demand, then we were to be crushed.

I realized this was the beginning of the end, yet even so I went on as if nothing was happening.

After the search, the next move was to try to evict us from our apartment. After our son and daughter-in-law emigrated, the two of us continued to live in the same apartment in which our son had been born and my parents had died. By Soviet standards it was a big apartment. Its total area greatly exceeded the regular allowance of living space (nine square meters per person); but my husband, as a research scholar, had a right to twenty square meters of extra space, and I, as an advocate, was permitted an extra ten square meters, which together accounted for more than the total area of our apartment. Under Soviet law there were no grounds for evicting us. One day, after coming home from an unpleasant, not to say disgraceful, scene in our local housing office, I said, "What fools they are. Why are they trying to evict us now? They only have to wait until you and I are fired from our jobs"—which we expected to happen any minute—"and then they can evict us without any trouble, because then we won't have the right to extra space."

Almost immediately the attempts to evict us ceased.

On Thursdays my husband was free to work at home or in a library, but Thursday, May 19, 1977, his department chief called early in the morning and asked him to come to the institute on a matter of urgency—a piece of research was needed for the draft text of the new Soviet Constitution. When my husband arrived he was asked to verify two draft passages whose wording was so urgently required that it had to be given over the phone. At one o'clock, when the work was finished, the same department chief said that they must now go together to another building, which housed the governing body of the institute, to get some new instructions. In that way my husband was taken to a special meeting of the Academic Council, the group of department heads and other senior figures who oversaw the administration of his institute, and on whose agenda there was one item: his dismissal.

The order for his expulsion from the Institute was published the same day. While my husband was working on the urgent drafts of the new Constitution, his chief, it turned out, had been sitting in the next room drafting the text of the expulsion order. What surprised and angered me most about the whole business was that my husband's boss, a legal scholar and a Ph.D., with whom my husband had worked for eleven years on the best of terms, had behaved like a sneaky little police spy or *agent provocateur*.

So on May 19 my husband became unemployed.

Friday passed without incident and we went to the *dacha* for the weekend. Early Monday morning the local housing officer came to the apartment. "We know you're no longer working and have no further right to extra space. You must vacate. An eviction order is being filed in court."

The KGB had followed my advice and waited until one of us was fired. Still, we were determined to resist to the last—and if we still lost, then we could always survive in one room. The only terrible threat was the possible arrest of my husband. Everything else faded into insignificance.

On June 15 I had a visit from Ida Milgrom, the mother of Anatoly

Shcharansky, a member of the Moscow group for monitoring the fulfillment of the Helsinki Agreement and a champion of Jews' right to emigrate. More than a year had passed since his arrest on the unfounded charges of espionage for the USA. Ida knew I had lost my access to political trials, but she hoped to be able to pull strings and have me granted a "once-only" access to defend her son. She had come back to me only after asking all the other advocates I had recommended; none of them wanted to challenge in court the guilt of someone charged with espionage.

I agreed to defend him.

The next day Ida went to see one of the deputy chairmen of the Moscow College of Advocates, who categorically refused to give me a once-only access. That evening he called up to scold me long and loud for not saying I was sick or too busy to take the case.

The weekend passed, and on Monday morning, as I was setting off for court to make a defense speech, I was urgently summoned to the office of the College of Advocates Presidium.

I was received by the two deputy chairmen and shown a letter dated June 17 and signed by the Procurator of Moscow. It recommended that I be expelled from the College of Advocates. It referred to the search and to my husband's authorship of an "anti-Soviet" manuscript, and, of course, to my meetings with foreign journalists named in the Soviet press as agents of the CIA.

"You realize, don't you, that we can't do anything for you?" they said.

I certainly did realize it. It was beyond their power.

A few minutes later my husband and I were walking toward the courthouse where I was to give my last defense speech. Konstantin tried to comfort me, but it was unnecessary. I was calm, as though this terrible disaster had never occurred, as though I were not coming to the end of my professional life.

Everything that happened afterward—the demand that we leave the Soviet Union or face my husband's arrest, the ten days of feverish preparations and packing, the KGB's kind help in booking air tickets to Vienna and obtaining the necessary documents—all that went by like a speeded-up newsreel.

For me, my life in the Soviet Union ended when my thirty-seven years in the Soviet courts ended. I delivered my last defense speech on June 20, 1977.

INDEX

Galanskov, Yurii (*cont.*)
  Litvinov and trial of, 207
  NTS links with, 262–63, 264, 277–
    278, 282, 284, 296, 304
  opposition to violence of, 262
  poetry readings organized by, 258
  in prison camp, 259–61
  psychiatric examination of, 270, 295
  Pushkin Square demonstration and,
    175, 178, 181, 195
  trial as viewed by, 274
  ulcer of, 258
  see also Ginzburg-Galanskov trial
Galanskova, Ekaterina, 258–61
General Procurator of the USSR, 52
Ginzburg, Alexander, 48–49, 52, 162,
    172, 261–308
  charges against, 261–62, 265–66
  defense counsel of, 262
  Litvinov and trial of, 207
  prisoner exchange and, 257
Ginzburg-Galanskov trial (1967–68),
    257–308
  appeals of, 309–10, 314
  Ariya's closing speech in, 302–3
  audience in, 279–80, 289–90, 300,
    307
  Brox-Sokolov's testimony in, 288–
    289, 292–94
  bugging of, 300
  clashes between clients in, 264, 278,
    282, 284, 296
  in "closed session," 276–77
  defense counsel free from
    punishment for, 307
  defense counsel's strategy in, 277–
    279
  Dobrovolsky's plea in, 263, 278
  Dobrovolsky's testimony in, 267,
    269–72, 282–86
  ethical problems in, 263–64, 280–82
  as farce, 308
  foreign agents in, 273–74, 282, 285
  Galanskov's "last word" in, 307
  Galanskov's plea in, 263–64, 278
  Galanskov's testimony in, 272–74,
    278, 296
  Ginzburg's "last word" in, 307

  Ginzburg's testimony in, 272, 296
  Gubanov's testimony and, 287–88
  insufficient pretrial preparation time
    for, 274, 276–78
  judge in, 274–76, 286
  judge's manipulation of, 285–92
  Kaminskaya endangered by, 303–4,
    309
  Kaminskaya's closing speech in, 302,
    303–6
  Kaminskaya's home bugged due to,
    229
  Kaminskaya's strategy in, 262–64,
    277–79, 280–85, 296
  Katz's testimony in, 291–92
  KGB investigation of, 265–74
  Lashkova's plea in, 263, 278
  Lashkova's testimony in, 272, 297–
    298
  Lunts's testimony in, 295
  NTS materials in, 262–64, 277–78,
    282–86, 296, 300, 304
  postponement of, 278–79, 293
  press agents at, 279–80
  prosecutor's closing speech in, 299–
    300
  prosecutor's questions in, 283
  psychiatric examinations for, 270,
    295
  secrecy of, 276
  sentencing in, 308
  Shveisky's closing speech in, 301–2
  street audience of, 290–91, 308
  Topeshkina's testimony in, 290–91
  Vinogradov's attendance request
    for, 290
  Yepifanov's testimony in, 286
  Zolotukhin's closing speech in, 302,
    306–7
Gnedin, Yevgeny, 20
Gollan, John, 306
Golovanov (printer), 265, 289
Gorbachev, Investigator, 144–47, 148–
    155
  see also Case of the Two Boys, third
    trial
Gorbanevskaya, Natalya, 209–10, 255
Grani, 282, 284

Kaminskaya, Dina Isaakovna (*cont.*)
first political defense speech of, 199–
201
first professional appointment of,
26–36
first professional rebuke of, 201, 341
heritage of, 42
Jewish background of, 15, 41–43
KGB eviction of, 346–47
KGB pressure for emigration of,
345–48
KGB search of, 324–26, 346
KGB surveillance of, 228–30, 328–
329, 342–48
Kirilov's warning to, 120–21
method for preparing defense by,
246
as political advocate, 37–50, 62, 335–
336
professional education of, 12–15, 23–
24
professional expulsion of, 348
during purges, 18–20, 21
sister of, 12, 17, 20, 42
sociability of, 17–18
son of, 144, 342
Zolotukhin's Party expulsion and,
311–19
Kaminskaya, Olga (mother), 15–18, 20
Kaminsky, Isaak (father), 12, 15–18, 20
Karasev, Judge, 142–43, 145
Kareva, Judge, 126–40
see also Case of the Two Boys,
second trial
Kats, Leonid Zakharovich, 26–28
Katz, Ludmila, 291–92
KGB (NKVD):
access system of, 31–33
in Bukovsky case, 175, 178–80, 183,
184, 187–88, 191, 203
Chronicle of Current Events and,
255
in College of Advocates, 28
in "doctors' plot," 41–42
evidence fabricated by, 46
in Gabay-Djamilev trial, 335–40
in Ginzburg-Galanskov trial, 264–
308

NTS compromised by, 294
in Red Square trial, 210, 212, 226–
228, 231–32, 240–41, 245, 252
in Sinyavsky-Daniel case, 164, 167–
168
surveillance methods of, 342, 345
trial investigations by, 51
Kharkov University, 16
Khaustov, Viktor (Vitka), 175
conviction of, 186–87
defense counsel of, 192
plea of, 192
Khrushchev, Nikita:
liberalism of, 58
Stalin denounced by, 267
Kirilov, Judge, 82–85, 99–121
slanders of, 125
see also Case of the Two Boys, first
trial
Klepikova, Ira, 66–68, 77–78, 110–11,
127–28, 153
Klimov, Ivan, 27
Kogan, Pavel, 21
Komsomol, 174, 191
Komsomol Vigilante Squad, 174–75,
186, 194, 197
Koshkin (prosecutor), 148–56
Kosterin, Alexei, 331
Kostopravkina, Alexandra, 70–72, 76
Babyonisheva harassed by, 131
court reprimand of, 108
hostility toward defense counsel by,
123–24
Kirilov slandered by, 125
testimony of, 104–5
see also Case of the Two Boys; *and
specific trials*
Kostopravkina, Marina, 66–69
see also Case of the Two Boys; *and
specific trials*
Kosygin, Aleksei, 168
Kovalev, Sergei, 346
Kozopolyanskaya, Irina, 65, 78–79, 81,
86, 140
Krasin, Viktor, 334–35
arrest of, 334
KGB press conference and, 334–35
testimony of, 334